Travel Discount Coupon

This coupon entitles
when you book yo

GLOBAL TRAVEL NETWORK®
RESERVATION SERVICE

Hotels ♦ Airlines ♦ Car Rentals ♦ Cruises
All Your Travel Needs

Here's what you get: *

♦ A discount of $50 USD on a booking of $1,000** or more for two or more people!

♦ A discount of $25 USD on a booking of $500** or more for one person!

♦ Free membership for three years, and 1,000 free miles on enrollment in the unique Miles-to-Go™ frequent-traveler program. Earn one mile for every dollar spent through the program. Earn free hotel stays starting at 5,000 miles. Earn free roundtrip airline tickets starting at 25,000 miles.

♦ Personal help in planning your own, customized trip.

♦ Fast, confirmed reservations at any property recommended in this guide, subject to availability.***

♦ Special discounts on bookings in the U.S. and around the world.

♦ Low-cost visa and passport service.

♦ Reduced-rate cruise packages.

Visit our website at http://www.travnet.com/Frommer or call us globally at 201-567-8500, ext. 55. In the U.S., call toll-free at 1-888-940-5000, or fax 201-567-1838. In Canada, call toll-free at 1-800-883-9959, or fax 416-922-6053. In Asia, call 60-3-7191044, or fax 60-3-7185415.

* To qualify for these travel discounts, at least a portion of your trip must include destinations covered in this guide. No more than one coupon discount may be used in any 12-month period, for destinations covered in this guide. Cannot be combined with any other discount or program.
** These are U.S. dollars spent on commissionable bookings.
*** A $10 USD fee, plus fax and/or phone charges, will be added to the cost of bookings at each hotel not linked to the reservation service. Customers must approve these fees in advance.

Valid until December 31, 1997. Terms and conditions of the Miles-to-Go™ program are available on request by calling 201-567-8500, ext 55.

NOR123

Frommer's 97

New Orleans

by Lisa M. Legarde

Macmillan • USA

ABOUT THE AUTHOR

Lisa M. Legarde was born in New Orleans and still has wonderful childhood memories of Mardi Gras and artists "on the fence" at Jackson Square. She loves Cajun food and music and is passionate about jazz.

MACMILLAN TRAVEL

A Simon & Schuster Macmillan Company
1633 Broadway
New York, NY 10019

Find us online at **http://www.mgr.com/travel** or
on America Online at Keyword **Frommer's.**

ISBN 0-02-860906-9
ISSN 0899-2908

Editor: Jim Moore
Production Editor: Laura Yockey
Map Editor: Douglas Stallings
Design by Michele Laseau
Digital Cartography by John Decamillis and Ortelius Design
All Maps copyright © Simon & Schuster, Inc.

SPECIAL SALES

Contents

List of Maps

AN INVITATION TO THE READER

In researching this book, I discovered many wonderful places—hotels, restaurants, shops, and more. I'm sure you'll find others. Please tell me about them, so I can share the information with your fellow travelers in upcoming editions. If you were disappointed with a recommendation, I'd love to know that, too. Please write to:

Lisa M. Legarde
Frommer's New Orleans '97
Macmillan Travel
1633 Broadway
New York, NY 10019

AN ADDITIONAL NOTE

Please be advised that travel information is subject to change at any time—and this is especially true of prices. We therefore suggest that you write or call ahead for confirmation when making your travel plans. The authors, editors, and publisher cannot be held responsible for the experiences of readers while traveling. Your safety is important to us, however, so we encourage you to stay alert and be aware of your surroundings. Keep a close eye on cameras, purses, and wallets, all favorite targets of thieves and pickpockets.

WHAT THE SYMBOLS MEAN

✪ **Frommer's Favorites**
Hotels, restaurants, attractions, and entertainment you should not miss.

Ⓢ **Super-Special Values**
Hotels and restaurants that offer great value for your money.

The following abbreviations are used for credit cards:

AE	American Express	EU	Eurocard
CB	Carte Blanche	JCB	Japan Credit Bank
DC	Diners Club	MC	MasterCard
DISC	Discover	V	Visa
ER	enRoute		

Introducing New Orleans

Pristine French Quarter courtyards, lacy wrought-iron balconies, antebellum Garden District mansions—and everywhere the aroma of chicory coffee. This is one of the faces New Orleans presents to the world. As you walk the narrow streets, lined with well-kept centuries-old buildings that are flush with fancy ironwork, the city's past will seem palpably alive—it's easy to imagine that the frock-coated gentlemen and hoop-skirted ladies of bygone days are strolling the sidewalks beside you or taking their leisure in the elegant courtyards and restaurants.

But like all true eccentrics, New Orleans has another side: steamy jazz, Mardi Gras beads, and pickpockets, all mixed up with the smell of stale beer, fruity hurricanes, and cigarettes. This dichotomy has run throughout its history: New Orleans was a capital of the great Mississippi riverboat industry that Mark Twain wrote about, as well as a haven for swashbuckling privateers, such as Jean Lafitte. It was a city of the southern gentility, with their lavish balls and elegant homes, as well as a raucous port where sailors could blow a month's pay in one night on wine and women.

It is the blending of those two faces that makes New Orleans so wonderful. Part of the spirit of partying on Bourbon Street is standing in the middle of all of that intriguing French Quarter architecture. And sitting in one of those lovely courtyards at sunrise wouldn't be quite so memorable if you couldn't hear the last strains of an all-night jam session drifting down from the club on the corner.

At no time does the city come together more completely, though, than when it celebrates. From Carnival to the Jazz and Heritage Festival, New Orleanians find some reason to get together and throw a party at least once a month. And these celebrations all have two things in common: music and food. Jazz, Cajun, and zydeco music were born in and around New Orleans; Cajun and Creole cooking pulled themselves up out of the bayou as well.

But history, music, food, and good times aside, New Orleans wouldn't be N'Awlins without the people: artists "on the fence" around Jackson Square; musicians sitting in at jazz clubs or Preservation Hall; shopkeepers displaying exquisite imports alongside inexpensive souvenirs; taxi drivers hopping out to open doors; natives happily sharing tables with tourists at the Café du Monde for an any-hour café au lait and beignets. Don't bother worrying about seeing all the sights; New Orleans is best experienced by sitting around talking to the natives and doing your best to live like one. New Orleanians are a cultural hodgepodge, a population gumbo that comes from a colorful, checkered history, and they've created a city unlike any other.

1 Frommer's Favorite New Orleans Experiences

- **Beignets and Café au Lait at Café du Monde:** A visit to New Orleans just wouldn't be the same without a trip to Café du Monde for a powdered-sugared plateful of those mouthwatering "doughnuts." Every time I return to New Orleans I can't resist running straight to Café du Monde to sit at the always-sticky, sugarcoated tables.
- **A Day of Play on Magazine Street:** Spend the entire day rooting around in the antique shops, galleries, and bookstores that line the 6-mile stretch of Magazine Street from Canal Street to Audubon Park. If you're lucky, you might come across a real find.
- **Bourbon Street After Dark:** You can't visit New Orleans without spending at least one night cruising up and down Bourbon Street. Music of every sort flows out windows and doors, and people from all walks of life gather in the various music halls, watering holes, and on the street.
- **Shopping in the French Market:** Whether you're shopping for souvenirs or gathering goods for a picnic in the park, the French Market is a great place to begin. Make your way through the throngs to stands stocked with fresh fruits, vegetables, and seafood. After that, head down to the end of the market and bargain with salespeople for everything from T-shirts to leather goods and jewelry.
- **A Ride on the Riverboat Casino:** I have to admit, I was skeptical about the riverboat casinos, but after I spent three hours on board, I was itching to go back. It's fun anytime, but it's a great rainy day activity.
- **Jazz at Preservation Hall:** Drop your three bucks in the hat and squeeze your way into one of the country's most time-honored jazz centers. Whether you sit up front or stand in the back and sway with the crowd you're guaranteed to get an earful of great music.
- **The Historic Streetcar:** A ride on the streetcar (except at rush hour) is a lovely way to see the uptown section of New Orleans. Get off at the point where St. Charles Avenue turns into Carrollton Avenue and enjoy the view of the Mississippi from the grass-covered levee.
- **A Walk Through the Garden District:** If you let it, a few hours wandering around the Garden District, especially on a warm spring day, will take you back in time to the way it was in the Old South.
- **An Arts Crawl Along Julia Street:** There are many new and wonderful contemporary art galleries in New Orleans's Warehouse District that shouldn't be missed. A day spent in this area of town will entertain and reward serious and window shoppers alike.
- **A Rainy Afternoon in Napoleon House:** You can't beat the atmosphere at Napoleon House, and there's no better place to go during an afternoon rainstorm. Locals have a particular fondness for this bar/cafe with its slow-whirring ceiling fans, low lights, and piped-in opera music, so it's a great place to mix with the natives. Five minutes here and you'll understand why it's long been a favorite haunt of artists and writers.
- **Live Entertainment at the House of Blues:** When Dan Ackroyd opened a branch of the original House of Blues (located in Cambridge, Massachusetts) on Decatur Street, it altered the face of the New Orleans music scene. On any night you'll be

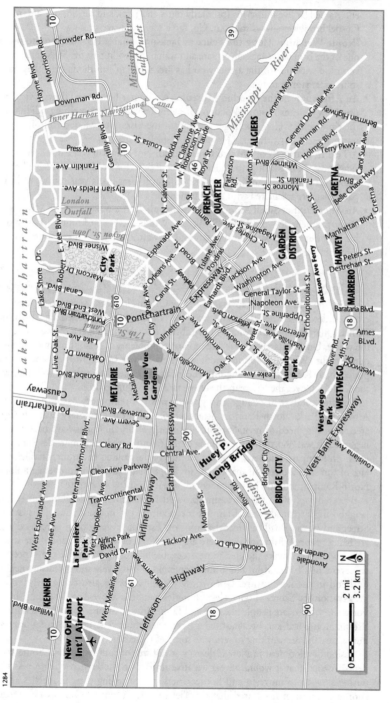

entertained by live musicians (primarily blues and jazz), and the Sunday-afternoon Gospel brunch is always sold out. Go, tap a toe, and leave smiling.

- **People-Watching Along the Fence at Jackson Square:** It's wonderful to sit on one of the benches at Jackson Square and watch the world pass by. Strike up a conversation with one of the artists who has "set up shop" on the fence—they have some great stories to tell.
- **An Afternoon in the Voodoo Museum:** No matter how many times I visit the tiny New Orleans Historic Voodoo Museum, I always find something I didn't see the time before. Here you'll get a lesson in the history of voodoo from its roots to the present day through a fascinating display of artifacts.
- **A Trip to Blaine Kern's Mardi Gras World:** Not only will you enjoy a free ferry ride across the Mississippi to Algiers, but you'll be in for a real treat at Blaine Kern's Mardi Gras World where artists work on Mardi Gras floats year-round. Kids, in particular, are fascinated with the experience.
- **An After-Dinner Stroll Along the Mississippi:** Take a walk along the Mississippi River promenade—the Moon Walk and Woldenberg Riverfront Park—before heading out to the bars and nightclubs. On warmer nights you can even catch a refreshing breeze here.

2 The City Today

Much of the national news coverage of New Orleans in recent years has focused on crime. Indeed, over the last several years the crime rate has increased, and even the French Quarter, a place in which I have always felt safe, has taken a marked turn for the worse. Unfortunately, this is due in part to problems of corruption in the police department. With the appointment of a new mayor (Marc Morial) and a new police chief (Richard J. Pennington), the locals are hopeful that things will improve soon. Indeed, over the last year, the crime rate has begun to drop.

Another catalyst of change and growth was the temporary casino located in Armstrong Park. North Rampart Street, off of which the temporary casino is situated, is in dire need of revitalization, and many of the buildings have been sorely neglected. It was hoped that the coming of the casino would bring more development to North Rampart, but news in recent months of the casino's bankruptcy has left the fate of this area a question mark. It is my hope that plans for improvement along North Rampart will still be implemented, but it's just too soon to tell.

By extension, plans for the casino brought restoration and development to the neighboring Esplanade area. Many of the beautiful old mansions along Esplanade Street and Bayou Road (a street that runs off Esplanade) have been purchased and are being restored. Additionally, there are plans for a new bus route and more street lights, which will make the area more accessible and much safer. We can expect to see several new bed-and-breakfast hotels opening in this lovely and promising neighborhood in the near future. Uptown, Magazine Street is also being targeted by preservationists. Scores of once-elegant homes had been allowed to deteriorate here. Fortunately, there are people like Lisa and Eddie Breaux, owners of the McKendrick-Breaux House bed-and-breakfast, who have taken more than just a passing interest in the area and are working to renovate some of these stately homes.

Casino development in New Orleans was not free of controversy, and some residents worried that it would have a negative impact on the French Quarter. As big business began to move in and homeowners started selling their properties at an enormous profit, many feared that the Vieux Carré (it means "Old Square" and is pronounced *view ka-RAY*) was in danger of becoming completely commercialized.

For years, T-shirt and souvenir shops have been taking the places of old French Quarter shops simply because they can more easily generate the profits needed to meet the neighborhood's rising rents. If rents continue to skyrocket, more small businesses will be forced to move out, and local concern for the area may be diminished. There is, however, a school of thought that says an increase in the French Quarter economy will be good for the neighborhood. Only time will tell, and with the closing of the casino, developments in the Quarter are even more uncertain.

Cultural development continues throughout the city. The Warehouse District has been experiencing growth with the addition of more contemporary art galleries and an expansion of the Louisiana Children's Museum (one of the best in the nation). The Audubon Institute is building an insectarium at the riverfront, and the Aquarium of the Americas has just completed an expansion with the addition of an IMAX theater and a gallery for changing exhibits. New Orleans, especially with the addition of the House of Blues, continues to attract musicians and music fans from around the world. You'll still find jazz being played in several venues on Bourbon Street, but look farther afield to places like Frenchmen Street in the Faubourg Marigny for clubs with a more low-key atmosphere.

It's clear that New Orleans is on the move, and only time will tell how all of these changes will affect the face of the city. I, for one, am keeping my fingers crossed for the French Quarter, and I have high hopes for the Esplanade area and for Magazine Street.

3 History 101

New Orleans, the largest city in Louisiana and one of the chief cities of the South, is situated at the mouth of the Mississippi-Missouri river system and is bounded by Jefferson Parish and the Mississippi to the west, Lake Pontchartrain to the north, Lake Borgne to the east, and St. Bernard Parish and the Mississippi to the south. Its location is no accident, but it was a feat of modern construction that allowed the city to grow into what it is today.

In 1718 a Canadian-born Frenchman, Jean-Baptiste Le Moyne, Sieur de Bienville, set out to find a suitable location for a settlement to protect France's holdings in the New World from British expansion. His brother, Pierre Le Moyne, Sieur d'Iberville, had planted a cross at the great bend of the Mississippi River in 1699, and de Bienville found this place a strategic point for his "city." Although it was almost 110 miles inland from the Gulf of Mexico by river, the city had an easy portage route to a little stream (Bayou St. John) that provided easy water transportation directly into Lake Pontchartrain. From a military standpoint, this was a convenient "back door" for defense or escape, should the fortunes of war turn against the French. And, of course, it was a perfect trade route inland to the nearby Native American villages and their fabled gold, which de Bienville's superiors in France were

Dateline

- 1718 City founded by Jean-Baptiste Le Moyne, first governor of Louisiana.
- 1726 Capuchin monastery erected.
- 1730 Ursuline convent completed.
- 1762 Louis XV secretly cedes New Orleans and all of Louisiana west of the Mississippi to Spain.
- 1783 Treaty of Paris confirms Spanish possession.
- 1788, 1794 Fire destroys much of the city; new brick buildings replace wood.
- 1795 Treaty of Madrid opens port to Americans; trade thrives.
- 1800 Louisiana again becomes French possession.
- 1803 United States purchases Louisiana.
- 1812 The *New Orleans,* a steam vessel, arrives from Pittsburgh.
- 1815 Battle of New Orleans.

continues

- 1834 Medical College of Louisiana founded, forerunner of Tulane University.
- 1837 First Mardi Gras parade.
- 1840 Antoine Alciatore, founder of Antoine's, arrives from Marseilles. New Orleans is by this point the fourth-largest city in the United States, second only to New York as a port.
- 1850 Commerce booming; cotton accounts for 45% of total commerce; city becomes greatest slave market in the country.
- 1853–55 Yellow fever epidemic.
- 1861 Louisiana secedes from the Union.
- 1862 City captured by Adm. David Farragut.
- 1865–77 Reconstruction; carpetbaggers swarm into the city.
- 1871 Audubon Park created.
- 1880 Railroad arrives.
- 1882 Canal Street illuminated by electric light.
- 1884 Cotton Centennial Exposition (World's Fair).
- 1885 Joe "King" Oliver born.
- 1890 Jelly Roll Morton born.
- 1892 First electric streetcar operated along St. Charles Avenue.
- 1897 Sidney Bechet born.
- 1900 Louis Armstrong born.
- 1906 Barney Bigard, clarinetist/tenor saxophonist, born.
- 1911 Razzy Dazzy Spasm Band performs in New York, where its name is changed to Razzy Dazzy *Jazz* Band.
- 1917 Original Dixieland Jazz Band attains height of popularity.
- 1921 Arnaud's established.
- 1927 Levee at Poydras erected.

continues

convinced would soon be shipped to them from Louisiana.

Following the plan of a late French medieval town, a central square (the Place d'Armes) was laid out, with streets forming a grid around it. A church, government office, priest's house, and official residences fronted the square, and earthen ramparts dotted with forts were built around the perimeter. In honor of the duc d'Orléans, then the regent of France, the little town was named New Orleans.

Today we know this section of the city as the Vieux Carré and the Place d'Armes as Jackson Square. Rude huts of cypress filled in with moss and clay were erected, and a tiny wooden levee was raised against the mighty river, which persisted in flooding periodically, turning streets into rivers of mud.

The fabled gold turned out to be just that, a fable. But there were furs aplenty, and de Bienville needed settlers to work as trappers, to run farms to feed the colony, and to fight off hostile tribes. The French government saw this as a perfect opportunity to rid itself of all its misfits at home and sent to New Orleans the dregs of its prisons, some bonded servants, and slaves from French Caribbean settlements. They were the first ingredients of New Orleans's population gumbo. Among them were "fallen women" who, according to today's New Orleanians, somehow managed to leave no direct descendants: Almost everyone proudly traces his or her ancestry to French or Spanish nobility and the respectable "casket girls" brought over by Ursuline nuns in 1727 (carrying all their worldly goods in casket-like trunks), with never a mention of those earlier women of the streets.

Lured by the first real estate scam in this country's history (a flamboyant speculator named John Law painted the appealing picture of a virtual paradise on earth in the new settlement), wealthy Europeans, aristocrats, merchants, exiles, soldiers, and a large contingent of German farmers arrived to find only mosquitoes, a raw frontier existence, and swampy land that resisted all but the most heroic efforts to put it to productive use. But the Europeans stayed on, and as they tamed the land, the colony prospered and attracted more and more members of the aristocratic class. Social life began to take on the complexion of European court life. By 1763 yet another seasoning was added to the pot: Acadians from Nova Scotia fleeing British rule. You'll find their descendants living a little to the west of New Orleans, still engaged in farming and trapping, still speaking their unique brand of French, and proudly calling themselves "Cajuns."

French to the core from the very beginning, New Orleanians were horrified to learn that Louis XV had given their city to his cousin, Charles III of Spain, in 1762 with the secret Treaty of Fontainbleu. Their resentment forced the first Spanish governor to leave, and it wasn't until Don Alexander O'Reilly, known as "Bloody O'Reilly," was dispatched by the Spanish Crown with 3,000 soldiers in 1769 that revolutionary ideas were firmly squelched (after the execution of five French patriots) and Spanish rule was accepted as a reality. With a Gallic shrug, French aristocracy mingled with Spanish nobility, intermarried, and created a new "Creole" culture.

Tragic fires struck in 1788, destroying more than 850 buildings, and again in 1794 in the midst of rebuilding. From the ashes emerged a completely new city, dominated by the proud Spanish style of brick-and-plaster buildings replete with arches, courtyards, balconies, and, of course, attached slave quarters. Even today you'll see tile markers giving Spanish street names at every corner in the "French" Quarter.

The new city was much coveted by both the English and the Americans. France, recognizing its blunder in giving the city away, wanted it back. Control of the lucrative trade conducted along the Mississippi River was at stake, and with all sorts of plots flying about, Governor Carondelet reinforced the wall around the city and armed its five forts with cannons pointing outward to fend off invaders and inward to ward off any internal uprising. France finally regained possession in 1800, with a surprisingly quiet transfer of ownership, and held on for three years while Napoleon negotiated the Louisiana Purchase with the United States for the paltry (as it turned out) sum of $15 million. To the Creole society, this was almost as appalling as Spanish rule had been to the French settlers, for they considered all Americans barbarians who would surely bring about the end of the sophisticated Vieux Carré lifestyle.

Shunned by existing New Orleans society, the newly arrived Americans settled across Canal Street (so named because a drainage canal was once planned along its route, although it was never actually constructed) and set about showing the "downtown" snobs that they were no strangers to culture. Splendid mansions rose in what is now the Garden District, and a segregated social life took shape. But not for long. Yankee commercialism (which made "uptown" into a boomtown) brought industry and wealth much needed by the downtowners, and the vitality of warm-blooded downtown society drew uptowners like a magnet. Besides, both were forced to join forces against hurricanes, yellow fever epidemics, and floods. Such a spirit of unity grew between the two sections that when Andrew Jackson needed volunteers in 1814 to protect New Orleans against British attack, some 5,000 citizens responded—from both sides of Canal Street. Even the infamous (but much revered in New Orleans) privateer Jean Lafitte joined in, supplying cannons and ammunition that swung the balance in favor of the Americans. Ironically the Battle of New Orleans—which left

- **1938** Tennessee Williams arrives in New Orleans; Huey P. Long Bridge built over Mississippi River.
- **1939** French Quarter Residents Association formed, an agent for preservation.
- **1956** Lake Pontchartrain Causeway completed.
- **1960** Public schools integrated.
- **1969** Bacchus krewe organized.
- **1973** Parades banned in the Vieux Carré.
- **1975** Superdome opens.
- **1977** Ernest N. "Dutch" Morial becomes first African-American mayor.
- **1984** Louisiana World Expo.
- **1992** Louisiana State Legislature authorizes a land-based casino to be built in New Orleans.
- **1993** State Casino Board awards operating contract of land-based casino to Harrah's Jazz Company.
- **1995** Harrah's Casino goes belly-up.

some 2,000 British casualties as opposed to only a small number of American dead and wounded—took place on January 8, 1815, two weeks *after* a peace treaty had been signed, unbeknownst to either side at New Orleans.

From then until the Civil War, New Orleans gloried in a prosperity unmatched anywhere in the country. Wealthy cotton and sugar planters left upriver mansions from time to time to occupy luxurious town houses and to attend festivals, opera, theater, banquets, parades, and spectacular balls (including "Quadroon Balls," where beautiful mulatto girls were displayed to the male gentry as possible mistresses). Hardworking Irish and German immigrants arrived in vast numbers to add their own dash of spice to the already exotic culture. Canals and levees were built to keep the city alive and a little drier; steamboats plied the river serving the cotton trade and pleasure-seeking passengers; politics and gambling became passionate pastimes; and there was a lively trade in the slaves who supported the plantation economy on their oppressed backs. Federal troops put an end to all that when they marched in in 1862 during the Civil War and stayed until 1877, through a bitter Reconstruction period. New Orleans would never again be quite so flamboyant, but it was far from dead.

Like the rest of the defeated South, the city went about the business of rebuilding its economic life without the dependency on slavery that had brought about its downfall. By 1880 port activity had begun to pick up and industrial activity drew from the business world more and more visitors, many of whom became residents. And a new group of immigrants, Italians, came to put their unique mark on the city. Through it all there survived an undiminished enthusiasm for fun. Gambling again thrived in more than 80 establishments, there were almost 800 saloons, and scores of "bawdy houses" openly engaged in prostitution (illegal but uncontrolled). New Orleans was earning a reputation for open vice, and there were some who felt that something should be done to counteract such publicity.

In 1897 Alderman Sidney Story thought he had the answer. He moved all illegal (but highly profitable) activities into a restricted district along Basin Street, next door to the French Quarter. Quickly nicknamed "Storyville," the district boasted fancy "sporting palaces" with elaborate decor, musical entertainment, and a variety of ladies of pleasure. Visitors and residents could purchase a directory (the "Blue Book"), which listed alphabetically the names, addresses, and races of more than 700 prostitutes, ranging from those in the "palaces" to the poorer inhabitants of wretched, decaying shacks called "cribs" on the blocks behind Basin Street. African-American musicians came into their own when they moved from the streets into ornate bordellos to entertain patrons with the music we know as jazz. Although jazz itself predates Storyville, here it gained the popularity that sent it upriver and into this country's musical heritage. When the secretary of the navy decreed in 1917 that our

Impressions

The soft, balmy air, with its strange scents of fermenting molasses, semi-baked sugar, green coffee, pitch, Stockholm tar, brine, of mess-beef, rum and whiskey-drippings, contributed a great deal towards imparting the charm of romance to everything I saw. The people I passed appeared to me to be nobler than any I had yet seen. They had a swing of the body wholly un-English, and their facial expressions different from those I had been accustomed to . . . . These people knew no master, and had no more awe of their employers than they had of their fellow-employees.

—Sir Henry Morton Stanley, Autobiography, 1909

Population Gumbo

The French and Spanish were the first to arrive in New Orleans, and their descendants, both Caucasian and African American, call themselves Creoles; their cuisine of highly spiced French and Spanish dishes has become internationally famous. Another major part of the cultural mix was introduced when large numbers of Acadians, expelled by the British from Atlantic Canada in 1763, settled in the Bayou Country to the west of New Orleans. Today these people proudly call themselves Cajuns and retain one of the nation's most distinctive cultures.

Well over 50% of New Orleanians are African American; unlike in many of the South's major cities, race relations here have always been characterized by at least a degree of harmony. In antebellum days, free people of color constituted an important minority, and today the city has sizable African-American upper- and middle-class populations. New Orleans is also home to significant populations of Irish, German, Italian, Anglo, and Cuban peoples.

armed forces should not be exposed to so much open vice (without, it might be added, any visible support from the troops), Storyville closed down and disappeared without a trace.

In recent years, New Orleans has built its port into the largest in the United States and the second busiest in the world. (Amsterdam is first.) It ranks near the top in tourism in this country (conventions alone bring in over one million visitors each year) and is one of the top travel destinations in the United States for foreign visitors. Drainage problems have been conquered by means of high levees, canals, pumping stations, and great spillways, which are opened to direct floodwater away from the city.

Outside the French Quarter, the city's face has changed considerably over recent years. The 1984 World's Fair left a legacy of high-rise luxury hotels and a reconstructed waterfront on the fair's site, in what was a derelict warehouse district. New Orleans's emergence as a major financial center (with more than fifty commercial banks) has brought with it the construction of soaring office buildings, mostly in the Central Business District.

But as hard as the present may press itself on New Orleans, it will never completely push out the past. Yesterday lives on in the architecture and lifestyle of the French Quarter, Garden District mansions, and colorful steamboats ferrying passengers around the harbor. While New Orleans is moving ahead into the future, it steadfastly refuses to break its ties to the past, a past that has made it so unique among American cities.

4 The Rhythms of New Orleans

When most people think of New Orleans music, they think of jazz—specifically Dixieland jazz, or "trad" jazz as they call it in Europe. In fact, New Orleans is considered the birthplace of jazz—one of the more remarkable American contributions to western culture—which spread from the Crescent City to such centers as Chicago, New York, Kansas City, and the West Coast and eventually became celebrated throughout the world. The New Orleans area is also home to two other distinctive types of music—Cajun and zydeco—that are enjoying increasing popularity nationally and internationally.

A CENTURY OF JAZZ

Jazz developed in the late 19th century from the work songs, spirituals, and blues sung by African Americans; all of these were rooted in the rhythms and sounds they brought from their homelands. But jazz did not enter the mainstream until it was played and recorded by white bands such as the New Orleans Rhythm Kings and the Original Dixieland Jazz Band, which first brought jazz north. Much later, in the 1930s, jazz's popularity was boosted further by racially mixed bands, led by such figures as Benny Goodman, that performed at major venues like Carnegie Hall.

The earliest jazz bands were called "spasm" bands; they played outside the theaters, saloons, and brothels of the city and employed a makeshift group of instruments—cigar-box fiddles, old kettles, cowbells, pebble-filled gourds, harmonicas, bull fiddles constructed from half a barrel, and various whistles and horns. Equally colorful were the names of the players, ranging from Stalebread Charley to Warm Gravy. One of these groups, the Razzy Dazzy Spasm Band, actually played New York in 1911, and there its name was changed to the Razzy Dazzy *Jazz* Band.

Jazz is improvisational music, and as a result no performance is ever the same—each depends on the personalities, musicianship, and inspirations of the individual players. New Orleans jazz is played by small bands, usually featuring cornet or trumpet; clarinet; trombone; and a rhythm section that includes bass, drums, guitar or banjo, and sometimes piano. When the bands march, as they often do at festivals and funerals, the bass and piano are replaced by a tuba. The difference between the original New Orleans style and the many incarnations of jazz that have followed lies primarily in the original New Orleans emphasis on counterpoint and ensemble—the contrapuntal, improvisational melodic flow between the three lead instruments and the rhythm section. In the big bands of the 1920s and 1930s, for example, emphasis had shifted to a single melodic line played by a virtuoso performer.

In the 19th century, New Orleans was one of the nation's great trading ports, and its society was a lively ethnic mix of Creole, Spanish, and African American elements; it was a lot more relaxed and fun-loving than the typical American Protestant city. Storyville, New Orleans's red-light district, with its brothels, honky-tonk saloons, and gambling dens, was an ideal environment for the growth of jazz. The pioneer African American New Orleans jazz band led by cornet player Buddy Bolden had been formed in the 1890s, but it was not until the all-white Original Dixieland Jazz Band made its first record in 1917 that jazz became widely popular. As long as Storyville existed, New Orleans was the center of the jazz world, but when it closed in 1917, many of the musicians left for northern cities. Kid Ory, King Oliver, Louis Armstrong, Jelly Roll Morton, Barney Bigard, and Johnny Dodds carried the New Orleans torch to Chicago, New York, and elsewhere, eventually evolving distinct sounds of their own.

Gradually the New Orleans style was modified, and a single melodic line with a star performer replaced the ensemble approach to music. With each decade jazz evolved as new performers improvised and experimented, producing new styles for each generation. In the late 1920s swing originated in Kansas City and Harlem, promoted by the big bands of jazz giants Duke Ellington and Count Basie, as well as by groups led by Fletcher Henderson, Glenn Miller, Benny Goodman, Jimmy Lunceford, Artie Shaw, and Tommy Dorsey.

In the late 1930s and 1940s the big band sound was replaced by small groups (often just three or four musicians) playing bebop. With more elaborate rhythms, more convoluted melodies, and a stronger focus on virtuosity, bebop was a beautiful, fiercely improvisational style whose premier exponents were Charlie Parker, Dizzy Gillespie, and Thelonius Monk.

Cool jazz was exactly that—rooted in bebop, but bluesier and with a loping tempo. It was developed in the late 1940s and early 1950s by such seminal figures as Miles Davis, John Coltrane, Lester Young, Stan Getz, and pianist Dave Brubeck. New trends have followed ever since—the neo-bop of Sonny Rollins and Art Blakey; the third-stream combination of classical music and jazz of Charles Mingus and George Lewis; the avant-garde sounds of Ornette Coleman, Archie Shepp, and Roland Kirk; and the various marriages of jazz to Latin, rock, and practically everything else being played.

But New Orleans started it all, and many of the original performers were born in the Crescent City, like the two early giants of jazz, Louis Armstrong and Sidney Bechet. Louis Armstrong learned to play cornet in the Colored Waif's Home in New Orleans. He started playing with Kid Ory's band and made several trips between 1918 and 1921 with a Mississippi riverboat band. In 1922 King Oliver lured him to Chicago to play second trumpet behind him, but soon Louis was building a reputation as a brilliant virtuoso soloist. Possessed of an unforgettable, gravelly vocal style, he organized several bands of his own and appeared on Broadway, as well as in several American and foreign films. The great clarinetist and soprano saxophonist Sidney Bechet was born in New Orleans and began his musical career with his brother's band in 1911. He also played with King Oliver's band but made his greatest name abroad in Europe, where he settled for the last 20 years of his life.

Pianist/composer Jelly Roll Morton, born Ferdinand Joseph La Menthe in Gulfport, Mississippi, began his career in Storyville. A colorful figure whose moods and cantankerous personality led many to disparage him, he claimed that he had single-handedly invented jazz. While this is clearly not the case, he was nevertheless one of the great composers of early jazz, the creator of such great tunes as "Dead Man Blues," "Jelly Roll Blues," "King Porter Stomp," "Sidewalk Blues," and "Wolverine Blues."

King Oliver, born in Abend, Louisiana, began playing in the Onward Brass Band in 1904 and established himself as a leading cornet player in New Orleans. He left in 1918 to form his own band in Chicago, and from 1920 to 1923 led the Creole Jazz Band there, popularizing the New Orleans sound in Chicago and elsewhere in the North. Other famous New Orleans jazz artists have followed—Al Hirt and Pete Fountain, to name two.

There's still a flourishing jazz scene in the city, but don't expect to hear jazz emanating from every club on Bourbon Street as in decades past. Rock and roll, country, and rhythm and blues have replaced jazz on Bourbon Street; today there are only a few places to hear jazz in the French Quarter, the foremost being Preservation Hall. The other serious jazz clubs are outside the Quarter, like Pete Fountain's in the Hilton Hotel.

Jazz, however, is still alive and well, and a new generation of local musicians such as Wynton and Branford Marsalis are among those pushing the music into the future. Their father, Ellis Marsalis, continues to play at venues throughout the city—he's a frequent guest, along with Charmaine Neville, at Snug Harbor. Harry Connick, Jr. (son of the local district attorney who—only in New Orleans—moonlights as a cabaret singer) calls New Orleans home and also plays some of the clubs here when he's in town.

CAJUN & ZYDECO

While jazz remains the prodigal son of musical genres born in New Orleans, Cajun and zydeco also gained fame in the Crescent City. Associated with the bayous and swamps of Lafayette and surrounding areas, these upbeat musical styles were born out

---

Swamp Pop: When Cajun Starts Rockin'

When "swamp pop" or "swamp boogie" developed in the 1950s, producers felt that the traditional Cajun sound needed to be Americanized to win mainstream audiences. Swamp pop was the result—good ole American rock 'n' roll with an unmistakeable Cajun twist. At the time perhaps the producers were right: The first Cajun musicians to make their mark on the national music charts all played swamp pop. These original hits included Bobby Charles's "See Ya Later Alligator" and Phil Phillips's "Sea of Love."

Originally swamp pop was just rock 'n' roll performed by the sons of Cajun musicians—they had grown up hearing that chanky-chank Cajun sound, and its influence came through even when they played rock 'n' roll. Today musicians like Zachary Richard are intentionally blending the sounds. Jimmy Buffet's Margaritaville Cafe, Tipitina's, and Mid-City Lanes Rock 'n' Bowl sometimes feature swamp pop bands.

---

of Acadian folk music. Traditionally played on homemade percussion instruments, violins, triangles, and accordions and rooted in the French ballads of the 1900s, Cajun dance music is upbeat and somewhat reminiscent of bluegrass and country music. Many Cajun songs are still sung in the Acadian dialect of French, so you probably won't understand some of it, but it's really music to dance to, so you won't even notice.

Cajun music was popular in the early part of this century, but never gained widespread popularity. The American folk revival of the 1960s, however, changed all that. At the 1964 Newport Jazz Festival, a traditional Cajun band played before a national audience for the first time, and received a standing ovation. During the 1970s, with the coming of age of musicians like Dewey Balfa, Bruce Daigreport, and Eddie LeJeune, Cajun music finally began to acquire a national following.

While the Acadians were out playing their traditional Cajun sound, their black Creole neighbors were listening and began experimenting with the Cajun rhythms and melodies. By blending it with R&B, blues, and traditional African music they produced what is perhaps the world's most infectious dance music: zydeco. Older generation zydeco performers like John Delaphose rely only on the accordion, drums, and trademark "rub board" (or washboard) vest to produce their sound. Clifton Chenier single-handedly brought zydeco into the modern era, adding electric guitars, driving basslines, saxophones, and trumpets to the traditional zydeco core to produce a hard-rockin', foot-stompin' sound. Check out his *Bogalusa Boogie* (Arhoolie, 1976) for the definitive zydeco introduction.

Some popular groups to look for today include Buckwheat Zydeco, Willis Prudhomme and Zydeco Express, Grammy winner Queen Ida Guillory and the Bon Temps Band, and the incomparable Boozoo Chavis. You can spend an evening cutting a rug to popular traditional Cajun and zydeco tunes at Mulate's and Michaul's on St. Charles (see Chapter 11 for more details).

5 Voodoo

To some, voodoo is synonymous with New Orleans. That's no surprise, really, since voodoo has been practiced widely in the city for almost 200 years.

Some say that voodoo's roots lie in a religion called Vodu from the African kingdom of Dahomey. The Africans believe in the god Zombi, who was said to have been a snake that granted sight to the first people on earth—thus the presence of snakes in voodoo ceremonies. Though snakes are harbingers of evil in the Judeo-Christian tradition, they're an omnipotent force that performs acts of good in voodoo. When large numbers of Africans from the kingdom of Dahomey were transported into the French West Indies as slaves, they brought their religious rituals with them.

By the early 19th century, thousands of African slaves had been brought to the state of Louisiana from the French West Indies. As the slaves moved from Africa into the French West Indies and then into Louisiana, they began to incorporate some of the imagery, iconography, and ritual of Catholicism, learned from their masters, into the traditional African beliefs and rituals they had brought with them. This blending of tribal African religion and Catholicism produced the modern religion of voodoo.

Voodoo so terrified an 18th-century Spanish governor of Louisiana that he refused to allow any more slaves to be imported from the Caribbean, but his decree was in vain, as many French planters (who came from the Caribbean) settled in New Orleans and brought their slaves with them.

Voodoo has a history of being matriarchal, and it is believed that the first organized voodoo ceremony took place in an abandoned brickyard on Dumaine Street and was presided over by Sanite Dede, one of the great voodoo queens. It is interesting to note that the voodoo queens were always free women of color, never slaves. Because police constantly raided the voodoo ceremonies, they moved around from one location to another. Voodoo ceremonies were eventually deemed illegal, except on Sunday. Congo Square in today's Armstrong Park was one of the places in which ceremonies were allowed to take place. Many people used to go to Congo Square on Sunday to watch the singing, chanting, and dancing. It is thought, however, that what went on in that particular public meeting place was nothing like the serious voodoo rituals that took place in secret.

Witnesses to one such ceremony, held on one of voodoo's most important nights, June 23 (St. John's Eve), claimed that they saw naked dancers almost flying in a whirling frenzy around a bonfire and a cauldron, into which they threw live chickens, snails, frogs, black cats, and, of course, snakes. (Some thought that the voodooists stole white babies and sacrificed them during their ceremonies, but this has never been substantiated.) The voodoo queen would dance with the snake while others beat rhythmically on tom-toms. They became like animals—throwing each other to the ground; clawing and biting at each other; having mad, frenzied sex as if in a trance; and ending in an exhausted heap of sweaty, bloodied, naked bodies.

The presence of voodoo in New Orleans today is not nearly as large as it was in the 19th century during the time of Marie Laveau (see feature "Marie Laveau: New Orleans's Voodoo Queen"), but it does still exist—there's a voodoo shop on Bourbon Street and a museum and shop on Dumaine Street, and believers still mark the tombs of both Marie Laveaus (mother and daughter) with red crosses.

Impressions

What little I have seen of this I like perhaps better than any town in the Union. There are pictures on the Quays: there are old French houses: there are streets which look for all the world like Harvre—the sweet kind of French tongue is spoken in the shops . . . . There is capital ordinaire Claret for dinner—The faces are not Yankee faces with their keen eager narrow eyes, there are many fat people—these are interesting facts.
—W. M. Thackeray, Letter to Anne and Harriet Thackeray, 7–10 March 1856

Marie Laveau: New Orleans's Voodoo Queen

One of the most famous names in voodoo around New Orleans is Marie Laveau, a legendary 19th-century voodoo queen. She lived in a house at 1022 St. Ann St., and her voodoo powers were much sought after, even by the city's respectable Catholic families. Their most common request was for succor in turning errant lovers and husbands into ardent and attentive slaves; Marie sold love potions and charms that were purported to work such wonders.

There were actually two Marie Laveaus: a mother and daughter. The original Marie Laveau was said to have had exceptional beauty, even up to her death, but some believe that when the first got too old to continue as voodoo queen, her daughter took over, assuming her mother's identity. Regardless of when the first gave way to the second, people were terrified of Marie Laveau's powers. It is said that she got rid of other queens through her "gris-gris" (*gree-gree*), killing them with her voodoo powers. Due to the fear that Laveau instilled in local politicians, she became one of the great political forces of her day.

Today, people come from all over to leave gifts and offerings on the tombs of both Marie Laveaus. The original voodoo queen is buried in St. Louis No. 1 Cemetery just steps from the Basin Street entrance. The tomb bears the inscription "Marie Philomen Glapion dece'de'e le 11 Juin 1897," but even without the inscription it is easily identifiable—believers mark it with red crosses. Followers also mark a tomb in St. Louis No. 2 Cemetery with red crosses, believing it to be the tomb of the younger Marie Laveau—but nearly every Protestant and Catholic cemetery in town claims to possess the daughter's remains.

6 Famous New Orleanians

Louis Armstrong (1900–71)   One of the all-time jazz greats, "Satchmo" spent part of his boyhood singing in a quartet on the streets of New Orleans. He learned the cornet at the Colored Waif's Home and went on to become perhaps the greatest of all jazz trumpeters, influencing the form and style of all who followed him. His unique vocal style, with a versatile but gravelly voice that brought a warm, confident glow to every tune he touched, is best heard on songs such as "What a Wonderful World," "Caboret," "Hello Dolly," and "Mack the Knife." He became an international star and also appeared in such films as *Pennies from Heaven*. He died in Corona, Queens.

Sidney Bechet (1897–1959)   As a young man, this clarinetist and soprano saxophonist played with the great musicians of New Orleans before moving to Chicago to join the orchestra of Will Marion Cook, with whom he traveled to Europe. He made headlines in London and later returned to play with Duke Ellington and others in New York along 52nd Street. In 1949 he moved to Paris permanently and died there.

Ernest J. Bellocq (ca. 1880–ca. 1945)   A commercial photographer in New Orleans during the early decades of this century, Bellocq made a series of portrait photographs, discovered only after his death, of Storyville "ladies of the evening"; they capture with unusual clarity the romantic legend of New Orleans as a city of unbridled sensuality.

George Washington Cable (1844–1925)   His first book, *Old Creole Days,* was successful and was followed by a number of local genre novels, including *The Creoles* *of Louisiana* (1884), *Bonaventure* (1888), *The Cavalier* (1901), and *The Flower of the Chapdelaines* (1918).

Truman Capote (1924–84)   With *In Cold Blood* (1966), a fictionalized account of a Kansas mass murder, he pioneered the genre of the nonfiction novel. He also wrote *Other Voices, Other Rooms* (1948), *Breakfast at Tiffany's* (1958), and other works, but *In Cold Blood* is considered his masterpiece. His later life was largely destroyed by drugs and alcohol and a constant round of socializing to the detriment of his talent.

Harry Connick, Jr. (b. 1967)   He began playing the piano at the tender age of three, and before he hit puberty he had already worked with a local band on a recording. During his musical development he studied with Ellis and Delfeayo Marsalis and James Booker and was a student at the prestigious New Orleans Center for the Creative Arts (a high school program). The recipient of three Grammy awards, Connick first attracted national attention with the soundtrack to *When Harry Met Sally,* and continues to experiment with new styles, ranging from big band to funk.

Pete Fountain (b. 1930)   This clarinetist and saxophonist began his career in New Orleans in the 1940s playing with Monk Hazel's Band, the Junior Dixieland Band, and others. His great success came when he teamed with Lawrence Welk in 1957, and he went on to TV and radio stardom during the 1960s; during these years he also opened his club on Bourbon Street. Today he performs regularly at his club in the New Orleans Hilton.

Louis Moreau Gottschalk (1829–69)   This pianist and composer was the first American composer to achieve recognition in Europe. Among his piano pieces are "Polka de Salon," "La Savane," "Bamboula," "Souvenir de Porto Rico," and "Ojos Criollos." He also composed songs and orchestral works.

Shirley Ann Grau (b. 1929)   Born in New Orleans, her stories of life in the South were first published in *The New Yorker, The Saturday Evening Post,* and *Mademoiselle.* Later, her books *The Black Prince* and the Pulitzer Prize–winning *Keepers of the House* were published to wide critical acclaim.

Lafcadio Hearn (1850–1904)   Most often associated with Japan, he lived in New Orleans for 10 years beginning in 1877. Among the works he wrote about the city are *Chita* and *Gombo Zhebes;* the latter is a book of Creole proverbs.

Lillian Hellman (1905–84)   This playwright's first stage success, *The Children's Hour* (1934), a drama about a child accusing two teachers of lesbianism, caused a sensation. Other successes followed, like *The Little Foxes, Watch on the Rhine,* and the film *Julia,* which was adapted from her autobiography, *Pentimento.* Politically sympathetic to Communism, she was subpoenaed to appear before the House Committee on Un-American Activities and became even more famous when she refused to testify about others, saying, "I can't cut my conscience to fit this year's fashions."

Al Hirt (b. 1922)   He took up the trumpet at eight and went on to a career with the New Orleans Philharmonic in addition to playing clubs. He became a major recording star, with such hit singles as "Java."

Mahalia Jackson (1911–72)   This gospel singer and civil rights worker learned to sing in the church choir before moving to Chicago in 1927. After making her first recording in 1934, she went on to achieve wide attention with "Move on Up a Little Higher" (1945) and to debut at Carnegie Hall in 1950. She was dedicated to devotional songs and refused to sing the blues.

Marie Laveau (c. 1795–1890)   New Orleans infamous voodoo queen (see feature "Marie Laveau: New Orleans's Voodoo Queen" for more information).

George Lewis (1900–68)   This clarinetist/alto saxophonist was working in brass bands by 1919. Unlike many other jazz musicians, he stayed in New Orleans and led various bands playing regularly at Manny's Tavern in the 1940s. In the 1950s he played Bourbon Street.

Branford Marsalis (b. 1960)   The oldest of Ellis and Dolores Marsalis's six sons, Branford Marsalis began his music career at age four when he learned to play the piano. He later traded the piano for clarinet so he could play in the school band. Over the years he has played with his brother Wynton as well as with The Grateful Dead, and recently ended a stint as music director and arranger for *The Tonight Show with Jay Leno*. Today this Grammy-winning jazz artist plays with his band, Buckshot LeFonque.

Ellis Marsalis (b. 1934)   Literally the father of a great family of jazz musicians, Ellis Marsalis is considered to be the premier jazz pianist in New Orleans today. During his college years, Ellis played with saxophonist Harold Battiste, drummer Edward Blackwell, and clarinetist Alvin Batiste. He has also played with the esteemed Al Hirt and, through his career as an educator (both at Xavier University and the New Orleans Center for the Creative Arts), has influenced more than a few of today's greatest jazz musicians (including Harry Connick, Jr.).

Wynton Marsalis (b. 1961)   A member of a true jazz family (See Ellis Marsalis and Branford Marsalis, above), Wynton Marsalis is living proof that jazz is alive and well in New Orleans. A prodigiously talented trumpeter, he is known for his virtuosic solos and as an active proponent of traditional modern jazz.

Jelly Roll Morton (1890–1941)   A pianist and composer, he was born in Gulfport, Mississippi, but by 1906 was playing piano in Storyville brothels. By 1923 he had moved to Chicago. His most famous recordings are those made with the Red Hot Peppers between 1926 and 1930. Colorful and cantankerous, he claimed to have single-handedly invented jazz, and indeed he did compose some great tunes, including "Jelly Roll Blues" and "Black Bottom Stomp." In the 1930s his personal ensemble style was eclipsed by the big band sound.

Walker Percy (1916–90)   Born in Alabama, this novelist lived for many years in a suburb of New Orleans, and most of his works have the city as background. Among his famous works are *The Moviegoer* (1961), *The Last Gentleman* (1966), and *Love in the Ruins* (1971).

Anne Rice (b. 1941)   New Orleans–born Anne Rice has authored a number of best-selling gothic horror novels, including cult favorites *Interview with the Vampire* and *The Vampire Lestat*. Her novel *Lasher* is set in Rice's Garden District mansion. Rice currently lives on First Street in the Garden District.

Sarah Walker (1867–1919)   Born in Delta, Louisiana, she became famous as Madam C. J. Walker, one of the first successful African-American female entrepreneurs and philanthropists. She invented a method for straightening hair, established a factory in Indianapolis, and built a major business.

Andrew Young (b. 1932)   Most famous for his controversial stint as U.S. ambassador to the United Nations, Young, a New Orleans native, has been active in American politics for 30 years. He was a leader in the civil rights movement, has been a U.S. congressman, was an adviser to Jimmy Carter through the early and mid-1970s, and most recently was a two-term mayor of Atlanta, Georgia (1982–89). As ambassador to the U.N., Young was an outspoken advocate of third world nations until he was forced to resign in 1979 after meeting secretly with a member of the PLO.

7 A Taste of New Orleans

Reflecting the cultural diversity of its population, New Orleans's cuisine is a tasty gumbo of French provincial, Spanish, Italian, West Indian, African, and Native American influences, all tied together with down-home southern cooking. Those who return time after time to the city do so as much for the food as for the music, the sightseeing, and Mardi Gras. Indeed, dining out in New Orleans can truly be called entertainment.

Provincial French recipes brought to the New World by early settlers fast took on a subtle twist with the use of native herbs and filé (ground sassafras leaves) from Native Americans. Saffron and peppers arrived with the Spanish somewhat later. From the West Indies came new vegetables, spices, and sugarcane, and when slave boats arrived, landing many a black woman in the kitchens of white slave owners, an African influence was added. Out of all this came the distinctive Creole culinary style unique to New Orleans. Italian immigrants later on added yet another dimension to the city's tables, and, through it all, traditional Old South dishes were retained virtually intact. Along with their love of exciting combinations of international cuisines, the people of New Orleans have inherited an appreciation for fine service in elegant surroundings. Their sense of fun also delights in gourmet dishes that appear in the plainest of settings, as well as in eating the plainest of meals (such as boiled crawfish or red beans and rice) in the fanciest of eateries. Many New Orleanians eat out at least three times a week, and they may stretch out an evening to include cocktails at a favorite spot, an appetizer (such as oysters Rockefeller) at another, an entrée at still another, and perhaps a dessert in a favorite courtyard setting. For many the evening is not complete without a stop at the Café du Monde for café au lait. By all means follow their example and double or even triple the number of restaurants you get to sample during even a short stay.

THE CUISINE   Both *Cajun* and *Creole* have come to mean "New Orleans." What's the difference between the two cuisines? Chiefly it lies in their origins. Cajun cooking came from country folk—the Acadians who left France for Nova Scotia in the 1600s and made their way to the swamps and bayous of rural Louisiana after being expelled from Canada by the British in the 1700s. Their much-loved French dishes traveled with them, but along the way the recipes were adapted to ingredients available locally. Their cuisine tends to be quite robust and hearty, with sausage, duck, poultry, pork, and seafood prepared in a rich roux (a seasoned sauce of fat—usually butter—and flour that lends a distinctive flavor) and served over rice. Creole dishes, on the other hand, were developed by French and Spanish city dwellers. Delicate sauces and attention to presentation are characteristic of "haute Creole," while "low Creole" favorites, such as red beans and rice, are likely to come to the table with as little fanfare as Cajun food.

In practice, however, the two cuisines have effected such a happy marriage in New Orleans that it's often difficult to distinguish between them. Internationally famed Paul Prudhomme, of K-Paul's Louisiana Kitchen, says simply that what has emerged is "Louisiana food." He goes on to say, "Nowhere else have all the ethnic groups merged to combine all these different tastes, and the only way you'll know the difference, honey, is to live 'em!" Suffice it to say that no matter how a New Orleans restaurant classifies its culinary offerings, you're bound to find one or two examples of Cajun and Creole cooking on the menu.

The much-loved spices of these two popular cuisines are onions (both green and yellow), bay leaf, thyme, parsley, cloves, allspice, cayenne pepper, filé, and Tabasco.

There is a whole family of sausages: boudin (*boo-DAN*), which contains onions, spices, pork, and rice and comes in white or red; chaurice (*cho-REECE*), which is a hard sausage used chiefly for flavoring beans or soups; andouille (*ahn-doo-WE*), which is also hard and a bit saltier than chaurice; and delicious smoked sausages. Seafood is everywhere—in fact, I find it next to impossible to order anything else when I'm in town. Oysters on the half shell (usually simply called "raw oysters" in New Orleans) are just the beginning of an oyster feast that includes soups; stews; pies; baked specialties, such as oysters Rockefeller (on the half shell in a creamy sauce, with spinach—so named because that was the only name rich enough for the taste); an oyster loaf (which elevates "sandwich" into the realm of a delicacy); and a host of other creations. Crabs, shrimp, and crawfish are used in imaginative recipes or served plain, hot or cold. Gumbo is a thick soup, always served with rice, usually containing crab, shrimp (sometimes oysters), and okra in a roux base. Jambalaya is made with meat and seafood combined with rice and seasonings. Beef and veal (you may see either on a menu as *daube,* pronounced *dohb*) take on added luster in New Orleans restaurants, as do classic French and Italian dishes. There's also a special quality to the French bread, with its crisp, flaky crust and its insides as light as a feather.

Two mainstays of any native's diet are red beans and rice and "po-boy" sandwiches, which once cost a nickel. This sandwich is made with a long, skinny bread loaf and can contain anything from roast beef and gravy; to ham and cheese; to fried fish, shrimp, soft-shell crabs, or oysters (in which case it becomes an oyster loaf). One of the largest (and tastiest) sandwiches you'll ever see is the muffuletta—a mountain of Italian sausages and meats with an unusual olive salad (consisting of pickled carrots and celery, capers, olives, and other delights) piled onto an eight-inch round Italian "bun."

DRINKS   Never let it be said that New Orleanians neglect the libations that precede, accompany, and follow a proper meal. As a matter of fact, they lay claim to adding the word *cocktail* to our modern vocabulary. A Monsieur Peychaud, who presided over the bar at 437 Rue Royale in the early 19th century, took to serving small drinks in egg cups—*couquetiers* in French—and Americans took to ordering them using a mangled version of the word. Since then more than a few inspired concoctions have appeared on the scene, among them the Sazerac (bourbon or rye with bitters), the Ramos gin fizz (gin, egg whites, and orange-flavored water), and the Hurricane (rum and passion fruit punch). If you're a cocktail drinker you'll find yourself right at home here.

As for coffee, you'll find it strong, hot, and black, with or without chicory (which adds a slightly bitter flavor—it was first used to stretch scarce coffee beans during the Civil War). Chicory coffee just might be what the Turks had in mind when they declared that the beverage should be "black as hell, strong as death, and sweet as love." Stouthearted purists drink it black and won't take it any other way, but most natives mix it half-and-half with hot milk for café au lait. And at least once during your stay, end a meal with café brûlot (*cah-FAY brew-LOW*), a lovely mixture of coffee, spices, and liqueurs served in a special cup, with ladle and chafing dish, and flamed at your table.

Restaurants pride themselves on their wine lists. If you are doubtful as to what to order with your entrée, don't worry—your waiter will know. And to top it all off, there are also several local beers, including Dixie, Abita Turbo Dog, and Blackened Voodoo.

TERMS TO KNOW   Here's a list of terms that will help you navigate any New Orleans menu:

andouille (*ahn-doo-WE*) Spicy Cajun sausage made with pork.

beignet (*bin-YEA*) A cross between a doughnut and a cruller, liberally sprinkled with powdered sugar.

café brûlot (*cah-FAY brew-LOW*) Coffee mixed with spices and liqueurs and served flaming.

crawfish (*CRAW-fish*) A tiny, lobsterlike creature plentiful in the waters around New Orleans and eaten in every conceivable way.

dirty rice A popular menu item, this rice only looks dirty because of the spices in which it's cooked—usually chicken livers and gizzards, onions, chopped celery, green bell pepper, cayenne, black-and-white peppers, and chicken stock.

dressed "Served with the works"—as when ordering a sandwich.

eggs hussarde Poached eggs with hollandaise and marchand de vin sauce with tomatoes and ham. Marchand de vin is a wine sauce flavored with onions, shallots, celery, carrots, garlic, red wine, beef broth, and herbs.

eggs sardou Legend has it that this dish was created especially for French playwright Victorien Sardou (author of *La Tosca*) by Antoine Alciatore. It includes poached eggs, artichoke bottoms, anchovy fillets, hollandaise, and truffles or ham as a garnish.

étouffée (*ay-too-FAY*) A Cajun stew (usually containing crawfish) served with rice.

filé (*FEE-lay*) A thickener made of ground sassafras leaves. Filé is frequently used to thicken gumbo.

grillades (*gree-YADS*) Thin slices of beef or veal smothered in a tomato- and beef-flavored gravy. Often served with grits.

grits Grains of dried corn that have been ground and hulled, grits are a staple of the southern breakfast table. They are most frequently served with butter and salt (not maple syrup or brown sugar) or red-eye gravy.

gumbo A thick, spicy soup, always served with rice.

hurricane A local drink of rum and passion fruit punch.

hush puppies Fried balls of cornmeal, often served as a side dish with seafood.

jambalaya (*jum-ba-LIE-ya*) A jumble of yellow rice, sausage, seafood, vegetables, and spices.

lagniappe (*lan-YAP*) A little something extra you've neither paid for nor deserve—like the 13th doughnut when you order a dozen.

muffuletta One of the tastiest sandwiches you'll ever have—Italian sausage, deli meats, one or two kinds of cheese, olive salad (pickled olives, celery, carrots, cauliflower, and capers), and oil and vinegar, piled onto a round loaf (about eight inches in diameter) of Italian bread that is specially made for these incredible sandwiches.

pain perdu (*pan PAIR-du*) Literally translated, "lost bread," this is New Orleans's version of French toast, and it's made with French bread (at home, it's a good way to use up that day-old bread). You'll find a large variety of toppings on pain perdu as you make your way around New Orleans. My favorite is a chocolate version made by Emeril Lagasse.

pralines (*PRAW-lines*) A very sweet confection made of brown sugar and pecans—they come in "original" and creamy styles.

shrimp Creole Shrimp in a tomato sauce that's seasoned with what's known around town as "the trinity": onions, garlic, and green bell pepper.

tasso A local variety of ham. You won't be surprised to learn that this is no weak little honey baked ham: it's smoked and seasoned with red pepper.

8 Recommended Books & Recordings

BOOKS

FICTION   Early fiction that is still worth reading to get a flavor of New Orleans life includes George Washington Cable's stories and novels, the most famous being his *Old Creole Days,* published in 1879. His not-always-flattering portrait of the Creoles was corrected by Grace King in her short stories and her novel *The Pleasant Ways of St. Medard* (1916). Lyle Saxon and Roark Bradford also wrote books about the legendary figures and tales associated with New Orleans, including Saxon's *Fabulous New Orleans* (1988) and Bradford's Civil War novel *Kingdom Coming,* which contains a lot of information about voodoo. As a riverboat captain, Mark Twain visited the city often, and his *Life on the Mississippi* contains a substantial number of tales of New Orleans and its riverfront life.

William Faulkner lived on Pirates Alley and wrote *Pylon,* which is set in New Orleans, as well as a series of short stories about the city. He penned *Soldier's Pay* while living on Pirates Alley. Tennessee Williams was inspired during his brief stay in the city to write *A Streetcar Named Desire; The Rose Tattoo* also is set in the city. Frances Parkinson Keyes lived in the city for more than 25 years on Chartres Street. Her most famous works are *Dinner at Antoine's* and *Madame Castel's Lodger.*

Perhaps the city's best-known contemporary writer is Anne Rice, whose best-selling vampire chronicles, which include *Interview with the Vampire* (later made into a film) and *Mnemnoch, the Devil,* are set in New Orleans. Her novel *Lasher* (Random House, 1993) is set in her stately home on First Street in the Garden District. Other notable modern writers include Walker Percy and Shirley Ann Grau. The former's novel *The Moviegoer* (1961) has Carnival Week as a background; the latter's most famous novel, *The Keepers of the House,* won the Pulitzer in 1964. Another Pulitzer also went, albeit posthumously, to John Kennedy Toole's *A Confederacy of Dunces,* a marvelous comic portrait of New Orleans life that you would do well to read before or during your visit. Ellen Gilchrist is another nationally recognized contemporary fiction writer whose work you might want to delve into. Her collection of short stories, *In the Land of Dreamy Dreams* (University of Arkansas, 1985), is a wonderful series of portraits of life in wealthy Uptown New Orleans.

There are several choices in new fiction as well. *Light Sister, Dark Sister,* by Lee Walmsley, is set against a New Orleans background. *With Extreme Prejudice,* by Frederick Barton, is a murder-thriller that takes readers from the mean streets of New Orleans to the picturesque Garden District. For a novel that captures the racial tension of New Orleans, look for *Glass House* by Christine Wiltz. Valerie Martin's *The Great Divorce* is a retelling of Dr. Jekyll and Mr. Hyde set in contemporary antebellum New Orleans.

HISTORY   If you're looking to bone up on New Orleans history before you leave, *A Short History of New Orleans* (Lexicos, 1982) by Mel Leavitt will help. *The WPA Guide to New Orleans* also contains some excellent social and historical background and provides a fascinating picture of the city in 1938.

Impressions

*It is the most congenial city in America that I know of and it is due in large part,
I believe, to the fact that here at last on this bleak continent the sensual pleasures
assume the importance which they deserve . . . .*
— Henry Miller, *The Air-Conditioned Nightmare,* 1945

There are many guides to Mardi Gras, including Robert Tallant's *Mardi Gras* and Myron Tassin's *Mardi Gras and Bacchus: Something Old, Something New,* both published by Pelican.

For the definitive account of Storyville, you can't beat Al Rose's *Storyville, New Orleans, Being an Authentic Illustrated Account of the Notorious Redlight District* (University of Alabama Press, 1974).

Other books worth reading include Lyle Saxon's *Fabulous New Orleans* (Pelican, 1988), *New Orleans: Facts and Legends* by Raymond Martinez and Jack Holmes (Hope Publications, 1980), and *The French Quarter and Other New Orleans Scenes* by Joseph A. Arrigo (Pelican, 1980).

If you're interested in women's history, I'd recommend *Women and New Orleans* by Mary Gehman; it's fascinating and well written.

ART, ARCHITECTURE & ANTIQUES   New Orleans is famous for its architecture, and there's an abundance of books available on this subject. *New Orleans Architecture* is a helpful and interesting series—each volume deals with a different area of the city, such as the Garden District, the Lower Garden District, Esplanade Ridge, and the Vieux Carré. The series is published by Friends of the Cabildo, which also published a small book on historical landmarks of New Orleans.

Another book you might want to refer to is *The Great Houses of New Orleans* by Curt Bruce (Knopf, 1977).

Antique lovers will appreciate a little book called *New Orleans Furniture* (The Knapp Press), which has color photographs with descriptive captions that help explain Louisiana antiques.

FOR KIDS   The **Greater New Orleans Tourist and Convention Commission** has just published a guidebook that is specifically for kids, with activities, such as dot-to-dots, and stories so your children can follow along as you sightsee. If you're interested, you should contact them directly at 1520 Sugar Bowl Dr., New Orleans, LA 70112 (☎ **504/566-5055**).

Additionally your kids might enjoy Mary Alice Fontenont's Clovis Crawfish Series (Pelican), a series of books whose main character is a crawfish struggling with everyday issues.

COOKBOOKS   There's no greater source of information about the history of food and its ingredients than local cookbooks. In New Orleans you can get cookbooks of all sorts at bookstores around town, as well as in some of the specialty food shops. Just about every popular New Orleans restaurant has published a cookbook or two. Among them are Emeril's, Antoine's, K-Paul's, Commander's Palace, and Dooky Chase. One of my favorite cookbooks is Craig Claiborne's *Southern Cooking* (Times Books, 1987). It features recipes from all over the South, but there are a large number of them that are specific to New Orleans. *River Roads Recipes* (Junior League of Baton Rouge, 1959) is a popular old standby. The Junior League of New Orleans has also gathered a collection of local recipes in *The Plantation Cookbook* (Trice Publishing, 1989). Finally, John Folse's *The Encyclopedia of Cajun and Creole Cuisine*

(The Encyclopedia Cookbook Committee, 1983) features simple recipes and is a good place to start if you'd like to try your hand at Cajun and Creole cooking.

MUSIC   There are scores of books available on the music of New Orleans, but the following list should get you started:

John Broven's *South to Louisiana: The Music of the Cajun Bayous* (Pelican, 1987) gives an interesting and detailed introduction to the music of the Cajun people.

For a look at specific time periods, people, and places in the history of New Orleans jazz, try reading William Carter's *Preservation Hall* (Norton, 1991); John Chilton's *Sidney Bechet: The Wizard of Jazz* (Oxford University Press, 1988); Humphrey Lyttleton's *The Best of Jazz: Basin Street to Harlem 1917–30* (Taplinger, 1982); and Gunther Schuller's *Early Jazz: Its Roots and Musical Development* (Oxford University Press, 1968). Al Rose's *Storyville, New Orleans* (University of Alabama Press, 1974) (mentioned above) is an excellent source of information about the very beginnings of jazz. The book also includes some wonderful photography by Ernest Bellocq.

If you'd rather get your information straight from the men who helped put jazz on the map, read Louis Armstrong's *Satchmo, My Life in New Orleans* (Da Capo Press, 1986) and Sidney Bechet's *Treat It Gentle* (Da Capo Press, 1960). Both autobiographies are captivating. *Jazz Makers: Essays on the Greats of Jazz* (Da Capo Press, 1979), by Nat Shapiro and Nat Hentoff, is also excellent. Other books of note published by Da Capo are Samuel B. Charters's *Jazz: New Orleans 1885–1963* (1983) and Leonard Feather's *The Encyclopedia of Jazz* (1965).

RECORDINGS

New Orleans has been so central to the history of jazz that it would be impossible to list all the great recordings here. There are several books currently available that do just that, provide discographies that cover the history of the music, including Len Lyon's *The 101 Best Jazz Albums: A History of Jazz on Records* (Morrow, 1980); Brian Priestly's *Jazz on Record: A History* (Billboard, 1991); and James McCalla's *Jazz: A Listener's Guide* (Prentice Hall, 1982).

Whether they play jazz, rhythm and blues, Cajun, or zydeco, New Orleanian musicians have always had a particularly infectious good-time sensibility. Listening to any of the following recordings (many are anthologies) will help you get a feel for it.

JAZZ   Louis Armstrong: *Louis Armstrong and Earl "Fatha" Hines 1928* (Smithsonian); *The Genius of Louis Armstrong* (Columbia); *Ella and Louis* (Verve); *What a Wonderful World* (MCA). Sidney Bechet: *Bechet of New Orleans* (Columbia); *Jazz Classics Vol. 1 and 2* (Blue Note). Kid Ory: *Kid Ory's Creole Jazz Band* (Folklyric). King Oliver: *The Immortal King Oliver* (Milestone); *King Oliver's Jazz Band 1923* (Smithsonian). Jelly Roll Morton: *Jelly Roll Morton 1923–24* (Milestone); *The Complete Jelly Roll Morton, Vols. 1–4* (RCA).

RHYTHM & BLUES   Dirty Dozen Brass Band: *Mardi Gras in Montreux: Live* (Rounder, 1985). Dr. John: *Gris Gris* (Atco, 1968); *Gumbo* (Atco, 1972). Meters: *Cissy Strut* (Island, 1975); *Rejuvenation* (Reprise, 1974). Neville Brothers: *Yellow Moon* (A&M, 1989). Professor Longhair: *New Orleans Piano* (Atco, 1953). Anthologies: *Ace Story, Vol. 1* (Ace, 1981); *New Orleans Jazz and Heritage Festival* (Island); *New Orleans Party Classics* (Rhino).

CAJUN & ZYDECO   Balfa Brothers: *J'ai Vu La Lupe, Le Renard et La Belette* (Rounder, 1977). Buckwheat Zydeco: *100% Fortified Zydeco* (Black Top Records, 1988). Clifton Chenier: *Bogalusa Boogie* (Arhoolie, 1976); *Classic Clifton* (Arhoolie, 1981); *Zodico Blues & Boogie* (Specialty, 1993). Anthology: *Louisiana Cajun Music Special* (Ace, 1977); *Alligator Stomp: Cajun and Zydeco Classics* (Rhino).

Mardi Gras & Other Festivals

2

New Orleans means "festival"—if you don't believe it, try this simple little free-association test. What's the first thing that comes to mind when someone says "New Orleans"? Mardi Gras, right? Well, that's the biggie, of course, but it's only one of this lively city's celebrations. There's something about the frame of mind here that just won't tolerate inhibitions—whether there's a declared celebration in progress or not.

As for officially designated festival days, a calendar of events issued by the New Orleans Metropolitan Convention and Visitors Bureau lists no fewer than 26 spread over the year that are observed either in the city proper or in its neighboring parishes. There's a festival of jazz and food; a celebration of spring, when women don the costumes of long ago and shepherd the public through gorgeous old mansions; numerous food festivals that celebrate the fine art of eating as it's practiced around here; and, well, you get the idea. If there's any possible reason to celebrate, New Orleans throws a party.

I can't, of course, cover them all in these pages. I'll tell you about some of the most interesting, and you can find others listed in the "Calendar of Events" in Chapter 3. If you take my advice, you'll also write or call ahead to the **New Orleans Metropolitan Convention and Visitors Bureau,** 1520 Sugar Bowl Dr., New Orleans, LA 70112 (☎ **504/566-5055**), to see what else might be happening when you visit. If, however, you don't see anything spectacular listed for the dates of your trip, don't worry—New Orleans is the kind of city that makes you feel festive from the moment you arrive.

1 Mardi Gras

Mardi Gras, of course, is the mother of all festivals. Volumes could be written about its history, and almost any native you encounter will have his or her own store of Mardi Gras tales. What follows here is a thumbnail sketch of its background and a quick rundown on present-day krewes, parades, and balls.

To begin with, the name *Mardi Gras* means "Fat Tuesday" in French, and that's a very appropriate name because it is always celebrated on the Tuesday before Ash Wednesday—the idea being that you have an obligation to eat, drink, and be as merry as you possibly can before the 40-day Lenten season of fasting and repentance sets in. The name *Carnival* is Latin in origin (from *carnisvale*, meaning "farewell to flesh") and refers to the six- to eight-week stretch from Twelfth Night, or January 6, to Mardi Gras Day. In New Orleans, the Carnival season is officially opened by the Krewe of Twelfth Night Revelers ball, the only ball that has a fixed date.

THE ROOTS OF REVELRY: MARDI GRAS HISTORY

Where did the custom start? Nobody knows for certain, but some historians see a relationship to ancient tribal rites connected with the coming of spring. And a glorious, sin-filled, pagan orgy that highlighted mid-February for ancient Romans may also have been an early ancestor of today's Mardi Gras. The Christian church did its best to stamp out such wild goings-on, but about all it succeeded in doing was insisting on a strict period of fasting and praying to follow the festive season. So although New Orleans can properly claim Mardi Gras for its own in the United States, its spirit of revelry belongs to the history of the world.

When the French explorer Pierre Le Moyne, Sieur d'Iberville, and his group of colonizers camped along the Mississippi in 1699, he didn't bother with keeping records, other than to note that the date was March 3. We don't know for sure, therefore, what that day's activities were in the little camp. What we *do* know is that March 3 was the day before Ash Wednesday in that year, and that he named the spot, some 12 miles north of the river's mouth, "Point du Mardi Gras."

It wasn't long after New Orleans was established in 1718 that the French began an organized celebration of Mardi Gras, although their celebration rather paled in comparison to today's revelry, consisting largely of private masked balls and parties, with street dancing limited to the poor (but lighthearted) elements of the population. When the Spanish governors took up residence, they slapped a ban on such doings, and the Americans who began arriving in 1803 continued the ban. It wasn't until 1823 that French Quarter Creoles persuaded the city government to permit the masquerade balls once more, and by 1827 it was legal to wear masks in the streets on the great day. When those street maskers started marching in processions that might— by a *big* stretch of the imagination—be called parades is uncertain, but in 1837 the *Daily Picayune* published for the first time an account of a Mardi Gras parade.

For the next few years things began to get out of hand, with so much wildness in the streets that it seemed inevitable that the city government would have to do something to quell the disorderliness. The future of Mardi Gras in New Orleans was very much in doubt, as newspapers and citizens aroused by street violence called for a permanent end to the festival. It took six new residents of the city, who had formerly lived in Mobile, Alabama, to turn things around. Determined to save Mardi Gras and restore some semblance of order and dignity to its observance, they met with 13 friends in what was known as "the club room" over the Gem bar at 127 Royal St. What came out of that meeting was a secret society, the Mistick Krewe of Comus, dedicated to preserving the institution of Carnival. They actually coined the "krewe" appellation, and they planned the first formal, torch-lit parade that was the pattern for all that have followed. Still adhered to, as well, is the practice of building each krewe's parade around a central theme, as did the Krewe of Comus in the first parade. It was from the Comus krewe, too, that New Orleanians took the practice of forming secret societies and ending each parade with private fancy balls that are always preceded by an elaborate tableau.

The Civil War put a temporary halt to things, but Comus was parading again by 1866. In 1870 a krewe known as the Twelfth Night Revelers was founded and added two new customs that still endure: They began the throwing of trinkets to onlookers (the first thrower was dressed as Santa Claus), and they were the first to have an

---

Some Mardi Gras Tips

Catching a Throw If someone throws you something from a float or a balcony and it actually makes it to the ground, don't go after it with your hands—step on it first to let everyone around you know that it's yours. When interest in what's under your foot wanes, it's safe to pocket the treasure. Otherwise, you'll probably end up with several broken fingers.

Parking Parking in New Orleans during Mardi Gras can be both costly and next to impossible, so you're best off to leave your car at the hotel and walk or take a cab to your intended spot along the parade route. Parking along the parade route is not allowed two hours before and two hours after the parade. In addition, although you'll see people leaving their cars on "neutral ground" (the median in the street), it is illegal to park there and the chances are good that you'll be towed. Parking and driving around the French Quarter are also restricted. If your hotel is in the French Quarter you can probably get a pass that will allow you access to your hotel's parking area.

Liquor Laws Liquor laws in New Orleans are quite lax. Many bars are open 24 hours during Mardi Gras, and drinking is allowed on the street. However, for safety reasons, you are required to have drinks in plastic "geaux" (or "go") cups.

Crime Not surprisingly, the streets of New Orleans are a haven for pickpockets during Mardi Gras. Take precautions.

---

official "queen" reign over their ball. A royal visit in 1872 contributed something more to New Orleans's Mardi Gras traditions. The grand duke of Russia, Alexis Alexandrovitch Romanov, followed his ladylove, a musical-comedy actress named Lydia Thompson, from New York when she came to star in *Bluebeard*. The city went all out to welcome him, and when it was learned that his favorite song was Lydia's favorite burlesque tune, "If Ever I Cease to Love You," every band in the Rex parade was asked to play it—that sprightly melody is now the official song of Mardi Gras. Incidentally, the prestigious Krewe of Rex was born that year when a group of citizens banded together to raise money for an impressive welcome ceremony for the duke. The royal colors (purple for justice, green for faith, and gold for power) were also adopted as the festival's official colors.

Today's traditional ending of Mardi Gras had its beginning in 1882, when Rex and his queen called on the Court of Comus at that krewe's ball. The Krewe of Rex also began throwing medallions instead of trinkets in 1884, and the "doubloons" that came many years later are an outgrowth of that substitution. The doubloons, usually of aluminum or anodized gold, show the krewe's coat of arms on one side and the parade theme of the year on the other—they're a marvelous souvenir of Mardi Gras if you're lucky enough to catch one (you can purchase them at some stores, but somehow that just isn't the same). They have become highly prized, so hold on to any you may acquire—some serious collector may someday offer a good price. The best way to come by one is to stand in the crowd and yell, "Throw me something, mister," along with everyone else as the floats pass by.

New Orleans's African Americans entered the Mardi Gras scene through a fun-filled back door. In 1909 a black man named William Storey mocked the elaborately garbed Rex by prancing after his float wearing a lard can for a crown. Storey was promptly dubbed "King Zulu." By 1916 his followers had grown so in numbers that they formed the Zulu Social Aid and Pleasure Club, and for years they observed Mardi Gras by wandering all over town, from one barroom to another that would extend hospitality to King Zulu. These days the Zulus get the day off to a start when his majesty arrives by boat (at the foot of Canal Street) at 7am, and they follow a set parade route through the city's streets on proper floats instead of the banged-up trucks and wagons they used in their early years. They're worth getting up early to see just for their grass skirts and sometimes outrageous makeup and masks. Besides the monarch in his colorful raiment, there's a "Provident Prince" and a "Big Shot of Africa" to look for, all decked out in the Good Lord only knows what. The most notable King Zulu was probably Louis Armstrong in 1949. In 1980 Armstrong's good friend Woody Herman realized a longtime dream when he donned blackface and was crowned king of the Zulus.

Other early morning Mardi Gras groups not to be missed are the "walking clubs," with names such as Jefferson City Buzzards, the Pete Fountain Half Fast, and Peggy Landry's Silk Stocking Strutters. To quote Arthur Hardy (author of a Mardi Gras guidebook), these clubs are "sometimes mistakenly named 'marching clubs'—actually, they *never* march; some do walk, but more than a few stumble!" You can catch these "marchers," who as much as the krewe parades embody the spirit of the day, anywhere along their St. Charles Avenue route (between Poydras and Washington).

WHAT TO SEE & DO

What can you expect to see and take part in if you come to New Orleans for Mardi Gras? First, you must remember that this is, primarily, a party New Orleans throws for itself—those spectacular balls are private, attended only by members and their invited guests. Attendance is by invitation, not by ticket, except, that is, for the Bacchus supper dance (and even those tickets are usually hard to come by). If you should be invited to a krewe ball, there are a few things you should know. You'll be a spectator, not a participant, and unless you're a woman and have been issued a "call-out" card, you'll be seated in a separate section to view the tableau after the previous year's queen and her court have been escorted to seats of honor and masked-and-costumed krewe members have taken their reserved, up-front seats. Members, who guard their secrecy not just during Mardi Gras but year-round, are always in costumes and masks—for men it's white tie and tails if the invitation reads *de rigueur*, tuxedos if it reads only *formal*. Women, of course, are always in ball gowns. Those lucky "call-out" women will be seated separately from other guests (even their escorts) until the dancing begins and they've been called out by the krewe member who sent them the card. After a turn around the floor, they'll be given a krewe favor (a souvenir representative of that year's ball theme) and returned to their escorts. As members of the krewe and their ladies continue dancing, the current "royal court" will repair to the queen's supper, where friends and guests will be entertained the rest of the night—and into the morning.

One of the nicest things about New Orleans's private party is that the whole world is invited to come and look, and there are a whole slew of not-so-private entertainments. If you think this town's restaurants and nightclubs and bars and jazz clubs are pretty special most of the time, you should see them during Carnival! You can, in fact, form your own informal "krewe" of friends and have a ball that might be as much fun as those private ones, just by making the rounds in a group.

Whatever else you do or don't do, you surely won't miss seeing a Mardi Gras parade—if, that is, you come during the final 11 days of Carnival. You'll know one's coming when you hear the scream of motorcycle sirens and a herd of motorized police come into view. They'll be followed by men on horseback (sometimes mounted police, sometimes krewe members) who clear the edges of the streets for the approaching floats. The king's float is first in line, with his majesty enthroned and waving to the mass of cheering humanity with his scepter. Then will come a float with a banner proclaiming the theme of the parade. After that, each float will illustrate some facet of the theme. And it's a grand sight—the papier-mâché lions or elephants or flowers or fanciful creatures or whatever are sometimes enormous (there are people in New Orleans who work all year designing and building Mardi Gras floats), and there's much use of silver and gold tinsel that sparkles in the sunlight or the light of torches. Those torches, or flambeaux, are carried by costumed dancers. Each float has masked krewe members who wave and throw doubloons and souvenirs. In some of the parades, the floats keep coming until you think there's no end to them—in one recent year, Bacchus had 23 and Rex had 25. Each krewe has its designated time and parade route (which makes a current Mardi Gras guidebook invaluable) and most follow some part of St. Charles Avenue, sometimes a portion of Jackson Street as well, and Canal Street, and end up at the Municipal Auditorium, where all parades disband—except the renegade Bacchus, which has a Rivergate terminus. Because there are more than 50 parading krewes and only 11 days in which to do the parading, the streets are seldom empty, day or night, during this period. And the rollicking, costumed crowd filling the streets is as much something to see as the parades themselves. Every conceivable manner of costume appears, and maskers made bold by their temporary anonymity carry on in the most outrageous, hilarious manner imaginable. A great good humor envelops the whole scene.

On Mardi Gras, the last day of Carnival, the walking clubs are out at the crack of dawn, King Zulu arrives around 9am, the Rex parade is midmorning, and Comus closes the day with its evening parade (about 6:30pm). The high point of the final day is probably when Rex, the only Mardi Gras king whose identity is disclosed, arrives on his majestic float. It is a very high honor to be chosen Rex, and the selection always comes from among prominent men in the city, most well past the first blush of youth. Rex's queen, on the other hand, is always one of the current year's pack of debutantes. Although they make for a pretty ill-matched royal couple, there've never been any reports of incompatibility between the rulers-for-a-day. The choosing of Rex and his queen is done in the strictest secrecy, adding to the excitement that attends their first public appearance in the parade.

Another thing that's nice about Carnival in New Orleans is the fact that it doesn't cost the city one red cent, except the cost of extra police for the parades and that of cleaning up the streets after Fat Tuesday. This is truly a private celebration, planned, executed, and paid for by New Orleanians themselves—and I'll wager that if none of us dropped in for the festivities, the celebration would not change one iota.

PLANNING YOUR FESTIVAL

Now for the practicalities. First, you can't really just drop in. If you do, you may find yourself sleeping in Jackson Square or on a sidewalk somewhere. Accommodations are booked solid in the city itself and in the nearby suburbs, *so make your plans well ahead and book a room as soon as the plans are finalized*. It is no exaggeration to say that you should make your plans a full year or more in advance. Prices are usually higher during Mardi Gras, and most hotels and guest houses impose minimum-stay requirements.

If you want to join the maskers in costume it's best to plan ahead and come prepared; there are, however, several shops in town that specialize in Mardi Gras costumes and masks (see Chapter 10). One of the most reasonable is the **Mardi Gras**

Mardi Gras from 1997 to 2000

You can always figure out the date of Mardi Gras because it falls exactly 46 days before Easter. If you can't find your calendar, or just can't be bothered with the math, the following will help:

February 11, 1997

February 24, 1998

February 16, 1999

March 7, 2000

Center, 831 Chartres St. (☎ **504/524-4384**). If you come early enough they can custom-make a costume to your specifications; if not, they are well stocked with new and used costumes, wigs, masks, hats, and makeup.

When you arrive, remember that while the huge crowds add to the general merriment, they also make it more difficult to get in and out of restaurants in a hurry. And your progress from one part of town to another will be slowed down considerably. So be sure to come in a relaxed frame of mind and with enough mental flexibility for the delays to be a source of enjoyment and not irritation—after all, who knows what you may see while waiting.

You'll enjoy Mardi Gras more, too, if you've done a little homework before your trip. Contact the **New Orleans Metropolitan Convention and Visitors Bureau,** 1520 Sugar Bowl Dr., New Orleans, LA 70112 (☎ **504/566-5055**), and ask for their current Mardi Gras information.

CAJUN MARDI GRAS

For a really unique Mardi Gras experience, drive out to Cajun Country. Lafayette, a booming but charming town in the very heart of French Acadiana, celebrates Carnival in a manner quite different from New Orleans's fete—a manner that reflects the Cajun heritage and spirit. (For their full story, see Chapter 12.) There are three full days of activities leading up to Mardi Gras that are designed to *laissez les bons temps rouler* ("let the good times roll"—an absolute creed around these parts during Carnival). This is, in fact, second in size only to New Orleans's celebration, and there's one *big* difference—the Cajuns open their final pageant and ball to the general public. That's right, you can don your formal wear and join right in.

Instead of Rex and his queen, the Lafayette festivities are ruled by King Gabriel and Queen Evangeline. They are the fictional hero and heroine of Longfellow's epic poem *Evangeline*, which was based on real-life lovers who were separated during the British expulsion of Acadians from Nova Scotia just after the French and Indian War, and their story is still very much alive here among the descendants of those who shared their wanderings. Things get off to a joyous start with the Children's Krewe and Krewe of Bonaparte parades and ball the Saturday before Mardi Gras, following a full day of celebration at Acadian Village. On Monday night Queen Evangeline is honored at the Queen's Parade. The King's Parade, held the following morning, honors King Gabriel and opens a full day of merriment. Lafayette's African-American community stages the Parade of King Toussaint L'Ouverture and Queen Suzanne Simonne about noon, just after the King's Parade. And following that, the Krewe of Lafayette invites everyone to get into the act as its parade winds through the streets. Krewe participants trot along on foot or ride in the vehicle of their choice—some very imaginative modes of transportation turn up every year. The Mardi Gras climax, a brilliantly beautiful, exciting formal ball presided over by the king and queen and their royal court, takes place that night. Everything stops promptly at midnight, as Cajuns and visitors alike depart to observe the solemnity of Lent with the fondly remembered glow of Mardi Gras to take them through to Easter.

Out in the Cajun countryside that surrounds Lafayette, there's yet another form of Mardi Gras celebration, and I'll guarantee you won't find another like it anywhere else in the world. It's very much tied to the rural lifestyle of these displaced people who have created a rich culture out of personal disaster. And since Cajuns firmly believe that nothing is ever quite as much fun alone as it is when shared, you're entirely welcome to come along. The rural celebration goes like this: Bands of masked men dressed in patchwork costumes and peaked hats (*capichons*) set off on Mardi Gras morning on horseback, led by their *capitaine*. They ride from farm to farm, asking at each, "Will you receive the Mardi Gras?" ("*Voulez-vous recevoir le Mardi Gras?*") and dismounting as the invariable "Yes" comes in reply. Then each farmyard becomes a miniature festival, as the revelers "make monkeyshines" (*faire le macaque*) with song and dance, much drinking of beer, and other antics loosely labeled as "entertainment." As payment for their show, they demand, and get, "a fat little chicken to make a big gumbo."

When each band has visited its allotted farmyards, all the bands head back to town, where everyone else has already begun the general festivities. There'll be dancing in the streets, rowdy card games, storytelling, and the like until the wee hours, and you may be sure that all those "fat little chickens" go into the "gumbo gros" pot to make a "big gumbo." It's a really "down home" sort of festival. And if you've never heard Cajun music (see "The Rhythms of New Orleans" in Chapter 1) or eaten gumbo cooked by real Cajuns, you're in for a treat.

You can write or call ahead for full particulars on both these Mardi Gras celebrations. Contact **Lafayette Parish Convention and Visitors Commission,** P.O. Box 52066, Lafayette, LA 70505 (☎ **318/232-3808** or 800/346-1958 in the United States, 800/543-5340 in Canada).

2 New Orleans Jazz & Heritage Festival

By the time mid-April rolls around, Easter has passed, the Mardi Gras is a fond memory of this year and a grand expectation for next, and New Orleanians turn to another celebration: the New Orleans Jazz and Heritage Festival (Jazz Fest). The festival began 26 years ago, when producer George Wein (who founded the Newport Jazz Festival, among others) organized a concert involving 300 musicians. It was held in Congo Square and included artists such as Duke Ellington, Al Hirt, Pete Fountain, and Mahalia Jackson. It got off to a slow start, with only about 150 people in the audience, but over the years it has become one of this country's greatest music festivals.

The Jazz and Heritage Festival actually combines two fetes, as its name implies. From one weekend to another (usually the last weekend in April and the first weekend in May), musicians, mimes, artists, craftspeople, and chefs head out to the Fairgrounds Race Track on the weekends and settle into hotel ballrooms, jazz joints, concert halls, and a special evening concert site to put on a never-ending show of what New Orleans is all about. More than 4,000 performers turn up—and that's not counting the street bands. Big-name jazz, rock, pop, R&B, Cajun, zydeco, Latin, ragtime, Afro-Caribbean, folk, rap, country, bluegrass, and gospel musicians are drawn to this festival, and they very happily share 11 stages out at the fairgrounds with lesser-known and local groups. Some of the artists who attended last year's festival were Dr. John, Bela Fleck and the Fleckstones, Allen Toussaint, Indigo Girls, Buckwheat Zydeco, the Neville Brothers, Joan Osborne, Phish, the Dave Matthews Band, The Radiators, Wynton Marsalis, Van Morrison, and Joan Baez. You can find your favorites and stand in front of the stage all day long or make the rounds and come back to see which new group has taken the stage. Remember that this is a New Orleans festival—completely unstructured with the emphasis on pure enjoyment.

If this sounds like a lot of entertainment, keep in mind that this is only what's happening out at the fairgrounds; on weeknights, street bands are everywhere, and if you can't find a performance of your kind of music going on somewhere, it must not exist. And if traditional jazz happens to be your preference, you'll be in heaven.

As for the "heritage" part of the festival, local craftspeople and imported artisans arrive at Jazz Fest en masse with their wares. Demonstrations are offered throughout the festival. You might get to see Louisiana Native American basket making; Cajun accordion, fiddle, and triangle making; decoy carving; boat building; and Mardi Gras Indian beading and costume making. Contemporary arts and crafts, like jewelry, furniture, hand-blown glass, and paintings, are also featured. At Congo Square you'll find an open marketplace filled with contemporary and traditional African (and African-influenced) crafts and performing artists. Additionally, delicious food is available from about 50 booths: Red beans and rice, jambalaya, gumbo, crawfish, sweet-potato pie, oysters, fried chicken, andouille, boudin, po-boys, crabs, and shrimp are always featured. You can also get Caribbean, African, Spanish, Italian, and soul food. And, there's plenty of cold beer available to wash everything down. There's just nothing quite like munching fried chicken from the Second Mount Triumph Missionary Baptist Church booth in an outdoor setting where the air is filled with strains of traditional jazz, ragtime, reggae, and the blues.

To find out about the current dates, the artists who will be there, and where they'll be performing in concert during the week, contact the **New Orleans Jazz and Heritage Festival,** 2000 Royal St., New Orleans, LA 70177 (☎ **504/522-4786**). Tickets, which should be purchased as early as February, are available through Ticketmaster. To inquire about mail orders call **504/522-5555.** To order tickets by phone, or to get ticket information, call **504/522-5555** or 800/488-5252 outside Louisiana. To order by fax call 504/379-3291. Tickets for the festival cost $10 in advance and $15 at the gate for adults, and $1.50 in advance and $2 at the gate for children. Evening events and concerts (tickets should be ordered in advance for these events as well) may be attended at an additional cost (usually between $17.50 and $30, depending on the concert).

A word about Jazz Fest parking and transportation: Basically, it's next to impossible to park at the fairgrounds. There are a small number of places available at a cost of $10 a day; however, I don't know anyone who has ever been lucky enough to get a space there (certainly not for the entire weekend). I strongly recommend that you take public transportation or one of the available shuttles. The Regional Transit Authority operates bus routes from various pickup points to the fairgrounds. For schedules and information, call **504/248-3900.** Taxis, though probably scarce, will also take you to the fairgrounds at a special event rate of $3 per person (or the meter reading if it is higher). I recommend **United Cabs** (☎ **504/524-9606**). The New Orleans Jazz and Heritage Festival will provide information about shuttle transportation, which is usually available at an additional cost to the ticket price.

Note: If you're flying to New Orleans specifically for the Jazz and Heritage Festival, you should consider calling **Continental Airlines** (☎ **504/581-2965** or

800/525-0280). They're the official airline for the Jazz and Heritage Festival and they offer special fares during the event. Before you call Continental, call the festival's information line and ask for the Jazz Fest promotional code.

3 Other Top Festivals

SPRING FIESTA

One of the best times of the year to visit New Orleans is during the five-day-long Spring Fiesta, which has been going on since 1935. This is one time you can get to see the inside of some of those lovely old homes ordinarily closed to the public. Hostesses clad in antebellum dress will escort you through the premises and provide all sorts of information and anecdotes about these homes and historic buildings. In the French Quarter, there are balcony concerts by sopranos rendering numbers sung there in the past by Jenny Lind and Adelina Patti. Out on River Road, there are plantation home tours; and as a highlight there is the gala "Night in Old New Orleans" parade, which features carriages bearing passengers dressed as prominent figures in the city's history and some of the best marching bands in town.

Spring Fiesta usually takes place during one week in April. For full details, reservations, and a schedule of the admission fees (around $15 for City Tours, $45 for Country Estate Tours) for some of the homes, you can write to **Spring Fiesta Association,** 826 St. Ann St., New Orleans, LA 70116 (☎ **504/581-1367**). You can order tickets by mail, or you can purchase tickets at the French Market Gift Shop, 824 Decatur St., as well as at Gray Line Tour Desks. For a list of locations, contact the Spring Fiesta Association.

TENNESSEE WILLIAMS FESTIVAL

In late March or early April, New Orleans honors one of its most illustrious writers. Tennessee Williams, although not born here, once said, "If I can be considered to have a home, it would have to be New Orleans . . . which has provided me with more material than any other city." During the three-day Tennessee Williams/New Orleans Literary Festival, many of his plays are performed, and there are symposiums and panel discussions on his work, as well as walking tours of his favorite French Quarter haunts. For dates and details, contact the **University of New Orleans,** Metro College Conference Services ED 122, New Orleans, LA 70148 (☎ **504/286-6680**).

Without the Food It's Not a Party

Just about every New Orleans celebration, from Jazz Fest to Mardi Gras and everything in between, includes food in one way or another. There are, however, a few annual events whose primary focus is on local cuisine. The Great French Market Tomato Festival is a two-day June event celebrating the diversity of the tomato. The Gumbo Festival, held in Bridge City each October, showcases that favorite New Orleans dish. In Breaux Bridge, the Louisiana Crawfish Festival is held each year in May; if you love crawfish, this event is not to be missed. Other festivals to look out for, especially if you're a fan of international cuisine, are the Greek Festival in May; the Reggae Riddums Festival, featuring African and Caribbean cuisine, in June; and the Carnaval Latino, also in June.

See the "Calendar of Events" in Chapter 3 for exact dates and other details on these events.

FRENCH QUARTER FESTIVAL

The three-day French Quarter Festival in early April (April 11 through 13 in 1997) is a spectacular conglomeration of all the ingredients of the unique French Quarter's rich gumbo of life. There are scores of free outdoor concerts, patio tours, a parade, a battle of jazz bands, art shows, children's activities, and talent and bartender competitions. As if that weren't enough, Jackson Square is transformed into the world's largest jazz brunch, when about 40 leading restaurants turn out to serve Cajun/Creole specialties such as jambalaya, gumbo, and crawfish fettucine. For exact dates and other information, write to **French Quarter Festivals,** 100 Conti St., New Orleans, LA 70130 (☎ **504/522-5730**).

CREOLE CHRISTMAS

Trust New Orleans! A few days simply are not enough for this lively city to celebrate Christmas, so the entire month of December is designated "Creole Christmas." There are all sorts of gala events sprinkled throughout the month's calendar, including tours of 19th-century homes decorated for the holiday, candlelight caroling in Jackson Square, cooking demonstrations, a madrigal dinner, gingerbread house demonstrations, and special Reveillon menus at select French Quarter restaurants (including Arnaud's, Begue's, the Rib Room, and Alex Patouts). Special "Papa Noël" rates are offered by hotels citywide from December 5 through December 25. For full details, contact **French Quarter Festivals,** 100 Conti St., New Orleans, LA 70130 (☎ **504/522-5730**).

FESTIVALS ACADIENS

This is a Cajun Country celebration—or rather, six celebrations—held during the third week of September in Lafayette. These festivals, lumped under the heading Festivals Acadiens, pay tribute to the culture and heritage of Cajun families who have been here since the British expelled them from their Nova Scotia homeland 200 years ago. The festive week includes the Bayou Food Festival, the Festival de Musique Acadienne, the Louisiana Native Crafts Festival, the Acadiana Fair and Trade Show, the RSVP Senior Fair and Craft Show, and Downtown Alive.

At the **Bayou Food Festival,** you'll be able to taste the cuisine of more than 30 top Cajun restaurants. Specialties such as stuffed crabs, crawfish étouffée, oysters Bienville, shrimp Creole, oysters Rockefeller, shrimp de la Teche, catfish en brochette, jambalaya, chicken-and-sausage gumbo, smothered quail, and hot boudin are everyday eating for Cajuns, and this is a rare opportunity to try them all. The Bayou Food Festival is held in Girard Park adjacent to the music festival. Admission is free.

The Festival de Musique Acadienne began in 1974 when some Cajun musicians were engaged to play briefly for visiting French newspaper editors. It was a rainy night, but some 12,000 Cajun residents showed up to listen. The walls rang for three solid hours with old French songs, waltzes, two-steps, Cajun rock rhythms, zydeco, and the special music some have dubbed "Cajun Country." Since then it has become an annual affair, with more than 50,000 visitors usually on hand. Because of the crowds, the festival is now held outdoors in Girard Park, where fans can listen in grassy comfort. Performed almost entirely in French, the music includes both traditional and modern Cajun styles, including zydeco (a form that combines the blues with more traditional Cajun sounds). The music starts early and ends late, and there's no charge to come to the park and listen. All money from sales of food and beverage stands goes to fund public service projects of the Lafayette Jaycees.

You'll see native Louisiana artisans demonstrating their skills at the **Louisiana Native Crafts Festival.** All crafts must have been practiced before or during the early 1900s, and all materials used must be native to Louisiana. Meeting these criteria are such arts as woodcarving of all types (with an emphasis, it seemed to me, on duck decoys), soap making, pirogue (pronounced *PEE-rogue*—it's a Cajun canoe, one variety of which is made from a dugout cypress log) making, chair caning, doll making, palmetto weaving, Native American–style basket weaving, quilting, spinning, dyeing, pottery making, jewelry making, and alligator skinning.

The **Acadiana Fair and Trade Show** is put on by Lafayette merchants and businesspeople, and there's an indoor display of their goods and services, plus an outdoor carnival with rides, a midway, and games. It's sponsored by the Lafayette Jaycees, and free shuttle bus service for the public from one festival to another is provided by the city.

The elders who have passed crafts down to many of the younger Cajuns you'll see at the Native Crafts Festival have their day in the sun at the **RSVP Senior Fair and Craft Show** (the RSVP stands for Retired Senior Volunteer Program). They're all over 60, and it's a rare treat to meet them and see their homemade articles and listen to them talk of the old days.

Downtown Alive (☎ 318/268-5566) features a free band playing outside on the streets of downtown Lafayette every Friday from April through June and September through November. The show starts at 5:30, usually runs until 8, and proceeds from the refreshments benefit Downtown Lafayette Unlimited, a nonprofit organization that works to help develop the downtown and promote Cajun music.

You can visit the **Acadian Village** any time of the year, but during Festivals Acadiens, special events are often scheduled. If you have any interest at all in Acadiana's history, you'll find this little village an interesting trip back in time. Homes and buildings here are not models or reconstructions—they're all original old Acadian homes that have been restored and moved to the village to create (or, as the Cajuns say, "reassemble") a typical 1800s village. It's a tranquil, charming spot.

For exact dates and full details on Festivals Acadiens, write or call the **Lafayette Parish Convention and Visitors Commission,** P.O. Box 52066, Lafayette, LA 70505 (☎ **318/232-3808** or 800/346-1958 in the United States, 800/543-5340 in Canada).

RAYNE FROG FESTIVAL

To prove my point that just about anything is cause for celebration in New Orleans and its environs, let me tell you about the **Rayne Frog Festival.** It's held in Cajun Country, just a few miles west of Lafayette. The Cajuns can hold their own when it comes to drumming up festivals—a harvest, a new season, a special tradition, or just the job of being alive—and in this case they simply turn to the lowly frog as an excuse for a *fais-dodo* (dance) and a waltz contest. Not to forget the reason for it all, things get under way with frog races and frog-jumping contests—and if you arrive without your frog, there's a "Rent-a-Frog" service. To wind things up, there's a lively frog-eating contest. The Rayne Frog Festival is held in September. For dates and full details, contact **Lafayette Parish Convention and Visitors Commission,** P.O. Box 52066, Lafayette, LA 70505 (☎ **318/232-3808** or 800/346-1958 in the United States, 800/543-5340 in Canada).

3 Planning a Trip to New Orleans

This chapter is devoted to the when, where, and how of your trip to New Orleans—the advance-planning issues required to get it together and take it on the road. Costs, how to get there, and where to obtain more information about New Orleans are all covered below.

Foreign visitors should also consult Chapter 4, "For Foreign Visitors," for information on entry requirements, getting to the United States, and more.

1 Visitor Information & Money

VISITOR INFORMATION

I would advise even the most seasoned traveler to write or call ahead to the **New Orleans Metropolitan Convention and Visitors Bureau,** at 1520 Sugar Bowl Dr., New Orleans, LA 70112 (☎ **504/566-5055**), for their brochures and information about the city. They're extremely friendly and helpful, and you can easily get any information you can't find in this book from them. Another source of information is the **Greater New Orleans Black Tourism Network** (☎ **504/523-5652**).

MONEY

High season rates are in effect through any of the major festivals (see Chapter 2), as well as at other times throughout the spring. New Orleans is also quite popular in the fall. Summer months are the least expensive, mainly because the heat and humidity make traveling at this time less appealing.

Some people still prefer to carry traveler's checks for the security they offer; one major issuer is **American Express** (☎ **800/221-7282**). However, if you've got a cash card, there are automated teller machines (ATMs) throughout the city. You might want to check with your bank before you leave home because sometimes it will have a list of ATM locations that will accept your card. If your bank is connected to the **Plus** network, call 800/843-7587 for their ATM locater; **Cirrus** provides the same service if you call 800/424-7787. Some centrally located ATMs in New Orleans are First National Bank of Commerce (240 Royal St.), Hibernia National Bank (701 Poydras St.), and Whitney National Bank (228 St. Charles Ave.).

What Things Cost in New Orleans	U.S. $
Taxi from the airport to the Central Business District or French Quarter	21.00
Bus from airport to downtown	1.10
Streetcar fare (one-way)	1.00
Double at the Hotel Inter-Continental (very expensive)	210.00–240.00
Double at Place d'Armes Hotel (moderate)	100.00–160.00
Double at Hotel Villa Convento (inexpensive)	79.00–85.00
Lunch for one at Port of Call (moderate)	10.00
Lunch for one at Petunia's (inexpensive)	8.50
Dinner for one at Antoine's (expensive)	50.00
Dinner for one at Mike Anderson's Seafood (moderate)	30.00
Dinner for one at the Camellia Grill (inexpensive)	15.00
Bottle of beer	2.00–5.00
Coca-Cola	1.00–1.50
Cup of coffee	.50–1.50
Roll of ASA 100 Kodacolor film, 36 exposures	7.50
Admission to New Orleans Museum of Art	6.00
Theater ticket at Le Petit Theatre	18.00–25.00

2 When to Go

CLIMATE

The average mean temperature in New Orleans is 70°F, but the thermometer can drop or rise considerably in a single day. The high humidity can make relatively mild temperatures feel uncomfortably cold or uncomfortably warm. The city's climate will be pleasant almost any time of year except July and August, which can be exceptionally muggy. If you do come during those months, you'll quickly learn to follow the natives' example and stay out of the noonday sun and duck from one air-conditioned building to another. And even in the rain (an average of 63 inches falls annually), you'll be able to get around without difficulty, mainly because it comes in great downpours that don't last too long.

If you're coming to New Orleans in the dead of summer, T-shirts and shorts are absolutely acceptable (except in the city's finest restaurants). In the spring and fall, something a little warmer is in order; in the winter, you'll probably need a lightweight coat or jacket.

New Orleans's Average Temperatures & Rainfall

	Jan	Feb	Mar	Apr	May	June	July	Aug	Sept	Oct	Nov	Dec
High (°F)	56	58	62	69	76	81	83	83	79	71	61	57
High (°C)	13	14	16	19	23	25	26	26	24	20	15	14
Days of Rainfall	10	9	9	7	8	10	15	13	10	5	7	10

NEW ORLEANS CALENDAR OF EVENTS

For more information on the major New Orleans events, see Chapter 2.

January
- **The USF&G Sugar Bowl Classic.** This is New Orleans's oldest yearly sporting event (it originated in 1934). The football game is the main event, but there are also tennis, swimming, basketball, sailing, running, and flag-football competitions. New Year's Day.

February
- **Lundi Gras** celebrations take place on the Monday before Mardi Gras Day at Spanish Plaza. It's a free, annual outdoor event that features fireworks, a parade, and a masked ball. For more information, contact New Orleans Riverwalk, 1 Poydras St., New Orleans, LA 70130 (☎ **504/522-1555**).
- ✪ **Mardi Gras.** The culmination of the two-month-long Carnival season, Mardi Gras is *the* annual blow-out. The entire city stops working and starts partying early in the morning.

  Where: All over the city something will be happening. Nowadays, however, the great parades go through the Central Business District instead of the French Quarter. **When:** For 1997 the date is February 11. **How:** Contact the New Orleans Metropolitan Convention and Visitors Bureau, 1520 Sugar Bowl Dr., New Orleans, LA 70112 (☎ **504/566-5055**).

March
- **Black Heritage Festival** honors African-American cultural contributions to New Orleans. Write or call the Black Heritage Foundation, P.O. Box 60131, New Orleans, LA 70160 (☎ **504/827-0112**) for more info.
- **St. Patrick's Day Parades.** There are two of them; one takes place in the French Quarter beginning at Molly's at the Market (1107 Decatur St.), and the other goes through the Irish Channel neighborhood following a parade route that begins at Race and Annunciation streets and ends at Jackson Street. For information on the French Quarter parade, call **504/525-5169**; for the Irish Channel parade, call **504/565-7080**.
- ✪ **Tennessee Williams New Orleans Literary Festival.** This is a four-day series of events, including theatrical performances, readings, discussion panels, master classes, musical events, and literary walking tours dedicated to the playwright.

  Where: Events occur all over the city. **When:** Late March. **How:** Call or write University of New Orleans, Metro College Conference Services ED 122, New Orleans, LA 70148 (☎ **504/286-6680**).
- ✪ **Spring Fiesta.** The fiesta, which begins with the crowning of the Spring Fiesta queen, is more than half a century old. If you come during this time, you'll be able to visit some of the city's historic private homes, courtyards, and plantation homes on tours created specially for Spring Fiesta.

  Where: Locations throughout the city. **When:** Late March to early April. **How:** For a current schedule, call or write Spring Fiesta Association, 826 St. Ann St., New Orleans, LA 70116 (☎ **504/581-1367**).

April
- ✪ **The French Quarter Festival.** This is a relatively new event, just over a decade old, that celebrates New Orleans's history. It's kicked off with a parade down Bourbon Street, and, among other things, you can join people dancing in

the streets, learn the history of jazz, visit historic homes, and take a ride on a riverboat.

Where: All over the French Quarter. **When:** Mid-April. **How:** Call or write French Quarter Festivals, Inc., 100 Conti St., New Orleans, LA 70130 (☎ **504/ 522-5730**).

✪ **The New Orleans Jazz and Heritage Festival.** Jazz Fest is so popular that the city, as it does during Mardi Gras, tends to sell out its lodging, sometimes up to a year in advance. Thousands of musicians, cooks, and craftspeople come together to strut their stuff. If you like jazz, Cajun, zydeco, or New Orleans rhythm and blues with that shuffling, "second-line" rhythm, don't miss the event.

Where: Fair Grounds Race Track and various venues throughout the city. **When:** Usually the last weekend in April and the first weekend in May. **How:** Call or write Jazz Fest, P.O. Box 53407, New Orleans, LA 70153 (☎ **504/ 522-4786**).

• **The Crescent City Classic.** This 10,000-meter road race, bringing an international field of top runners to the city, begins at Jackson Square and ends at Audubon Park. For more information, call or write Classic, 8200 Hampson St., Suite 217, New Orleans, LA 70118 (☎ **504/861-8686**).

May

• **Greek Festival** takes place every year at the Hellenic Cultural Center and features Greek folk dancing, specialty foods, crafts, and music. For more information about this three-day event, call or write the Holy Trinity Cathedral, 1200 Robert E. Lee Blvd., New Orleans, LA 70122 (☎ **504/282-0259**).

June

• **The Great French Market Tomato Festival.** A celebration of the diversity of the tomato. The two-day event features cooking and tastings in the historic French Market. For more information call or write P.O. Box 51749, New Orleans, LA 70151 (☎ **504/522-2621**).

• **Reggae Riddums Festival.** A gathering of calypso, reggae, and soca musicians is held annually in City Park. Like all other New Orleans festivals, this three-day extravaganza includes both ethnic foods and arts and crafts. For more information call or write Ernest Kelly, P.O. Box 6156, New Orleans, LA 70174 (☎ **504/ 367-1313** or 800/367-1317).

July

• **Go Fourth on the River.** New Orleans's annual July 4th celebration. Events begin in the morning at the New Orleans riverfront and continue into the night, culminating in a spectacular fireworks display. For more information call or write Anna Pepper, 610 South Peters St., Suite 301, New Orleans, LA 70130 (☎ **504/ 528-9994**).

• **New Orleans Wine and Food Experience.** Wine and food tastings are held in antique shops and art galleries throughout the French Quarter. Seminars by wine makers and local chefs, vintner dinners, and grand tastings are also offered. More than 150 wines and 40 restaurants are featured every day. For information call or write Mary Reynolds, P.O. Box 70514, New Orleans, LA 70172 (☎ **504/ 529-9463**). Late July.

August

• **African Heritage Festival International.** This three-day event celebrates the culture and music of the local African-American community. There's food, dance, arts and crafts, and activities for the kids. For more information call or write the African Heritage Foundation, 1683 N. Claiborne Ave., New Orleans, LA 70116 (☎ **504/949-5610**).

October

- **Art for Arts' Sake.** The season begins with gallery openings throughout the city. Julia, Magazine, and Royal streets are where the action is. For more information contact the Contemporary Arts Center, 900 Camp St., New Orleans, LA 70130 (☎ **504/523-1216**).

- **Swamp Festival.** Sponsored by the Audubon Institute, the Swamp Festival takes place over two weekends (at the end of September and the beginning of October) and features hands-on contact with Louisiana swamp animals. Admission to the festival is free with zoo admission. For information call or write the Audubon Institute, 6500 Magazine St., New Orleans, LA 70118 (☎ **504/861-2537**).

- **Louisiana Jazz Awareness Month.** This is one of the highlights of October. There are nightly concerts (some of which are free), television and radio specials, and lectures. The events are sponsored by the Louisiana Jazz Foundation. For more information and a schedule of events call the Louisiana Jazz Federation at **504/522-3154.**

- **Gumbo Festival.** In a city that loves its food, this festival showcases one of the city's favorites. There are a number of events that highlight Cajun culture, and the entertainment is continuous. The Gumbo Fest is held in Bridge City. For information contact the Gumbo Festival, P.O. Box 9069, Bridge City, LA 70094 (☎ **504/436-4712**).

- **New Orleans Film and Video Festival.** New Orleans's film festival is a relatively young event. Canal Place Cinemas and other theaters throughout the city screen award-winning local and international films and host writers and directors. The event lasts one week. Admission prices range from $3 to $12. Call **504/523-3818** for 1997 dates.

- ✪ **Halloween.** Halloween in New Orleans can be even more spectacular than Mardi Gras in terms of the costumes you're likely to see while walking the streets of the French Quarter. Events include Boo-at-the-Zoo (October 30 and 31) for children, a number of costume parties (including a Monster Bash at the Ernest N. Morial Convention Center), the Anne Rice Vampire Lestat Extravaganza, and the Moonlight Witches Run.

  Where: All over the city, but the French Quarter, as always, is the center of action. **When:** October 31. **How:** Contact the New Orleans Metropolitan Convention and Visitors Bureau, 1520 Sugar Bowl Dr., New Orleans, LA 70112 (☎ **504/566-5055**).

December

- **A New Orleans Christmas.** New Orleans's holiday events include candlelight caroling in Jackson Square and the old New Orleans homes dressed up especially for the occasion. Restaurants offer multicourse Reveilion dinners and hotels throughout the city offer "Papa Noël" rates. For information contact French Quarter Festivals, 100 Conti St., New Orleans, LA 70130 (☎ **504/522-5730**). Events are held throughout December.

- **New Year's Eve.** The countdown to 1998 will take place in Jackson Square (one of the country's biggest street parties). Revelers watch a lighted ball—à la New York City—as it drops from the top of Jackson Brewery. For further details contact the New Orleans Metropolitan Convention and Visitors Bureau, 1520 Sugar Bowl Dr., New Orleans, LA 70112 (☎ **504/566-5055**).

3 Getting There

BY PLANE

THE MAJOR AIRLINES   No fewer than 13 airlines fly to New Orleans's Moisant International Airport; among them are **American Airlines** (☎ 800/433-7300); **Continental Airlines** (☎ 504/581-2965 or 800/525-0280); **Delta Airlines** (☎ 800/221-1212); **Northwest Airlines** (☎ 800/225-2525); **Southwest Airlines** (☎ 800/435-9792); and **TWA** (☎ 504/529-2585).

NEW ORLEANS INTERNATIONAL AIRPORT   New Orleans's airport is located 15 miles west of the city in Kenner. You'll find information booths scattered around the airport and in the baggage claim area, and a branch of the **Travelers Aid Society** (☎ 504/464-3522) is also here.

From the airport you can reach the Central Business District by bus for $1.10. The bus leaves the airport and goes to the downtown side of Tulane Avenue between Elks Place and South Saratoga Street every 12 to 15 minutes from 6 to 9am and from 3 to 6pm, every 23 minutes at other times. Buses run from 6am to 6:30pm. For information call **504/737-9611.**

You can also get to your hotel by **Airport Shuttle** (☎ 504/522-3500). The ride will cost $10 per person (one-way), and the van will take you directly to your hotel. There are airport shuttle information desks (staffed 24 hours) in the airport. *Note:* If you plan to take the airport shuttle back to the airport when you depart, you must call a day in advance and let them know what time your flight is leaving. They will then tell you what time they will pick you up.

A taxi from the airport will cost you $21; if there are three or more passengers, the fare will be $8 per person.

If you want to ride in style from the airport to your hotel contact **Olde Quarter Livery** (☎ 504/595-5010). Express transfer service from New Orleans International Airport is available at a rate of $50 for a four-passenger stretch limousine and $65 for a six-passenger limousine. You'll be greeted by a uniformed chauffeur and escorted to the car, which will be waiting just outside the airport's baggage claim area. Drivers are prompt and efficient—you'll never be left waiting.

BY CAR

You can drive to New Orleans via I-10, U.S. 90, and U.S. 61 and across the Lake Pontchartrain Causeway on La. 25.

It's a good idea to call before you leave home to ask for directions to your hotel. Most hotels have parking facilities (for a fee); if they don't, they'll give you the names and addresses of nearby parking lots.

AAA (☎ 800/926-4222) will assist members with trip planning, service aids, and emergency services.

Renting a Car   All major national car rental companies are represented at the airport, including **Alamo** (☎ 800/327-9633); **Avis** (☎ 800/331-1212); **Budget** (☎ 800/527-0700); **Dollar** (☎ 800/800-4000); **Hertz** (☎ 800/654-3131); and **National** (☎ 800/227-7368). See "Getting Around" in Chapter 5 for more information on car rental and driving in New Orleans.

BY TRAIN

Amtrak trains reach New Orleans's **Union Passenger Terminal,** 1001 Loyola Ave. (☎ 504/524-7571 or 800/USA-RAIL for Amtrak information and schedules), from Los Angeles and intermediate points; New York, Washington, and points in between;

and Chicago and intermediate points. Using the All Aboard America fares, you'll pay $188 to $208 from New York or Chicago, and $248 to $288 from Los Angeles. Amtrak, too, frequently offers senior-citizen discounts and other packages, some with a rental car, so be sure to check when you reserve.

Amtrak also does an especially good job with tour packages, which can be arranged through your local Amtrak Tour Desk. Options might range from a ticket with hotel accommodations to an air/rail package—take the train and then fly back to your destination, or choose from eight other combinations of tour packages. Prices will change, of course, during the life of this book, but from past experience it is safe to say that Amtrak tours will be genuine moneysavers.

The train station is located in the Central Business District, and there will be plenty of taxis outside the main entrance of the passenger terminal. It will be a short ride to your hotel if you're staying in the French Quarter or the Central Business District.

BY BUS

Greyhound-Trailways buses come into the **Union Passenger Terminal** (☎ **800/ 231-2222** for fares and schedules from the New Orleans bus station) from points throughout the country. Arriving by bus will also bring you directly to the Central Business District. I'd recommend taking a cab from the bus terminal to your hotel. There should be taxis out front, but if there aren't, the number for **United Cabs** is **504/522-9771.**

For Foreign Visitors 4

This chapter will provide some specifics about getting to the United States as quickly and effortlessly as possible, plus some helpful tips about how things are done in New Orleans—from mailing a postcard back home to making a long-distance telephone call.

1 Preparing for Your Trip

ENTRY REQUIREMENTS

Document Regulations Canadian citizens may enter the United States without visas; they need only proof of Canadian residence.

Citizens of the United Kingdom, New Zealand, Japan, and most western European countries traveling with valid passports may not need a visa for fewer than 90 days of holiday or business travel to the United States, provided that they hold a round-trip or return ticket and enter on an airline or cruise line participating in the visa-waiver program. (Note that citizens of these visa-exempt countries who first enter the United States may then visit Mexico, Canada, Bermuda, and/or the Caribbean Islands and then reenter the United States, by any mode of transportation, without needing a visa. Further information is available from any U.S. embassy or consulate.)

Citizens of countries other than those stipulated above, including Australia, must have a valid passport, with an expiration date at least six months later than the scheduled end of the visit to the United States, and a tourist visa, available without charge from the nearest U.S. consulate. To obtain a visa, the traveler must submit a completed application form (either in person or by mail) with a $1^1/_2$-inch-square photo and demonstrate binding ties to the residence abroad.

Usually you can obtain a visa at once or within 24 hours, but it may take longer during the summer rush from June to August. If you cannot go in person, contact the nearest U.S. embassy or consulate for directions on applying by mail. Your travel agent or airline office may also be able to provide you with visa applications and instructions. The U.S. consulate or embassy that issues your visa will determine whether you will be issued a multiple- or single-entry visa and any restrictions regarding the length of your stay.

MEDICAL REQUIREMENTS

No inoculations are needed to enter the United States unless you are coming from, or have stopped over in, areas known to be suffering from epidemics, particularly of cholera or yellow fever.

If you have a disease requiring treatment with medications containing narcotics or drugs requiring a syringe, carry a valid signed prescription from your physician to allay any suspicions that you are smuggling drugs.

CUSTOMS REQUIREMENTS

Every adult visitor may bring in, free of duty: (1) 1 liter of wine or hard liquor; (2) 200 cigarettes or 100 cigars (but no cigars from Cuba), or 3 pounds of smoking tobacco; and (3) $100 worth of gifts. These exemptions are offered to travelers who spend at least 72 hours in the United States and who have not claimed them within the preceding six months. It is altogether forbidden to bring into the country foodstuffs (particularly cheese, fruit, cooked meats, and canned goods) and plants (vegetables, seeds, tropical plants, and so on). Foreign tourists may bring in or take out up to $10,000 in U.S. or foreign currency with no formalities; larger sums must be declared to U.S. Customs on entering or leaving.

Foreign tourists to New Orleans can arrange to have a refund check mailed to them on taxes paid on purchases made in the city if they go to the Louisiana Tax Free Shopping Refund Center, located in the New Orleans International Airport. Present the clerk there with sales receipts and vouchers from merchants, your passport, and a round-trip international ticket of less than 90 days. For more information contact the New Orleans Metropolitan Convention and Visitors Bureau, 1520 Sugar Bowl Dr., New Orleans, LA 70112 (☎ **504/566-5055**).

INSURANCE

There is no national health system in the United States. Because the cost of medical care is extremely high, we strongly advise every traveler to secure health coverage before setting out.

You may want to take out a comprehensive travel policy that covers (for a relatively low premium) sickness or injury costs (medical, surgical, and hospital); loss of or theft of your baggage; trip-cancellation costs; guarantee of bail in case you are arrested; costs of accident, repatriation, or death. Such packages (for example, "Europe Assistance" in Europe) are sold by automobile clubs at attractive rates, as well as by insurance companies and travel agencies.

MONEY
CURRENCY & EXCHANGE

The U.S. monetary system has a decimal base: one American dollar ($1) = 100 cents (100¢).

Dollar bills commonly come in $1 ("a buck"), $5, $10, $20, $50, and $100 denominations (the last two may not be welcome when paying for small purchases and are not accepted in taxis). There are also $2 bills (seldom encountered).

There are six denominations of coins: 1¢ (one cent or "a penny"), 5¢ (five cents or "a nickel"), 10¢ (ten cents or "a dime"), 25¢ (twenty-five cents or "a quarter"), 50¢ (fifty cents or "a half dollar"), and the rare $1 piece.

Note: The "foreign-exchange bureaus" so common in Europe are rare in the United States, and nonexistent outside major cities. Try to avoid having to change foreign money, or traveler's checks denominated other than in U.S. dollars, at a small-town bank, or even a branch in a big city; in fact, leave any currency other than U.S. dollars at home—it may provide more nuisance to you than it's worth.

TRAVELER'S CHECKS

Traveler's checks denominated in U.S. dollars are readily accepted at most hotels, motels, restaurants, and large stores. But the best place to change traveler's checks is at a bank. Do not bring traveler's checks denominated in other currencies.

CREDIT CARDS

The method of payment most widely used is the credit card: Visa (BarclayCard in Britain), MasterCard (Eurocard in Europe, Access in Britain, Chargex in Canada), American Express, Diners Club, Discover, and Carte Blanche. You can save yourself trouble by using plastic rather than cash or traveler's checks in most hotels, motels, restaurants, and retail stores. You must have a credit card to rent a car. It can also be used as proof of identity (often carrying more weight than a passport), or as a "cash card," enabling you to draw money from banks that accept them.

SAFETY
GENERAL SAFETY TIPS

While tourist areas are generally safe, crime is on the increase everywhere, and U.S. urban areas tend to be less safe than those in Europe or Japan. Visitors should always stay alert. This is particularly true of large U.S. cities. It is wise to contact the New Orleans Metropolitan Convention and Visitors Bureau if you're in doubt about which neighborhoods are safe. In New Orleans, avoid deserted areas (like the outer edges of the French Quarter), especially at night. Don't go into any city parks at night unless there is an event that attracts crowds—for example, New Orleans's festivals and concerts in the parks. Generally speaking, you can feel safe in areas where there are many people and many open establishments.

Avoid carrying valuables with you on the street, and don't display expensive cameras or electronic equipment. Hold on to your pocketbook and place your billfold in an inside pocket. In theaters, restaurants, and other public places, keep your possessions in sight.

Remember also that hotels are open to the public, and in a large hotel, security may not be able to screen everyone entering. Always lock your room door—don't assume that once inside your hotel you are safe and no longer need to be aware of your surroundings.

DRIVING SAFETY

Question your rental agency about personal safety, or ask for a brochure of traveler safety tips when you pick up your car. Obtain written directions, or a map with the route clearly marked, from the agency showing how to get to your destination. And, if possible, arrive and depart during daylight hours.

Recently more and more crime in all U.S. cities has involved cars and drivers, most notably carjacking. If you drive off a highway into a doubtful neighborhood, leave the area as quickly as possible. If you have an accident, even on the highway, stay in your car with the doors locked until you assess the situation or until the police arrive. If you are bumped from behind on the street or are involved in a minor accident with no injuries and the situation appears to be suspicious, motion to the other driver to follow you to the nearest police precinct or well-lighted service station. *Never* get out of your car in such situations.

If you see someone on the road who indicates a need for help, do *not* stop. Take note of the location, drive on to a well-lighted area, and telephone the police by dialing 911.

Park in well-lighted, well-traveled areas if possible. Always keep your car doors locked, whether attended or unattended. Look around you before you get out of your car and never leave any packages or valuables in sight. If someone attempts to rob you or steal your car, do *not* try to resist the thief/carjacker—report the incident to the police department immediately.

2 Getting to the U.S. from Overseas

MAJOR AIRLINES

No matter which airport you connect through, you should cultivate patience and resignation before setting foot on U.S. soil. Getting through immigration control and customs may take as long as two to three hours on some days, especially on summer weekends, so have your guidebook or something else to read. Make a very generous allowance for these delays when you are planning connections between international and domestic flights.

See also "Getting There" in Chapter 3 for information on alternative low-cost fares.

From the United Kingdom and Ireland   Many airlines offer service from the United Kingdom or Ireland to the United States. There are no direct flights from London to New Orleans, but the following airlines will book you through on a connecting flight.

American Airlines (☎ 0181/572-5555 in London, 0345/789-789 elsewhere in the U.K.) connects through Chicago; **British Airways** (☎ 0345/222-111 throughout Europe) connects through Philadelphia or Charlotte, NC; **Continental Airlines** (☎ 0800/776-464 in the U.K.) connects through Newark, NJ or Houston; **Delta Airlines** (☎ 0800/414-767 in the U.K.) connects through Atlanta or Cincinnati; **United Airlines** (☎ 0181/990-9900 in London, 0800/888-555 elsewhere in the U.K.) connects through Washington DC-Dulles or Chicago; **Virgin Atlantic** (☎ 01293/747-747 in the U.K.) connects through either New York, Newark, Miami, or Orlando.

Residents of Ireland can call **Aer Lingus** (☎ 01/844-4777), which flies to New York, where you can connect to a New Orleans flight on their partner airline, TWA.

From Australia and New Zealand   **Qantas** (☎ 008/112-121 toll free in Sidney and Melbourne, or 2/957-0111 in Sidney, 7/234-3747 in Brisbane) flies into Los Angeles, then puts you on a Delta or American Airlines flight to New Orleans. You can also take **United** (☎ 237-8888 in Sidney, 602-2544 in Melbourne, 008-230-322 elsewhere in Australia), which connects through San Francisco or Los Angeles.

Air New Zealand (☎ 09/357-3000 in Auckland or 03/379-5200 in Christchurch) connects through Los Angeles on a local carrier such as Delta.

From Canada   **Air Canada** (in Canada ☎ 800/268-7240 in Toronto or 800/663-3721 in Vancouver), flies from Toronto and Montreal to Newark, and from Calgary and Vancouver to Houston. From both cities, your connecting flight would be on Continental Airlines.

Many American carriers also serve similar routes. The toll-free numbers in Canada for some of the major airlines follow. **American Airlines** (☎ 800/433-7300) connects through Chicago or Dallas, **Continental Airlines** (☎ 800/231-0856) flies from Montreal and Toronto, connecting through Newark (they partner with Air Canada to service other Canadian cities), **Delta** (☎ 800/241-4141) connects through Atlanta or Cincinnati, **TWA** (☎ 800/221-2000) flies from Toronto only, connecting through at St. Louis, and **United Airlines** (☎ 800/241-6522) flies from Toronto, Calgary, and Vancouver, connecting through Chicago.

ARRIVING IN THE U.S.

The visitor arriving by air, no matter what the port of entry, should cultivate patience and resignation before setting foot on U.S. soil. Getting through immigration control may take as long as two hours on some days, especially summer weekends. Add the time it takes to clear U.S. Customs and you will see that you should make very generous allowance for delay in planning connections between international and domestic flights—an average of two to three hours at least.

In contrast, for the traveler arriving by car or by rail from Canada, the border-crossing formalities have been streamlined to the vanishing point. And for the traveler by air from Canada, Bermuda, and some places in the Caribbean, you can sometimes go through Customs and Immigration at the point of departure, which is much quicker and less painful.

3 Getting Around the U.S.

BY PLANE   Some large American airlines (for example, TWA, American Airlines, Northwest, United, and Delta) offer travelers on their transatlantic or transpacific flights special discount tickets under the name **Visit USA,** allowing travel between any U.S. destinations at minimum rates. They are not on sale in the United States and must, therefore, be purchased before you leave your foreign point of departure. This system is the best, easiest, and fastest way to see the United States at low cost. You should obtain information well in advance from your travel agent or the office of the airline concerned, since the conditions attached to these discount tickets can be changed without advance notice.

For further information about travel to and arriving in New Orleans see "Getting There" in Chapter 3.

BY TRAIN   International visitors can buy a **USA Railpass,** good for 15 or 30 days of unlimited travel on Amtrak. The pass is available through many foreign travel agents. Prices in 1996 for a 15-day pass were $239 off-peak, $354 peak; a 30-day pass costs $349 off-peak, $435 peak. (With a foreign passport, you can also buy passes at some Amtrak offices in the United States, including locations in San Francisco, Los Angeles, Chicago, New York, Miami, Boston, and Washington, D.C.) Reservations are generally required and should be made for each part of your trip as early as possible.

Visitors should also be aware of the limitations of long-distance rail travel in the United States. With a few notable exceptions (for instance, the Northeast Corridor line between Boston and Washington, D.C.), service is rarely up to European standards: Delays are common, routes are limited and often infrequently served, and fares are rarely significantly lower than discount airfares. Thus, cross-country train travel should be approached with caution.

BY BUS   Greyhound, the nationwide bus line, offers an Ameripass for unlimited travel for seven days ($269), 15 days ($469), and 30 days ($569). Bus travel in the United States can be both slow and uncomfortable, so this option is not for everyone.

FAST FACTS: For the Foreign Traveler

Automobile Organizations   Auto clubs will supply maps, suggested routes, guide-books, accident and bail-bond insurance, and emergency road service. The major auto club in the United States, with 955 offices nationwide, is the **American Automobile Association (AAA)**. Members of some foreign auto clubs have recip-rocal arrangements with AAA and enjoy its services at no charge. If you belong to an auto club, inquire about AAA reciprocity before you leave. AAA can provide you with an International Driving Permit validating your foreign license. You may be able to join AAA even if you are not a member of a reciprocal club; call **800/222-4357**. In addition, some automobile rental agencies now provide these ser-vices, so you should inquire about their availability when you rent your car.

Business Hours   Banks are open weekdays from 9am to 3pm, although there's 24-hour access to the automatic tellers (ATMs) at most banks and other outlets. Generally, offices are open weekdays from 9am to 5pm. Stores are open six days a week with many open on Sundays, too; department stores usually stay open until 9pm one day a week.

Climate   See "When to Go" in Chapter 3.

Currency and Exchange   You will find currency-exchange services in major air-ports with international service. Elsewhere, they may be quite difficult to come by. In New Orleans, a very reliable choice is **Thomas Cook Currency Services,** located at 111 St. Charles Ave. (☎ **504/524-0700**). The company has been in busi-ness since 1841 and offers a wide range of services. They also sell commission-free foreign and U.S. traveler's checks, drafts, and wire transfers; they also do check collections (including Eurochecks). Their rates are competitive and service is excellent.

Exchange services are also offered at the **First National Bank of Commerce** (210 Baronne St.) and the **Whitney National Bank's International Department** (228 St. Charles Ave.). In addition, any hotels will exchange currency if you are a registered guest.

Drinking Laws   See "Liquor Laws" in "Fast Facts: New Orleans" in Chapter 5.

Electric Current   The United States uses 110–120 volts, 60 cycles, compared to 220–240 volts, 50 cycles, as in most of Europe. Besides a 100-volt converter, small appliances of non-American manufacture, such as hair dryers or shavers, will require a plug adapter with two flat, parallel pins.

Embassies and Consulates   All embassies are located in Washington, D.C.; some consulates are located in major cities, and most nations have a mission to the United Nations in New York City.

Listed here are the embassies and East and West Coast consulates of the major English-speaking countries. Travelers from other countries can get telephone numbers for their embassies and consulates by calling "Information" (directory assistance) in Washington, D.C. (☎ 202/555-1212).

The embassy of **Australia** is at 1601 Massachusetts Ave. NW, Washington, DC 20036 (☎ 202/797-3000). The consulate in New York is located at the International Building, 630 Fifth Ave., Suite 420, New York, NY 10111 (☎ 212/408-8400). The embassy of **Canada** is at 501 Pennsylvania Ave. NW, Wash-ington, DC 20001 (☎ 202/682-1740). The consulate in New York is located at 1251 Avenue of the Americas, New York, NY 10020 (☎ 212/596-1600). The embassy of **Ireland** is at 2234 Massachusetts Ave. NW, Washington, DC 20008 (☎ 202/462-3939). The consulate in New York is located at 345 Park Ave.,

New York, NY 10022 (☎ 212/319-2555). The embassy of **New Zealand** is at 37 Observatory Circle NW, Washington, DC 20008 (☎ 202/328-4800). The consulate in New York is located at 780 Third Ave., Suite 1904, New York, NY 10017-2024 (☎ 212/832-4038). The embassy of the **United Kingdom** is at 3100 Massachusetts Ave. NW, Washington, DC 20008 (☎ 202/462-1340). An honorary consulate operates in New Orleans at 321 St. Charles Ave. (☎ 504/524-4180). The consulate in New York is located at 845 Third Ave., New York, NY 10022 (☎ 212/745-0200).

Emergencies   Call 911 for fire, police, and ambulance. If you encounter such traveler's problems as sickness, accident, or lost or stolen baggage, call Traveler's Aid, an organization that specializes in helping distressed travelers whether American or foreign. Check the local telephone directory for the nearest office.

Holidays   On the following national legal holidays, banks, government offices, post offices, and many stores, restaurants, and museums are closed: January 1 (New Year's Day), third Monday in January (Martin Luther King Day), third Monday in February (Presidents' Day), last Monday in May (Memorial Day), July 4 (Independence Day), first Monday in September (Labor Day), second Monday in October (Columbus Day), November 11 (Veterans Day/Armistice Day), last Thursday in November (Thanksgiving Day), and December 25 (Christmas Day). The Tuesday following the first Monday in November, Election Day, is a legal holiday in presidential election years.

Information   See "Visitor Information and Money" in Chapter 3.

Legal Aid   If you are stopped for a minor infraction (for example, of the highway code, such as speeding), never attempt to pay the fine directly to a police officer; you may be arrested on the much more serious charge of attempted bribery. Pay fines by mail, or directly into the hands of the clerk of the court. If accused of a more serious offense, it is wise to say and do nothing before consulting a lawyer. Under U.S. law, an arrested person is allowed one telephone call to a party of his or her choice. Call your embassy or consulate.

Mail   If you want your mail to follow you on your vacation and you aren't sure of your address, your mail can be sent to you, in your name, c/o General Delivery at the main post office of the city or region where you expect to be. The addressee must pick it up in person and produce proof of identity (driver's license, credit card, passport, etc.).

Generally to be found at intersections, mailboxes are blue and carry the inscription "U.S. Mail." If your mail is addressed to a U.S. destination, don't forget to add the five-figure postal code, or ZIP (zone improvement plan) code, after the two-letter abbreviation of the state to which the mail is addressed (LA for Louisiana, CA for California, NY for New York, and so on).

Medical Emergencies   For an ambulance, dial 911. For information on hospitals and doctors in New Orleans see "Fast Facts: New Orleans" in Chapter 5.

Newspapers and Magazines   *The New York Times,* widely available in large cities, and the magazines *Newsweek* and *Time* cover world news. European newspapers and magazines are available in large cities. See "Fast Facts: New Orleans" in Chapter 5 for information on local publications.

Post   See "Mail," above.

Radio and Television   There are dozens of radio stations (both AM and FM), each broadcasting talk shows, continuous news, or a particular kind of music—classical, country, jazz, pop, gospel—punctuated by frequent commercials.

Television plays a major part in American life—there are four major coast-to-coast networks (ABC, CBS, Fox, and NBC), plus the Public Broadcasting System (PBS) and a slew of cable channels. For information about radio and television stations in New Orleans, see "Fast Facts: New Orleans" in Chapter 5.

Safety   See "Safety" in "Preparing for Your Trip," above.

Taxes   In the United States there is no VAT (value-added tax) or other indirect tax on a national level. Every state, and each city in it, is allowed to levy its own local tax on all purchases, including hotel and restaurant checks, airline tickets, and so on. In New Orleans, the sales tax rate is 9%.

Telephone and Fax   The telephone system in the United States is run by private corporations, so rates, especially for long-distance service, can vary widely—even on calls made from public telephones. Local calls in the United States usually cost 25¢.

Generally, hotel surcharges on long-distance and local calls are astronomical. You are usually better off using a public pay telephone, which you will find clearly marked in most public buildings and private establishments, as well as on the street. Outside metropolitan areas, public telephones are more difficult to find. Stores and gas stations are your best bet.

Most long-distance and international calls can be dialed directly from any phone. For calls to Canada and other parts of the United States, dial 1 followed by the area code and the seven-digit number. For international calls, dial 011 followed by the country code, city code, and the telephone number of the person you wish to call.

For reversed-charge or collect calls, and for person-to-person calls, dial 0 (zero, *not* the letter "O") followed by the area code and number you want; an operator will then come on the line, and you should specify that you are calling collect, or person-to-person, or both. If your call is international, ask for the overseas operator.

For local directory assistance ("Information"), dial 411; for long-distance information, dial 1, then the appropriate area code and 555-1212.

Note that all calls to area codes 800 and 888 are toll free. However, calls to numbers in area codes 700 and 900 (chat lines, bulletin boards, etc.) can be very expensive—usually 95¢ to $3 per minute.

Most hotels have fax machines available for guest use, and some hotel rooms are even wired for guests' fax machines. You'll probably also see signs for public faxes in the windows of local shops.

Telephone Directory   There are two kinds of telephone directories available to you. The general directory is the so-called *White Pages*, in which private and business subscribers are listed in alphabetical order. The inside front cover lists the emergency numbers for police, fire, ambulance, and other vital numbers (like the coast guard, poison-control center, crime-victims hotline, and so on). The first few pages are devoted to community-service numbers, including a guide to long-distance and international calling, complete with country codes and area codes.

The second directory, printed on yellow paper (hence its name, *Yellow Pages*), lists all local services, businesses, and industries by type of activity, with an index at the back. The listings cover not only such obvious items as automobile repairs by make of car, or drugstores (pharmacies), often by geographical location, but also restaurants by type of cuisine and geographical location, bookstores by special subject, places of worship by religious denomination, and other information that the tourist might otherwise not readily find. The *Yellow Pages* also include city plans or detailed area maps, often showing postal ZIP codes and public transportation routes.

Time   The United States is divided into six time zones. From east to west these are: eastern standard time (EST), central standard time (CST), mountain standard time (MST), Pacific standard time (PST), Alaska standard time (AST), and Hawaii standard time (HST). New Orleans is in central standard time.

Always keep the changing time zones in mind if you are traveling (or even telephoning) long distances in the United States. For example, noon in New York City (EST) is 11am in New Orleans (CST), 10am in Denver (MST), 9am in Los Angeles (PST), 8am in Anchorage (AST), and 7am in Honolulu (HST). When it is noon in London (GMT, or Greenwich mean time), it is 7am in New York.

Daylight saving time is in effect from 1am on the first Sunday in April until 2am on the last Sunday in October, except in Arizona, Hawaii, part of Indiana, and Puerto Rico.

Tipping   Waiters and taxi drivers are tipped between 15% and 20%. Bellhops should be tipped $1 per bag; airport porters should be tipped 50¢ for a small bag, $1 for a larger one.

Toilets   Often euphemistically referred to as rest rooms, public toilets are nonexistent on the streets of New Orleans. They can be found, though, in bars, restaurants, hotel lobbies, museums, department stores, and service stations—and will probably be clean (although ones in the last-mentioned category sometimes leave much to be desired). Note, however, that some restaurants and bars display a notice that "Toilets are for use of patrons only." You can ignore this sign, or better yet, avoid arguments by paying for a cup of coffee or soft drink, which will qualify you as a patron. The cleanliness of toilets at railroad stations and bus depots may be questionable; some public places are equipped with pay toilets that will require you to insert one or two dimes (10¢) or a quarter (25¢) into a slot on the door before it will open. In rest rooms with attendants, leaving at least a 25¢ tip is customary.

THE AMERICAN SYSTEM OF MEASUREMENTS

Length

1 inch (in.)			=	2.54cm			
1 foot (ft.)	=	12 in.	=	30.48cm	=	.305m	
1 yard (yd.)	=	3 ft.			=	.915m	
1 mile	=	5,280 ft.					=	1.609km

To convert miles to kilometers, multiply the number of miles by 1.61 (example: 50 mi. × 1.61 = 80.5km). Also use to convert speeds from miles per hour (m.p.h.) to kilometers per hour (kmph).

To convert kilometers to miles, multiply the number of kilometers by .62 (example: 25km × .62 = 15.5 mi.). Also use to convert kilometers per hour to miles per hour.

Capacity

1 fluid ounce (fl. oz.)			=	.03 liter		
1 pint (pt.)	=	16 fl. oz.	=	.47 liter		
1 quart (qt.)	=	2 pints	=	.94 liter		
1 gallon (gal.)	=	4 quarts	=	3.79 liters	=	.83 Imperial gal.

To convert U.S. gallons to liters, multiply the number of gallons by 3.79 (example: 12 gal. × 3.79 = 45.58 liters).

To convert liters to U.S. gallons, multiply the number of liters by .26 (example: 50 liters × .26 = 13 U.S. gal.).

To convert U.S. gallons to Imperial gallons, multiply the number of U.S. gallons by .83 (example: 12 U.S. gal. × .83 = 9.96 Imperial gal.).

To convert Imperial gallons to U.S. gallons, multiply the number of Imperial gallons by 1.2 (example: 8 Imperial gal. × 1.2 = 9.6 U.S. gal.).

Weight

1 ounce (oz.)		=	28.35g			
1 pound (lb.)	= 16 oz.	=	453.6g	=	.45 kg	
1 ton	= 2,000 lb.	=		907kg	=	.91 metric ton

To convert pounds to kilograms, multiply the number of pounds by .45 (example: 90 lb. × .45 = 40.5kg).

To convert kilograms to pounds, multiply the number of kilos by 2.2 (example, 75kg × 2.2 = 165 lb.).

Area

1 acre		=	.41ha		
1 square mile	= 640 acres	=	2.59ha	=	2.6 sq. km

To convert acres to hectares, multiply the number of acres by .41 (example: 40 acres × .41 = 16.4ha).

To convert hectares to acres, multiply the number of hectares by 2.47 (example: 20ha × 2.47 = 49.4 acres).

To convert square miles to square kilometers, multiply the number of square miles by 2.6 (example: 80 sq. mi. × 2.6 = 208 sq. km).

To convert square kilometers to square miles, multiply the number of square kilometers by .39 (example: 150 sq. km × .39 = 58.5 sq. mi.).

Temperature

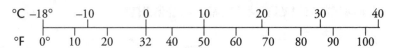

To convert degrees Fahrenheit to degrees Celsius, subtract 32 from °F, multiply by 5, then divide by 9 (example: 85°F − 32 × $^5/_9$ = 29.4°C).

To convert degrees Celsius to degrees Fahrenheit, multiply °C by 9, divide by 5, and add 32 (example: 20°C × $^9/_5$ + 32 = 68°F).

Getting to Know New Orleans

New Orleans is a small city, so you'll come to know it quite well, even if you have only a week, and the people are extraordinarily helpful and friendly. If you still need some help getting your bearings and getting around, you'll find listed below just about everything you need to know.

1 Orientation

VISITOR INFORMATION

You'll be way ahead if, as far in advance as possible, you contact the **New Orleans Metropolitan Convention and Visitors Bureau,** 1520 Sugar Bowl Dr., New Orleans, LA 70112 (☎ **504/566-5055**), for their brochures on such subjects as sightseeing, dining, entertainment, and shopping. The Convention and Visitors Bureau can also be reached by E-mail at tourism@nawlins.com. If you have a special interest, they'll help you plan your visit around appropriate activities. The internet address for the Convention and Visitors Bureau is http://www.nawlins.com. Other internet addresses worth checking out are http://www.nola.com and http:www.neworleans.net. From those addresses you'll also be able to access other New Orleans–specific sites.

Once you've arrived in the city, you also might want to stop by the **Visitor Information Center** at 529 St. Ann St. (☎ **504/566-5031**), in the French Quarter. The center is open daily from 9am to 5pm and has excellent walking- and driving-tour maps and booklets on restaurants, accommodations, sightseeing, special tours, and almost anything else you might want to know about. The staff is friendly and knowledgeable about not only New Orleans but the entire state of Louisiana as well. In addition you might keep an eye out for the mobile **Info a la Cart** sites around town.

CITY LAYOUT

The French Quarter, where the city began, is a 13-block-long area between Canal Street and Esplanade Avenue running from the Mississippi River to North Rampart Street. Because of the bend in the river, much of the city is laid out at angles that render useless such mundane directions as north, south, east, and west. New Orleans solved this directional problem long ago by simply substituting *riverside, lakeside, uptown,* and *downtown*. It works, and you'll catch on quickly if you keep in mind that North Rampart Street is the "lakeside" boundary of the Quarter, Canal Street marks the beginning of "uptown," and the Quarter is "downtown." As for building numbers, they begin at 100 on either side of Canal. In the Quarter they begin at 400 at the river (that's because four blocks of numbered buildings were lost to the river before the levee was built). Another reminder of Canal Street's boundary role between new and old New Orleans is the fact that street names change when they cross it (that is, Bourbon Street "downtown" becomes Carondelet "uptown").

MAPS   Consult the free four-color fold-out map included in this guide. If you want others before you leave home, call the New Orleans Metropolitan Convention and Visitors Bureau (see above) and they'll send them to you. Otherwise, stop by there or the Visitor Information Center when you arrive and pick them up. If you rent a car, be sure to ask for maps of the city—the rental agents have good ones. Major bookstores also sell good city maps. If you're planning excursions outside the city, the places listed above also supply state maps.

NEIGHBORHOODS IN BRIEF

The French Quarter   Made up of about 90 square blocks, this section is also known as the Vieux Carré and is bounded on the south by Canal Street, the west by North Rampart Street, the east by the Mississippi River, and the north by Esplanade Avenue. It is the most historic and the best preserved area in the city.

Canal Street/Central Business District   There's no street more central to the life of New Orleans than Canal—the location of *everything* is described in reference to its relation to Canal Street. It took its name from a very shallow ditch that was dug along this border of the French Quarter in its early days. Although the ditch was given the rather grand name of canal, it was never large enough to be used for transport.

The Central Business District (CBD) is roughly bounded by Canal Street on the north and the elevated Pontchartrain Expressway (Bus. I-90) to the south, between Loyola Avenue and the Mississippi River. There are pleasant plazas, squares, and parks sprinkled among all the commercial high-rise buildings of the CBD, and some of the most elegant of the luxury hotels are located in this area.

The Warehouse District   With the revitalization of an area once devoted almost entirely to abandoned warehouses into an upscale residential neighborhood, the area between Julia and St. Joseph streets has become a mecca for artists. The area is just loaded with galleries (listed in Chapter 10) that show the works of contemporary artists. The Contemporary Arts Center, 900 Camp St. (see Chapter 8 for a full listing) just beyond St. Joseph toward Howard Avenue, has facilities for presenting not only art exhibitions but also performances. Also in this area, you will find the Louisiana Children's Museum (see "Especially for Kids" in Chapter 8 for more details).

The Garden District   Located uptown and bounded by St. Charles Avenue (lakeside) and Magazine Street (riverside) between Jackson and Louisiana avenues, it remains one of the most beautiful areas in the city because of the old Victorian homes that line the streets. Unfortunately, most of the gardens that used to exist around the outsides of the homes no longer exist and some of the houses are in disrepair, but you can still get some idea of what it used to be like.

The Irish Channel   The area between the Garden District (Magazine Street) and the river is known locally as the Irish Channel because it was home to hundreds of Irish immigrants during the 1800s. These days it is an interesting, although somewhat seedy, section of town. It houses many of New Orleans's poor, just as it did in

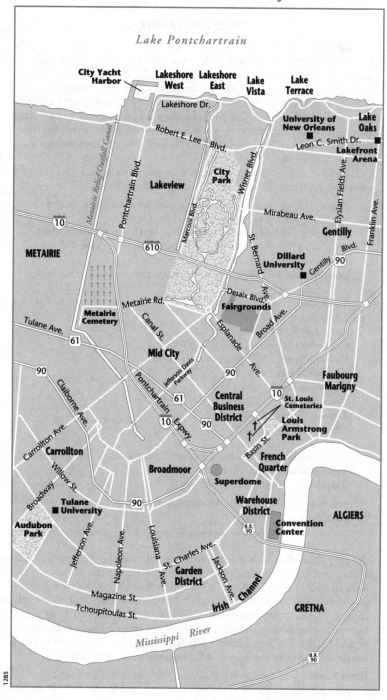

Lake Pontchartrain

City Yacht Harbor · Lakeshore West · Lakeshore East · Lake Vista · Lake Terrace

Lakeshore Dr.

Robert E. Lee Blvd.

University of New Orleans · Lake Oaks

Leon C. Smith Dr. · Lakefront Arena

Metairie Relief Outfall Canal

Pontchartrain Blvd.

Lakeview

City Park

Wisner Blvd.

Marconi Blvd.

Elysian Fields Ave.

Franklin Ave.

Mirabeau Ave.

Gentilly

10

METAIRIE

610

St. Bernard Ave.

Dillard University

Gentilly Blvd.

90

Metairie Rd.

Desaix Blvd.

Fairgrounds

Tulane Ave.

Metairie Cemetery

Canal St.

61

Mid City

Jefferson Davis Parkway

Esplanade Ave.

Broad Ave.

90

Faubourg Marigny

90

Claiborne Ave.

Pontchartrain Expwy.

61

Central Business District

10

St. Louis Cemeteries

Louis Armstrong Park

Carrollton Ave.

Carrollton

Willow St.

10

90

Broadmoor

Basin St.

French Quarter

Broadway

Superdome

Warehouse District

ALGIERS

Tulane University

90

B.R. 90

Convention Center

Audubon Park

Jefferson Ave.

Napoleon Ave.

Louisiana Ave.

St. Charles Ave.

Jackson Ave.

Garden District

Irish Channel

GRETNA

Magazine St.

Tchoupitoulas St.

Mississippi River

B.R. 90

1285

Speak Like a Native

The local lingo comes with tones, accents, and pronunciations that may surprise you. Don't expect to hear a lot of "y'alls" or other Deep South expressions; be prepared instead for a sort of southern Brooklynese. There are, of course, all sorts of dialects around town, as you'd expect from the variety of ethnic backgrounds represented in New Orleans, but somehow they *all* seem to have developed a little bit along the lines of speech in New York's Brooklyn. Unless you stick to the Garden District and university campuses, you should know before you arrive that "toin" translates to turn, "erl" means oil, and even the most cultured downtowner is likely to slip in "de" for the.

To help you sound less like a "foreigner" as you move around town, here are some words and street names that are given the native twist:

bayou   BY-you (a marshy, sluggish stream, usually feeding into a river or lake; also, the swamplands of southern Louisiana)

banquette   ban-KET (a French word for bench that means "sidewalk" in New Orleans, since early wooden sidewalks were elevated above muddy streets)

neutral ground   (a uniquely New Orleans term meaning a "median" in the roadway)

Vieux Carré   view ka-RAY

Conti Street   CON-teye

Burgundy Street   bur-GUN-dee

Carondelet Street   car-ONDE-let (not lay)

Calliope Street   CAL-i-ope (not cal-I-opee)

Chartres Street   charters

Dauphine Street   daw-FEEN

Iberville Street   EYE-bur-vill

Bienville Street   bee-EN-vill

Orleans Street   or-LEENS
  but

New Orleans   noo OR-lyuns (or, better yet, nor-luns)

Tchoupitoulas Street   chop-a-TOOL-us

Terpsichore Street   TURP-sick-ory

You're sure to hear others that sound peculiar, but don't question, just follow the lead of those who live here.

the early days when Irish immigrants struggled to establish themselves in New Orleans and lived along these streets. An illuminating sidelight to the city's history is the fact that between 1820 and 1860 the more than 100,000 Irish newcomers were considered more "expendable" than costly slaves—many were killed while employed doing dangerous construction work and any other manual labor. In spite of that, there was a toughness and lively spirit that gave the Irish Channel a distinctive neighborhood flavor. Today it is mostly populated by African Americans and Hispanic Americans, and there is still a sort of "street camaraderie" alive here.

Basin Street   You remember Basin Street, of course—the birthplace of jazz. But some people will tell you that Storyville (the red-light district along Basin Street) served only as a place for jazz, which had been around a long time, to come in off the streets. It did that all right—jazz bands became the house entertainment in the many ornate "sporting palaces" that offered a wide variety of "services," primarily of the sex-for-hire variety. King Oliver, Jelly Roll Morton, and Louis Armstrong were among the jazz greats who got their start on Basin Street in the brothels between Canal Street and Beauregard Square. Storyville operated with reckless abandon from 1897, when Alderman Sidney Story proposed a plan for the concentration of illegal activities in this area, until an official of the U.S. Navy had it closed down in 1917.

What you'll find today is a far cry from what was there in those rowdy days. A low-income public housing project now sprawls over the site, and statues depicting Latin American heroes dot the landscape. Simón Bolívar presides over the Canal and Basin streets intersection; there's also a statue of Mexico's Benito Juárez with the inscription "Peace is based on the respect of the rights of others"; and finally a likeness of Gen. Francisco Morazón, a hero of Central America, given to the city by Honduras and El Salvador, is last in line at Basin and St. Louis streets.

Faubourg Marigny *Faubourg* means "suburb," and Marigny is the name of a prominent early New Orleans family. For some years the area (beginning with Frenchmen Street) had been going downhill; these days, however, small businesses, a good hotel (The Frenchmen, see Chapter 6), several good eateries, and many popular music spots are revitalizing Frenchmen Street and its smaller tributaries. Because of Faubourg Marigny's proximity to the Quarter, the restaurants and entertainment there are included with those of the Quarter.

NETWORKS & RESOURCES

If you need more help than what's listed here, call the New Orleans Metropolitan Convention and Visitors Bureau (☎ **504/566-5055**) or the numbers for the organizations listed and ask them for references.

FOR STUDENTS New Orleans has two major colleges, both only a short ride on the streetcar from the French Quarter or the Central Business District. Both Tulane and Loyola universities have student unions that are open to the public, so if you're missing your peers, jump on the streetcar and head for the student unions.

FOR AFRICAN AMERICANS The **Greater New Orleans Black Tourism Network** (☎ **504/523-5652**) can provide information on tourism that is of interest to black Americans or to others who are interested in African-American culture as it pertains to New Orleans.

FOR GAY MEN & LESBIANS You'll find an abundance of centers serving gay and lesbian interests, from bars to restaurants to community services to certain businesses. Here are some numbers you might find useful if you need some help finding your way.

The **Gay and Lesbian Community Center** is located at 816 N. Rampart St. (☎ **504/524-8334**). The **NO/AIDS** task force has a 24-hour hotline (☎ **504/945-4000**). *Ambush* magazine, 828-A Bourbon St., New Orleans, LA 70116 (☎ **504/522-8049**), is the Gulf South weekly entertainment/news publication for the gay and lesbian community. You can access Ambush through the internet at http://www.ambushmag.com. *Impact Gulf South Gay News* is another popular area publication. **Grace Fellowship** (☎ **504/944-9836** or 504/949-2325) and **Vieux Carré Metropolitan Community Church,** 1128 St. Roch (☎ **504/945-5390**) are both religious organizations that support gays and lesbians.

FOR SENIORS & THE DISABLED "Rollin' by the River," a guide to wheelchair-accessible restaurants and clubs in the French Quarter, is available for a handling fee of $2.25 (they'll send it on receipt of your check or money order) from the **Advocacy Center for the Elderly and Disabled**, 210 O'Keefe Ave., Suite 700, New Orleans, LA 70112 (☎ **504/522-2337**). Seniors are welcome to use this number as well.

For information about specialized transportation systems, call **LIFT** at **504/827-7433.**

2 Getting Around

BY PUBLIC TRANSPORTATION

DISCOUNT PASSES You can obtain a **VisiTour** pass that will entitle you to an unlimited number of rides on all streetcar and bus lines. It costs $4 for one day, $8 for three days. Ask at your hotel or guest house where you can get the VisiTour pass. You can also call the **Regional Transit Authority** for information at **504/248-3900.**

BY BUS New Orleans has an excellent public bus system, and you can get complete information on which buses run where by calling 504/248-3900 or by picking up an excellent city map at the Visitor Information Center, 529 St. Ann St. in the French Quarter. All fares at press time are $1 (you must have exact change, and transfers are an extra 10¢), except for expresses, which are $1.25.

Along the riverfront, buses made up to look like vintage streetcars, affectionately known as the "Ladies in Red," run for 1.9 miles from the Old Mint, across Canal Street, to Riverview. The fare is $1.25, there are convenient stops along the way, and there's ramp access for the disabled—a great step-saver as you explore this lively area of the city.

BY STREETCAR One treat you really should allow yourself is the 1¹/₂-hour ride down St. Charles Avenue on the famous old streetcar line, which has been named a national historic landmark (see "A Streetcar Tour" in Chapter 9). The trolleys run 24 hours a day at frequent intervals, and the fare is $1 each way (you must have exact change). Board at Canal and Carondelet streets (directly across Canal from Bourbon Street in the French Quarter), sit back, and look for landmarks in this part of town.

The end of the line is at Palmer Park and Playground at Clairborne Avenue, but if you want to mount a shopping expedition at the interesting Riverbend Shopping Area (see Chapter 10), get off at Carrollton. It will cost you another $1 for the ride back to Canal Street. If you would like to transfer from the streetcar to a bus it will cost you 10¢.

BY CAR

The following is a list of car-rental agencies with their local and toll-free numbers and addresses:

Avis, 2024 Canal St. (☎ 504/523-4317 or 800/331-1212); **Budget Rent-A-Car,** 1317 Canal St. (☎ 504/467-2277 or 800/527-0700); **Dollar Rent-A-Car,** 1910 Airline Hwy., Kenner (☎ 504/467-2285); **Hertz,** 901 Convention Center Blvd. No. 101 (☎ 504/568-1645 or 800/654-3131); **Swifty Car Rental,** 2300 Canal St. (☎ 504/524-7368); **Value Rent-A-Car,** 1701 Airline Hwy., Kenner (☎ 504/469-2688).

Rental rates vary according to the time of your visit and from company to company, so call ahead and do some comparison shopping. Ask lots of questions and try different dates and pickup points; ask about any corporate or organizational discounts. *Note:* If you're staying for a week or more, be sure to ask about weekly rates—stay away from the daily rates.

Comparatively speaking, driving in New Orleans isn't too difficult. But traffic cops are absolute murder on illegal parking, handing out tickets right and left. For that reason, I strongly suggest that you put the car away for any French Quarter sightseeing (it's more fun, anyway, on foot) and use it only for longer jaunts out of congested areas. Most hotels provide parking for their guests (although a daily fee is usually charged); smaller hotels or guest houses (particularly in the French Quarter) may not have parking facilities but will be able to direct you to a nearby public garage.

French Quarter driving is more difficult than driving in some other areas of the city. All streets there are one-way, and on weekdays during daylight hours, Royal and Bourbon streets are closed to automobiles between the 300 and 700 blocks. Driving is also trying in the Central Business District, where congested traffic and limited parking make life difficult for the motorist. It is much smarter to park the car and use the public transportation provided in both areas.

BY TAXI

Taxis are plentiful in New Orleans and respond quickly to telephone calls. They can be hailed easily on the street in the French Quarter and in some parts of the Central Business District and are usually in place at taxi stands at the larger hotels. Otherwise, telephone and expect a cab to appear in three to five minutes. In my experience, at least two out of three drivers will get out to open doors for you at both ends of the ride. Rates are $1.70 when you enter the taxi and $1 per mile thereafter. During special events (like Mardi Gras and Jazz Fest) the rate is $3 per person (or the meter rate if it's greater) no matter where you go in the city. The city's most reliable company is **United Cabs** (☎ **504/524-9606**).

Touring tip: Most taxis can be hired for an hourly rate for up to five passengers—a hassle-free and economical way for a small group to tour far-flung areas of the city (the lakefront, for example). Out-of-town trips cost double the amount on the meter.

ON FOOT

In my opinion, the *only* way to see the French Quarter (and some parts of the Garden District) is by foot. It's easy to find your way around both of these small areas, and they are crammed with things you won't want to miss. Only by strolling can you really soak up the charm of both these sections. In the Quarter, look through iron gates or down alleyways for glimpses of lovely patios and courtyards and above street level for interesting facades and incredibly delicate, lacy iron railings. Along Bourbon Street, intersperse strolls with stops to listen to live jazz groups playing at open-door saloons—there's nonstop music most of the day. In the Garden District, be sure to allow enough time to drink in the beauty of the formal gardens surrounding the fine old mansions.

BY FERRY

One of New Orleans's nicest treats is absolutely free. It's the 25-minute (round-trip) ferry ride across the Mississippi from the foot of Canal Street to Algiers. It's a joy, whether you go by day for a view of the busy harbor or at night when the lights of the city reflect in the mighty river. If you'd like to do some West Bank driving, the ferry carries both car and foot passengers.

FAST FACTS: New Orleans

Airport   See Chapter 3.

American Express   The American Express office (☎ **504/586-8201**) is located at 158 Baronne St. in the Central Business District.

Area Code   The area code for New Orleans is 504.

Baby-Sitters   It's best to ask at your hotel about baby-sitting services—they might even have one of their own. They'll give you all the information you need, including rates. If your hotel doesn't offer any help in finding child care, try calling **Accent on Children's Arrangements** (☎ **504/524-1227**).

Business Hours   As far as businesses and stores go, New Orleans is generally a 9 to 5 town. Some stores, particularly in the French Quarter, open late and, as a consequence, stay open later. Just call before you go to be sure. Banking hours are generally 9am to 3pm weekdays, although some banks stay open later one day per week, and some offer limited Saturday hours. There is no official closure law for bars, so many stay open into the wee hours.

Car Rentals   See "Getting Around" earlier in this chapter.

Climate   See "When to Go" in Chapter 3.

Convention Center   The **Ernest N. Morial Convention Center** is located at 900 Convention Center Blvd. (☎ **504/582-3000**).

Driving Rules   See "Getting Around" earlier in this chapter.

Embassies/Consulates   See Chapter 4.

Emergencies   For fire, ambulance, and police, just dial 911 in an emergency.

Holidays   See "When to Go" in Chapter 3.

Hospitals   Should you become ill during your New Orleans visit, most major hotels have in-house staff doctors on call 24 hours a day. If there's not one available in your hotel or guest house, call or go to the emergency room at **Ochsner Medical Institutions,** 880 Commerce Rd. W. (☎ **504/842-3460**), or the **Tulane University Medical Center,** 1415 Tulane Ave. (☎ **504/588-5800**).

Information   See "Visitor Information" earlier in this chapter.

Libraries   The **New Orleans Public Library** (☎ **504/596-2550**) is located at 219 Loyola Ave. It's open Monday to Thursday from 11am to 6pm, and Saturday from 11am to 5pm. Consult the phone book for other branch locations throughout the city.

Liquor Laws   Alcoholic beverages are available in New Orleans around the clock, seven days a week. You are allowed to drink on the street, but only as long as your libation is in a plastic cup or container. Although the legal drinking age is 21 years, I've seen people much younger taking their seats at the bar.

One warning: Although the police may look the other way if they see a pedestrian who's had a few too many (as long as he or she is peaceful and not bothering anyone else), they have no tolerance at all for those who are intoxicated behind the wheel.

Maps   See "City Layout" earlier in this chapter.

Newspapers/Magazines   To find out what's going on around town, you might want to pick up a copy of the *Times-Picayune* or *New Orleans Magazine. Offbeat Publications* is a monthly guide to the city's evening entertainment, art galleries, and special events. It can be found in most hotels. *Where Magazine* and *Arrive Magazine,* also published monthly, are good resources for visitors. *This Week Magazine* is an informative weekly publication for visitors.

Photographic Needs　One of the city's most complete camera shops is the **K&B Camera Center,** 227 Dauphine St. (☎ **504/524-2266**), with a wide selection of cameras and other electronics, as well as film, camera, and darkroom supplies. Fast film developing is also available. It is open Monday through Friday from 8am to 6pm, Saturday from 8am to 2pm. **Fox Photo Labs** at 414 Canal St. (☎ **504/529-6120**) and **French Quarter Camera,** 809 Decatur St. (☎ **504/529-2974**), also offer one-hour film processing.

Post Office　The main post office is located at 701 Loyola Ave. There's also a post office in the World Trade Center. If you're in the Vieux Carré, you'll find a post office at 1022 Iberville St. There's another one at 610 S. Maestri Place. If you've got something large or fragile to send home and don't feel like hunting around for packing materials, go to **The Wooden Box Packing and Shipping Co.,** 816 South Peters (☎ **504/568-0281**), or **Prytania Mail Services,** 5500 Prytania St. (☎ **504/897-0877**); both places will pack and ship items for a surcharge.

Safety　While visiting any unfamiliar city you should be careful, but in New Orleans in particular, don't walk alone at night, and do not go into the cemeteries alone at any time during the day or night. Ask around locally before you go anywhere—people will tell you if you should take a cab instead of walking or taking public transportation. Most important, if someone holds you up and demands your wallet, purse, or other personal belongings, don't resist.

Taxes　Sales tax in New Orleans is 9%. An additional 2% tax is added to hotel bills for a total of 11%.

Taxis　See "Getting Around" earlier in this chapter.

Time and Temperature　For information without leaving your room, call **504/465-9212** for weather and **504/976-1111** for the time.

Time Zone　New Orleans observes central standard time, the same time zone as Chicago.

Transit Information　Local bus routes and schedules can be obtained from the **RTA Ride Line** (☎ **504/248-3900**).

Useful Telephone Numbers　You can reach the **Travelers Aid Society** at **504/525-8726. Union Passenger Terminal,** 1001 Loyola Ave., provides bus information (☎ **504/524-7571**) and train information (☎ **504/528-1610**).

6 Accommodations

Despite the annual influx of hundreds of thousands of visitors needing a place to stay, New Orleans has managed to keep historic districts, such as the French Quarter, free of those high-rise monstrosities that deface many a formerly gracious and historic city. Indeed, it is almost impossible to tell if some of the new French Quarter hotels have been built from scratch or lovingly placed inside the shell of an older building, so faithful has been the dedication to preserving the Quarter's architectural style. Even motor hotels (which have alleviated the ever-present problem of on-street parking) have a look that is distinctly New Orleans.

You'll find those high-rise hotels, of course, but they're more appropriately located uptown, in commercial sections, where they seem to fit just fine.

With the arrival of legalized gambling, there came a need for more hotel rooms. Old office buildings were quickly bought up by hotel developers and as such, several new hotels are scheduled to open within the next two years. However, now that Harrah's casino has gone belly-up, developers are wondering whether they may have moved too fast to buy property. Only time will tell, of course, but my opinion is that if the city continues to work on cleaning up its crime problem, the people will come even without the casino.

Some new hotels set to debut in 1997 are the Queen and Crescent Hotel, the Omni Crescent Hotel, and the Wyndham Riverfront Hotel. They're not yet open as this book goes to press, but they promise to be quite lovely.

As for guest houses, they really do make you feel like a guest. Presided over by New Orleanians (or others, charmed by the city, who picked up and moved here) and imbued with a special brand of hospitality, many are furnished with antiques and all provide a very homelike atmosphere. After spending time in numerous New Orleans guest houses, I'd recommend them over hotel-style accommodations. You'll be treated as one of the family, and there's no better way to experience the history of New Orleans, as most guest house owners know the background history of their home and are more than willing to share it with you.

A sort of passkey to the lively people who live in New Orleans is **Bed and Breakfast Reservation Service,** 1021 Moss St. (P.O. Box 52257), New Orleans, LA 70152 (☎ **504/488-4640** or 800/ 729-4640). Personable Hazell Boyce can put you up in luxury in

19th-century, turn-of-the-century, or modern residences. Or you can opt for a cottage in the French Quarter or Garden District areas. Prices range from $35 to $225 single or double occupancy, and she delights in arranging modest lodging for students. Hazell will send you free listings that include rates and locations upon request.

One word of warning: In spite of the thousands of rental rooms in New Orleans, there are times when there isn't a bed to be had. Advance reservations (a good idea whatever the season) are a must during spring, fall, and winter. If your trip will coincide with Mardi Gras or Jazz Fest, it isn't an exaggeration to say that you should book as far as a year in advance. Sugar Bowl week and other festival times also flood New Orleans with visitors and require advance planning for accommodations, and of course, there's always a chance that a big convention will be in town, making it difficult to find a room. It's conceivable that you might run across a cancellation and get a last-minute booking, but the chances are remote, to say the least. You should also be aware that rates frequently jump more than a notch or two for Mardi Gras and other festival times, and in some cases there's a four- or five-night minimum requirement.

If you want to miss the crowds and lodgings squeeze that mark the big festivals, consider coming in the month immediately following Carnival (after "Fat Tuesday," the last day before Lent) or in the summer months (though they are often unbearably hot and muggy) when the streets are not nearly as thronged.

Since I am convinced that the only place to stay is in the French Quarter—the very heart and soul of New Orleans—I'm listing accommodations there first. But if circumstances make another location more desirable for you, you'll find listings outside the Quarter in this chapter as well. Note that there are no recommendable inexpensive hotels in the French Quarter. If you're on a budget and must stay here, consider staying at one of the guest houses. On the whole, however, you will have a better selection of inexpensive lodgings outside the Quarter. Note that there are two hostels in New Orleans; both are listed at the end of this chapter.

The hotels listed in this chapter are divided into four price categories. Those listed as **very expensive** will cost upwards of $200 a night for a double room; **expensive** hotels start in the neighborhood of $160 a night; **moderate** hotels offer double rooms for between $80 and $160. Any hotel in New Orleans where you can get a comfortable room for under $80 is considered **inexpensive.** Rates given are for double rooms and do not include the city's 11% hotel tax. Reduced single-occupancy rates are often offered; inquire when you make reservations. Unless otherwise noted in a particular hotel or guest house listing, all accommodations in New Orleans have private baths.

1 Best Bets

- **Best for a Romantic Getaway:** The **Melrose Mansion,** 937 Esplanade Ave. (☎ **504/944-2255**), is an excellent choice. Your visit will begin with a ride in a chauffeured stretch limousine, and when you arrive at the Melrose, you'll be greeted by the butler. Rooms are furnished with exquisite antiques, and some feature deep Jacuzzi tubs. Service here is impeccable.
- **Best Moderately Priced Hotel:** For my money, the **Bourbon Orleans,** 717 Orleans St. (☎ **504/523-2222**), is the best value in New Orleans. It's centrally located, has excellent amenities (coffeemakers in rooms, in-room movie systems, and marble baths), and rivals some of the city's more expensive hotels in elegance and quality of service.

New Orleans Accommodations

Avenue Plaza Suite Hotel & Spa 4
The Columns 2
Crowne Plaza New Orleans 9
Fairmount Hotel 16
Holiday Inn Downtown-Superdome 15
House on Bayou Road 20
Hotel Inter-Continental 13
Hotel LaSalle 17
Le Meriden Hotel 12

Le Pavillion Hotel 14
McKendrick-Breaux House 6
Melrose Mansion 18
Mechling's Guest House 19
New Orleans Hilton Riverside Hotel 8
Nicholas M. Benachi House 21
Park View Guest House 1
The Pelham 11
Pontchartrain Hotel 5

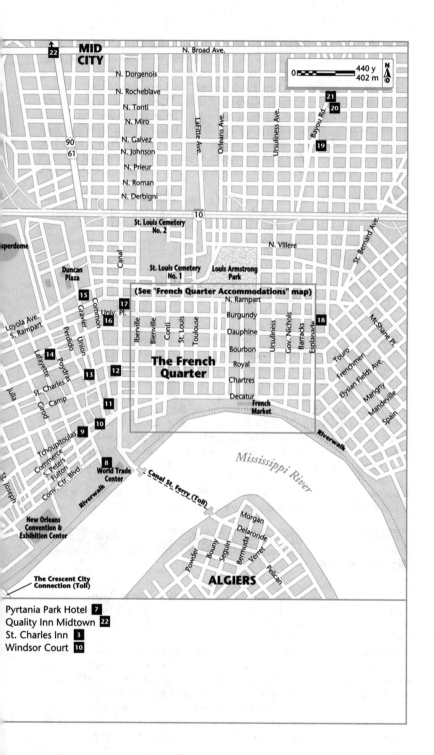

Pyrtania Park Hotel **7**
Quality Inn Midtown **22**
St. Charles Inn **3**
Windsor Court **10**

- **Best Guest House Value:** At the **McKendrick-Breaux House,** 1474 Magazine St. (☎ **504/586-1700**), you get the kind of service you'd expect at a larger, more expensive hotel (like ice brought to your room every evening), and your hosts seem to know instinctively just how much (or how little) attention you need. Rooms and bathrooms are exceptionally large, and cable TV and telephones are standard. The claw-foot bathtubs in the rooms in the main house are an added luxury.
- **Best Location:** If you want to stay right in the French Quarter, you'll be hard pressed to find a hotel better located than the **Omni Royal Orleans** at 621 St. Louis St. (☎ **504/529-5333**). The Omni Royal happens to be one of the city's most elegant hostelries, and it also features the Rib Room, one of New Orleans's best restaurants.
- **Best Modern Hotel:** You'll want for nothing in the luxury, high-rise **Hotel Inter-Continental,** 444 St. Charles Ave. (☎ **504/525-5566**). All rooms, even the standard ones, have such special touches as minibars and mini-TVs in the dressing alcoves. There's a health club with pool, butler service on the executive floor, business services, and an excellent restaurant here as well.
- **Best Health Club:** The hands-down winner is the **New Orleans Hilton Riverside Hotel,** 2 Poydras St. (☎ **504/561-0500**). Their Rivercenter Racquet and Health Club features outdoor and indoor tennis courts, squash and racquetball courts, a rooftop jogging track, aerobics classes, tanning beds, massage, a hair salon, and a golf studio.
- **Best Gay-Friendly Hotel:** The **New Orleans Guest House,** located on the outer edge of the French Quarter, just off North Rampart Street, at 1118 Ursulines St. (☎ **504/566-1177**), is a favorite with the visiting gay and lesbian community (the clientele is not entirely gay, however). A lush courtyard with bubbling fountains and unique garden statues, individually decorated rooms, and reasonable rates also make this place one of the best buys in the city.
- **In a Class by Itself:** Of all the hotels in New Orleans, **The Windsor Court,** 300 Gravier St. (☎ **504/523-6000**), stands head and shoulders above the rest. The hotel's lovely public areas are a veritable treasure trove of fine art. Most guest rooms are suites featuring Italian marble bathrooms, fine fabrics, balconies or bay windows, living rooms, kitchenettes, and dressing rooms. If you choose one of the two-bedroom penthouse suites, you'll have the added luxury of your own private library and a terrace that overlooks the mighty Mississippi.

2 In the French Quarter

VERY EXPENSIVE

✪ Omni Royal Orleans
621 St. Louis St., New Orleans, LA 70140. ☎ **504/529-5333** or 800/THE-OMNI in the U.S. and Canada. Fax 504/529-7089. 346 rms, 16 suites. A/C TV TEL. $175–$250 double; $350–$1,000 suite. Children 17 and under free with parents. AE, CB, DC, DISC, MC, V. Valet parking $14 per day with in/out privileges.

Considered *the* place to stay by many veteran visitors, the elegant Omni Royal Orleans is certainly one of the most beautiful French Quarter hotels. The present-day hotel opened its doors in 1960 on the site of the 1836 St. Louis Exchange Hotel, one of this country's most splendid hostelries of the mid-19th century. The St. Louis Exchange was a center of New Orleans social life until the final years of the Civil War, when it first became a hospital for wounded soldiers from both the North and the South, then served for a time as the state capitol building and a meeting place of the

French Quarter Accommodations

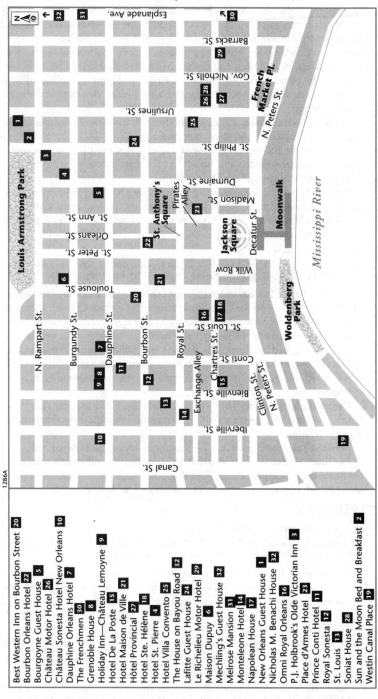

Best Western Inn on Bourbon Street 20
Bourbon Orleans Hotel 22
Bourgoyne Guest House 5
Château Motor Hotel 26
Château Sonesta Hotel New Orleans 10
Dauphine Orleans Hotel 7
The Frenchmen 30
Grenoble House 8
Holiday Inn—Château Lemoyne 9
Hotel De La Poste 15
Hotel Maison de Ville 21
Hôtel Provincial 27
Hotel Ste. Hélène 18
Hotel St. Pierre 4
Hotel Villa Convento 25
The House on Bayou Road 32
Lafitte Guest House 24
Le Richelieu Motor Hotel 29
Maison Dupuy 6
Mechling's Guest House 32
Melrose Mansion 31
Monteleone Hotel 14
Napoleon House 17
New Orleans Guest House 1
Nicholas M. Benachi House 32
Omni Royal Orleans 16
P.J. Holbrook's Olde Victorian Inn 3
Place d'Armes Hotel 23
Prince Conti Hotel 11
Royal Sonesta 12
St. Louis 13
Soniat House 28
Sun and the Moon Bed and Breakfast 2
Westin Canal Place 19

carpetbagger legislature, and finally was destroyed by a 1915 hurricane. In its heyday of gala soirees and eminent visitors, it was also the innovator of the "free lunch" for noontime drinkers, establishing a tradition of top-notch noontime cuisine that survives even today. The Omni Royal Orleans has proved a worthy successor, with a lobby of marble and brass and crystal chandeliers. Furnishings are truly sumptuous in the guest rooms. All rooms come equipped with umbrellas, irons, and ironing boards, and bathrooms include such amenities as terry-cloth bathrobes and makeup mirrors.

Dining/Entertainment: The classic Rib Room is a favorite dining spot for many natives (see Chapter 7), and there's soft music after 8pm in the elegant Esplanade Lounge. Touché Bar offers light meals and excellent mint juleps. The rooftop, poolside, palm tree–bordered La Riviera bar and restaurant is a terrific lunch spot, with unobstructed views of the French Quarter.

Services: Concierge, baby-sitting service, emergency mending and pressing services, complimentary shoe shine, nightly turn-down service, 24-hour room service.

Facilities: Health club, heated pool, beauty and barber shops, florist, sundries shop and newsstand, business center.

Westin Canal Place

100 Iberville St., New Orleans, LA 70130. ☎ **504/566-7006** or 800/228-3000. 438 rms. A/C MINIBAR TV TEL. $235–$298 double. AE, CB, DC, DISC, MC, V. Parking $12.

The Westin Canal Place has one of the most convenient locations in town—right on the Mississippi River on the Canal Street edge of the French Quarter. Its window-walled 11th-floor lobby is a masterpiece of Carrara marble, fine paintings, and antiques. Each room has a marble foyer and bath, fine furnishings, as well as phones with call waiting and voice mail. The Westin Guest Office program (for an additional $20) includes use of an in-room combination copier/printer/fax machine, free office supplies, and the use of an in-room coffeemaker. Sweeping river and French Quarter views are truly special here.

Dining/Entertainment: The lobby makes a lovely setting for afternoon tea. The Green Bar and The Riverbend Grill restaurant are just steps away. There is also a Sunday jazz brunch.

Services: Full concierge service, 24-hour room service, multilingual staff.

Facilities: Heated pool, privileges at a nearby 18-hole golf course, special elevator descending directly to Canal Place shopping center where guests can enjoy use of the Health Center or visit the barbershop, beauty salon, and stores.

EXPENSIVE

Best Western Inn on Bourbon Street

541 Bourbon St., New Orleans, LA 70130. ☎ **504/524-7611** or 800/535-7891. 186 rms. A/C TV TEL. $155–$235 double. AE, DC, DISC, MC, V. Parking $9.

This hotel sits on the site of the 1859 French Opera House, the first ever built in the United States; it burned down in 1919. All rooms have a Deep South decor and king-size or double beds, and some have balconies overlooking Bourbon Street. Both the Sing-a-Long piano bar and the Bourbon Street Cafeteria (a self-service restaurant featuring Creole and Cajun cooking) are popular with guests. There is a fitness center, and the hotel offers room service, concierge services, and laundry/valet service. Prices hinge on whether your room faces Bourbon Street or has a balcony.

Chateau Sonesta Hotel New Orleans

800 Iberville St., New Orleans, LA 70130. ☎ **504/586-0800** or 800/SONESTA. 255 rms. A/C MINIBAR TV TEL. $145–$215 double, $275–$575 suite. Extra person $35. AE, MC, V. Valet parking $14.

The Chateau Sonesta Hotel is one of the city's newest hostelries. Located at the site of the former D. H. Holmes Canal Street Department Store, built in 1849, the hotel maintains its 1913 facade. If you decide to stay here you'll have easy access to the historic French Quarter. Guest rooms are large, and many feature balconies overlooking either Bourbon or Dauphine streets. Videos are available for rental. Phone systems with voice mail, conference calling, data port, and modem capabilities are state of the art.

Dining/Entertainment: La Chatelaine Restaurant and The Clock Bar are open daily.

Services: Concierge, room service, baby-sitting service, nightly turndown.

Facilities: Indoor and outdoor pools, exercise room, gift shop.

Dauphine Orleans Hotel

415 Dauphine St., New Orleans, LA 70112. ☎ **504/586-1800** or 800/521-7111. Fax 504/586-1409. 109 rms. A/C MINIBAR TV TEL. $145–$190 double; $170–$370 suite; $150–$220 patio suite. Rates include continental breakfast. Extra person $15. Children under 12 free in parents' room. AE, MC, V. Valet parking $12.

There's a sort of casual elegance at the Dauphine Orleans Hotel. All rooms have recently been upgraded with marble bathrooms (equipped with bathrobes and hair dryers), new solid wood headboards and feather pillows on the beds, and new/modern or upgraded period furnishings, making the Dauphine Orleans one of the French Quarter's loveliest properties. There are three secluded courtyards at the Dauphine, and history lurks around every corner. The hotel's main building was once the studio of the famous John James Audubon, and the "patio suites" across the street from the main building were originally built in 1834 as the home of New Orleans merchant Samuel Herrmann. In 1991 when the cottages, located adjacent to the main hotel, were renovated, many intriguing aspects of the building were uncovered. The original construction of the cottages was brick between posts, and the nails that can now be seen in the wood posts are thought to have come from the famous Lafitte's Blacksmith Shoppe. Hidden fireplaces have been uncovered, and in a room that was once the kitchen, antique pots and pans were discovered under the floor. While all of the rooms here are nice, I am partial to the cottage rooms.

Dining/Entertainment: May Baily's, the hotel's bar, was once a notorious "sporting house" (brothel), and guests are given a copy of the original 1857 license, which still hangs on the wall. The Coffee Lounge is where continental breakfast is served daily from 6:30 to 11am. Complimentary afternoon tea is also served daily from 3 to 5pm.

Services: Complimentary French Quarter and downtown transportation, morning paper delivered to your door.

Facilities: Pool, guest library, small fitness room.

Hotel Maison de Ville

727 Toulouse St., New Orleans, LA 70130. ☎ **504/561-5858.** 23 rms. A/C MINIBAR TV TEL. $165–$205 double; $375–$525 cottage. AE, MC, V. Valet parking $17.

Unique among New Orleans's luxury hotels is the small, European-style Hotel Maison de Ville. Dating from before 1742, the Maison has been restored to an old-time elegance marked by marble fireplaces, fine French antiques, gilt-framed mirrors, rich swagged drapes, and matching quilted bedspreads. Guest rooms surround a brick courtyard (one of the loveliest in the Quarter) with a tiered fountain and palm trees. It was here, at one of the wrought-iron tables, that Tennessee Williams reworked *A Streetcar Named Desire;* his usual room was today's room 9. Another famous tenant, John Audubon, lived in one of the seven cottages now operated by the hotel while painting the Louisiana portion of his *Birds of America*. The cottages, with brick walls, beamed ceilings, and slate or brick floors, are furnished with antiques and reflect a warm country elegance. All rooms are equipped with VCRs.

Dining/Entertainment: The Maison's service includes a breakfast of fresh orange juice, croissants or muffins, and steaming chicory coffee served on a silver tray in your room, in the parlor, or on the patio. Complimentary sherry and port are served in the afternoon and evening. The Bistro, the hotel's restaurant, is intimate and inviting.

Services: Morning and evening newspapers delivered to your room; shoe-polishing service.

Maison Dupuy

1001 Toulouse St., New Orleans, LA 70112. ☎ **504/586-8000** or 800/535-9177. Fax 504/525-5334. 198 rms, 10 suites. A/C TV TEL. $95–$205 deluxe double. $250–$800 suite. AE, DC, MC, V. Valet parking $12 when available.

Maison Dupuy is a lovely hotel comprising seven town houses. It's ideally located for French Quarter sightseeing and is the perfect size for those who like their privacy but also like to be recognized by the staff.

Rooms are quite large, done in dusty rose and blue-green, and each has a desk, comfortable armchairs, and either two double beds or one king-size bed. All have modern bathrooms with standard amenities, and some have balconies that face either the courtyard or the street.

In the courtyard you can relax, swim, enjoy a cocktail, or just take in the beautiful surroundings.

Dining/Entertainment: The hotel's restaurant, Le Bon Creole, serves breakfast, lunch, and dinner. The hotel also does a Sunday "Champagne Jazz Brunch Buffet." The Cabaret Lautrec Lounge has live entertainment and is a perfect place to relax. There is also a courtyard patio bar that is open during fair weather.

Services: Room service, twice-daily maid service, same-day laundry and dry cleaning.

Facilities: Heated outdoor pool, health club.

Monteleone Hotel

214 Royal St., New Orleans, LA 70140. ☎ **504/523-3341** or 800/535-9595. 600 rms. A/C TV TEL. $145–$210 double-double or king-double; $290–$400 suite. Extra person $25. Children under 18 free in parents' room. Package rates available. AE, CB, DC, MC, V. Parking $11.

The largest French Quarter hotel, the Monteleone has been operated by four generations of Monteleones. Covering almost an entire block, it seems to keep expanding over the years without losing a trace of its trademark charm. Service at the Monteleone is surprisingly personal for a hotel of its size. The hotel offers accommodations that range in style from luxurious, antique-filled suites to more modern, comfortable family rooms.

Dining/Entertainment: Le Café restaurant is a favorite with native New Orleanians, and the revolving Carousel Bar also draws the locals.

Services: Room service.

Facilities: Heated rooftop swimming pool (open year-round) and fitness center.

Royal Sonesta

300 Bourbon St., New Orleans, LA 70140. ☎ **504/586-0300** or 800/766-3782. 500 rms. A/C MINIBAR TV TEL. $160–$280 double; $325–$1,100 suite. Package and seasonal rates may be available. AE, CB, DC, DISC, MC, V. Parking $14.

The Royal Sonesta is adorned with lacy New Orleans balconies, and its rooms are furnished with period reproduction pieces. Many overlook inner patios or the pool, and these are preferable to rooms facing Bourbon Street, which can be noisy. This is an ideal French Quarter location—within walking distance of almost everything.

Dining/Entertainment: Begue's restaurant carries on the tradition of an older New Orleans eating spot of the same name, while Desire offers fresh seafood and an oyster bar. The Can Can Cafe features live Dixieland jazz.

Services: Concierge, room service (until 2am).

Facilities: Pool, exercise room, business center.

St. Louis

730 Bienville St., New Orleans, LA 70130. ☎ **504/581-7300** or 800/535-9706. 70 rms. A/C TV TEL. $164–$294 double; $324–$755 suite. Children under 12 free in parents' room. AE, CB, DC, MC, V. Valet parking $12.

Another lovely small hotel right in the heart of the French Quarter is the St. Louis. The original hotel, a favorite gathering place of area plantation owners, was built in the early 19th century at the corner of Royal and Saint Louis streets, but was destroyed by fire in the early 1900s. Today's hotel was built under the direction of William Henderson in 1968 and was officially opened in 1972. The current owners purchased the St. Louis in 1980. The building surrounds a lush, fountained courtyard and is decorated in high Parisian style, with antique furniture, crystal chandeliers, and gilt-framed original oil paintings. Some rooms have private balconies overlooking Bienville Street, and all overlook the central courtyard. Suites have private courtyards.

Dining/Entertainment: This is the home of an elegant, four-star French restaurant, Louis XVI (see Chapter 7 for a detailed description).

Services: Full concierge services, complimentary daily newspaper, room service from Louis XVI restaurant.

✪ Soniat House

1133 Chartres St., New Orleans, LA 70116. ☎ **504/522-0570** or 800/544-8808. Fax 504/522-7208. 31 rms. A/C TV TEL. $145–$235 standard room; $235–$375 suite; $550 two-bedroom suite. AE, MC, V. Valet parking $14 per day.

Built in 1829 by wealthy plantation owner Joseph Soniat Dufossat, the Soniat House is an interesting combination of Creole style and Greek Revival detail. Rodney and Frances Smith purchased the three-story house in 1982 and have done an excellent job of creating the perfect blend of guest house and hotel.

The doorman will welcome you through the impressive plant-lined carriageway that leads to a fountained courtyard (breakfast is served here after 9am upon request). Most of the rooms have balconies and face the courtyard.

All rooms are different in size and decor; furnished with French, English, and Louisiana antiques; and feature polished hardwood floors covered with antique Oriental rugs. Also, all have phones in the bathrooms, and some hold paintings on loan from the New Orleans Museum of Art. Room 27, which is a deluxe room, has crochet lace canopied twin beds, exposed brick walls, a small fireplace, and an antique armoire. One of the two-bedroom suites, which has its own elevator, is located on the third floor. It has exposed cypress-wood beams, skylights, and an interesting collection of antique furniture, as well as a bed fabricated by one of New Orleans's foremost artists. In 1995 seven new suites were added to the Soniat House in the renovated Soniat family town house (located directly across Chartres Street from main buildings). All have Jacuzzi baths, custom decor, and antique furnishings. Children over 12 are welcome in rooms that accommodate three persons.

Dining/Entertainment: Available every morning after 7am is a "southern continental" breakfast. It consists of freshly baked homemade biscuits, strawberry preserves (specially made for the Soniat House), fresh orange juice, and café au lait; it's $7 extra but worth every penny. There is a fully stocked honor bar in the parlor next to the reception area.

Services: Same-day cleaning and laundry service; evening turndown; 24-hour concierge.

MODERATE

⑤ Bourbon Orleans Hotel

717 Orleans St., New Orleans, LA 70116. ☎ **504/523-2222.** Fax 504/525-8166. 161 rms, 50 suites. A/C MINIBAR TV TEL. $115–$150 petit queen or twin; $135–$225 deluxe king or double-double; $150–$225 junior suite; $210–$325 town house suite; $230–$400 town house with balcony. Extra person $20. AE, DC, DISC, MC, V. Parking $12.

You can't miss the Bourbon Orleans Hotel: Its pale salmon and moss green exterior takes up an entire block of the French Quarter. The Orleans Ballroom, located within, dates from the 1800s and is the oldest part of the hotel. It was constructed in 1815 as a venue for the city's masquerade, carnival, and quadroon balls. In 1881 the building was sold to the Sisters of the Holy Family, who were members of the South's first order of African-American nuns. The sisters converted the ballroom into a school, and there they remained for 80 years until the building was sold to real estate developers from Baton Rouge who turned it into an apartment hotel. Today the hotel occupies three buildings and has recently undergone a $6 million renovation. Public spaces are lavishly decorated with gorgeous chandeliers, Oriental rugs, and marble flooring, and guest rooms have recently been completely redecorated, and a state-of-the-art movie system is available in each. Coffeemakers are supplied in all the rooms, and you can order room service through your TV. A voice-mail system is operational in all guest rooms. There are standard-size rooms, as well as bilevel suites that have a living room with a pull-out queen sofa. Bathrooms are outfitted with Italian marble, telephones, and hair dryers.

Dining/Entertainment: Café Lafayette is the hotel's restaurant, and there is an elegant lobby bar that features a nightly cocktail hour.

Services: Room service, same-day dry cleaning, business service, nightly shoe shine, daily morning newspaper.

Facilities: Pool.

⑤ Château Motor Hotel

1001 Chartres St., New Orleans, LA 70116. ☎ **504/524-9636.** 45 rms. A/C TV TEL. $84–$104 double. Rates include continental breakfast. Seniors receive 10% discount. AE, CB, DC, MC, V. Free parking.

The Château Motor Hotel is one of the best buys in town. Each room is distinctively decorated. Some have king-size four-poster beds, while others feature painted iron beds, and all have armchairs and/or couches. There are even a few bed/living-room combinations. Its outdoor swimming pool is surrounded by a flagstone-paved courtyard dotted with chaise lounges. Continental breakfast and the morning newspaper are complimentary daily.

The Frenchmen

417 Frenchmen St., New Orleans, LA 70116. ☎ **504/948-2166** or 800/831-1781. 27 rms. A/C TV TEL. $84–$135 double. Rates include breakfast. AE, MC, V. Free parking.

Situated in two 19th-century buildings, which were once grand New Orleans homes, the Frenchmen is a small inn with an excellent reputation. As you walk in, its elegant lobby sets the tone, and each of the rooms is individually decorated and furnished with beautiful antiques. Standard rooms have one double bed, some rooms have private balconies, and others have a loft bedroom with a sitting area. A pool and Jacuzzi are located in the inn's tropical courtyard. Restaurants, shops, and nightlife are just steps away from this secluded hotel.

Holiday Inn—Château LeMoyne

301 Dauphine St., New Orleans, LA 70112. ☎ **504/581-1303** or 800/holiday. 171 rms. A/C TV TEL. $150–$185. Extra person $25. AE, CB, DC, DISC, MC, V. Valet parking $10.

A friend urged me to inspect this Holiday Inn, saying, "It's not like any Holiday Inn you've ever seen." She was right: Although it is, in fact, a member of that chain, it is so distinctly French Quarter that you'd never associate it with any of those highway stopover hostelries. Housed in buildings more than a century old, with arched colonnades and winding staircases, the place exudes character and charm. Patios and converted slave-quarter suites add to the old New Orleans flavor, and bedrooms are furnished in a comfortable traditional style. There's a restaurant on the premises for breakfast only, otherwise it's room service until 10pm. There's also a bar. Hotel facilities include a swimming pool. If you plan to do much sightseeing or business outside the French Quarter, the Château LeMoyne's location is ideal—only minutes away from the Central Business District and the streetcar that takes you to the Garden District. And, of course, anything in the Quarter is within easy walking distance.

Hotel De La Poste

316 Chartres St., New Orleans, LA 70130. ☎ **504/581-1200** or 800/448-4927. Fax 504/ 523-2910. 100 rms. A/C TV TEL. $150–$185 double; $180–$215 junior suite. Children under 16 free in parents' room. Package rates, AAA, and senior-citizen discounts available. AE, CB, DC, MC, V. Valet parking $12.

Right in the heart of the Quarter, the recently remodeled Hotel De La Poste has spacious and comfortable rooms, most of which overlook either the courtyard and fountain or one of the more interesting French Quarter streets. The courtyard has a magnificent staircase leading to a second-level outdoor patio. There is an outdoor pool, *USA Today* is delivered daily to your room, all guest room phones feature voice mail and data ports, and complimentary coffee, tea, and apples are available. Services include valet laundry service, concierge tours, room service, a 24-hour bellman, and baby-sitting . Also within the hotel is Ristorante Bacco, run by sibling restaurateurs Cindy and Ralph Brennan. Location, accommodations, and service are all first rate.

Hôtel Provincial

1024 Chartres St., New Orleans, LA 70116. ☎ **504/581-4995** or 800/535-7922. Fax 504/ 581-1018. 100 rms. A/C TV TEL. $90–$175 double. Summer package rates are available. AE, CB, DC, MC, V. Parking available on premises.

There are no fewer than five patios—and each is a jewel—at the family owned Hôtel Provincial. The building dates from the 1830s, and rooms are high-ceilinged, each one decorated distinctively with imported French and authentic Creole antiques. My favorite holds a huge carved mahogany double bed with a high overhanging canopy topped by a carved tiara. Gaslights on the patios and the overall feeling of graciousness make this establishment a real delight, a tranquil refuge from the rigors of sightseeing or nighttime revelry. The pleasant restaurant serves breakfast, lunch, and dinner at moderate prices.

Hotel Ste. Hélène

508 Chartres St., New Orleans, LA 70130. ☎ **504/522-5014** or 800/348-3888. Fax 504/ 523-7140. 26 rms. A/C TV TEL. $125–$185 double. Rates include continental breakfast. AE, CB, DC, DISC, JCB, MC, V. Parking is about $14 in nearby lot.

Located right in the middle of the French Quarter, not far from Jackson Square, Hotel Ste. Hélène is a no-frills kind of place with an ideal location. Here you can be a part of the action, but far enough away from Bourbon Street to escape the noise and mayhem that begins just before dusk.

When you enter the hotel's small but lovely lobby, you'll be greeted by a friendly staff who will direct you through the inner courtyard to your room. With a trickling fountain, greenery, and exposed brick walls, the inner courtyard is the center of the hotel. The rooms vary mainly in size and the type of bed they hold. Room 103, for example, is standard, small in size, with twin beds—ideal for a single traveler. It's also a good bet for families, as it connects to room 104, which is a bit bigger, with a queen-size bed, a couch, and a desk. The superior rooms have king-size beds and balconies. All are clean and comfortable.

The outer courtyard has a flagstone patio with cast-iron tables and chairs at which you can have your breakfast every morning. There is also a small swimming pool.

Hotel St. Pierre

911 Burgundy St., New Orleans, LA 70116. ☎ **504/524-4401**, 800/535-7785, or 800/ 225-4040. Fax 504/524-6800. 74 rms and suites. A/C TV TEL. $120 double; $135 king or double-double; $139–$169 suite. Rates include morning coffee and doughnuts. Extra person $20. Children under 12 are free in parents' room. AE, CB, DC, DISC, MC, V. Free parking.

Hotel St. Pierre is located only two blocks from Bourbon Street. Guest rooms here are surrounded by beautiful courtyards, and because of the original floor plan of the old Creole home, room sizes vary greatly throughout the hotel. The Sammy Davis Jr. Suite has two double beds, floral bedspreads, and exposed brick. Some of the rooms are located in the old slave quarters, and most of them have king-size beds. Half of the rooms have fireplaces. A breakfast of coffee and doughnuts is available each morning in the breakfast room. There are two outdoor pools.

Hotel Villa Convento

616 Ursulines St., New Orleans, LA 70116. ☎ **504/522-1793.** Fax 504/524-1902. 24 rms. A/C TV TEL. $79–$95 double; $105 and $125 suite. Additional person $10 extra. Rates include continental breakfast. AE, CB, DC, DISC, MC, V. Parking is available in public parking area at the riverfront ($15 per day).

The Hotel Villa Convento, really a small inn, in many respects resembles a guest house because of the personal touch of its owner/operator, the Campo family. The building is a Creole town house with individually decorated rooms. Some open to the tropical patio, others open to the street; many have balconies. The lovely "loft" rooms are unique family quarters, each with a king-size bed on the entry level and twin beds in the loft. A continental breakfast is served in the courtyard, and guests who prefer breakfast in bed may have a tray to take it to their rooms.

Le Richelieu Motor Hotel

1234 Chartres St., New Orleans, LA 70116. ☎ **504/529-2492** or 800/535-9653 in the U.S. and Canada. Fax 504/524-8179. 88 rms, 17 suites. A/C TV TEL. $95–$140 double; $160–$475 suite. Extra person or child $15. Ask about French Quarter Explorer and Honeymoon packages. AE, CB, DC, DISC, JCB, MC, V. Free parking.

The Le Richelieu Motor Hotel is housed in what was once a row mansion and then a macaroni factory. They're proudest here of their VIP suite, which has three bedrooms, a kitchen, and even a steam room; but the "ordinary" guest rooms I saw were all quite nice and much less expensive. Most have brass ceiling fans, many have refrigerators and balconies, and all overlook either the French Quarter or the courtyard. Bathrooms are large and are outfitted with hair dryers. There's a pool in the large courtyard, with lunch service poolside. The Terrace Café is the hotel's restaurant, and the Terrace Lounge is the bar. Le Richelieu is the only French Quarter motel with free self-parking on the premises—you keep your car keys, so there's no wait for an attendant to bring your car. Local calls are also free.

Place d'Armes Hotel

625 St. Ann St., New Orleans, LA 70116. ☎ **504/524-4531** or 800/366-2743. 79 rms. A/C TV TEL. $100–$160 double. Rates include continental breakfast. AE, CB, DC, DISC, MC, V. 24-hour parking next door for $10.

The lovely Place d'Armes has one of the most magnificent courtyards in the Quarter, as well as a swimming pool. All rooms are homey and furnished in traditional style; many are wallpapered. Be sure that you ask, however, for a room with a window when you reserve—there are some interior rooms without windows (not all bad, but still, a window is better). The complimentary breakfast is served in a breakfast room, and the location, just off Jackson Square, makes sightseeing a breeze.

Prince Conti Hotel

830 Conti St., New Orleans, LA 70112. ☎ **504/529-4172** or 800/366-2743. 49 rms. A/C TV TEL. $120–$150 double. Rates include continental breakfast. AE, DC, DISC, MC, V. Valet parking $10.

Prince Armand de Conti, the French nobleman who helped back Bienville's expedition to found New Orleans, would be proud of his namesake, with its small lobby beautifully furnished in the French château fashion and the delicate iron grillwork lining the outside of the second-story rooms. The nicest things at the Prince Conti Hotel, though, are the friendly, helpful staff and the comfortable guest rooms, many furnished with antiques and period reproductions. A continental breakfast is served in the hotel's breakfast room. The restaurant is open Tuesday through Saturday from 5pm.

GUEST HOUSES
EXPENSIVE

Grenoble House

329 Dauphine St., New Orleans, LA 70112. ☎ **504/522-1331.** 17 suites. A/C TV TEL. $185–$285 one-bedroom suite; $235–$375 two-bedroom suite. Rates include continental breakfast. Weekly rates available. AE, MC, V. Parking is available at nearby lot.

The Grenoble House is truly an elegant home away from home. The suites are beautifully and uniquely furnished with a mix of fine antiques and the best of modern fittings—all have fully equipped kitchens. This is an old French Quarter town house built around a courtyard that features a swimming pool with heated whirlpool spa and a barbecue pit. Suites all have king- or queen-size beds (the more expensive have the king-size), and there's a sofa bed in each living room. A very special "extra" here is the personal, attentive service—they'll book theater tickets, restaurant tables, and sightseeing tours and even arrange for a gourmet dinner to be brought to your suite or for a private cocktail party on the patio if you want to entertain friends.

MODERATE

Lafitte Guest House

1003 Bourbon St., New Orleans, LA 70116. ☎ **504/581-2678** or 800/331-7971. 14 rms. A/C TV TEL. $85–$165 double. Rates include continental breakfast. Extra person $22.20. AE, DC, MC, V. Parking $7.50.

If you think a Bourbon Street address automatically means a noisy, honky-tonk environment, think again. The Lafitte Guest House is located beyond the hullabaloo in a quiet, pleasant residential area of the Quarter. The three-story brick building, with wrought-iron balconies on the second and third floors, was constructed in 1849 and has been completely restored. There are marble fireplaces, exposed brick walls, and 14-foot ceilings. Rooms are furnished with a blend of modern reproduction pieces and beautiful Victorian antiques, and each room is individually sized and decorated. Room 5 is described as a "New York loft"–style apartment, and it overlooks the hotel's lush courtyard. Room 23 has an incredible cypress fireplace; and room 40, with two queen-size beds and a pull-out couch, can accommodate up to six people and covers the entire top floor of the hotel. A continental breakfast of fresh juice, croissants, jam, butter, and coffee or tea; wine and cheese in the parlor during the "happy hour"; and the daily newspaper are all included in the room rate.

New Orleans Guest House

1118 Ursulines St., New Orleans, LA 70116. ☎ **504/566-1177.** 14 rms. A/C TV. $79–$89 queen or twin; $89–$99 king or two full beds. Rates include continental breakfast. Extra person $25. AE, MC, V. Free parking.

The New Orleans Guest House is impossible to miss—the exterior is painted hot pink, a clue to its gay-friendly, though by no means exclusive, character. It is located just on the fringe of the French Quarter, across North Rampart Street, on the border of a less than desirable neighborhood (you may feel safer taking a taxi at night). Ray Cronk and Alvin Payne have been running this renovated Creole cottage, dating from 1848, for more than 10 years now. There are rooms in the main house and some in what used to be the old slave quarters. Each is decorated with period furniture and has a unique color scheme. If bright colors scare you, don't worry; the colors inside the guest house aren't quite as arresting as those outside. You're sure to find most of the guest rooms absolutely restful and tastefully done, although recently some readers have complained about the maintenance, especially in room 9. Those rooms in the slave quarters are a little smaller than the ones in the main house, but I actually prefer the smaller ones because they all open onto the lush New Orleans–style courtyard. To get to the slave quarter rooms you walk through the covered patio, then out into the sunlight and a veritable tropical garden where you'll find a banana tree, more green plants than I could count, and some intricately carved old fountains that Ray and Alvin have restored to working order. There is a new covered breakfast room with an outdoor patio where you'll be served croissants, fruit, and coffee, tea, or hot chocolate at cozy white-clothed tables. Also located in the courtyard is a beer machine, soda machine, and an ice maker.

✪ P. J. Holbrook's Olde Victorian Inn

914 N. Rampart St., New Orleans, LA 70116. ☎ **504/522-2446** or 800/725-2446. 6 rms. A/C. $115–$170 double. Rates include full breakfast. Senior-citizen discount. Weekly rates available. AE, MC, V. Parking on street only.

Walking into P. J.'s is like walking through time into an old Victorian home. The entire house is done in Victorian style—from the "gathering room" to the dining room. P. J. has gone to the ends of the earth, it seems, to find the perfect pieces, draperies, color schemes, and curios. Even the names of the guest rooms, such as Chantilly, Wedgwood, Chelsea, and Greenbriar, were thoughtfully chosen, and each room is decorated just as its name suggests. Most of them have fireplaces, and Chantilly even has a balcony, with a cast-iron table and chairs and hanging plants, that looks out over North Rampart Street. Each room has its own bathroom, although there are a couple of units with their own private baths across the hall.

P. J. herself is a most gracious host who will look after your every need and cook up a breakfast that could probably keep you going for an entire week. A typical breakfast here consists of some kind of bread (usually banana or cinnamon), fruit, eggs (all different ways), biscuits, some type of potato, juice, and coffee or hot tea. You can have this feast in the dining area just outside the kitchen; in your room; or in the courtyard, at one of the tables on which there are always white cloths and flowers floating in little bowls.

P. J.'s is located near the corner of St. Philip Street, next door to the Landmark Hotel. You'll have to look carefully for the modest, hand-painted sign out front. Upon arrival you'll be treated to freshly baked goodies and a cup of hot tea or lemonade.

The house is nonsmoking, so if you're a smoker be prepared to light up outside. P. J. has a lovely dog, Olivia, who guards the house and charms the guests, so don't bring any pets. Be sure to sit and chat with P. J. and her staff—they've got some great New Orleans stories to tell. (If you ask nicely, they might even tell you about Uncle Leo.)

INEXPENSIVE

Sun & the Moon Bed & Breakfast

1037 N. Rampart St., New Orleans, LA 70116. ☎ **504/529-4652.** 2 rms. A/C TV MINIBAR. $75 double. Rate includes continental breakfast. No credit cards. Parking is available.

Kelly and Taina Mechling are the proprietors of this cozy little bed-and-breakfast, whose Spanish name is El Sol y la Luna. They have charmingly furnished and decorated two rooms in Southwest style. Both of the rooms have good-sized, comfortable sleeping and sitting areas. The bathrooms are clean and fully equipped. Here you have the added extra of a minirefrigerator in your room, so you can store goodies for midnight snacking. There also are balconies overlooking the courtyard (which features a large fruit-bearing banana tree) between the main house and the guest quarters. Each guest room has a separate entrance, which creates a nice sense of privacy. Continental breakfast can be served in your room or on the deck. Maid service is daily.

Kelly and Taina also run Trade Folk Art Import Export (see Chapter 10 for more details) and Mechling's Guest House (see below).

GUEST HOUSES JUST OUTSIDE THE FRENCH QUARTER
VERY EXPENSIVE

✪ Melrose Mansion

937 Esplanade Ave., New Orleans, LA 70116. ☎ **504/944-2255.** Fax 504/945-1794. 8 rms. A/C MINIBAR TV TEL. $225–$250 double; $325–$425 suite. AE, DISC, MC, V. Free parking.

The Melrose Mansion is one of the most splendid guest houses in the city; if you choose to stay here, you will be met at the airport by a chauffeured stretch limousine, which will whisk you to this guest house on the outer limit of the French Quarter. Rosemary and Melvin Jones have lovingly restored this three-story 1884 Victorian mansion, with its square turret set at a jaunty angle in one corner, to combine the utmost in luxury with the warm, personal hospitality of a private home. Enormous bath towels, fine soaps, and rooms with names (such as "Miss Kitty's Room") rather than numbers all contribute to the hospitality. Its architectural style is hard to pin down—in Rosemary's words, it is "a bit of Victorian Gothic, Victorian Italianate, along with a suggestion of the baroque and the classic, as seen in the upper-level Corinthian capitals." The old house has a rich and varied history (ask about Miss Kitty—she was an ex-stripper with a seagoing lover—who lived out her last years here).

Guest rooms are furnished with marvelous antiques, and the créme de la créme has to be the Donecio Suite, with a magnificent rice four-poster bed, a marble bathroom complete with Jacuzzi and separate dressing room, and a wide balcony on which breakfast often is served. (Lady Bird Johnson was its first tenant and gave it a rave review.) The mansion's elegant drawing room is the focal point for gatherings for afternoon tea or wine and cheese. Breakfast comes with silver coffee service, beautiful china and crystal, fresh-baked muffins, and fresh fruit and can be served in your room, on the balcony, or at poolside. The Parc Henry Suite, atop the original carriage house and overlooking the pool, sleeps three or four. The Sol Owens Suite houses a fitness and health area with a Life Cycle, treadmill, Stair Master, and weight machine. But the best feature of this place may well be its staff. Rosemary and Melvin are always on hand; there is a wonderfully hospitable butler; and a staff member is always available during the day to make sure that you've got everything you could possibly need. Book as far in advance as possible.

EXPENSIVE

✪ The House on Bayou Road

2275 Bayou Rd., New Orleans, LA 70119. ☎ **504/949-7711.** 4 rms, 2 cottages. A/C TEL. $145–$225 double. Rates include breakfast. MC, V. Free parking.

If you want to stay in a rural plantation setting, but still want to be near the French Quarter, The House on Bayou Road might be just the place for you. Located just off Esplanade Avenue, this intimate Creole plantation home, built in the late 1700s for a colonial Spanish diplomat, has been lovingly restored by owner Cynthia Reeves. As you enter the antique-filled double parlor you'll feel like you're stepping back in time. The individually decorated rooms are each named for a bayou and have a light, airy quality. Cynthia has paid extraordinary attention to every detail. The Bayou St. John Room (the old library) holds a queen, four-poster rice bed, has a working fireplace, and is decorated with a masculine color scheme. Bayou Delacroix also has a queen-size four-poster rice bed, but it is decorated with floral prints and has a wonderfully large bathtub. Bayou Cocodrie holds a brass-and-iron half-canopy bed with mosquito netting and can be joined with the Bayou Barataria Room, which has a queen-size pencil-post four-poster bed. The large cottage, which is completely separate from the main house, has three rooms that can be rented separately or as a whole. It's perfect for a large family. The small Creole cottage, located next door to the large cottage, is a great romantic getaway spot. It has a queen-size four-poster bed, a queen sofa sleeper, Jacuzzi tub, wet bar, and a porch with a swing and rocking chairs. The grounds are beautifully manicured, and you can sit either outside on the patio or in the screened-in porch. A swimming pool is available for guest use. In the morning guests are treated to a full plantation-style breakfast, and during the day and in the evening there is access to a minirefrigerator filled with beverages.

The House on Bayou Road also offers Cuisine Eclairée cooking classes as a special package.

MODERATE

Mechling's Guest House

2023 Esplanade Ave., New Orleans, LA 70116. ☎ **504/943-4131** or 800/725-4131. Fax 504/944-0956. 5 rms. A/C. $95–$155 double. Rates include full breakfast. AE, MC, V. Free parking.

Keith and Claudine Mechling (pronounced *mek-ling*) worked with their son and daughter-in-law (Kelly and Taina) for several years to restore this 1860s mansion, but they have moved on and Kelly and Taina now own the guest house. The guest rooms are on the first floor of the house and retain as many of the original fixtures, windows, and woodwork as could be salvaged. For instance, Claudine and Keith searched through the debris and painstakingly pieced together the leaded-glass window in the front door. They found that they were missing only one piece, which they were able to have replicated. They cleaned the original fireplace mantels, some of which are black onyx marble and are quite stunning. Kelly and Taina are still working on different parts of the property, including the second floor of the main house and the slave quarters in back. The rooms are quite large, and most have fireplaces. The front bedroom, tastefully done in peach, is especially unique because the bathroom is actually part of the room, just as it was in the original house, and it is curtained off. There is a claw-foot bathtub and a tile floor. The rest of the room is carpeted, and its focal point is a queen-size canopy bed. The other rooms are equally unique and beautifully decorated.

If you choose to stay with the Mechlings you'll be within walking distance of the French Quarter and City Park, but don't walk alone at night—keep the number for United Cab handy. Kelly and Taina are wonderful hosts and will gladly give you sightseeing advice as you have your breakfast. Ask them to point out the old slave jail next to an enormous old oak tree.

Nicolas M. Benachi House

2257 Bayou Rd., New Orleans, LA 70119. ☎ **504/525-7040** or 800/308-7040. 4 rms. A/C TEL. $85–$130 double. Free parking.

This lovely bed-and-breakfast was originally constructed in 1858 for Nicholas M. Benachi, who was a cotton broker, consul of Greece, and founder of the New Orleans Greek Orthodox Congregation. It was from this house, situated on a road that connected the Mississippi River with surrounding bayous, that Mr. Benachi and his friends would set out on hunting expeditions, and the house became known as the Rendezvous des Chasseurs. Jim Derbes, a lawyer and university instructor, is the fourth owner of the house, and it was under his loving care that it was restored to its current condition. Furnishings in the downstairs public rooms are of the Victorian, Rococo Revival, Gothic, Classical, and Empire styles. The dining room features a lovely nine-foot rococo mirror as well as exquisite carpentry by New Orleans cabinetmakers Mallard, Barjon, and Seignouret. The guest rooms are named for the Benachi children, and each has a ceiling fan. Belasario's room holds a lovely Victorian double bed and writing desk. Marie's room is located at the front of the house and features a balcony with outdoor seating. It joins Irene's room (a good choice for families); these rooms share a bath and are both furnished with reproduction antiques. My favorite room, though, is Pandia's room, located on the first floor. The rococo revival dresser and American mahogany double bed are quite beautiful. After your arrival Jim will give you a tour of the house and property. Televisions are available on request, and smoking is allowed outdoors only. The Nicolas M. Benachi House has been designated a landmark by the Orleans Parish Landmarks commission and the Historic Districts Landmarks Commission (from whom Mr. Derbes received the 1985 Honor Award for restoration).

APARTMENTS

Bourgoyne Guest House

839 Bourbon St., New Orleans, LA 70116. ☎ **504/525-3983** or 504/524-3621. 5 apartments. A/C TEL. Studios $77 double; Blue Suite $100 double, $125 triple, $140 quad. Green Suite $110 double; $135 triple; $160 quad. MC, V. Pay parking nearby.

If you're on a budget, the Bourgoyne is a good place to set up home during your stay in New Orleans. Behind the front gate and through the stone carriageway is a quaint courtyard. Each studio room has a fully equipped kitchenette, a bathroom, and a double bed. The studios (and bathrooms) are small and a bit outdated, but functional. The larger apartments, or suites, have kitchens, sitting areas, TVs, and room to sleep three or four. If you're staying in the Green Suite, you'll climb the winding staircase to the third floor and enter into the spacious sitting and dining area. The apartment is sparsely furnished with antiques and brass light fixtures. The focal point of the Green Suite is the bed in the main bedroom. It is covered with a green velvet spread and has an enormous, partially draped mirror hanging on the wall above it. Also, a balcony overlooks Bourbon Street. Don't worry about the noise level in the larger apartments as the guest house is far enough up Bourbon Street to be unaffected by the sounds of an average day or night. However, if you're planning to stay in the studio rooms and you're a light sleeper you'll do well to find a room elsewhere.

Napoleon House

500 Chartres St., New Orleans, LA 70130. ☎ **504/524-9752.** 1 apartment. A/C TV TEL. $125–$250. Weekly and monthly rentals are available. AE, DISC, MC, V. No parking available.

If you'd like to experience French Quarter living as a temporary "local," I can't think of a better place to do it than in the one apartment that Sal Impastato, owner of the historic Napoleon House, has made available. The three-room upstairs apartment, with two balconies, was the longtime residence of his uncle, and its furnishings are what might be called "New Orleans homey"—several antique pieces intermingle happily with rather well-worn furnishings of indeterminate age but definite comfort. The apartment is right in the heart of the Quarter, with one of the city's best pubs and light-meal restaurants downstairs.

3   Outside the French Quarter

You will find a wide price range of hotels and motels outside the French Quarter, whether you wish to be near the universities, in the Central Business District, or on the outskirts of town.

For those of you who prefer the predictability of a chain hotel, there's a **Marriott** at 555 Canal St. (☎ **504/581-1000** or 800/228-9290) and a **Hyatt** at 500 Poydras Plaza (☎ **504/561-1234**).

VERY EXPENSIVE

✪ Fairmont Hotel

At University Place, 123 Baronne St., New Orleans, LA 70140. ☎ **504/529-7111** or 800/527-4727. 672 rms, 60 suites. A/C TV TEL. $185–$230 double. Extra person $25. AE, DC, DISC, MC, V. Parking $10.

New Orleanians still sometimes think of it as the Roosevelt, and today's Fairmont Hotel upholds the tradition of elegance left by its predecessor. There's the feel of luxury from the moment you enter the magnificent newly renovated marble and gilded-columned lobby. The rooms are spacious, with high ceilings and such extras as an electric shoe buffer. Beds are luxuriously outfitted with the finest all-cotton sheets, down pillows, and comforters, and bathroom amenities are custom made for the hotel. Bathrooms are also outfitted with scales and oversized bath towels. For the business traveler, the Fairmont offers in-room computer hookups and fax machines in the suites. In short, the Fairmont is a "grand hotel" in the old manner that offers midtown convenience as a bonus.

Dining/Entertainment: For many years, the sophisticated Blue Room presented headliner entertainers—perhaps you remember those old radio broadcasts "from the Blue Room of the Hotel Roosevelt in downtown New Orleans." I'm happy to report that although it was redecorated in recent years, that lovely blue-and-gold decor and French period furnishings have changed very little since the days of my visits years ago. These days, the Blue Room is used for private functions only, except for

Sunday, when there's a sumptuous brunch (see Chapter 7). An addition is Bailey's, a casual bistro-style eatery that serves breakfast, lunch, and dinner daily. For fine dining, there's the romantic Sazerac Restaurant.

Services: 24-hour room service, twice-daily maid service, concierge, baby-sitting service, activities desk, valet/laundry service.

Facilities: Rooftop health club, pool, tennis courts, beauty shop, business center, gift shop, newsstand, currency exchange.

✪ Hotel Inter-Continental

444 St. Charles Ave., New Orleans, LA 70130. ☎ **504/525-5566** or 800/327-0200. 480 rms, 32 suites. A/C MINIBAR TV TEL. $210–$240 double; $350–$1,700 suite. AE, CB, DC, DISC, MC, V. Valet parking $12.

The Hotel Inter-Continental rises in red granite splendor in the heart of the Central Business District. It is within walking distance of the French Quarter and the Mississippi River attractions. Its luxurious rooms and suites feature writing desks, separate conversation/dressing areas, minibars, built-in hair dryers, and telephones and TVs in the bathrooms. The furnishings in both the guest rooms and the public areas are a blend of classic and contemporary styling.

The Governor's Floor (the 14th) is reminiscent of Louisiana's romantic past, and the suites feature period antiques, reproductions, artifacts, and decorations that represent the six heads of state for whom the rooms are named. All the rooms on this floor are decorated individually in blues and cream. The floor has a VIP lounge, which entitles guests to a complimentary continental breakfast and evening cocktails. The Governor's Lounge is stocked with popular periodicals.

Dining/Entertainment: The large marble lobby showcases a cocktail lounge, gourmet meals are served in the Veranda Restaurant (see Chapter 7 for a full listing), and Pete's Pub, on the first floor, serves lunch daily.

Services: 24-hour room service, laundry and valet service, shoe-shine service.

Facilities: Health club and pool, barber shop and beauty salon, gift shop, business center.

Le Meridien Hotel

614 Canal St., New Orleans, LA 70130. ☎ **504/525-6500.** 494 rms. A/C MINIBAR TV TEL. $180–$260 double; $500–$1,500 suites. AE, CB, DISC, MC, V. Valet parking $12.

The Le Meridien Hotel is one of the city's most dramatic hotels, with lots of marble and a spectacular indoor waterfall. All rooms have multiple-line telephones and a desk and sitting area. Accommodations here are either king- or twin-bedded and are decorated in pleasant neutral tones. There is a complete health club on the premises, and rooms for nonsmokers are available. Le Meridien Hotel is an excellent place for viewing Mardi Gras festivities.

Dining/Entertainment: La Gauloise is the hotel's Parisian-style bistro. The Jazz Meridien Club is the hotel's jazz lobby bar and features entertainment Monday through Saturday.

Services: 24-hour concierge, 24-hour room service, laundry service, baby-sitting service, complimentary shoe shine, nightly turndown, business center.

Facilities: Health club, sauna, heated outdoor pool, massage and aerobics, beauty salon, gift shop, jewelry store, art gallery.

Pontchartrain Hotel

2031 St. Charles Ave., New Orleans, LA 70140. ☎ **504/524-0581** or 800/777-6193. Fax 504/529-1165. 102 rms. A/C TV TEL. $95–$380 based on single occupancy. Extra person $25. Seasonal packages and special promotional rates available. AE, CB, DC, DISC, MC, V. Parking $10 per night.

Named in honor of comte de Pontchartrain from the court of Louis XVI, the elegant Pontchartrain Hotel is located in the Garden District on the St. Charles Streetcar line, making it easily accessible from the French Quarter. This landmark hotel (erected in 1927) is a grand structure built in a Moorish architectural style, and the rooms are beautifully furnished. In fact, many original furnishings and antiques are still found in the guest rooms. The service will make you feel like a pampered favorite within minutes of your arrival—the staff is accustomed to treating guests well because the hotel is a favorite of dignitaries, celebrities, and even royalty. Everything in this New Orleans institution is in the continental tradition at its finest.

The hotel and its cafe are settings for part of author Anne Rice's novel *The Witching Hour.*

Dining/Entertainment: The gourmet cuisine of the Caribbean Room (see Chapter 7) is internationally known. Special low-salt, low-cholesterol menus are available on request. You can have breakfast in Café Pontchartrain and stop for a drink in the Bayou Bar.

Services: 24-hour room service, complimentary shoe shine, complimentary newspaper, nightly turn-down service.

✪ Windsor Court

300 Gravier St., New Orleans, LA 70140. ☎ **504/523-6000** or 800/262-2662. Fax 504/596-4513. 319 rms and suites. A/C TV TEL. $235–$320 standard guest room; $310–$405 junior suite; $390–$580 full suite; $590–$990 two-bedroom suite. Children under 12 free in parents' room. AE, CB, DC, MC, V. Valet parking $15.

The pink granite facade of the centrally located, 24-story Windsor Court makes it one of the city's loveliest hotels. Two classic touches are the English tea served in Le Salon (in the first-floor lobby) and accompanied by live chamber music and two corridors that are minigalleries displaying original 17th-, 18th-, and 19th-century works of art. Italian marble and antique furnishings distinguish public spaces.

Each suite is individually decorated and features large bay windows or a private balcony overlooking the river or the city, a private foyer, a large living room, a bedroom entered through French doors, a marble bath, separate his-and-her dressing rooms, and a "petite kitchen." Both suites and standard guest rooms are exceptionally spacious and beautifully furnished with four-poster and canopy beds. Most of the rooms here are suites, and this hotel is particularly popular with celebrities. The Windsor Court Hotel is truly a standout.

Dining/Entertainment: The Polo Club Lounge has the ambience of a private English club; the Grill Room Restaurant serves breakfast, brunch, lunch, and dinner; Le Salon, the lobby lounge, serves afternoon tea, cocktails, and sweets and has chamber music and piano music during the day and evening.

Services: 24-hour suite service (much more than your average room service), full concierge service.

Facilities: Among the guest facilities are a health club with a resort-size pool, sauna, and steam room. Numerous conveniences are available for business travelers, who might want to conduct conferences in the privacy of their own suites or in the specially planned meeting spaces.

EXPENSIVE

Crowne Plaza New Orleans

300 Poydras St., New Orleans, LA 70130. ☎ **504/525-9444.** 441 rms. A/C TV TEL. $200 double; $375–$675 suite. AE, CB, DC, DISC, MC, V. Valet parking $12; self-parking $8.50.

The Crowne Plaza New Orleans has recently renovated guest units, suites, an Executive Floor, and a restaurant, deli, and lounge. It's an attractive hotel that includes among its many amenities a pool with poolside beverage service, an exercise room, and free in-room movies. Suites and the 22 rooms on the luxury-level Executive Floor come with a complimentary continental breakfast and refreshments, refrigerators, and a private cocktail lounge.

New Orleans Hilton Riverside Hotel

2 Poydras St., New Orleans, LA 70140. ☎ **504/561-0500** or 800/445-8667. Fax 504/568-1721. 1,602 rms. A/C MINIBAR TV TEL. $275–$295 double; $580–$1,870 suite. Special packages available. AE, CB, DC, DISC, JCB, MC, V. Parking $12 for 24 hours.

The New Orleans Hilton Riverside Hotel, at the Mississippi River, has perhaps more than any other new hotel integrated itself successfully into the lifestyle of the city. Located in what some are calling the "River Quarter," the Hilton sits right at the riverfront, adjacent to the World Trade Center of New Orleans and the New Orleans Convention Center, yet it somehow manages to avoid the sterile imperson-ality projected by so many large hotels. Maybe it has to do with a decor that makes use of warm colors such as tea rose and emerald green; Italian oak and mahogany paneling; travertine marble; and deep-pile, hand-woven carpeting. The 90-foot, nine-story, multilevel atrium creates a feeling of space, but it is so well designed that there is none of that rattle-around boxiness that always makes me a little nervous. Guest rooms are spacious, and most have fabulous views of the river or the city; all are furnished in a country French manner, using muted colors and draperies keyed to the etched toile of the wall coverings. Light-softening sheer curtains let you take full advantage of those gorgeous views. The epitome of luxury is to be found on the 24th, 25th, 26th, and 27th tower floors, which hold 150 guest rooms, includ-ing 16 elegant suites. A concierge is there to help you, and a private lounge and an honor bar with TV and comfortable furniture completes the towers picture. The third part of the Hilton complex is its 456-room, low-rise Riverside complex perched on the edge of the Mississippi. There are six luxurious suites and eight courtyards, with fountains and lush tropical foliage, opening to the river.

Dining/Entertainment: The atrium is broken up into attractive centers, such as the English Bar, Le Café Bromeliad, and the French Garden Bar. There are in fact seven restaurants and lounges within the complex. You will know past doubt that the Hilton has won New Orleans's approval when you learn that Pete Fountain moved his jazz club from the Quarter to a third-floor replica here. A relatively new addition to the Hilton is the Flamingo Casino: 20,000 square feet of gambling space on board a riverboat.

Services: 24-hour room service, concierge service, laundry/valet/pressing service, airport transportation, shoe-shine service.

Facilities: Guests are eligible for membership in the hotel's Rivercenter Racquet and Health Club, which includes outdoor and indoor tennis courts, squash and rac-quetball courts, a rooftop jogging track, aerobics classes, tanning beds, massage, a hair salon, and a golf studio.

The Pelham

444 Common St., New Orleans, LA 70130. ☎ **504/522-4444** or 800/659-5621. Fax 504/539-9010. 60 rms, A/C TV TEL. $149–$229 double. AE, DC, DISC, MC, V. Parking $12 a day.

If you're not interested in staying right in the French Quarter, want more indepen-dence than is offered at a bed-and-breakfast, and would like to be as far away from conventioneers as possible, the recently opened Pelham is an excellent choice. The small hotel, located in a beautifully renovated building that dates from the late 1800s, is cozy and attractively decorated. Fabric-covered walls lend a homelike feeling to this English-style property. Centrally located rooms are generally less bright than those on the exterior of the building, but I had no complaints with any of them.

MODERATE

Avenue Plaza Suite Hotel & Spa

2111 St. Charles Ave., New Orleans, LA 70130. ☎ **504/566-1212** or 800/535-9575. Fax 504/
525-6899. 250 rms. A/C TV TEL. $89–$199 double. AE, DC, DISC, MC, V. Parking $8.

Located in the picturesque Garden District on the historic St. Charles Avenue
Streetcar line, the Avenue Plaza Hotel and Spa features, after a $7 million renova-
tion, completely refurbished suites and public spaces. Each suite in this 18th-century
antebellum home has a kitchenette and is attractively furnished. Special amenities are
the Mackie Shilstone Pro Spa, Health Club, and Salon. There is a rooftop sundeck
and a courtyard swimming pool. A cafe and lounge are located on the premises.

The Columns

3811 St. Charles Ave., New Orleans, LA 70115. ☎ **504/899-9308.** 19 rms (9 with bath).
A/C TEL. $75–$175 double. Rates include continental breakfast. AE, MC, V. Parking available
on the street.

The Columns, built in 1883 by Simon Hernsheim, a wealthy tobacco merchant, is
one of the greatest examples of a late 19th-century Louisiana residence. You'll be
impressed by the grand, columned entrance, and once inside you'll feel as though
you've stepped back in time. Its architectural style is Italianate, or pre–Queen Anne,
and most of the original interior features still exist. The wide mahogany staircase is
truly awesome, as is the stained-glass, domed skylight above it. The Columns was the
setting of Louis Malle's film *Pretty Baby* and is listed in the National Register of
Historic Places.

The hotel's staff is very friendly; however, it looks as if the furnishings are becoming a bit run down. There's a lot more charm and character than elegance here these
days, but it's worth looking into because of the reasonable rates and the clean and
comfortable rooms. All the rooms and furnishings are different—some rooms have
wood sleigh beds, while others have double beds with intricately carved head- and
footboards. Many have couches and chairs, while some are much too small to
accommodate such furnishings. The rooms with baths have claw-foot tubs, and the
rooms without baths come equipped with sinks.

The hotel's restaurant, Albertine's Tea Room, is open for lunch, dinner, and Sunday brunch, and the Victorian lounge is open for evening cocktails.

Holiday Inn Downtown—Superdome

330 Loyola Ave., New Orleans, LA 70112. ☎ **504/581-1600.** Fax 504/522-0073. 297 rms.
A/C TV TEL. $94–$209 double; $350 suite. Extra person $15. Children 19 and under free in
parents' room. AE, CB, DC, DISC, JCB, MC, V. Parking $10.

The 18-story Holiday Inn Downtown—Superdome is centrally located, with easy
access to New Orleans's business and financial centers, as well as the Louisiana
Superdome and the French Quarter. Each room has a balcony and city view, and the
hotel has a collection of jazz scene murals available for public viewing. In addition,
the dining room here holds an interesting collection of New Orleans streetcar paintings. The Mardi Gras Lounge offers cocktails and after-dinner drinks nightly. There
is a rooftop heated pool.

⑤ Le Pavillon Hotel

833 Poydras St., New Orleans, LA 70140. ☎ **504/581-3111** or 800/535-9095. Fax 504/
522-5543. 220 rms, 7 suites. A/C TV TEL. From $109 double; from $395 suite. AE. Parking
available.

Established in 1907 and the first hotel in New Orleans to have elevators, Le Pavillon
truly is, as they bill it, "the belle of New Orleans." It is, in fact, a member of

Historic Hotels of America. The lobby is stunning, with high ceilings, grand columns, plush furnishings, Oriental rugs, detailed woodwork, and 11 crystal chandeliers imported from Czechoslovakia. Each hall features massive Louisiana antiques and has 14 original paintings from the hotel's fine-arts collection.

The standard guest rooms are similar in terms of furnishings but differ in size by virtue of the hotel's original floor plan, which for the most part has remained intact. The "Bay Rooms" are standard, with two double beds and bay-window treatments—one of the many special features of the old hotel.

The Pavillon also has some fine suites for very reasonable rates. If you like art deco, you're sure to love the two-bedroom art deco suite. Another of the two-bedroom suites is the marvelous Antique Suite. All the furnishings are antiques, and the collection includes pieces by Mallard, C. Lee (who, as a slave, studied under Mallard), Mitchell Rammelsberg, Belter, Badouine, and Marcotte. The beds have feather mattresses and elaborate canopies. If you can afford it and want a real taste of old New Orleans, ask about this one—you won't be disappointed.

Guests are treated to complimentary peanut-butter-and-jelly sandwiches and a glass of milk each evening in the lobby. You really can't beat this place—affordable rates, more than pleasant surroundings, a central location, and PB&J every night!

Dining/Entertainment: The Gold Room, the hotel's large dining room, is open for breakfast, lunch, and dinner daily. A beautiful room, it has a working fireplace, which makes for a cozy atmosphere. The hotel lounge is the Gallery, which serves complimentary hors d'oeuvres Monday to Friday from 4 to 7pm.

Services: 24-hour room service, complimentary shoe shine, full concierge service.

Facilities: Heated rooftop pool, fitness center, and whirlpool spa.

Prytania Park Hotel

1519 Terpsichore St., New Orleans, LA 70130. ☎ **504/524-0427** or 800/862-1984. Fax 504/522-2977. 62 rms. A/C MINIBAR TV TEL. $109 double; $119 suite. Rates include continental breakfast. Seasonal rates are available. Extra person $10. Children under 12 free. Special packages available. AE, CB, DC, DISC, MC, V. Free parking.

Centrally located in the historic Garden District and offering a choice of contemporary or old-world setting, the Prytania Park is a charming hotel run with the same personal attention as a guest house. The Victorian Building, which dates from 1834, is beautifully restored and furnished in period hand-carved English pine. The Victorian town house rooms also have high ceilings and exposed brick walls. The 49 streamlined rooms in the modern addition retain the New Orleans architectural ambience but have more contemporary furnishings than the 13 rooms in the original part of the hotel; they open onto landscaped courtyards and feature the conveniences of microwave ovens and refrigerators. The St. Charles Avenue Streetcar line is half a block away, providing quick and easy access to the French Quarter (15 blocks away) and all the major attractions.

The hotel is situated in the heart of the uptown restaurant district; cuisine and prices here vary widely enough to fit all kinds of gastronomic yearnings and budgets.

INEXPENSIVE

Hotel La Salle

1113 Canal St., New Orleans, LA 70112. ☎ **504/523-5831** or 800/521-9450 in the U.S. Fax 504/525-2531. 57 rms (42 with bath). A/C TV TEL. $45 double without bath, $64 double with bath. Children under 12 free in parents' room. AE, DC, DISC, JCB, MC, V. Free parking.

You'll find convenience and comfort at budget prices only half a block outside the French Quarter at the Hotel La Salle. The no-frills rooms are plainly furnished, clean, and comfortable and come with or without private bath. There's an old-fashioned air to the small lobby with its high ceilings, overhead fans, carved Austrian wall clock, and old-time wooden reception desk. Free coffee is always available in the lobby, and guests receive a complimentary newspaper daily. This is a favorite with European visitors who appreciate bathroom-down-the-hall savings.

Quality Inn Midtown

3900 Tulane Ave., New Orleans, LA 70119. ☎ **504/486-5541** or 800/486-5541. Fax 504/488-7440. 102 rms. A/C TV TEL. $69–$300 double; $180–$300 suite. Extra person $10–$20. AE, DC, DISC, MC, V. Free parking.

The Quality Inn Midtown is located only about five minutes from the Central Business District. All the rooms have balconies; many face the courtyard, are spacious, and have double beds. The hotel's French Quarter–style courtyard features a swimming pool and Jacuzzi. There is free shuttle service available daily to the French Quarter and convention center. Guests also have use of coin-operated laundry facilities, and movies are free. A restaurant and lounge are open daily.

St. Charles Inn

3636 St. Charles Ave., New Orleans, LA 70115. ☎ **504/899-8888** or 800/489-9908. Fax 504/899-8892. 40 rms. A/C TV TEL. $75 double. Rate includes continental breakfast. AE, DC, DISC, MC, V. Parking $3 outdoors.

The St. Charles Inn is only five minutes away from Tulane and Loyola universities and 10 minutes from the French Quarter or Louisiana Superdome via the trolley. Each room has either two double beds or a king-size bed. Facilities here include a lounge and a restaurant, and there are extras like continental breakfast served in your room and a complimentary morning newspaper.

GUEST HOUSES

If you're in New Orleans to visit Tulane University, Loyola University, or Newcomb College, or if you just want to stay out of the hustle and bustle of downtown, you'll want to know about these conveniently located guest houses.

⑤ The McKendrick-Breaux House

1474 Magazine St., New Orleans, LA 70130. ☎ **504/586-1700.** 5 rms. A/C TV TEL. $90–$135 double. Rates include breakfast. Limited free off-street parking is available.

You'd be hard pressed to find more gracious hosts than Lisa and Eddie Breaux, owners of the McKendrick-Breaux House. The young couple saved the two houses on their property from ultimate destruction. The original building was built in 1865 by Scottish immigrant Daniel McKendrick, but was virtually unrecognizable by the time the Breauxes got their hands on it in 1992. Lisa and Eddie first had the building shored up with metal ties, gutted the structure, and then started from scratch (original medallions, some woodwork, and some flooring remain). The downstairs parlor and adjoining dining room is where breakfast is served each morning. Rooms are located both in the main house and in the building directly across the quiet courtyard (which was once the site of a bar). All rooms are extremely spacious and are furnished with antiques and family collectibles. Bathrooms are large as well. The ones in the main house have beautiful claw-foot tubs, while those in the building opposite are huge and have modern fixtures. Fresh flowers greet you on arrival, and Lisa and Eddie will supply your room with a bucket of ice every evening. Breakfast consists of cereal, fruit, some sort of pastry, juice, and coffee or tea. Lisa and Eddie do their best to accommodate all their guests' needs, and they'll also help plan day and evening activities. In short, you'll want for nothing if you choose to stay here.

Note: At press time there were plans in the works to add two more rooms to the upper floor.

Park View Guest House

7004 St. Charles Ave., New Orleans, LA 70118. ☎ **504/861-7564.** 23 rms (17 with bath). A/C TEL. $75–$80 double without bath, $80–$90 double with bath. Rates include continental breakfast. Extra person $10. AE, MC, V. On-street parking.

On the far edge of Audubon Park is the Park View Guest House, a rambling Victorian structure built in 1884 as a hotel for the Cotton Exposition. It has been on the National Register of Historic Places since 1981. Simply entering the building is like a trip to another era: A front door that sparkles with etched-glass panels admits you to the wide central hall with gleaming crystal chandeliers. A lovely stained-glass window is the focal point of the large lounge furnished with comfortable sofas and chairs. All the rooms are furnished in antiques and reflect an old-fashioned comfort that's hard to resist; some have balconies. There's a large dining room, with windows overlooking the park, where a continental breakfast is served daily. All guests have the use of a refrigerator and ice machine anytime.

AIRPORT HOTELS

Downtown New Orleans is only a 15-minute drive from the airport (located in nearby Kenner), so even if you're only going to be in town overnight you can still take a room in one of the hotels mentioned above without inconveniencing yourself. However, if you'd rather just stay near the airport, there are several hotels from which to choose. If you want to spend a night in Kenner in style, make a reservation at the **New Orleans Airport Hilton,** located at 901 Airline Hwy., Kenner, LA 70062 (☎ **504/469-5000** or 800/445-8667). The 312-room Hilton features a lighted tennis court, fitness center, putting green, gift shop, restaurant, and business center. **The Holiday Inn New Orleans—Airport,** 2929 Williams Blvd., Kenner, LA 70062 (☎ **504/467-5611** or 800/465-4329), is a less-expensive alternative. It also has a restaurant, exercise room, pool, and sauna. Both hotels offer airport transfer.

4 Hostels & Campgrounds

HOSTELS

The **Marquette House New Orleans International Hostel,** 2253 Carondelet St., New Orleans, LA 70130 (☎ **504/523-3014**; fax 504/529-5933), is located in a century-old home, which is reminiscent of antebellum New Orleans. A communal kitchen, dining area, reading rooms, a garden patio, and laundry facilities are all available to guests. Dormitory beds go for $11 to $14 a night, and private rooms with shared bath are $28 to $31. In addition, there are 12 suites with private bath. Weekly rates are available, and there is free on-street parking at the hostel.

The **YMCA International Hotel** at 920 St. Charles Ave., New Orleans, LA 70130 (☎ **504/568-9622**), charges $29 for a single room, $35 for a double, $41 for a triple, and $46 for a quad. A room key deposit of $5 is required and refundable at checkout. Rooms are air-conditioned and have TVs. Within walking distance of the French Quarter, it has a fitness facility (free for hotel guests), an indoor pool, and a restaurant.

CAMPGROUNDS

There are two KOA campgrounds, one on each side of town. The **KOA New Orleans East,** 56009 Hwy. 433, Slidell, LA 70461 (☎ **504/643-3850**), is three-quarters of a mile east of I-10 on La. 433 (Exit 263). The country setting includes two pools, a recreation room, and miniature golf. Riverboat, swamp, and city tours are available. Rates (for two) are $17.95 for a tent site, $22.95 for a full hook-up site, and $28.50 for a "Kamping Kabin." An extra person is $3.50. The **KOA New Orleans West,** 1129 Jefferson Hwy. (La. 48), River Ridge, LA 70123 (☎ **504/467-1792** or 800/562-5110) is to the west of the city and also welcomes tenters as well as vehicles. You can swim in the pool as well as buy provisions in the on-site store. City and boat tours are available; if you want to "do" the French Quarter on your own, city transportation and rental cars are available. Rates (for two) are $21.95 for tenting and $26.95 for a full hook-up site; there is a $3 charge for each extra person.

Good eating in New Orleans is by no means confined to the French Quarter—you'll find it all over town. What you'll find here are some of my favorites. It simply isn't possible to list them all, so explore on your own, you'll be certain to find others.

New and relatively new openings of particular note include Gabrielle (on Esplanade Avenue) and the Pelican Club, NOLA, and Bacco (all in the French Quarter). I personally guarantee you a good time if you try any one of those four. Of course, there may be some even newer ones opened by the time you get there, so ask at your hotel, or ask a local (no one knows food like a native New Orleanian!).

To make life easier for you as you move around the city, restaurants in this chapter are listed by area first. Under each geographical breakdown, you'll find the most **expensive** (with most entrées over $20) listed first, then **moderate** places (most entrées in the $10 to $20 price range), and **inexpensive** places last (most entrées under $10). Area boundaries for this purpose are rather broad: "downtown" (remember, that's *downriver* from Canal Street) is outside the French Quarter but on the same side of Canal Street; the Central Business District is roughly the area upriver from Canal, extending to the elevated expressway (U.S. 90); "uptown" includes everything upriver from Canal and as far as Carrollton toward the lake, including the Garden District; Metairie is New Orleans's next-door neighbor in Jefferson Parish; the "lake," of course, means the area along the shores of Lake Pontchartrain. Turn back to the Greater New Orleans map in Chapter 1 and you'll get the general idea.

1 Best Bets

- **Best Spot for a Business Lunch: Mr. B's Bistro & Bar,** 201 Royal St. (☎ **504/523-2078**), is the perfect place to cut a deal. The atmosphere is casual but classic, and wood-and-glass partitions break up the otherwise large dining room, keeping noise levels low.
- **Best Wine List:** The wine cellar at **Brennan's,** 417 Royal St. (☎ **504/525-9711**), is virtually unsurpassed in the city of New Orleans. There's a good selection of less-expensive California wines, some moderately priced French wines, as well as some more

New Orleans Dining

Bailey's  **22**
Bon Ton Café **16**
Bluebird Cafe **5**
Brigsten's **4**
Caribbean Room **9**
Casamento's **6**
Christian's **23**
Commander's Palace **7**
Copeland's **4**

Delmonico Restaurant **10**
Emeril's **13**
Ernst's Café **12**
Gautreau's **1**
Graham's **17**
Kabby's Seafood Restaurant **14**
Mark's on the Avenue **18**
Mother's **15**
P.J.'s Coffee & Tea Company **6**

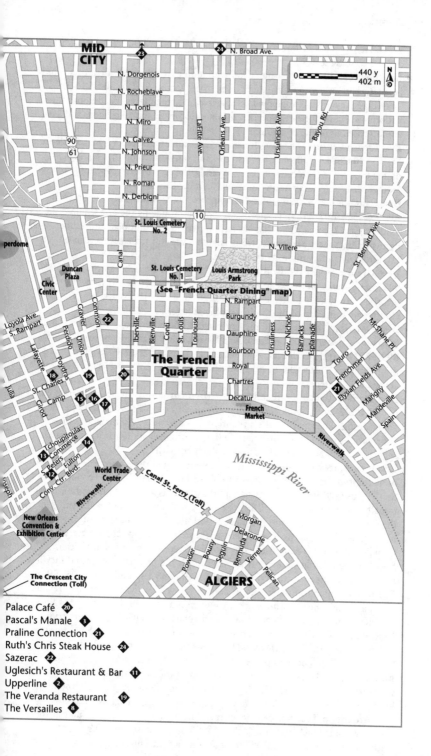

MID CITY

N. Broad Ave.

N. Dorgenois

N. Rocheblave

N. Tonti

N. Miro

N. Galvez

N. Johnson

N. Prieur

N. Roman

N. Derbigni

Lafitte Ave.

Orleans Ave.

Ursullines Ave.

Bayou Rd.

0 ___ 440 y / 402 m

N

90 / 61

10

St. Bernard Ave.

St. Louis Cemetery No. 2

N. Villere

perdome

Duncan Plaza

St. Louis Cemetery No. 1

Louis Armstrong Park

Civic Center

Canal

(See "French Quarter Dining" map)

N. Rampart

Burgundy

Dauphine

Bourbon

Royal

Chartres

Decatur

Iberville

Bienville

Conti

St. Louis

Toulouse

Ursullines

Gov. Nichols

Barracks

Esplanade

McShane Pl.

Loyola Ave.-S. Rampart

Gravier

Common

Union

Perdido

Lafayette

Poydras

St. Charles

Camp

Girod

The French Quarter

Touro

Frenchmen

Elysian Fields Ave.

Marigny

Mandeville

Spain

Julia

Tchoupitoulas

Commerce

S. Peters

Fulton

Conv. Ctr. Blvd.

French Market

World Trade Center

Canal St. Ferry (Toll)

Riverwalk

Mississippi River

Riverwalk

New Orleans Convention & Exhibition Center

Joseph

The Crescent City Connection (Toll)

Morgan

Delaronde

Powder

Bouny

Seguin

Bermuda

Verret

Pelican

ALGIERS

Palace Café ⊘20

Pascal's Manale ◆3

Praline Connection ◆21

Ruth's Chris Steak House ◆24

Sazerac ⊘22

Uglesich's Restaurant & Bar ◆11

Upperline ◆2

The Veranda Restaurant ◆19

The Versailles ◆8

expensive labels and a lovely selection of dessert wines. (The prices range from about $20 to $420.)

- **Best for Kids:** I haven't yet met a kid who didn't go wild for hot chocolate and beignets, best enjoyed at **Café du Monde,** 813 Decatur St. (☎ 504/581-2914). They especially love getting powdered sugar all over their faces. In addition, street performers around the cafe, especially the ones that make animal balloons and hats, are top entertainment for children.

- **Best French Cuisine:** The city's first French restaurant, **Louis XVI,** 829 Toulouse St. (☎ 504/581-7000), remains its best, and plush surroundings complete the dining experience. Tableside preparations add a flourish, but the superiority of the food is what keeps locals and visitors alike coming back.

- **Best Cajun:** It may have a fast-food atmosphere, but **Copeland's,** 4339 St. Charles Ave. (☎ 504/897-2325), is known citywide for producing the best Cajun dishes around. Chef George Rhode IV has an unwavering commitment to freshness—he makes his sauces and stocks from scratch—yet still manages to turn out an extraordinary variety of dishes every night.

- **Best Creole:** When the **Praline Connection,** 542 Frenchmen St. (☎ 504/943-3934), came on the scene a couple of years back, it quickly became the city's favorite place for good Creole cooking. Beans and rice, jambalaya, and crawfish étouffée are just a few of the specialties offered here.

- **Best Desserts:** There are a number of places in New Orleans where you'll find outstanding desserts, but **Commander's Palace,** 1403 Washington Ave. (☎ 504/899-8221), has them all beat. Their repertoire is unsurpassed: Creole bread pudding, bananas Foster cheese cake, anything flaming, anything chocolate, and always, lemon crepes.

- **Best Italian: Bacco,** brainchild of the Brennan family, at 310 Chartres St. (☎ 504/522-2426), took New Orleans by storm a couple of years ago and is still going strong. The emphasis is on tradition, but a Creole twist maintains the creative spirit expected of the Brennans. Dishes like penne with tomatoes and roasted eggplant and crawfish ravioli are among the best I've had.

- **Best New American:** When it comes to American food there's not a doubt in my mind (or in the minds of most New Orleanians) that **Emeril's,** 800 Tchoupitoules St. (☎ 504/528-9393), sets the pace in this town. As a base for his creations, nationally renowned chef Emeril Lagasse uses Creole preparations and then gives them an enormous kick into the nineties with the addition of modern American touches. What he ends up with is some of the freshest (he makes most everything, from ketchup to cheese, himself) and most innovative dishes in New Orleans.

- **Best Burgers:** Ask anyone in town where to get the best hamburger and they'll all tell you to head straight for **Port of Call,** 838 Esplande Ave. (☎ 504/523-0120), an appropriately casual hole in the wall at the edge of the French Quarter. I know people who won't leave town until they've downed one of Port of Call's giant burgers and enormous baked potatoes (always done to perfection).

- **Best Steaks:** Don't be turned off by the fact that **Ruth's Chris Steakhouse,** 711 N. Broad St. (☎ 504/486-0810), is a chain. Chefs there serve up the best beef around. You'll be hard pressed to find better anywhere else.

- **Best Outdoor Dining:** My personal favorite is the beautiful, quiet, and fairly secluded courtyard at Bayona. It's particularly lovely on a spring afternoon at lunch, and chef Susan Spicer's innovative international cuisine is hard to beat.

- **Best Afternoon Tea:** Everyone loves spending an afternoon in **Le Salon** at the Windsor Court hotel, 300 Gravier St. (☎ 504/523-6000), enjoying tea, scones, a little chamber music, and the Windsor's ultra-elegant surroundings.

- **Best Picnic Fare:** My personal favorite is **Central Grocery** (located on Decatur Street). Stop by there in the afternoon and pick up a muffaletta sandwich, drinks, and anything else you might desire from this wonderful Italian delicatessen and specialty food shop.
- **Best Views:** At **Bella Luna,** 914 N. Peters (☎ **504/529-1583**), you'll not only get great Italian food, but you'll be treated to the best moonlight view of the Mississippi available to diners in New Orleans.

2 Restaurants by Cuisine

AMERICAN & NEW AMERICAN

Bella Luna (French Quarter, *E*)
Bluebird Cafe (Central Business District, *I*)
Cafe Sbisa (French Quarter, *E*)
Emeril's (Central Business District, *E*)
G&E Courtyard Grill (French Quarter, *M*)
Mike's on the Avenue (Uptown, including the Garden District, *E*)
Napoleon House (French Quarter, *I*)
Nola (French Quarter, *E*)
Pelican Club (French Quarter, *E*)
Rémoulade (French Quarter, *M*)

CAFES

Café du Monde (French Quarter, *I*)
New Orleans Coffee and Concierge (French Quarter, *I*)
Royal Blend Coffee and Tea House (French Quarter, *I*)
St. Ann's Cafe and Deli (French Quarter, *I*)

CAJUN

Bon Ton Café (Central Business District, *M*)
Bozo's (Metairie, *I*)
Brigtsen's (Uptown, including the Garden District, *E*)
Copeland's (Uptown, including the Garden District, *M*)
Ernst's Café (Central Business District, *I*)
K-Paul's Louisiana Kitchen (French Quarter, *E*)

Olde N'Awlins Cookery (French Quarter, *M*)
Père Antoine Restaurant (French Quarter, *I*)
Petunia's (French Quarter, *I*)

COFFEE SHOPS

Bailey's (Central Business District, *M*)

COFFEE, TEA & SWEETS

Angelo Brocato's Ice Cream and Confectionery (French Quarter, *I*)
Café du Monde (French Quarter, *I*)
La Madeleine (French Quarter, *I*)
La Marquise (French Quarter, *I*)
P. J.'s Coffee and Tea Company (French Quarter, *I*)

CONTINENTAL

Sazerac (Uptown, including the Garden District, *E*)
The Veranda Restaurant (Central Business District, *E*)

CREOLE

Arnaud's (French Quarter, *E*)
Bacco (French Quarter, *E*)
Brigtsen's (Uptown, including the Garden District, *E*)
Commander's Palace (Uptown, including the Garden District, *E*)
Copeland's (Uptown, including the Garden District, *M*)
Court of Two Sisters (French Quarter, *E*)
Dooky Chase (Downtown, *M*)

Key to abbreviations: *E*=Expensive, *I*=Inexpensive, *M*=Moderate

Emeril's (Central Business District, *E*)
Ernst's Café (Central Business District, *I*)
Felix's Restaurant and Oyster Bar (French Quarter, *I*)
Gumbo Shop (French Quarter, *M*)
Mother's (Central Business District, *I*)
Mr. B's Bistro and Bar (French Quarter, *M*)
Olde N'Awlins Cookery (French Quarter, *M*)
Palace Café (Central Business District, *M*)
Père Antoine Restaurant (French Quarter, *I*)
Petunia's (French Quarter, *I*)
Praline Connection (French Quarter, *I*)
Ralph and Kacoo's (French Quarter, *M*)
Rémoulade (French Quarter, *M*)
Rita's Olde French Quarter Restaurant (French Quarter, *M*)
Royal Café (French Quarter, *M*)
Sazerac (Uptown, including the Garden District, *E*)
Tujague's (French Quarter, *M*)
Upperline (Uptown, including the Garden District, *E*)
The Veranda Restaurant (Central Business District, *E*)

ECLECTIC
Graham's (Central Business District, *E*)
Upperline (Uptown, including the Garden District, *E*)

FRENCH AND FRENCH/CREOLE
Antoine's (French Quarter, *E*)
Brennan's (French Quarter, *E*)
Broussard's (French Quarter, *E*)
Caribbean Room (Uptown, including the Garden District, *E*)
Christian's (Downtown, *M*)
Crozier's Restaurant Français (Metairie, *M*)

Galatoire's (French Quarter, *E*)
Louis XVI (French Quarter, *E*)
Palm Court Café (French Quarter, *M*)
Peristyle (French Quarter, *E*)
The Versailles (Uptown, including the Garden District, *E*)

HAMBURGERS
Camellia Grill (Uptown, including the Garden District, *I*)
Port of Call (French Quarter, *M*)

INTERNATIONAL
Bayona (French Quarter, *E*)
Gabrielle (just outside the French Quarter, *M*)
Gautreau's (Uptown, including the Garden District, *M*)
Le Bistro (French Quarter, *E*)

ITALIAN
Alberto's (French Quarter, *M*)
Bacco (French Quarter, *E*)
Bella Luna (French Quarter, *E*)
Dipiazza's (French Quarter, *M*)
Louisiana Pizza Kitchen (French Quarter, *I*)
Mama Rosa's (French Quarter, *I*)
Maximo's Italian Grill (French Quarter, *M*)
Napoleon House (French Quarter, *I*)
Pascal's Manale (Uptown, including the Garden District, *E*)
Peristyle (French Quarter, *E*)
Ristorante Carmelo (French Quarter, *M*)

LATE NIGHT/24 HOUR
St. Ann's Cafe and Deli (French Quarter, *I*)

SANDWICHES
Café Maspero (French Quarter, *I*)
Camellia Grill (Uptown, including the Garden District, *I*)
Mother's (Central Business District, *I*)
Uglesich's Restaurant and Bar (Central Business District, *I*)

SEAFOOD

Acme Oyster House (French Quarter, *I*)

Bozo's (Metairie, *I*)

Bruning's Seafood on the Lake (Lake Pontchartrain, *M*)

Café Maspero (French Quarter, *I*)

Casamento's (Uptown, including the Garden District, *M*)

Felix's Restaurant and Oyster Bar (French Quarter, *I*)

Kabby's Seafood Restaurant (Central Business District, *M*)

Mike Anderson's Seafood (French Quarter, *M*)

Olde N'Awlins Cookery (French Quarter, *M*)

Ralph and Kacoo's (French Quarter, *M*)

SEAFOOD/STEAKS

Delmonico Restaurant (Uptown, including the Garden District, *M*)

Rib Room (French Quarter, *E*)

Tavern on the Park (Uptown, including the Garden District, *M*)

SOUL FOOD

Dooky Chase (Downtown, *M*)

Praline Connection (French Quarter, *I*)

STEAKS

Pascal's Manale (Uptown, including the Garden District, *E*)

Ruth's Chris Steak House (Downtown, *M*)

3 In the French Quarter

EXPENSIVE

Antoine's

713 St. Louis St. ☎ **504/581-4422.** Reservations required. Main courses $14.25–$49. AE, DC, MC, V. Mon–Sat 11:30am–2pm and 5:30–9pm. FRENCH/CREOLE.

Who hasn't heard of Antoine's and dreamed of at least one meal in this legendary restaurant, run by the same family for more than 150 years? Once inside the ironwork-adorned building, you're in a world of white-tile floors, slowly turning antique ceiling fans, and 15 separate rooms that run the gamut from plainness to grandeur. As for the food, choose from such classics as oysters Rockefeller, alligator soup, chicken Rochambeau, and filet de boeuf marchand de vin; or settle for something simpler from a menu that lists more than 150 selections. To accompany your choice you have at your disposal one of the richest wine cellars in America. You won't have to bone up on your French as diners have had to do in the past; Antoine's has just added English translations to the menu. Baked Alaska is the favorite dessert here. Even with reservations, be prepared for a wait at peak hours. If you want to dine with locals, try for a table in the Annex. In the interest of attracting a lunchtime crowd, Antoine's has put together a less pricey lunch menu.

Arnaud's

813 Bienville St. ☎ **504/523-5433.** Reservations recommended. Main courses $15.50–$39.95. AE, DC, MC, V. Mon–Fri 11:30am–2:30pm; Sun–Thurs 6–10pm, Fri–Sat 6–10:30pm; brunch Sun 10am–2:30pm. CREOLE.

This favorite New Orleans restaurant has quite a history. Housed in buildings dating from the 1700s, Arnaud's was opened in 1918 by "Count" Arnaud Cazenave (the fictitious title was bestowed by locals in recognition of his grand manner and great love of life), and after his death in 1948 the old traditions were carried on for many years by his daughter. Then a decline set in that eventually led to the restaurant's desertion by even the most loyal of its wide clientele. But in late 1978 Archie and

Jane Casbarian fell in love with the old restaurant, bought it, and began a restoration that would have gladdened the old count's heart. The lovely mosaic-tile floors were patched and polished; the lighting fixtures, dark-wood paneling, original ceiling medallions, and antique ceiling fans were refurbished; Le Richelieu Bar was restored; a delightful Grill Bar was added; and the wood was stripped from interior columns to reveal beautiful fluted iron posts. Flickering gaslights now welcome you into the large dining room where potted palms, beveled-glass windows, and crystal chandeliers re-create a turn-of-the-century air. There also is the upstairs Germaine Wells Mardi Gras Museum, which holds an extensive private collection of Mardi Gras gowns owned by the late Mrs. Wells, the count's daughter and the restaurant's previous owner.

Best of all, of course, is the kitchen and the dining service. Formally dressed waiters, as knowledgeable, efficient, and friendly as they are stylish, see to your needs at tables laid with classic linen and set with sterling silver, original Arnaud china, fine crystal, and original water decanters. Executive chef Kevin Davis turns out specialties such as shrimp Creole, trout meunière, and a superb crème brûlée, and he constantly creates exciting new dishes. At lunch there's an inexpensive table d'hôte (fixed-price) selection along with an à la carte menu. The Sunday brunch features eggs Benedict, eggs André, several kinds of omelets (including Arnaud's red bean omelet), and grillades and grits, along with the jazz of Sam Alcorn Jr.'s Trio. This has been a favored place to eat, especially during Carnival season, with New Orleanians over the years, and I am happy to report that now it has reclaimed their devotion.

✪ Bacco

310 Chartres St. ☎ **504/522-2426.** Reservations recommended. Main courses $16.50–$21. AE, DC, MC, V. Mon–Sat 7–10am, Sun 8:30–10am; Mon–Sat 11:30am–2:30pm; brunch Sun 10:30am–2:30pm; daily 6–10pm. ITALIAN/CREOLE.

Located next door to the De La Poste Hotel, Bacco (owned and operated by brother and sister Ralph and Cindy Brennan) is a new addition to the New Orleans restaurant scene. The interior, with pink Italian marble floors, wall and ceiling murals, Venetian chandeliers, and Gothic arches, is as stunning as it is refreshing. At lunch you should try the pan fried polenta cake (served over spinach, oven roasted tomatoes, and finished with gorgonzola cream and spicy walnuts) or the Creole Italian gumbo (made with roasted goose, Italian sausage, chicken, and tasso) to start. Follow your appetizer with Louisiana crab cakes and fettuccine, a grilled chicken breast sandwich, or the delicious fried oyster Caesar salad. Begin your dinner with a Creole-Italian specialty, Bacco shrimp (spicy jumbo gulf shrimp roasted in the wood-burning oven, served in a garlic pepper oil) or the roasted artichoke. One of my favorite dinner entrées is the crawfish ravioli (homemade ravioli filled with crawfish tails, onions, sweet peppers, and Creole seasonings tossed in a sun-dried tomato pesto sauce). The hickory grilled pork chop, which is wrapped with apple-smoked bacon and served with a wild mushroom–sage sauce and sweet potato mash, is another good choice. There are daily specials as well. For dessert try the frozen cappuccino (homemade espresso ice served with Grand Marnier double cream and a biscotti), or the praline cinnamon ice-cream sandwich.

✪ Bayona

430 Dauphine St. ☎ **504/525-4455.** Reservations required at dinner; recommended at lunch. Main courses $9–$20. AE, CB, DC, DISC, MC, V. Mon–Fri 11:30am–2pm; Mon–Thurs 6–9:30pm, Fri–Sat 6–10:30pm. Closed Sun. INTERNATIONAL.

After bringing success to Le Bistro (see below), chef Susan Spicer decided to put her talents to use in a restaurant of her own. Bayona is her brainchild, and everyone who

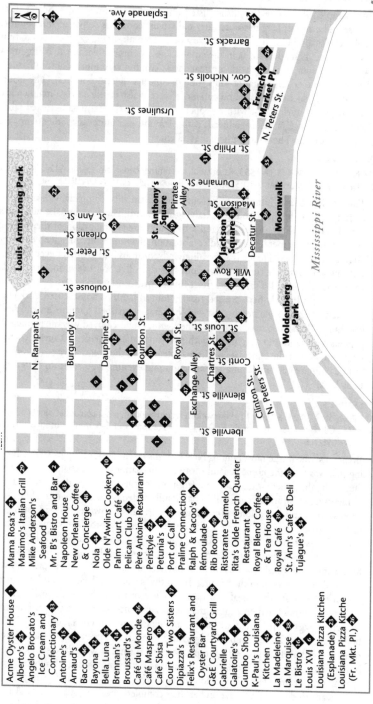

Acme Oyster House ❶
Alberto's ㉕
Angelo Brocato's Ice Cream and Confectionary ㉝
Antoine's ⑮
Arnaud's ❼
Bacco ㊻
Bayona ⑫
Bella Luna ㉟
Brennan's ⑭
Broussard's ⑰
Café du Monde ㊱
Café Maspero ㊼
Cafe Sbisa ㉚
Court of Two Sisters ㊼
Dipiazza's ⑨
Felix's Restaurant and Oyster Bar ❸
G&E Courtyard Grill ㉓
Gabrielle ㉓
Galatoire's ④
Gumbo Shop ㊲
K-Paul's Louisiana Kitchen ㊺
La Madeleine ㉜
La Marquise ㊳
Le Bistro ⑯
Louis XVI ❻
Louisiana Pizza Kitchen (Esplanade) ㉓
Louisiana Pizza Kitche (Fr. Mkt. Pl.) ㉖

Mama Rosa's ㉑
Maximo's Italian Grill ㉙
Mike Anderson's Seafood ❺
Mr. B's Bistro and Bar ❷
Napoleon House ㊸
New Orleans Coffee & Concierge ㊽
Nola ⑩
Olde N'Awlins Cookery ⑩
Palm Court Café ㉗
Pelican Club ⑲
Père Antoine Restaurant ⑲
Peristyle ㊸
Petunia's ㉓
Port of Call ㉓
Praline Connection ㉕
Ralph & Kacoo's ㊵
Rémoulade ❽
Rib Room ㊾
Ristorante Carmelo ㊷
Rita's Olde French Quarter Restaurant
Royal Blend Coffee & Tea House ⑱
Royal Café ㊴
St. Ann's Cafe & Deli ⑳
Tujague's ㉞

95

has sampled the innovative dishes listed on Bayona's menu agrees—Spicer never misses. The atmosphere in the century-old Creole cottage is convivial and comfortable yet elegant, but if you'd rather have a quiet open-air dining experience—and this is one of the best spots for it in the city—there are some tables in the courtyard as well. Begin your meal here with the goat cheese crouton with mushrooms in Madeira cream, or the cream of garlic soup (one of Spicer's signature dishes). The grilled shrimp with black-bean cake and coriander sauce is also excellent. As a main course, try the grilled duck breast with a pepper-jelly glaze or the Parmesan-crusted rabbit with a lemon-sage sauce. Sweetbreads with a lemon-caper butter is another of Spicer's signature dishes. The wine list here is excellent.

✪ Bella Luna

914 N. Peters. ☎ **504/529-1583.** Reservations recommended. Main courses $12–$24. AE, CB, DC, DISC, MC, V. Mon–Sat 6–10:30pm, Sun 6–9:30pm. ECLECTIC/CONTINENTAL.

The interior of Bella Luna is reminiscent of an Italian villa, complete with tile floors. In fact, you might think you're in Italy—that is, until you look out the window at the Mississippi River. The decor and setting here are an indication of the surprises you'll find on the menu: a splendid combination of almost every imaginable cuisine. German chef Horst Pfeifer is refreshingly adventurous and creative, even by New Orleans standards. He turns out delicious appetizers like Southwest duck enchiladas with roasted tomatillo salsa and fresh thyme with unflagging consistency. Main courses might include herb-crusted roasted loin of lamb or house-cured pork chop in a New Orleans–style pecan crust with horseradish mashed potatoes and an Abita beer sauce. Pastas also have a place on the menu. One I enjoyed was the penne with peppers, eggplant, and gorgonzola with a fontina sauce. The dessert menu changes frequently, but if the chocolate bellini napoleon is on the menu, give it a try. If you want a culinary adventure on a romantic moonlit evening, you can't do better than Bella Luna.

Brennan's

417 Royal St. ☎ **504/525-9711.** Reservations recommended. Main courses at dinner $28.50–$35. AE, CB, DC, DISC, JCB, MC, V. Daily 8am–2:30pm and 6–10pm. Closed Christmas. FRENCH/CREOLE.

Brennan's, one of the most famous New Orleans restaurants, occupies a 1795 building that was once the home of Paul Morphy, international chess champion. The restaurant has been here since 1946 and from the start has won a place in the hearts of residents and visitors alike. The Brennan family is dedicated to providing fine food, good service, and exceptional atmosphere. Be prepared, however, to wait for breakfast and lunch, even if you have a reservation—if that's a problem, come at dinner, when it's less crowded. The lush tropical patio here has to be seen to be believed, and there's a view of it from any table in the downstairs rooms. Elegance is the only word for the interior. "Breakfast at Brennan's" has become internationally famous, and you can breakfast here even in the evening. But if that's what you have in mind, take heed and don't plan another meal that day. You'll want to be able to do justice to the sumptuous dishes listed on a menu that tempts you with items such as eggs Hussarde (poached eggs atop Canadian bacon, and marchand de vin sauce, served with hollandaise sauce and accompanied by grilled tomato) and trout Nancy (filet of fresh trout sautéed and topped with lump crabmeat, sprinkled with capers and lemon-butter sauce). Even their omelets are spectacular. This is not your typical bacon-and-eggs affair, but breakfast in the tradition of antebellum days in the Quarter. If you really want to do it right, order one of their complete breakfast suggestions. A typical one begins with eggs Sardou (poached eggs atop creamed spinach and artichoke bottoms, served with hollandaise sauce), followed by grillades and grits, sautéed baby veal (served in a spicy Creole sauce with fines herbes and freshly cracked black pepper), and topped off by crepes Fitzgerald (cream cheese–filled crepes with a sauce of crushed strawberries flamed in maraschino) and hot chicory coffee. A marvelous eye-opener to begin with is an absinthe Suissesse (a legendary Brennan's drink that has the faint flavor of anisette). The dinner menu features oysters Rockefeller or escargots to start, followed by specials like steak Diane, tournedos chanteclair, and shrimp Creole. Desserts include the usual bananas Foster and crepes Fitzgerald, among others.

Broussard's

819 Conti St. ☎ **504/581-3866.** Reservations required. Main courses $19.50–$32.50. AE, CB, DC, DISC, MC, V. Daily 5:30–10pm. FRENCH/CREOLE.

This venerable New Orleans restaurant marked its 75th anniversary in 1995. Decor varies from opulent elegance in the Napoleon Room; to Italian rustic in the Magnolia Room, a smaller room overlooking the lush courtyard; to delightful French country style in the Josephine Room. This is where you'll experience some of the city's best French-Creole cooking. Those of you who may have dined at Broussard's in the past and were less than satisfied with your meal will understandably be doubtful, but take heart. Broussard's was purchased in 1993 by the Preuss family, and they have breathed new life into this landmark restaurant. Along with some of the old standbys, you'll find more innovative creations like pecan-stuffed salmon de la Salle in a Tabasco beurre blanc; snapper filet Ponchartrain baked with a piquant crabmeat filling and topped with a cayenne beurre blanc; and boneless duckling Normandy with an apple-bacon demi-glacé and served with braised cabbage. The flaming desserts, including crepes Broussard and bananas Foster, are superior. Other dessert items that shouldn't be missed are the chocolate marquis in a raspberry sauce and Broussard's specialty, Delice Madam P. There's a fairly strict dress code (no jeans, shorts, sneakers, or T-shirts).

✪ Cafe Sbisa

1011 Decatur St. ☎ **504/522-5565.** Reservations recommended. Main courses $11–$23. AE, DISC, MC, V. Sun–Thurs 5:30–10:30pm, Fri–Sat 5:30–11pm; brunch Sun 11am–3pm. NEW AMERICAN.

Located right across from the French Market, Cafe Sbisa is, after a brief closure, once again a local favorite. Cafe Sbisa first opened in 1899 and in the 1970s was one of the first to experiment with Creole cooking. The building is old, but the interior is classy and cosmopolitan in feeling. There are two floors of dining rooms (tables on the upper floor near the interior balcony are the best), and there is a small courtyard. Today, Sbisa is owned by the Napoli family, which has transformed the menu so dramatically that it's nipping at the heels of Emeril's (see below) in terms of creativity. The turtle soup, I think, is the best in the city, and I've also enjoyed the crabcakes with a roasted bell pepper velouté. My favorite entrée is the charcoal-grilled shrimp with a red Thai curry and barbecue relish. Desserts are equally creative and good; my favorite is the white chocolate bread pudding.

Court of Two Sisters

613 Royal St. ☎ **504/522-7261.** Reservations required at dinner. Main courses $15.50–$30; fixed-price $35; brunch $21. AE, CB, DC, DISC, MC, V. Daily 9am–3pm and 5:30–10pm. CREOLE.

One of the loveliest and most atmospheric of French Quarter restaurants is the Court of Two Sisters. There are entrances from both Royal and Bourbon streets into a huge courtyard filled with flowers, fountains, and low-hanging willows, with a wishing well at its center. The building and its grounds were designed by an early French territorial governor of Louisiana to create the atmosphere of his homeland, and the unusual name comes from the Shop of the Two Sisters, operated here in the late 1800s by two sisters, of course. You can dine outside amid all that lush planting or in the Royal Court Room. You'll know you've found a friendly establishment from the very first, because a sign just outside the door lists their hours as "Buffet Brunch 9am to 3pm, Dinner 5:30 to 10pm. Visiting and browsing allowed 3:30 to 5pm. Have a nice day." You can accept that invitation to browse and enjoy a cocktail in the courtyard. An innovation here is the daily Jazz Brunch Buffet, which features more than 60 dishes (meat, fowl, fish, vegetables, fresh fruits, homemade bread, and pastries) and a jazz band that strolls about, supplying the New Orleans sound. Delicacies such as shrimp Toulouse, crawfish Louise, and chicken Michelle are good bets at dinner. For dessert try the pecan pie or the crepes Suzette. There is a $15 per person minimum at dinner.

Galatoire's

209 Bourbon St. ☎ **504/525-2021.** Reservations not accepted. Main courses $12–$24. AE, MC, V. Tues–Sat 11:30am–9pm, Sun noon–9pm. Closed holidays. FRENCH.

This is a restaurant that draws its charm from a comfortable sense of its age; good, unfussy service; and a way with seafood that leaves many beaming. Galatoire's doesn't accept reservations (even the visiting Duke and Duchess of Windsor had to wait in line), so unless you can take a tip from the natives and go to lunch before noon or dinner before 6pm, you'll line up with everyone else. This restaurant has been family run since 1905, and its traditions remain intact and unchanging. With its mirrored walls and gleaming brass fixtures, Galatoire's is one of the loveliest dining rooms in town. Seafood dishes are quite good. Oysters Rockefeller is a nice way to begin. Trout seems to be the chef's favorite fish here, and it's served in a multitude of ways. Try the trout amandine or the trout Marguéry; as an alternative, the pompano meunière is perfectly broiled. There is a good selection of beef, veal, and lamb, as well. At lunch, you might opt for the oysters en brochette, the eggs Sardou, or the stuffed eggplant. The à la carte menu is the same at lunch and dinner. (*Tip:* If you go on a Sunday afternoon, you'll find yourself in the company of New Orleans family groups who have made Sunday dinner here a ritual for generations.) Jackets are required after 5pm and all day Sunday.

K-Paul's Louisiana Kitchen

416 Chartres St. ☎ **504/524-7394.** Reservations accepted for upstairs dining room only. Lunch $6.95–$14; dinner $20.95–$30. AE, MC, V. Mon–Sat 11:30am–2:30pm and 5:30–10pm. CAJUN.

This is the place that started all the hoopla about Cajun cooking when chef Paul Prudhomme spread its virtues across the entire country. This is also where you'll find the *hottest* interpretation of that cuisine—lots of pepper and other hot seasonings— as well as some of the best. Known for its blackened redfish and Cajun martini (only for the very brave or those with cast-iron innards), K-Paul's also specializes in fiery gumbo, chicken and rabbit from its own farm, and Cajun popcorn (fried crawfish tails). If they're on the menu (which changes daily) try the bronzed (just short of blackened and cooked with less butter) swordfish with "Crawfish Hot Fanny Sauce" or the eggplant pirogue filled with seafood and smothered with "Garlic Slam-Bam Sauce." Prudhomme's sweet potato pecan pie served with chantilly cream is probably your best bet for dessert.

The food aside, you'll have to decide if you really are prepared to wait in line (if you didn't reserve a table in the upstairs dining room) as much as an hour before gaining admittance to the plain, cafelike interior, where harried waitresses will serve you at wooden tables (sans tablecloths) that you'll share with other diners unless your party numbers four or more. Prices have soared to *very* expensive heights, and service might be a little less attentive than you'd expect, depending on how busy the restaurant is when you go.

Le Bistro

In the Hotel Maison de Ville, 733 Toulouse St. ☎ **504/528-9206.** Reservations recommended. Main courses $19.50–$23. AE, DC, MC, V. Mon–Sat 11:30am–2pm; daily 6–10:30pm. INTERNATIONAL.

Go to Le Bistro for some of the finest and most creative cooking in New Orleans. With white-clothed tables and a banquette running the length of the restaurant, the setting is both intimate and romantic—it seats only about 38. To start, there's crawfish with a spicy aioli or goat cheese wrapped in filo pastry with a sweet onion-thyme fricassee and a honey balsamic vinaigrette. Entrées might run the gamut from grilled sesame seed–crusted yellow fin tuna (served with couscous) to herb-crusted rack of lamb. The menu changes seasonally and there's an extensive wine list.

✪ Louis XVI

730 Bienville St. ☎ **504/581-7000.** Reservations recommended. Main courses $16.50–$30. AE, CB, DC, MC, V. Mon–Fri 7–11am, Sat–Sun 7am–noon; dinner daily 6–10pm. FRENCH.

Set in the small, stylish St. Louis Hotel, the Louis XVI is one of New Orleans's finest restaurants. The elegant 1920s Parisian-style dining rooms accented with brass and glass fixtures and fresh flowers look onto a lush courtyard complete with a sparkling fountain. Tuxedoed waiters serve specialties like beef Wellington tableside. The menu, like the decor, is decidedly French, although in recent years it has been lightened slightly with the addition of dishes like filet de poisson grille au beurre de mangue (grilled fish of the day with a composed butter of mango, orange, and cilantro). However, you'll still find traditional cream sauces over shrimp and scallops and filet mignon with béarnaise sauce here. Desserts like chocolate hazelnut cake and charlotte au chocolate et la banane (chocolate and banana mousse surrounded by lady fingers with Chantilly cream in an English rum sauce) are simple but enticing.

Nola

534 St. Louis St. ☎ **504/522-6652.** Reservations recommended. Main courses $16–$24. AE, DC, DISC, MC, V. Mon–Sat 11:30am–2pm; Sun–Thurs 6–10pm, Fri–Sat 6pm–midnight. NEW AMERICAN.

The brainchild of chef Emeril Lagasse (of Emeril's Restaurant), Nola is one of New Orleans's hottest new restaurants. A two-story establishment, Nola is modern and casual in atmosphere. Sculptures and photographs of food decorate the restaurant, but people don't come to Nola to *look* at food, they come here to enjoy Lagasse's culinary creations. At lunch, diners might begin with wood-oven baked pocket bread with garlic-infused oil, fresh basil, and Parmesan cheese, or a crabcake with piquant butter sauce. Entrées at lunch include cedar plank trout with citrus-horseradish crust and lemon-butter sauce served with a spicy slaw and smoked mushroom and tasso pizza with roasted garlic sauce (at dinner you'll find the same pizza on the menu, but as an appetizer). The Lafayette boudin stewed with beer, onions, cane syrup, and Creole mustard served on a sweet potato bread crouton is a great way to begin your dinner here. As a main course at dinner, the grilled free-range chicken with a brown sugar–cayenne rub, Caribbean style served with sweet potato casserole, guacamole and fried tortilla threads is excellent, as is the grilled double-cut pork chop with pecan-glazed sweet potatoes and Creole mustard served with a caramelized onion reduction sauce. On a simpler, but equally satisfying, note is the grilled New York strip served with garlic mashed potatoes and fried red onions. Desserts run the gamut from Nola turtle pie with caramel sauce to coconut cream pie to banana layer cake or chicory coffee crème brûlée. The wine list is well selected.

✪ Pelican Club

312 Exchange Alley. ☎ **504/523-1504.** Reservations recommended. Main courses $16.50–$21.50; fixed-price "early dinner" $19.50. AE, DC, DISC, MC, V. Daily 5:30–closing. Early dinner nightly 5:30–6pm. NEW AMERICAN.

The Pelican Club is located in a 19th-century Creole town house. Three distinctive dining rooms are decorated with art on consignment from area galleries. The overall cosmopolitan feeling here, combined with the talents of chefs Richard Hughes and Chin Ling, has drawn locals, visitors, and big-name stars alike to its tables over the past three years. Signature dishes here include veal and shrimp potstickers with garlic-chili and ginger-soy sauces to start (the two very different sauces complement the dish well); clay pot seafood with shrimp, scallops, fish, mussels, clams, and vegetables in a broth flavored with chili, garlic, lime, and cilantro as a main course (all the shellfish in this dish are done to perfection and the decidedly southwestern accents give the dish an unusual twist); and vanilla brandy crème brûlée for dessert. The Pelican Club has earned *Wine Spectator's* "Award of Excellence" for the past five years running.

Peristyle

1041 Dumaine St. ☎ **504/593-9535.** Reservations recommended. Main courses $18.50–$22.50. MC, V. Lunch Fri 11:30am–2:30pm; dinner Tues–Thurs 6–10pm, Fri–Sat 6–11pm. FRENCH/ITALIAN.

Peristyle, located on the edge of the French Quarter, is a charming place for dinner. Low light and dark wood accents set the scene for a wonderful meal. I enjoyed the beef carpaccio with shaved artichoke salad to start and moved on to the duck à l'orange. I've also enjoyed the salmon with a sorrel-wine sauce as a main course. Other great dishes include fried oysters on fennel with apple-bacon relish and seared foie gras with a cranberry preserve reduction. Desserts are simple, but fresh—try one of the tarts. The service staff here is extremely attentive, and the noise levels are low.

Rib Room

621 St. Louis St. ☎ **504/529-7045.** Reservations recommended. Main courses $22–$48. AE, MC, V. Daily 11:30am–3pm; Sun–Thurs 6–10:30pm, Fri–Sat 6–11pm. SEAFOOD/STEAKS.

Ask almost any New Orleans native for a list of favorite restaurants and chances are that the Omni Hotel's Rib Room will be at or very near the top. Arched windows, high ceilings, natural brick, and lots of wood give the dining room a decidedly Old English feel. Open rotisserie ovens accent the back. As you might guess, the specialty is beef—prime rib ranks highest in most patrons' esteem, but there are also filets, sirloins, brochettes, tournedos, and steak au poivre. Veal, lamb, and duckling also appear on the menu, as do trout, crab, oysters, and shrimp. Many consider at least one meal at the Rib Room as a must for any New Orleans visit.

MODERATE

⑤ Alberto's

611 Frenchmen St. ☎ **504/949-5952.** Reservations not accepted. Main courses $7.75–$16. DISC, MC, V. Mon–Sat 6–11pm. ITALIAN.

Alberto's is a small Italian eatery above the Apple Bar with one of the friendliest staffs in the city. Alberto Gonzalez, owner and chef, holds sway in a setting of bare wooden tables, lots of hanging greenery, and a whimsical stuffed parrot. The food here is New

Orleans with a touch of Italy—chicken Tasso with cream sauce, veal with artichoke hearts and shrimp, red snapper with crabmeat and capers cannelloni, and soft-shell crabs with crawfish tails (in season, of course) are a few of the specialties. The prices are amazingly low. Locals flock to this charming little place, so you may have a wait (not such a chore, with the 24-hour bar just downstairs). Frenchmen Street runs parallel to and one block behind Esplanade Avenue.

Dipiazza's

337 Dauphine St. ☎ **504/525-3335.** Reservations recommended for dinner. Menu items $3.50–$22.95. Fixed-price from $35. AE, CB, DC, MC, V. Mon–Thurs 6–10:30pm, Fri–Sat 6–11pm. ITALIAN.

You won't see this place if you're not looking carefully or if you're on the wrong side of the street. The name is on the front of the awning, which doesn't project too far over the sidewalk. It's a casual, cozy eatery that fills up quickly for dinner, so expect to wait if you're just dropping by. The standard Italian menu items like pasta, veal, chicken, and steak are traditionally prepared behind the wooden bar in the back. Daily specials usually bring an interesting twist to the menu. Grilled alligator makes for an unusual appetizer, and you'll usually find a grilled fish entrée or an excellent prime veal. For dessert, my favorite is the key lime cheesecake.

✪ G&E Courtyard Grill

1113 Decatur St. ☎ **504/528-9376.** Reservations recommended. Main courses $12.50–$22. AE, CB, DC, DISC, MC, V. Fri–Sun 11:30am–2:30pm; Sun–Thurs 6–10pm, Fri–Sat 6–11pm. NEW AMERICAN.

The G&E is another fantastic, relatively new arrival on the New Orleans dining scene. The front dining room, with a mural on one wall, is lovely; there's a nice bar as well. However, what really keeps diners coming back is the covered courtyard, where cast-iron chairs and glass-topped tables rest on terra-cotta tile. The best part? There actually is an open grill at the back of the courtyard where at least a dozen chickens can be seen slowly rotating on the rotisserie. On your left, as you walk into the courtyard, you'll also see some chefs at work.

Nearly seven years since its opening, people are still raving about chef/proprietor Michael Uddo's creations, and there's frequently a line out the door. Go with an open mind and try something new and exciting—you can't really go wrong here. The soft-shell crab rolls with caviar, wasabi, and a low-salt soy sauce or the shrimp cakes with homemade goat cheese, gingered black bean puree, and a garlic, tomato, and cilantro salsa are excellent starters. As an entrée, the rotisserie chicken in a mint, garlic, tomato, and balsamic sauce is unsurpassed. Another good choice is the grilled Gulf fish with chanterelle black lentil sauce served with a risotto cake. I also enjoyed the rotisserie roasted and tea smoked duck with a port and cranberry sauce and garlic mashed potatoes. For dessert I can't think of anything better than the G&E's exceptionally light tiramisu.

✪ Gabrielle

3201 Esplanade Ave. ☎ **504/948-6233.** Reservations recommended. Main courses $14.50–$24. AE, CB, DC, DISC, MC, V. Tues–Sat 5:30–10pm. Lunch is served 11:30am–2pm, Fri only Oct–May. INTERNATIONAL.

This uniquely shaped little restaurant on Esplanade Avenue, just outside the French Quarter, is gaining a big reputation around town. The white walls, hung with unpretentious pieces of art, and the white-clothed tables topped with fresh flowers create a casual and comfortable atmosphere for diners. The food here is superb (and something of a miracle, I think, considering the size of the kitchen). I started with the crab and corn soup, and with the first taste I knew I was in for a treat. The mixed sausage grill with two sauces is also a nice way to start your meal—chef Sonnier (who studied under Paul Prudhomme and Frank Brigtsen) specializes in delectable home-made sausages. As a main course I tried the panfried trout with shrimp and roasted pecan butter. The fish was tender and moist, and the flavors blended perfectly. Desserts are less sophisticated than they might be for a restaurant that rivals some of the best in the city, but I must say I enjoyed my "Peppermint Patti" enormously. It's made of chocolate cake, peppermint ice cream, and chocolate sauce. The lemon pie was also good. There is a small bar, and the wine list is quite nice. Gabrielle offers an early evening special Tuesday through Thursday from 5:30 to 6:15pm. You'll get a choice of three appetizers, two entrées, and two desserts for only $15.95.

⑤ Gumbo Shop

630 St. Peter St. ☎ **504/525-1486.** Reservations not required. Main courses $5.95–$14.95. AE, CB, DC, DISC, JCB, MC, V. Daily 11am–11pm. CREOLE.

In a building dating from 1795, the Gumbo Shop is just one block off Jackson Square. The atmosphere in both the small patio and the indoor dining room is informal. Murals of old New Orleans, ceiling fans, brass accents, and a fireplace with an antique mirror hung above the mantel add a unique charm to the restaurant. The seafood gumbo here is a meal in itself, and if you haven't yet tried jambalaya this is the place to do so. Other dishes include red beans and rice, shrimp Creole, salads, po-boys (ranging from regular ham and cheese to Cajun sausage), and homemade desserts (including just about everybody's favorite, southern pecan pie with ice cream). In addition to the regular menu, fresh fish entrées and dessert specialties are reoffered daily. There's a full bar, and you can also get wine by the bottle or the glass.

Maximo's Italian Grill

1117 Decatur St. ☎ **504/586-8883.** Reservations recommended. Main courses $8.95–$26.95. AE, DISC, MC, V. Daily 6–11pm. ITALIAN.

A friend of mine recommended Maximo's as one of his favorite spots in New Orleans. The restaurant is done in black and gray with a slatted wood ceiling and ceiling fans, and there is an open kitchen at the back of the dining room. You can sit on a stool at the granite counter surrounding the open kitchen, at a table, in a booth, or even on the balcony.

Most people enjoy beginning a meal here with the antipasto platter, on which you're likely to find lovely portobello mushrooms, prosciutto wrapped fruit, and a selection of olives. Pastas usually number more than a dozen in variety and come smothered with tomato sauce, tossed with garlic and oil, or dotted with clams. My favorite, and a house specialty, is the penne Rosa topped with sun-dried tomatoes, garlic, arugula, and shrimp. The chef's signature item is veal T-bone cattoche (pan roasted with garlic and fresh herbs). Go for the zabaglione or the Black Max (flourless chocolate cake) for dessert. This is a very popular spot, and rightly so; be sure to plan ahead and make reservations. The wine list here is excellent.

Mike Anderson's Seafood

215 Bourbon St. ☎ **504/524-3884.** Reservations not accepted. Main courses $9.95–$24.95; daily lunch specials under $8.95. AE, DISC, MC, V. Sun–Thurs 11:30am–10pm, Fri–Sat 11:30am–11pm. SEAFOOD.

This is an offshoot of the popular restaurant by the same name in Baton Rouge. As the name implies, seafood is the specialty here, and it comes in all varieties: fried, baked, boiled, or charbroiled. Especially good are the crawfish bisque and the craw-fish étouffée. The daily lunch specials, served weekdays, are a bargain, and they

Learn to Cook the Louisiana Way

Early on during your New Orleans visit, you're likely to develop an itch to dupli-cate some of the great dishes in your own home. Well, you can scratch that itch by signing up for lunch that comes with a liberal dash of learning at the **New Orleans School of Cooking,** 620 Decatur St. (☎ **504/731-6100** or 800/237-4841). It's a great way to learn the secrets of Creole cooking as local Louisiana cooks and chefs conduct entertaining and informative demonstrations of basic techniques, then serve the dishes you've just seen prepared. Groups are limited in number, so reserve as far in advance as possible; if classes are full, inquire about the possibility of special evening courses. The school is in the back of the Louisiana General Store, which is crammed full of cookbooks, Cajun and Creole seasonings, and a host of other New Orleans gift items. The session hours are 10am to 1pm Monday through Saturday. The school also has a free Louisiana gift catalog.

The **Creole Delicacies and Cooking School,** Store No. 116, Riverwalk, 1 Poydras St. (☎ **504/586-8832**), also offers cooking classes daily from 11am to 1pm. You'll learn to make everything from jambalaya to pralines. There is a gour-met shop (open 10am to 10pm daily) on the premises featuring a great collection of hot sauces and cookbooks.

Another way to get a lesson in Creole and Cajun cooking is to call **Cuisine Eclairée Ecole de Cuisine** at The House on Bayou Road Inn (listed in Chapter 6) at **504/945-0992** or 800/882-2968. The House on Bayou Road offers two- and five-night accommodations packages in combination with the cooking school. The two-day minicourse will teach you to plan a menu and prepare a meal. The five-day "Grand Class" includes visits to some of the best restaurants in New Orleans, as well as the preparation of a meal. Class sizes are limited, so call well in advance to make reservations. Courses are taught by Chef Elaine Lemm, who established Cuisine Eclairée in York, England.

change daily. On an average night you should be prepared to wait at least 15 min-utes for a table. While you wait, you can go upstairs, have a cocktail, and sit down to some appetizers. It's not the kind of place for a romantic evening—it can get pretty loud and crowded—but it's good food at extremely reasonable prices.

Mr. B's Bistro & Bar

201 Royal St. ☎ **504/523-2078.** Reservations recommended. Main courses $15.50–$26. AE, DC, MC, V. Mon–Sat 11:30am–3pm; daily 5:30–10pm; brunch Sun 10:30am–3pm. CONTEMPORARY CREOLE.

Mr. B's, owned and operated by Ralph and Cindy Brennan, is one of the most attractive restaurants in town, featuring polished oak floors, warm wood paneling, marble-topped tables, and large bay windows that look out onto Royal Street. In keeping with the bistro spirit, you can drop in for appetizers and a salad or a casual glass of wine or enjoy a full meal. Traditional New Orleans dishes, like seafood gumbo, Creole catfish fingers, and Louisiana turtle soup are featured on both the lunch and the dinner menus, but there are also some more contemporary, adventur-ous dishes offered. Some of my favorites are the skillet seared tuna with spicy ginger, red cabbage, warm mozzarella, and an herb–black pepper sauce; grilled fennel-crusted salmon in a smoked sweet onion cream sauce; and pasta jambalaya: Gulf shrimp, andouille sausage, duck, and chicken, tossed with spinach fettucine.

Recent items on the dessert menu included strawberry shortcake, tangerine meringue pie, and carrot cake. There's a jazz brunch on Sunday.

Olde N'Awlins Cookery

729 Conti St. ☎ **504/529-3663.** Reservations accepted for 5 or more. Breakfast $5.75–$12.50; main courses $5.75–$14.95 at lunch, $13.50–$20.75 at dinner. AE, MC, V. Daily 8am–11pm. CREOLE/CAJUN/SEAFOOD.

The Olde N'Awlins Cookery symbolizes several of the city's food traditions. The building it's housed in was built in 1849 as two private residences. The two were later combined into a rooming house, then it endured a (probable) stint as a brothel, and underwent service as a bistro bar and then a disco. Finally, after lying idle for two years, it was reopened as a restaurant. Since its opening in 1983, the family operated restaurant has dished up traditional Cajun and Creole favorites and attracted a loyal clientele from the ranks of city residents. Using the freshest of Louisiana seafood and local seasonings, the kitchen turns out specialties such as Cajun jambalaya, blackened redfish, and shrimp Creole, as well as soups, salads, and great desserts. In a rather plain setting that makes use of the original old brick and a delightful courtyard, informality is the keynote. With good prices and a lively, distinctly New Orleans ambience, this is one place where you won't mind a long wait to be seated.

Palm Court Café

1204 Decatur St. ☎ **504/525-0200.** Reservations recommended. Main courses $11–$14.95. AE, DISC, MC, V. Wed–Sun 7–11pm. FRENCH/CREOLE.

The Palm Court Café is not only a delightful place to enjoy Creole and French culinary specialties but also the repository of a jazz-record collection that will probably contain any classic you might be looking for. And Wednesday through Sunday from 8 to 11pm your food comes to the table accompanied by live music from top-line jazz performers. Owners Nina and George Buck have a long history in the recording business, as well as a passionate love of food. Gumbo, shrimp Creole, oysters bordelaise, Creole beef indienne, and jambalaya are just a few of the à la carte menu specials.

⑤ Port of Call

838 Esplanade Ave. ☎ **504/523-0120.** Reservations not accepted. Main courses $6–$19. AE, MC, V. Sun–Thurs 11am–1am, Fri–Sat 11am–3am. HAMBURGERS.

After a regular diet of Cajun and Creole food, I get to a point where I can't bear to look at another shrimp, oyster, or filet and can't wait to get my hands on a big, fat, juicy hamburger. That's when I head straight for Port of Call.

Outside you'll see a small sign lit by a red lamp, and perhaps a line. Inside you'll find a cozy wooden interior and an attentive and friendly staff. The mushrooms sautéed in wine sauce are well known around the city, and the hamburgers, which come with a baked potato, are quite a handful. There also are pizzas, excellent filet mignon, rib eye, and New York strip steaks. Because businesspeople come from all over the city to eat here, it's often jammed at regular eating hours, so try it at off hours or before 7pm, when people who work in the Quarter gather here to relax. Port of Call also has a take-out service.

Ralph & Kacoo's

519 Toulouse St. ☎ **504/522-5226.** Reservations not required. Main courses $6.95–$17.95. AE, DISC, MC, V. Mon–Thurs 11am–10:30pm, Fri–Sat 11am–11pm, Sun 11am–9:30pm. CREOLE/SEAFOOD.

You can't miss Ralph and Kacoo's large, colorful exterior as you walk down Toulouse, and the restaurant may well be crowded no matter when you go. Although your wait for a table here will be at the bar, surrounded by a lively crowd of patrons, it will seldom be for more than 15 to 20 minutes. Creole dishes, mostly seafood, are quite good, portions are more than ample and prices are reasonable, and due to the restaurant's high volume of business you can rest assured that everything is fresh. Start with the fried crawfish tails or the "killer" onion rings, and if you're adventurous, give the blackened alligator with hollandaise a try. For a main course you might try the trout Ruby, which is trout stuffed with lump crabmeat and topped with baby shrimp and hollandaise sauce; or try the mesquite grilled, blackened, or broiled mahimahi (when available) topped with green onions and served with a Cajun stuffed potato, coleslaw, and hush puppies. For those with restricted diets, there is a special "heart healthy" menu available. Ask about the luncheon specials.

Rémoulade

309 Bourbon St. ☎ **504/523-0377.** Reservations recommended. Full meal $15–$20. AE, CB, MC, V. Daily 11:30am–midnight. CREOLE/AMERICAN.

If you've been wanting to go to Arnaud's but can't afford it, can't get a reservation, or just don't feel like dressing up, I have the answer. It's Rémoulade, an offshoot of the famous Arnaud's (located next door). The brasserie atmosphere with piped-in jazz music and a kitchen that can be seen from every table in the house, is a pleasant and almost downright disrespectful alternative to the traditional atmosphere of Arnaud's. The menu is fun and eclectic; the food, not surprisingly, is excellent. Thin-crust pizzas with a wide variety of toppings are popular here, as are the seafood po-boys. Rémoulade also features some of the dishes Arnaud's made famous, like shrimp Arnaud (shrimp in a Creole mustard sauce) and oysters stewed in cream. It also pokes a bit of fun at tradition by serving a hot dog topped with rémoulade sauce (it's not bad, actually). The wine list comes from Arnaud's, so you won't be disappointed on that front either.

Ristorante Carmelo

541 Decatur St. ☎ **504/586-1414.** Reservations not required. Main courses $5.50–$9.50 at lunch, $9–$28 at dinner. AE, MC, V. Daily 11:30am–3pm; Sun–Thurs 5–11pm, Fri–Sat 5:30–11pm. ITALIAN.

Conveniently located near Jackson Brewery and Jackson Square, Ristorante Carmelo is a lovely spot for a relaxing lunch in the middle of a busy day of sightseeing, and the upstairs balcony offers a panoramic view of the Mississippi. The menu proclaims "At Carmelo you eat and drink Italian," and traditional Italian cuisine is exactly what you get. At dinner, fresh homemade pasta, including fettucine, ravioli, manicotti, and capellini are available. Fresh grilled grouper, swordfish, veal dishes, carpaccio, and calamari are among the house specialties as well. For dessert, the il Nostro Tiramisu is a must.

Rita's Olde French Quarter Restaurant

945 Chartres St. ☎ **504/525-7543.** Reservations not required. Main courses $5.95–$16.95. AE, CB, DC, DISC, MC, V. Daily 11am–10pm. CREOLE.

On the corner of Chartres and St. Philip, Rita's doesn't look like much on the outside, and you're likely to walk right by without even noticing it. Don't. When you walk in you'll feel right at home, maybe because of the friendly staff, maybe because of the portrait of Rita hanging high above everything in the room, maybe because you're likely to see members of Rita's family having dinner at the back table. There's nothing fancy here and the atmosphere is very casual; in fact, the pictures often hang a little crooked on the walls.

One of the nights I went, I had the special blackened catfish bathed in a very tasty Lea and Perrins and lemon sauce. I'm not crazy about catfish, but I'd have to say that this was some of the best I've ever had. Unlike average catfish, the variety used at Rita's is farm-raised and corn-fed, which gives it a sweet flavor. Also on the plate were sweet potatoes in a brown-sugar sauce, and they too were delicious. Another time I tried shrimp Creole—some of the best I've had in New Orleans. The oyster and artichoke soup is tasty as well and the gumbo is excellent. You shouldn't miss Rita's bread pudding (and you probably won't because they often bring out a complimentary dish when you're done with your meal)—it's on par with my mother's, and she makes a mean bread pudding.

Royal Café

700 Royal St. ☎ **504/528-9086.** Reservations not required. Main courses $4.75–$19.95. AE, MC, V. Mon–Fri 11:30am–3pm, Sat–Sun 10am–3pm; daily 5:30–10pm. CREOLE.

The Royal Café is a casual eatery, with dining rooms on both the ground and the second floors. But it is the upstairs balcony that appeals to most who come here. This balcony finds its way into almost every tourist's photos of New Orleans; along with your food, you enjoy a superb view of the French Quarter itself. Try New Orleans "lost bread" for breakfast (it's listed as "French Quarter toast" on the menu and it's available on Saturday and Sunday only), a spicy shrimp Creole or a po-boy at lunch, and the famous crabcakes at dinner. Should you have a bit of difficulty choosing, there's a terrific "Taste of New Orleans" sampler that gives you a cup of gumbo; a small bowl of red beans, sausage, and rice; followed by the aforementioned shrimp Creole—served with fresh-baked French bread.

Tujague's

823 Decatur St. ☎ **504/525-8676.** Reservations recommended. Five-course lunch $6.50–$12; six-course dinner $24–$26. AE, CB, DC, DISC, MC, V. Daily 11am–3pm and 5–11pm. CREOLE.

Tujague's (pronounced *two jacks)* is the second restaurant to occupy this site. The first was run by Madame Begue, who in 1856 began cooking huge "second breakfasts" for the butchers who worked in the French Market across the way. So well loved were her elaborate, leisurely meals that even today her name lives on in a modern eatery in the Royal Sonesta Hotel. Today Tujague's serves only lunch and dinner, but continues the original cook's tradition of serving whatever inspiration dictates that day. This is a favorite with New Orleanians, who seem not to mind that there's a very limited menu. At lunch, you have a choice of three entrées, which might include a specialty here, brisket of beef with horseradish sauce; their terrific shrimp rémoulade; and the freshest fish available that day. The five-course meal will consist of soup, salad, entrée, vegetable, dessert, and beverage. If something lighter appeals to you, choose gumbo served with a side dish of shrimp salad.

INEXPENSIVE

"Inexpensive" in the French Quarter can often mean "very, very good." That's due, I think, to two things: First, many traditional dishes here are made with low-cost ingredients (red beans and rice, for example); second, there are so many good cooks in this city who can make almost anything taste delicious. So whatever preconceived notions you bring with you about luncheonette-style eateries, be ready to revise them after trying one or two of the following.

⑤ Acme Oyster House

724 Iberville St. ☎ **504/522-5973.** Reservations not accepted. Oysters $3.50–$6; New Orleans specialties $5.25–$5.75; seafood $7.75–$9.75; po-boys $4–$5. AE, DC, JCB , MC, V. Mon–Sat 11am–10pm, Sun noon–7pm. SEAFOOD.

If you're an oyster lover, there's nothing quite like standing at the oyster bar in the Acme Oyster House, eating a dozen or so freshly shucked oysters on the half shell.

(You can have them at a table, but somehow they taste better at the bar.) If you can't quite stomach them raw, try the oyster po-boy off the sandwich menu, with beer, of course, as the perfect accompaniment. Acme offers fresh baked bread pudding and cheesecake on the dessert menu. This New Orleans institution is a fun place to eat—the shuckers behind the bar are as much a treat as those lovely oysters.

Café Maspero

601 Decatur St. ☎ **504/523-6250.** Reservations not accepted. Main courses $4–$8.50. No credit cards. Sun–Thurs 11am–11pm, Fri–Sat 11am–midnight. SEAFOOD/SANDWICHES.

The Café Maspero serves the largest portions I've run into—burgers, deli sandwiches, seafood, grilled marinated chicken, and so on—as well as an impressive list of wines, beers, and cocktails, all at low, low prices. This is a lively spot, especially following a concert, the opera, or the theater, when locals drop by in droves; it's not unusual to see patrons lined up for tables. Be assured, however, that it's worth your time to wait—the quality is as good as the portions are large.

Felix's Restaurant & Oyster Bar

739 Iberville St. ☎ **504/522-4440.** Reservations not required. Main courses $10–$16.95. AE, MC, V. Mon–Thurs 10:30am–midnight, Fri–Sat 10:30am–1:30am, Sun 10:30am–10pm. SEAFOOD/CREOLE.

If you get a yen for oysters, Felix's is the place to go. Like its neighbor, the Acme Oyster House, Felix's is almost legendary among New Orleanians, and it stays open quite late all week long. Sometimes crowded and noisy, it almost always looks disorganized, but if you pass it by on those grounds you'll be missing a real eating experience. Have your oysters raw, in a stew, in a soup, Rockefeller or Bienville style, in your spaghetti, or even in your omelet. In addition to the oysters, there's a selection of fried or grilled fish, chicken, steaks, spaghetti, and omelets, and the Creole cooking is quite good. It's possible to get things blackened to order.

Louisiana Pizza Kitchen

2800 Esplanade Ave. ☎ **504/488-2800.** Reservations not required. Pizzas $5.95–$7.95, pastas $4.50–$9.95. AE, CB, DC, DISC, MC, V. Daily 5:30–11pm. ITALIAN.

The Louisiana Pizza Kitchen is favored locally for its creative pies as well as for the atmosphere. Located on a quiet section of Esplanade Avenue, its dining room allows patrons a lovely view. While pastas also have a place on the menu, it's the pizza and Caesar salad that diners come for. Individually sized pizzas, baked in a wood-fired oven, are offered with a wide variety of toppings (shrimp pizza and roasted garlic pizza are two of the most popular). The best thing about the pizzas here is that your toppings won't get lost in an abundance of cheese and tomato sauce. Louisiana Pizza Kitchen is also located at 95 French Market Place (☎ **504/522-9500**) and 615 S. Carrollton Ave. (☎ **504/866-5900**).

Mama Rosa's

616 N. Rampart St. ☎ **504/523-5546.** Reservations not required. Pizzas $7.25–$13.50; specials $5–$7.50. MC, V. Tues–Thurs, Sun 10:30am–10:30pm; Fri–Sat 10:30am–11:30pm. ITALIAN.

Mama Rosa's "Little Slice of Italy" serves up a big slice of pizza. While the decor is nothing to brag about—typical red and white checkered linen tablecloths, a jukebox, and a bar—the pizzas are. You can get a 10- or 14-inch pizza with a variety of different toppings for very reasonable prices. The crusts are thick, and the more you put on them, the better they are. In fact, the slices are so thick, you could almost compare them to pan pizza. Of course, you can also get pasta, like spaghetti and manicotti, and the salads are big enough to be a full meal. You can even get mini muffalettas as appetizers. One of the big draws is Mama Rosa's homemade bread. The staff can be a bit surly, but most people don't go there for ambience; they go with one thing in mind: good, fast, inexpensive Italian food, and they get it.

Napoleon House

500 Chartres St. ☎ **504/524-9752.** Reservations required for large parties. Sandwiches and pastries $4.25–$10. AE, MC, V. Daily 11am–1am. AMERICAN/ITALIAN.

Giving in a bit to everyday wear and tear on the outside, Napoleon House, at the corner of Chartres and St. Louis streets, is so named because at the time of the death of the "Little Corporal" there was actually a plot (most likely absinthe induced) hatching in this 1797 National Landmark to snatch him from his island exile and bring him to New Orleans. The third floor was added expressly for the purpose of providing him with a home after the rescue. It wears its history with dignity. There's a limited menu of po-boys, Italian muffuletta sandwiches, and pastries; the jukebox plays only classical music. You can relax inside by the old bar or outside in the courtyard. This is a very popular spot with residents and many visiting celebrities. You can easily picture struggling artists and writers of days long past engaged in conversation at the little cafe tables or at the bar. If you're looking for some opera and a bit of old New Orleans, the best time to visit Napoleon House is after dark when the locals gather.

New Orleans Coffee & Concierge

334B Royal St. ☎ **504/524-5530.** Reservations not necessary. All items $1.67–$6.95. MC, V (in gallery only). Daily 8am–5pm. CAFE.

When I first discovered New Orleans Coffee and Concierge in 1992 it was a new addition to the French Quarter scene. I was sure it would be around for quite some time. Four years later it's more popular than ever. It has been transformed from a small cafe serving pastries and coffee into a full-service, bistro-style cafe offering breakfast and lunch, and there is a gallery that at press time was featuring the works of George Rodrique, world famous for his "Blue Dog" paintings. At breakfast you can get Belgian waffles, an omelet soufflé, bagels and lox, and brioche French toast. Items on the lunch menu include gumbo, crawfish pie, vegetable sandwiches, and salads. They're now serving the famous New Orleans beignets, and there's an exclusive Robert Mondavi Wine Bar available for your tasting pleasure all afternoon.

Père Antoine Restaurant

714 Royal St. ☎ **504/581-4478.** Reservations not required. Main courses $3.95–$14.95. No credit cards. Daily 9am–midnight. CAJUN/CREOLE.

Père Antoine is an attractive European-style place with huge mirrors in back and flowers out front. Specialties here include Cajun red snapper (cooked in a rich tomato sauce, a nice change from "blackened"), shrimp, and crawfish étouffée. The seafood platter, with catfish, shrimp, scallops, crab, and Cajun popcorn (deep-fried seasoned shrimp), is a real bargain. For lighter meals, there are soups and salads, sandwiches and burgers, omelets, and such New Orleans favorites as red beans and rice, jambalaya, and chicken Creole. Items on the breakfast menu, such as Belgian waffles and a "Louisiana Breakfast—The Rajun Cajun Omelet" (with smoked sausage, green peppers, onion, ham, and a Creole sauce) are available all day.

Petunia's

817 St. Louis St. ☎ **504/522-6440.** Reservations not required. Main courses $9.95–$18.95. AE, DISC, MC, V. Daily 8am–11pm. CAJUN/CREOLE.

Petunia's, located in an 1830s town house between Bourbon and Dauphine streets, dishes up enormous portions of New Orleans specialties like shrimp Creole, Cajun pasta with shrimp and andouille, and a variety of fresh seafoods. Breakfast and Sunday brunch are popular here, with a broad selection of crepes—they are billed as the world's largest (I can't prove it, but they probably are) at 14 inches. Crepe selections include the "St. Marie," which is a blend of spinach, cheddar, chicken, and hollandaise; and the "St. Francis," filled with shrimp, crab ratatouille, and Swiss cheese. If you have room for dessert, try the dessert crepes or the peanut butter pie.

✪ Praline Connection

542 Frenchmen St. ☎ **504/943-3934.** Reservations not accepted. Main courses $4–$13.95. AE, DC, DISC, MC, V. Sun–Thurs 11am–10:30pm, Fri–Sat 11am–midnight. CREOLE/SOUL FOOD.

The Praline Connection is famous around the city, but visitors probably wouldn't know about it unless it was recommended to them by a friend, as it was in my case. It's a bit out of reach because it's hidden away on Frenchmen Street, which is just behind Esplanade Avenue. If you get back there, you'll find that Frenchmen Street is a veritable treasure trove of restaurants and entertainment.

The interior is bright and airy, with stainless-steel ceiling fans and a black and white tiled floor. It's not the kind of place you'd go for a romantic dinner because the noise level can be quite daunting. The people who go to the Praline Connection go there to eat and have fun; you might even end up talking to the people next to you because sometimes there is not enough room to seat you at a private table, and you might have to wait to get that.

The food is wonderful, plentiful, and very reasonably priced. The fried chicken is crispy and juicy, and you can get it with almost any kind of beans and rice. There are red beans, white beans, and crowder peas, as well as okra, mustard greens, and collard greens. It's real southern soul cooking at its best. Praline Connection's newest menu items include fried soft-shell crawfish and barbecued ribs. At lunch you might try the Hog's Head Cheese with garlic toast to start followed by an oyster or smoked sausage po-boy. A small candy shop is attached (there are a few tables in there, and it's a little quieter than the main dining room) selling pralines as well as other candies. The friendly staff is smartly dressed in black and white with fedora hats. Praline Connection II at 901 South Peters St. (☎ **504/523-3973**) offers the same menu and a larger dining room.

St. Ann's Cafe & Deli

800 Dauphine St. ☎ **504/529-4421.** $2.25–$12.95. AE, DISC, MC, V. Open 24 hrs. CAFE DELI.

St. Ann's is a cozy little cafe on the corner of St. Ann and Dauphine streets. Inside there are a few cafe tables, giving the feeling that it's more of a local hangout than a tourist attraction. There's nothing fancy about it, and I probably wouldn't even have tried it out if it hadn't been for the raving recommendation of a friend who said that St. Ann's was one of the only things that kept her going when she was first moving into town. Everything here is homemade, and you can get a variety of foods, including sandwiches, pizzas, soups, and salads, as well as breakfast items. Lunch and dinner specials are offered daily, and there's a decent selection of beer and wine.

4 Downtown

Christian's

3835 Iberville St. ☎ **504/482-4924.** Reservations recommended. Main courses $13.25–$23.95. AE, CB, DC, MC, V. Tues–Fri 11:30am–2pm and 5:30–10pm; Sat 5:30–10pm. FRENCH/CREOLE.

Ever had a three-course meal in a church? Well, at Christian's, only about 10 minutes from the French Quarter, you can do just that. Started by Christian Ansel, this lovely restaurant serves seafood specialties, some of which are prepared with the most delicate of French sauces. Try the oysters Roland or the crawfish "Carolyn" (crawfish in a spicy cream sauce with brandy and Parmesan cheese) to start off; the sweet-breads with fresh mushrooms, sherry, and a demi-glacé sauce, or the shrimp en brochette (grilled shrimp with slices of onion and bell pepper served with a lemon butter sauce over angel hair pasta) as an entrée; and finish it off with café brûlot, baked Alaska, or profiteroles aux chocolate. There are specials available at lunch. The little church building remains unaltered on the exterior, and inside it's been beautifully restored.

Dooky Chase

2301 Orleans Ave. ☎ **504/821-2294.** Reservations recommended at dinner. Fixed-price $26; main courses $10.50–$19.50; Creole feast $39.50. AE, DC, MC, V. Daily 11:30am–midnight. SOUL FOOD/CREOLE.

Established in 1941, Dooky Chase has long been a favorite of the locals, but it's only just recently been recognized by critics farther afield as serving some of the best soul food in the city. And it's soul food with distinctive New Orleans touches, such as shrimp Dooky with its spicy rémoulade sauce, veal panne (served with jambalaya), and a delicious crawfish étouffée. The fried chicken here is terrific, some of the best I've had in a long time, and steaks also are on the menu. Try the praline pudding instead of the traditional bread pudding for dessert. If you're really in the mood to put on a few pounds, call and reserve a Creole feast for yourself.

While you're there, you might get to see the chef, Leah Chase, who is fast becoming known across the country as one of the great chefs of New Orleans. The decor seems plain, but take a look around, and you'll see that the owners are avid collectors of African-American art, a great deal of which is hanging in the restaurant. *Note:* After dark, it is best to go there by cab.

Ruth's Chris Steak House

711 N. Broad St. ☎ **504/486-0810.** Reservations recommended. Main courses $8.50–$28.50. AE, DC, MC, V. Daily 11:30am–11pm. STEAKS.

You won't get an argument locally if you pronounce that the best steak in town is served at Ruth's Chris Steak House. The specialty here is, in fact, prime beef, custom aged, cut by hand, and beautifully prepared. Cuts include filets, strips, rib eyes, porterhouses (for two or more), and more. All the beef prepared at Ruth's Chris Steak House is corn fed. Pork chops and one or two other meats appear on the menu, but this is primarily a steak house, and one that will not disappoint.

There's another Ruth's Chris at 3633 Veterans Blvd. in Metairie (☎ **504/ 888-3600**) and branches in Baton Rouge and Lafayette (see Chapter 12.)

5 Central Business District

EXPENSIVE

✪ Emeril's

800 Tchoupitoulas St. ☎ **504/528-9393.** Reservations recommended at dinner. Main courses $7.50–$25. AE, CB, DC, DISC, MC, V. Mon–Fri 11:30am–2pm and 6–10pm; Sat 6–10pm. CREOLE/NEW AMERICAN.

Emeril's was opened in March 1990 by Emeril Lagasse, who used to be head chef at Commander's Palace. He's another of the young, daring, but traditionally schooled chefs that everyone in New Orleans has been talking about as of late. He has gained national recognition with his own show, "The Essence of Emeril," on the Food Network.

The restaurant is located in the warehouse district, practically on gallery row. The building was, in fact, once a warehouse, and rather than cover the remaining traces of its history, Lagasse has incorporated exposed pipes in the interior design and created a wonderfully modern establishment.

Lagasse insists on making everything from scratch, including sausage and even ketchup. Emeril loves experimenting with new ingredients and preparations while still improving on the old stand-bys. His zealous approach to his work is quite contagious—the fever has been caught by his entire staff, who number among the best in New Orleans. To start, try the grilled homemade andouille sausage with his famous homemade Worcestershire sauce, or the smoked wild and exotic mushrooms in a homemade tasso cream sauce over angel hair pasta and topped with Parmesan Reggiano cheese. As an entrée you might have the grilled fresh fish of the day or the paneed Mississippi quail (sautéed in olive oil, until crisp and served with roasted garlic, smashed root vegetables, crispy bacon, green beans, stewed barbecue quail legs, and a drizzle of sweet barbecue sauce). If you don't have time for a full meal at Emeril's, go and have a look at the after-dinner menu, which features some pretty incredible desserts: banana cream pie with a banana-flavored crust and topped with caramel sauce and chocolate shavings, the homemade ice cream sandwich, and J. K. chocolate soufflé. Emeril now employs a full-time sommelier and the wine list recently won recognition and awards from *Wine Spectator* magazine.

✪ Graham's

200 Magazine St. ☎ **504/524-9678.** Reservations recommended, especially on weekends. Main courses $14–$24 at dinner. AE, CB, DC, DISC, MC, V. Breakfast daily 7–10:30am; lunch Mon–Fri 11:30am–2pm; dinner Sun–Thurs 6–10pm, Fri–Sat 6–11pm. ECLECTIC.

Graham's is one of New Orleans's most recently opened restaurants. From 1988 to 1994 Kevin Graham was the head chef at the Grill Room in the Windsor Court Hotel, which he helped to raise to a higher level of culinary excellence. Now he works his magic at his own place. The modern dining room here has soaring ceilings, tile floors, and few decorative accents. The food is even more impressive. Menus change very frequently, but if you get a chance, you should try the foie gras served with cubes of port-wine aspic and sauced with red currant jelly, ginger, mustard, and shallots. The veal chop I had, which was served with tomato sauce and accompanied by a white bean and fontina puree, was excellent. Desserts like profiteroles and the lemon tart are simple, but well-executed. The wine list is excellent.

The Veranda Restaurant

In the Hotel Inter-Continental, 444 St. Charles Ave. ☎ **504/525-5566.** Reservations recommended. Main courses $11.50–$22.50. AE, CB, DC, DISC, MC, V. Mon–Sat 11am–2pm and 5:30–10pm, Sun 5:30–9pm; brunch Sun 11am–2:30pm. CONTINENTAL/CREOLE.

The Veranda's chef, Willy Coln, is one of the most respected in New Orleans, and that's only the beginning. The atmosphere is both dramatic and comfortable. Its glass-enclosed garden courtyard (with an abundance of greenery) and private dining room make you feel as though you're dining in a stately New Orleans home, and Tuesday through Sunday a harpist makes dining at The Veranda all the more memorable.

The menu is varied, and it is doubtful that you'll find anything to complain about. I started with the excellent Louisiana crab cakes in a light Creole mustard sauce. The oyster and artichoke soup, offered daily, is always good. The smoked duck and wild mushroom strudel is also a top choice. For an entrée I enjoyed potato crusted redfish with baby bok choy and a ginger beurre blanc. The paneed rabbit with Creole mustard sauce and the heart-healthy vegetable strudel on tomato coulis and fresh artichoke ragout are done to perfection. Desserts are incredible, and I know because I tasted every one. You shouldn't pass up this hotel restaurant—it's worth the trip.

MODERATE

Bailey's

In the Fairmont Hotel, 123 University Place. ☎ **504/529-7111.** Reservations not required. All items $3–$17. AE, CB, DC, DISC, MC, V. Sun–Thurs 11am–1am, Fri–Sat 24 hours. COFFEE SHOP.

Bailey's is a cozy spot softly lit by Tiffany-style lamps and decorated with antiques. At any hour of the day you can order breakfast items such as waffles, pancakes, and omelets, or New Orleans specialties such as red beans and rice with hot sausage and a seafood platter. There also are sandwiches and burgers, as well as a nice selection of po-boys. The entrance is at Baronne Street.

Bon Ton Café

401 Magazine St. ☎ **504/524-3386.** Reservations required at dinner. Main courses $8.75– $14.50 at lunch, $18.75–$24.25 at dinner. AE, DC, MC, V. Mon–Fri 11am–2pm and 5–9:30pm. CAJUN.

You'll find the Bon Ton Café absolutely mobbed at lunch with New Orleans businesspeople and their guests. Such popularity is largely due to its owner, Al Pierce; his nephew, Wayne; and Wayne's wife, Debbie. Al and Wayne both grew up in the Bayou country, where Al learned Cajun cooking from his mother. He came to New Orleans in 1936, bought the Bon Ton in 1953, and since then has been serving up seafood gumbo, crawfish bisque, jambalaya, crawfish omelet, and other Cajun dishes in a manner that would make his mother proud. Wayne and Debbie are continuing the tradition. This is a small, utterly charming place that's not to be missed if you want to sample true Cajun cooking at its best (more subtle than Creole, making much use of shallots, parsley, bell peppers, and garlic). The lunch menu is partially à la carte; at dinner the menu is à la carte and fixed-price.

Kabby's Seafood Restaurant

2 Poydras St. ☎ **504/584-3880.** Reservations recommended. Main courses $17–$28.95. AE, CB, DC, MC, V. Daily 10:30am–2:30pm and 6–11pm. SEAFOOD.

Dining at Kabby's affords a lookout over the river through a 200-foot-wide, 14-foot-high window. It's a spectacular view. You enter the restaurant through a New Orleans courtyard foyer that features a bubbling fountain, custom-designed lamp-posts, and tropical plantings. At lunch, there are salads, sandwiches (oyster loaf, muffuletta, and so on), and other specialties. The dinner menu is more adventurous. To start, try the corn and crab chowder or the crabmeat stuffed oysters with a trio of dipping sauces. As a main course, the peppered duck breast (with andouille sausage dressing, sweet potato frites, and a natural duck reduction) is excellent, as is the salmon gratin. The warm pecan and chocolate tart is a good choice for dessert.

✪ Palace Café

605 Canal St. ☎ **504/523-1661.** Reservations recommended. Main courses $9.95–$20. AE, CB, MC, V. Lunch Mon–Sat 11:30am–2:30pm; brunch Sun 10:30am–2:30pm, dinner daily 5:30–7:30pm. CONTEMPORARY CREOLE.

Operated by Ti Martin, daughter of Ella Brennan of the famous New Orleans restaurateur family, the Palace Café is a grand cafe (situated in the old Werlein's music building) serving contemporary Creole seafood. Enter through the cafe's brass and glass revolving door and you will be immediately impressed by the spiral staircase in the middle of the restaurant. It's comfortable, the ground floor being almost entirely made up of booths—even for two. Deep green, creamy yellow, and brass lend an open, airy feel to the downstairs dining room. Upstairs you'll find a mural featuring local music giants, such as Aaron Neville, Harry Connick Jr., Ellis Marsalis, and Louis Armstrong.

No doubt you'll find something interesting on the menu. If you're an oyster lover, start with the oyster shooters (raw oysters served in a shot glass) or the oyster pan roast (oysters lightly poached in a rosemary cream sauce, served in the skillet). The crabmeat batons (ginger wrapped Louisiana crabmeat with wasabi cream and soy dipping sauce) are another good appetizer choice. The seafood boil features the day's fresh local seafood served on a raised platter (just the way it's done in the grand cafes of Paris). The crabmeat cheesecake is excellent, as is the grilled tuna. The double cut rotisserie pork chop with candied sweet potatoes was delicious and filling—I found it impossible to clean my plate. Also from the rotisserie is roasted pasture raised chicken, and it's done to perfection. Fresh, warm bread is served with each course, and you can get wines by the glass. For dessert, you should try the white chocolate bread pudding or the Mississippi mud pie. The staff is attentive and friendly. If you go for lunch there's likely to be a large business crowd present. Brunch on Sunday brings live blues entertainment by Betty Shirley.

INEXPENSIVE

Bluebird Cafe

3625 Prytania St. ☎ **504/895-7166.** Reservations not accepted. All menu items under $7. No credit cards. Mon–Fri 8am–3pm, Sat–Sun 7am–3pm. AMERICAN.

The charming eggshell blue dining room at the Bluebird Cafe is always packed, primarily with a local crowd of breakfast and lunch diners in the know. This place is one of the best in New Orleans to stop for a hearty, flavorful, inexpensive meal. Portions are enormous. Try the buckwheat pecan waffle or the cheese grits (my favorite); they even make their own sausage. If those delectable items don't appeal to you, you can always opt to "build your own" omelet.

Ernst's Café

600 S. Peters St. ☎ **504/525-8544.** Reservations not required. Main courses $6.50–$9.95. AE, DC, MC, V. Mon–Sat 11am–3pm. CAJUN/CREOLE.

There's been an eatery and bar run by the same family in the old brick building that now houses Ernst's Café since 1902. Its brick walls, high ceilings, and heavy timbered bar make it an interesting and attractive setting for excellent sandwiches, hamburgers, fried shrimp, salads, red beans and rice, and po-boys. If the weather is fine, eat outside.

⑤ Mother's

401 Poydras St. ☎ **504/523-9656.** Reservations not accepted. Menu items $1.75–$16.50. No credit cards. Mon–Sat 5am–10pm, Sun 7am–10pm. SANDWICHES/CREOLE.

You owe it to yourself to make at least one pilgrimage to Mother's, which is within walking distance of the Louisiana Superdome and a number of major hotels. When you go, be sure to allow time to stand in line—bankers line up with warehouse workers, dockworkers, and just about everybody else from this part of town for *the* best po-boy sandwiches in New Orleans. Made on crisp French bread fresh from the oven, the po-boys here are real creations. Many of them are served with a rich, thick, sloppy gravy, but the sandwiches are so good you won't mind the mess. Try the roast beef or ham—Mother's baked ham is said to be "the world's best." The restaurant's most sought-after po-boy is the Ferdi Special with baked ham, roast beef, shredded cabbage, and Creole mustard. There are plate lunches, too, such as the excellent gumbo, red beans, Jerry's award-winning jambalaya, and spaghetti pie, and they also serve one of the best breakfasts in the city. Mother's is always crowded, but don't let that throw you off—the line moves quickly.

Uglesich's Restaurant & Bar

1238 Barrone St. ☎ **504/523-8571.** Reservations not required. Lunch $6–$11. No credit cards. Mon–Fri 9:30am–4pm. SANDWICHES.

Uglesich's, at Erato Street near Lee Circle, is old and more than a little rundown in appearance (stacked cases of beer are some of the most decorative features this place has to offer), but it is well loved locally for its outstanding sandwiches of fried food. If you're a little homesick and just feel like being part of the neighborhood scene, with the added bonus of eating delicious, freshly prepared, inexpensive food, Uglesich's is the place. You won't regret the trip, but leave your jacket behind or you'll carry the fried smell all day.

6   Uptown (Including the Garden District)

EXPENSIVE

Brigtsen's

723 Dante St. ☎ **504/861-7610.** Reservations required a week or two in advance. Main courses $12–$24. AE, DC, MC, V. Tues–Sat 5:30–10pm. CAJUN/CREOLE.

In the Riverbend area, Brigtsen's occupies a small house and is presided over by Frank Brigtsen, a former chef at K-Paul's. Two of the most popular dishes right now are his roast duck with "dirty" rice and honey-pecan gravy, and broiled Gulf fish with a crabmeat Parmesan crust and lemon mousselline (Frank has a magic touch with seafood). The menu changes daily, but some items of note on a recent menu included stuffed chicken breast with Creole farmer's cheese, bacon, mushrooms, and red wine; and grilled beef tournedos with fried shallots and blue cheese in a balsamic roasted garlic sauce. For those on a budget, Brigtsen's offers "Early Evening" dinner specials Tuesday through Thursday from 5:30 to 6:30pm. The price, $14.95, includes a three-course dinner.

Caribbean Room

In the Pontchartrain Hotel, 2031 St. Charles Ave. ☎ **504/524-0581.** Reservations recommended. Main courses $19–$31.50. AE, DC, DISC, MC, V. Tues–Sat 6–10pm. FRENCH/CREOLE.

Since it opened in 1948, the Caribbean Room has won a list of culinary awards as long as your arm, and it really epitomizes New Orleans cuisine at its finest. The decor, like that of the rest of the hotel, is infused with a refined (almost understated) luxury. As for service, well, *impeccable* and *solicitous* come to mind. The kitchen turns out appetizer specialties such as oysters and bacon en brochette, crabmeat Remick served with tortilla chips, and bronzed shrimp (jumbo shrimp dusted with Cajun spices, seared in butter, and topped with a lobster and garlic demi-glacé). Brilliantly executed main courses like snapper Eugene (filet of snapper sautéed in butter and drizzled with a sauce of shallots, shrimp, lump crabmeat, lemon juice, and Worcestershire sauce) and duckling vert pres (slow-roasted half duckling on mixed greens with orange-fig gravy and poached pear) are the things that keep diners coming back, and the Mile-High Pie is what makes them stay for dessert.

✪ Commander's Palace

1403 Washington Ave. ☎ **504/899-8221.** Reservations required, sometimes days in advance. Main courses $22–$30; full brunch $20–$32; full dinner $29–$32. AE, CB, DC, MC, V. Mon–Fri 11:30am–2pm; daily 6–10pm; brunch Sat 11:30am–12:30pm and Sun 10:30am–1pm. HAUTE CREOLE.

The unusual, rather grand blue and white Victorian building at the corner of Washington Avenue and Coliseum Street was built as a restaurant in 1880 by Emile

Commander and is now owned by members of the Brennan family. Commander's Palace is a consistent favorite of locals and visitors alike. The patio, fountains, lush tropical plantings, and soft colors are a perfect backdrop for mouthwatering Creole specialties. To start your meal try the Soups 1-1-1, a half serving of turtle soup au sherry, Creole gumbo du jour, and the soup of the day. The corn-fried oysters with shoestring potatoes and a horseradish cream sauce are also excellent. Outstanding entrées include fresh Gulf fish with roasted pecans and a Creole meunière sauce; roasted Mississippi quail with a rock shrimp stuffing and a port-wine sauce; and garlic-crusted seared redfish served with smoked corn succotash topped with vegetable crisps. Commander's also has a nice roast rack of lamb for two with a mint-Madeira demi-glacé. There is an excellent wine list, and the menu offers suggestions with each entrée. If you're a jazz buff, don't miss their famous Jazz Brunch, featuring Joe Simon and his Dixieland band.

✪ Mike's on the Avenue

In the Lafayette Hotel, 628 St. Charles Ave. ☎ **504/523-1709.** Reservations recommended. Main courses at lunch $11–$15, at dinner $18–$26. AE, MC, V. Mon–Fri 11:30am–2pm; daily 6–10pm. NEW AMERICAN.

Located on the ground floor of the Lafayette Hotel, Mike's on the Avenue has become extremely popular with New Orleanians over the past few years. Chef Mike Fennelly is inspired not only in the creation of culinary delights—like his homemade Chinese dumplings filled with shrimp, ginger, and scallions with a Szechuan tahini sauce—but also in the creation of the canvases that decorate the walls of his restaurant. The cuisine, which Mike and his partner, Vicky, like to call eclectic, crosses the borders of many countries. For instance, traditional Louisiana crab cakes are emboldened with the spice of chiles and smoothed by a lobster cream. The pomegranate and rosemary marinated grilled lamb chops with jalapeño mint glaze and baked merlition stuffed phyllo triangles are excellent. Fennelly is daring with spices, and it pays off. Desserts are equally creative. My favorite is the brioche bread pudding. Before making reservations, you should know that this is not the place to go for a quiet, romantic dinner for two: The high ceilings and the prevalence of glass don't absorb the noise in this lively establishment.

Pascal's Manale

1838 Napoleon Ave. ☎ **504/895-4877.** Reservations recommended. Main courses $13.95–$22. AE, DC, DISC, MC, V. Mon–Fri 11:30am–10pm, Sat 4–10pm, Sun 4–9pm. Closed Sun Memorial Day through Labor Day. ITALIAN/STEAKS/SEAFOOD.

Locals still flock to Pascal's Manale for barbecued shrimp. It's crowded, noisy, and verges on expensive, but you'll leave as much a fan as any native. Don't expect fancy decor—the emphasis is on food and conviviality. (Sunday nights feel more like social gatherings than one could reasonably expect at a commercial restaurant.) Pascal's bills itself as an Italian–New Orleans steak house, but the presence of such specialties as veal Marsala, turtle soup, the combination pan roast, and those marvelous barbecued shrimp (a house creation) give the menu a decidedly different slant.

✪ Sazerac

In the Fairmont Hotel, 123 Baronne St. ☎ **504/529-4733.** Reservations recommended. Main courses $14.95–$24.95. Fixed-price $21. AE, CB, DC, DISC, MC, V. Mon–Fri 11:30am–2pm; daily 6–10pm. CREOLE/CONTINENTAL.

Named for New Orleans's most famous cocktail, Sazerac restaurant offers fine dining in one of the city's most elegant settings. The dining room features cut-glass chandeliers, lace-covered tables, and red velvet banquettes. The walls are hung with portraits of New Orleans and Louisiana notables from days gone by. A meal here begins with bread and butter (sculpted in the shape of a rose) and is followed by such appetizers as steak tartare (prepared tableside); grilled Abita quail with braised endive, black currants, and a port wine sauce; or smoked duck and andouille gumbo. Main courses include Louisiana Gulf shrimp (stuffed with lump crabmeat and fresh herbs); roasted rack of lamb (with fresh herbs and a whole-grain mustard crust, accompanied by fresh vegetables); or steak Diane. For dessert go for the sorbet served in illuminated ice swans. Brunch on Sunday features three special menus. The wine list is excellent. Jackets are recommended at dinner.

Upperline

1413 Upperline. ☎ **504/891-9822.** Reservations required. Main courses $8.95–$17.50. AE, DC, MC, V. Mon, Wed–Sun 5:30–9:30pm. ECLECTIC/CREOLE.

Upperline is a small, popular uptown place between St. Charles Avenue and Prytania Street whose walls are decorated with the colorful works of local artists. Chef Richard Benz continues a rich 14-year heritage of a varied, creative, Creole-inspired menu, keeping many old favorites and adding new ones of his own. The restaurant's most popular dishes of late include duck roasted with garlic and served with a port sauce; shrimp with jalapeño cornbread, fried green tomato, and rémoulade sauce; onion crusted redfish; and rack of lamb in a spicy Merlot sauce. If you can't decide, give the seven course "Taste of New Orleans" dinner a try. Upperline also hosts popular seasonal events like the garlic festival (all menu items, including dessert involve the use of garlic), the duck festival, and a Jane Austen dinner. Call ahead to see if one is running during your visit. While you eat you'll be surrounded by New Orleanians and out-of-town visitors alike, as well as lots of fresh flowers. For dessert try the warm honey-pecan bread pudding or the chocolate hazelnut mousse. An award-winning wine list focuses primarily on California selections.

The Versailles

2100 St. Charles Ave. ☎ **504/524-2535.** Reservations recommended. Main courses $20–$29. AE, MC, V. Mon–Sat 6–10pm. FRENCH/CREOLE.

For dining in high style, you just can't equal The Versailles. The lovely St. Charles Room looks out on tree-shaded St. Charles Avenue; the warm, red-walled Marie Antoinette Room is lit with huge cut-glass chandeliers; and the Trianon Room provides elegant seclusion. Of course, ambience is important, but what people really come for is the food. Chef Dennis Hutley creates specialties such as smoked venison with a pinot noir aspic, pan-roasted snapper in an almond crust (served on sautéed crabmeat with a poblano pepper cream sauce), and a delightful weiner schnitzel. Baking is done on the premises (try the hazelnut cake Marjolaine) and the wine cellar is outstanding. Valet parking is free.

MODERATE

Casamento's

4330 Magazine St. ☎ **504/895-9761.** Reservations not accepted. Main courses $2.40–$9.40. No credit cards. Tues–Sun 11:30am–1:30pm and 5:30–9pm. Closed mid-June to mid-Sept. SEAFOOD.

Another of the homey places so loved by people who live in New Orleans is Casamento's. The plain exterior fronts a warm, friendly restaurant decorated with Spanish tiles and lots of plants. Almost always crowded (mostly with locals), Casamento's has an excellent oyster bar and some of the best seafood plates in town at unbelievably low prices. Their oyster loaf is especially good, but then so are the fried soft-shell crabs and anything else that you might order here. Incidentally, don't confuse the oyster loaf with the oyster sandwich—the loaf is made with a large loaf of white bread toasted and buttered and filled with fried oysters and large enough for two; the sandwich comes on regular toast. The same goes for the shrimp loaf and the tenderloined trout loaf.

○ Copeland's

4339 St. Charles Ave. ☎ **504/897-2325.** Reservations recommended. Main courses $8–$15.95. AE, CB, DC, DISC, MC, V. Mon–Fri 11:30am–1:30pm; daily 6–10pm; brunch Sat 11:30am–12:30pm, Sun 10am–12:30pm. CAJUN/CREOLE.

Copeland's, uptown, almost operates on a fast-food basis, yet its dishes are so authentic and fresh that it has gained a loyal local following. The setting is attractive with dark wood, brass, and glass accents; all the ingredients are fresh; and the recipes have been collected from some of New Orleans's leading chefs. Copeland's current chef, George Rhode IV, worked in the kitchens of K-Paul's, Olde N'Awlins Cookery, and his own restaurant, George IV. The consistency of the food here is unsurpassed. Start with the onion mumm, a local favorite, or the hot crab claws. Blackened redfish here is excellent, as is the blackened prime rib. One of my top choices is the grilled chicken with spinach and bacon dressing topped with blue cheese. For dessert, the sweet potato and pecan bread pudding is a delicious twist on the traditional version.

Delmonico Restaurant

1300 St. Charles Ave. ☎ **504/525-4937.** Reservations not required. Main courses $16–$23. AE, DC, DISC, MC, V. Daily 11:30am–9pm. SEAFOOD/STEAKS.

A short streetcar ride from the Quarter, the Delmonico Restaurant was founded in 1895 and has been run by the La Franca family since 1911; many of the dishes on the menu actually come from old family recipes. Today it is overseen by sisters Angie Brown and Rose Dietrich, daughters of Tony Franca, the restaurant's original owner. Delmonico is essentially a comfortable, family style eatery, with a touch of elegance. As a dedicated seafood lover, I favor the trout meunière or the Delmonico seafood kebab (shrimp, oysters, trout, and red snapper), but the steaks, veal, and chicken dishes are also very good. Desserts are simple but acceptable.

Gautreau's

1728 Soniat St. ☎ **504/899-7397.** Reservations recommended. Main courses $12.50–$21. AE, MC, V. Tues–Sat 6–10pm. INTERNATIONAL.

Those of you who knew the old Gautreau's (which, after closing in 1989 was reopened by new owners) won't be disappointed to see that the new Gautreau's warm and modest decor has remained the same: the tin ceiling, the old New Orleans photographs, and the famous apothecary cabinet from the original drugstore that still holds a varied selection of wines. The menu, however, is quite another thing. Chef Rob Mitchell, a graduate of the Culinary Institute of America, has been working at Gautreau's since 1993 and in 1995 became the restaurant's head chef. The chef may have changed, but the quality of the food has not. Menus change seasonally, but if it's on the menu you should try the marinated shrimp and Dungeness crab served with sticky rice and an orange and honey soy sauce to start. Another outstanding choice might be the warm crisped duck confit with sherried flageolets, mustard, and sage. As an entrée, the sautéed tilapia and shrimp with basmati rice, arugula, and chile mango sauce is wonderful, as is the roasted chicken with wild mushrooms, garlic potatoes, and green beans. The pastry chef does a fine honey-orange crème brûlée and a delightful triple layer (chocolate, maple pecan, and almond) cheesecake.

Tavern on the Park

900 City Park Ave. ☎ **504/486-3333.** Reservations recommended. Main courses $15.95–$24.95. AE, CB, DC, JCB, MC, V. Tues–Fri 11:30am–2:30pm and 5–10pm; Sat 5–10pm or later. Closed Sun–Mon. SEAFOOD/STEAKS.

Just across from City Park, within sight of the famous "dueling oaks," the Tavern on the Park is a delightful re-creation of art deco eateries of the Prohibition era and is, in fact, the only remaining building from the Storyville era. The historic building is a marvelous setting for the restaurant's steak and seafood specialties, with broiled cold-water lobster, fresh trout, and superb steaks high on the list of local favorites. Balcony dining is available, weather permitting.

INEXPENSIVE

⑤ Camellia Grill

626 S. Carrollton Ave. ☎ **504/866-9573.** All items under $10. No credit cards. Sun–Thurs 9am–1am, Fri–Sat 9am–3am. HAMBURGERS/SANDWICHES.

If you're out in the Riverbend area, don't bypass the Camellia Grill. It's right on the trolley line and serves a great variety of sandwiches, omelets, salads, and desserts at low to moderate prices. The hamburgers are really special; the sandwiches are stuffed to overflowing with corned beef, ham, or whatever; and the omelets are enormous. This is one place in which you can count on having a filling meal at low cost, and although it's counter service and you may have a short wait for a seat, surprisingly, you'll be given a real linen napkin. That counter service is actually a bonus feature: It provides a front-row contact with the friendly, entertaining waiters on the other side.

7 Metairie

Bozo's

3117 21st St. ☎ **504/831-8666.** Reservations not required. Lunch $5–$10; dinner $12–$16. MC, V. Tues–Sat 11am–3pm; Tues–Thurs 5–10pm, Fri–Sat 5–11pm. CAJUN/SEAFOOD.

New Orleanians have much affection for this plain, unpretentious fish house; it's easy to see why when heaping plates of seafood appear cooked to perfection and served by friendly and efficient waitresses. Fried catfish—crisp and utterly delectable—is lightly breaded with cornmeal. Shrimp, oysters, crawfish, crabs, and almost anything that swims or lives in nearby waters make up the bulk of the menu, which also includes "Mama Bozo's" delectable chicken andouille gumbo; a few steak, chicken, and veal selections; and a good list of sandwiches. The prices are unbelievably low, starting with a bargain gumbo and topping out with the rib-eye steak. It's worth the trip.

Crozier's Restaurant Français

3216 W. Esplanade, N. Metairie. ☎ **504/833-8108.** Reservations recommended. Main courses $15.25–$19.50. AE, DC, DISC, MC, V. Tues–Sat 5:30–10pm. FRENCH.

Authentic French cooking accounts for this restaurant's long-standing popularity. There are no surprises here, just good old-fashioned French cuisine that would make any native French person (particularly those from the south of France) feel right at home. Begin with a very tasty, traditional onion soup or a salad of mixed greens. There's also a nice duck liver pâté and of course, the ever-present escargots. Entrées might include trout with pecans and a fish du jour; however, if you've had enough seafood on this trip to last you a while, chef Gerard Crozier makes a wonderful steak au poivre and an incredible grilled quail with a light demi-glacé. Traditional desserts like crème caramel, mousse au chocolate, and various tartlettes are a nice way to finish a meal here. The wine list is limited but good and moderately priced.

8 Lake Pontchartrain

Bruning's Seafood on the Lake

1924 West End Parkway. ☎ **504/282-9395.** Reservations not accepted Fri–Sat night. Main courses $5.50–$29.95. AE, DISC, MC, V. Sun–Thurs 11am–9:30pm, Fri–Sat 11am–10:30pm. SEAFOOD.

Bruning's has been serving a classic New Orleans seafood menu since 1859, and is now run by fifth- and sixth-generation Brunings who still use traditional family recipes. The fish here is some of the best and freshest around. You'll dine over the water with a beautiful view of Lake Pontchartrain. The broiled seafood is especially good, as is the seafood gumbo, and fried dishes show up grease-free. A good buy, if you can't make up your mind, is the generous seafood platter. There's a children's menu, and all entrées come with salad, toast, and a potato.

9 Coffee, Tea & Sweets

Angelo Brocato's Ice Cream & Confectionery

537 St. Ann St. ☎ **504/525-9676.** All items under $8. No credit cards. Mon–Fri 10am–6pm, Sat 10am–11pm, Sun 9am–8pm. ITALIAN PASTRY.

There's been a Brocato's in New Orleans since 1905, and except for a brief interruption, it has been in the French Quarter. It is the Brocato's on whom the city's most demanding hostesses have depended for three generations to cater those occasions for friends and special guests when sweets must reach the heights of sheer perfection. Happily you'll now find them back in new quarters, serving their fabulous ice cream, Italian ices, cannolis, and a whole feast of other pastries. There's another branch at 214 N. Carrollton Ave. (☎ **504/486-0078**).

✪ Café du Monde

In the French Market, 813 Decatur. ☎ **504/581-2914.** Coffee, milk, hot chocolate, and beignets $1. No credit cards. Daily 24 hrs. Closed Christmas Day. CAFE.

This is one of my favorites, an indispensable part of the New Orleans food scene. Across from Jackson Square and absolutely habit-forming, the delightful Café du Monde has been a favorite with New Orleanians for years. There are only four main items on the menu—coffee (black or au lait), milk, hot chocolate, and beignets (three to a serving)—and each item costs $1. (You can also get a soda served in a big plastic souvenir cup for $1.35.) Beignets (pronounced *bin-YEAS*), the official doughnuts of Louisiana, are square, deep-fried confections that come hot, crisp, and covered with confectioner's sugar. One order and a cup of café au lait can serve as breakfast, lunch, or a light dinner (after one of those "splurge" lunches) for the incredible price of $2. There's an indoor dining room, but sit outside under the awning to take advantage of the Mississippi River breeze and unexcelled people-watching. Besides your fellow diners, there's all of Jackson Square, with horse carriages lined up across from the cafe, as well as shoppers headed for the French Market and the occasional sidewalk musician. You'll find many a native here in the dawn or predawn hours.

La Madeleine

547 St. Ann St. ☎ **504/568-9950.** Pastries 85¢–$2.25; entrées $3.89–$9.25. AE, MC, V. Daily 7am–10pm. FRENCH BAKERY.

La Madeleine, at Chartres Street, is one of the French Quarter's most charming casual eateries. One of a chain of French bakeries, it has a wood-burning brick oven that turns out a wide variety of breads, croissants, and brioches. A glass case up front holds marvelous pastries to take out or eat in the cafeteria section, where quiches, salads, soups, sandwiches, and other light entrées are available. This restaurant is delightful for a continental breakfast or light lunch.

La Marquise

625 Chartres St. ☎ **504/524-0420.** Pastries 82¢–$5. No credit cards. Daily 7am–5pm. PASTRY.

The tiny La Marquise serves French pastries on the premises, either in a crowded front room that also holds the display counter or outside on a small but delightful patio. Maurice Delechelle is the master baker and guiding hand here, and you'd be hard pressed to find more delectable goodies. There are galettes bretonnes (butter cookies); pain au chocolat (a rectangle of croissant dough that has been wrapped around a chocolate bar, then baked); cygne swans (éclairs in the shape of swans filled with whipped cream); choux à la crème (cream puffs); and mille-feuilles (napoleons); as well as croissants, brioches, and a wide assortment of strudels and Danish pastries. La Marquise is almost always crowded; if the patio has no seats available, there's always Jackson Square just a few steps away for a dessert picnic. A larger La Marquise is at 617 Ursulines St.

P. J.'S Coffee & Tea Company

5432 Magazine St. ☎ **504/895-0273.** 80¢–$4. AE, MC, V. Daily 7am–11pm. COFFEE/PASTRIES.

P. J.'s is just the place if you're mad about tea or coffee—some 30 different teas and 47 types of coffee are sold here, where they do their own roasting. You can taste as many as 18 teas and three or four coffees on any given day. Their iced coffee is very special, made by a cold-water process that requires 12 hours of brewing. Their newest addition is granita prepared with P. J.'s own Espresso Dolce iced coffee concentrate frozen with milk and sugar and served as a coffee "slushee"—great on hot muggy days in New Orleans. Assorted pastries are available to go with the brew you choose. P. J.'s is also located at Tulane and Loyola universities, 644 Camp St., 2727 Prytania St., and 637 N. Carrollton Ave.

Royal Blend Coffee & Tea House

623 Royal St. ☎ **504/523-2716.** Pastry 75¢–$2.15; lunch $2.85–$4.95. MC, V (only accepted for orders over $10). Sun–Thurs 7am–8pm, Fri–Sat 7am–midnight. CAFE.

I'm not sure if I fell in love with this place because it's set back off the street and you walk through a courtyard to get to it or because the sparrows come in and eat crumbs off the floor. Whatever my reason, it's a great place. Order your light lunch (sandwiches, quiche, or salad) at the white tile-topped counter and take it out into the courtyard (where on Saturday afternoons, weather permitting, a guitarist serenades diners) to eat or stay inside at a blue and white tiled table. If you're just in the mood for coffee and pastry, they've got plenty of that, too, and the pastry menu changes daily. Royal Blend is also located at 222 Carondelet St. and at 244 Metairie Rd. in Metairie.

What to See & Do in New Orleans

8

In many respects the French Quarter *is* New Orleans—it's where it all began and is still the city's most popular sightseeing spot; many visitors never leave its confines. But I think that's a mistake. Sightseeing excursions into areas outside the French Quarter will allow you to feel the pulse of the city's commerce, see river activities that keep the city alive, stroll through spacious parks, drive or walk by the impressive homes of the Garden District, and get a firsthand view of the bayou/lake connection that explains why New Orleans grew up here in the first place.

At press time the Aquarium of the Americas had just completed an expansion with the addition of its new IMAX theater (the first ever to be housed in an aquarium). The Audubon Institute was working on an expansion that will include a 16-acre riverfront park (stretching from the Governor Nicholls and Mandeville Street Wharves), an open-air museum, a themed playground, and a performance pavilion. The greatest feature of the new riverfront park will be the living science museum that will include an insectarium and a butterfly pavilion. The Audubon Institute expects to display close to a million species of insects. The insectarium and riverfront park are scheduled to open in late 1996. In addition, a brand-new baseball stadium for the city's minor league team, the New Orleans Zephyrs, has recently been completed. Plans are also underway for the building of other sports facilities around the city.

Remember not to allow the quaintness of the city to deaden your safety senses—New Orleans is a major metropolis, with the usual urban crime problems. Particular areas to steer clear of at night include the outer edges of the French Quarter, the Garden District, and the cemeteries. Try not to walk alone at night, and stay in well-lit, heavily trafficked areas—better yet, take a cab.

SUGGESTED ITINERARIES

If You Have 1 Day

If you've got only one day in New Orleans, don't despair: The city is small enough for you to be able to get a taste of what it's all about in one day.

New Orleans Attractions

Aquarium of the Americas **9**
Beauregard-Keyes House **26**
Cabildo **19**
Confederate Museum **3**
Contemporary Arts Center **4**
Gallier House Museum **27**
Harrah's Temporary Casino **14**
Historic French Market **29**
Historic New Orleans Collection **16**

Lafayette No. 1 Cemetery **2**
Louisiana Children's Museum **5**
Louisiana Science Center **7**
Louisiana Superdome **1**
Musée Conti Wax Museum **15**
New Orleans
 Convention Center **6**
New Orleans Historic
 Voodoo Museum **25**

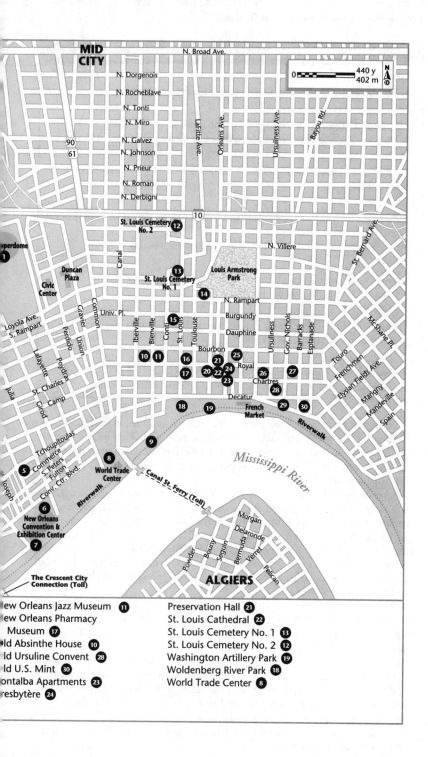

MID CITY

N. Broad Ave.

N. Dorgenois
N. Rocheblave
N. Tonti
N. Miro
N. Galvez
N. Johnson
N. Prieur
N. Roman
N. Derbigni

LaFitte Ave.
Orleans Ave.
Ursulines Ave.
Bayou Rd.

90
61

0   440 y
    402 m

N

10

St. Louis Cemetery No. 2 ⑫

uperdome ❶

Duncan Plaza

Canal

Civic Center

Loyola Ave.
S. Rampart

Gravier
Common
Union
Perdido
Poydras

Lafayette
St. Charles
Camp
Julia
Girod

Tchoupitoulas
Commerce
S. Peters
Fulton
Conv. Ctr. Blvd.

Univ. Pl.

St. Louis Cemetery No. 1 ⑬

⑭

Louis Armstrong Park

N. Villere

N. Rampart

Burgundy

Dauphine

Bourbon

Iberville
Bienville
Conti
St. Louis
Toulouse

⑮

⑩ ⑪   ⑯

⑰

⑳ ㉒ ㉓ ㉔ ㉑

㉕ Royal

Chartres

㉖

㉘

Decatur

Ursulines
Gov. Nichols
Barracks
Esplanade

Touro
Frenchmen
Elysian Fields Ave.
Marigny
Mandeville
Spain

McShane Pl.

St. Bernard Ave.

㉗

⑱   ⑲   French Market

㉙ ㉚

Riverwalk

⑨

Mississippi River

❽ World Trade Center

Canal St. Ferry (Toll)

Riverwalk

❺

❻

New Orleans Convention & Exhibition Center

❼

. Joseph

The Crescent City Connection (Toll)

Morgan
Delaronde
Powder
Bouny
Seguin
Bermuda
Verret
Pelican

ALGIERS

123

What's Special About New Orleans

Monuments
- Jackson Square Monument, in the heart of the French Quarter.

Buildings
- St. Louis Cathedral, on the edge of Jackson Square.
- The Old U.S. Mint, on Esplanade Avenue behind the old French Market.

Museums
- The New Orleans Historic Voodoo Museum, one of the only places like it in the United States.

Parks/Gardens
- Audubon Park, across from Tulane and Loyola universities, just off the streetcar line.
- City Park, with a wealth of activities as well as natural beauty.

Events/Festivals
- Mardi Gras, one of New Orleans's biggest and most spectacular events.
- Jazz Fest, hosting thousands of musicians every year.

Religious Shrines
- The tomb of the 19th-century voodoo queen Marie Laveau, a religious shrine to countless admirers who visit yearly.

Great Neighborhoods
- New Orleans's historic French Quarter, or Vieux Carré.
- The beautiful Garden District, with its old southern plantation homes.

I'd suggest that you get there early in the morning and head to Café du Monde for beignets and coffee. Then follow the walking tour of the French Quarter given in Chapter 9, which shouldn't take too long and will give you a nice sampling of New Orleans architecture, history, and shopping. For lunch, pick one of the restaurants that appeals to you along the way.

After you've had lunch, hop on the St. Charles Avenue streetcar; as you ride, follow along with the streetcar tour given in this book (see Chapter 9). If you're up for another walking tour, try either the tour of the Lower Garden District or the tour of the Garden District, also given in Chapter 9. They average about the same walking time as the French Quarter walking tour, but there aren't any shops, restaurants, or museums to distract you. Whatever you do, be sure to ride the streetcar all the way to the end of the line because you'll see some interesting architecture along the way and you'll get a real feel for the city.

When you get back from the afternoon's activities, you'll probably have a little time to go back to the hotel, rest for a bit, and wash up for dinner. I suggest dining somewhere in the French Quarter. Chapter 7 can help you choose a restaurant if there's not one you've already set your heart on.

After dinner, take a walk over to Bourbon Street—it should be in full swing by the time you finish your meal. If it's jazz you're looking for, it's a little difficult to find these days; however, there are two places right in the French Quarter that you might enjoy: The Palm Court Café on Decatur Street and Preservation Hall on St. Peter (see Chapter 11 for details on both).

If rock 'n' roll's more your style, you'll have no trouble finding it all along Bourbon Street—just pop in to any of the clubs.

Finally, before you go back to your hotel for a good night's sleep, make a stop at Lafitte's Blacksmith Shop on the corner of Bourbon and St. Philip (see Chapter 11 for details) for a nightcap. This is a place you really shouldn't miss, especially in the fall or winter—it has a working fireplace and is the perfect spot in which to unwind after a long day.

If You Have 2 Days

A two-day stay in New Orleans will probably be a lot less tiring than trying to see this fabulous city in only one day.

Day 1   I'd suggest that you take your time on the French Quarter walking tour I've worked out for you. Spend some time poking around in the galleries, shops, and museums. If you get up early you can either try to finish before lunch or work your way around to the French Market, where you might grab something on your way through, or maybe stop at Central Grocery for a muffaletta sandwich and either eat it there or, if it's warm enough, take it over to the banks of the Mississippi and watch the barges and steamboats chugging through the muddy waters.

After lunch, I'd suggest a trip over to the Aquarium of the Americas or perhaps a ride on one of the steamboats (most of them leave around 2pm; refer to "Organized Tours" later in this chapter for exact times and prices). By the time you're finished with that, you'll want to go back to the hotel for a break, then enjoy dinner, and then sample some nightlife (see Chapter 11 for details).

Day 2   If you'd like to get out of the Quarter and explore some of the Garden District, get on the streetcar and head out toward the Riverbend area. Take your time, getting out when you see something that interests you. On the way back to the Vieux Carré, stop in the Garden District and follow the walking tour supplied in Chapter 9 of this book. If you just can't get enough of that wonderful Victorian architecture and your legs can stand it, go ahead and do the walking tour of the Lower Garden District.

If you're not interested in architecture but are interested in art and antiques, I suggest that you head out to Magazine Street and nose around in the antique shops (see Chapter 10 for a listing of shops). On your way back, stop on Julia Street and go gallery hopping (see Chapter 10 for details), then head over to the Contemporary Arts Center (see "Museums and Galleries," below).

If you're out in this area late enough to be hungry for dinner, there are plenty of places to eat, so don't think you have to hurry back to the French Quarter, although you might want to do that to take in some nightlife later—after a couple of hurricanes at Pat O'Brien's in the Vieux Carré, you won't be feeling your throbbing feet any longer.

If You Have 3 Days

Days 1–2   Follow "If You Have Two Days," above.

Day 3   Do some exploring on the other side of the Quarter. Check out Esplanade Avenue with the walking tour listed in Chapter 9. Explore St. Louis Cemetery No. 3 (best not to go alone—try to join a guided tour using my suggestions later in this chapter) and City Park. Head back to the Quarter and check out the shops and sights you missed but wanted to see the last two days. Try a new spot for lunch, and go for a ride around the city in a horse-drawn buggy.

When evening comes, head over to Frenchmen Street to Alberto's (if you're in the mood for Italian cuisine) or the Praline Connection (if you'd rather have soul food) for dinner. There's a great place nearby to go to hear some jazz: Snug Harbor (see Chapter 11).

1 The French Quarter

The narrow old streets of the French Quarter are lined with ancient buildings (many a century and a half old) whose fronts are embellished with that distinctive lacy iron-work. Their carriage drives or alleyways are often guarded by more ironwork in the form of massive gates; through them you can often catch glimpses of some of the love-liest courtyards in the world. Secluded from street noises and nosy neighbors, the courtyards provide beauty, relaxation, and privacy—three qualities that have always been important to New Orleanians—and ventilate the homes. Of course, many of these venerable buildings now serve as entertainment centers that often ring with merriment that is anything but restful; and many more now house shops of every description. But above ground level most also have apartments (many quite luxurious), keeping to the old-world custom of combining commercial ventures with living space. A few are still in the hands of original-owner families.

Thanks to the Vieux Carré Commission, not even "progress" is allowed to intrude on a heritage that blends gaiety with graciousness, the rowdiness of Bourbon Street with the quiet residential areas, and the busyness of commerce with the sense of lei-sure and goodwill. Progress is here, all right, with all its attendant benefits, but New Orleans insists that it conform to the city's traditional way of life, not the other way around. There's not even a traffic light within the whole of the French Quarter—they're relegated to fringe streets—and street lights are of the old gaslight style. Do not worry about those absent traffic lights—automobiles are banned from Royal and Bourbon streets during a good part of the day, making these streets pedestrian malls, and the area around Jackson Square is a permanent haven for foot traffic because no vehicles are allowed.

Laid out in 1718 in an almost perfect rectangle by a French royal engineer named Adrien de Pauger, the French Quarter is easy to get around. And even in these high-crime days, you're relatively safe wandering its streets during daylight hours. After dark, as in most metropolitan areas, it's best to exercise caution when walking alone outside the centers of activity—in New Orleans, that means Bourbon, Royal, and Chartres streets and the streets that connect them (there's safety as well as fun in the numbers that throng those streets all night long).

Since this area is one of the major attractions in New Orleans, I would suggest that you turn to Chapter 9 and do the walking tour of the French Quarter. It will give you the best overview in terms of historic buildings and the city's history. Many other attractions that aren't covered in the walking tour will be covered in this chapter.

✪ Aquarium of the Americas
1 Canal St. ☎ **504/861-2537.** Aquarium $10.50 adults, $8 seniors, $5 children 2–12. IMAX $7.50 adults, $6.50 seniors, $5 children. Combination tickets $15 adults, $12 seniors, $9 children. Aquarium Sun–Thurs 9:30am–6pm, Fri–Sat 9:30am–7pm. IMAX Sun–Thurs 10am–6pm, Fri–Sat 10am–8pm. Shows every hour on the hour. Last ticket sold one hour before closing.

The one million-gallon Aquarium of the Americas is located on the banks of the Mississippi River, right on the edge of the French Quarter. Five major exhibit areas and dozens of smaller aquarium displays hold a wonderful collection of fish from North, Central, and South America and are exhibited in environments that mimic their natural ones. You can take a walk through the underwater tunnel in the Car-ibbean Reef exhibit and feel like you're swimming with the fish. A re-creation of the Gulf of Mexico houses a sampling of fish that you would see if you were swimming around in the Gulf—chances are you'll think twice about that after you've seen the sharks! There's also a wonderful tropical rain forest with piranha and tropical birds, plus a penguin exhibit. The aquarium has just added a 350-seat IMAX theater and a 12,000-square-foot changing exhibit gallery.

The Historic French Market
On Decatur St., just down from Jackson Square.

Legend has it that the French Market was originally used by the Native Americans as a bartering market. In 1812 it began to grow as an official market and in two later stages (one in 1822 and one in 1872) it was expanded. Today you'll find all sorts of shops lining the street here. Down toward the end there's a Farmer's Market where you can get everything from fresh produce and fresh fish to hot sauces, Cajun/ Creole mixes, and beignet mix. The Farmer's Market also has a few coffee and take-out stands, as well as souvenir shops. It's open 24 hours daily. The Flea Market, just a bit further down from the farmer's market, is a great place to shop for mementos and gifts for your friends back home. T-shirts, jewelry, hats, belts, crystals, and sunglasses are just some of the things you'll find as you browse among the tables here. It's a good place to test your bargaining skills. The Flea Market is open daily.

St. Louis Cathedral
615 Père Antoine's Alley ☎ **504/525-9585.** Free tours Mon–Sat 9am–5pm, Sun 1:30–5pm.

The oldest active cathedral in the United States, St. Louis Cathedral virtually dominates Jackson Square. This is actually the third building to stand on this spot. A hurricane destroyed the first in 1722. Then, on Good Friday 1788, the bells of its replacement were kept silent for religious reasons rather than ringing out the alarm for a fire that eventually went out of control and burned down more than 850 buildings, and the cathedral was once again destroyed. Rebuilt in 1794, largely through the generosity of Don Almonester (who is buried in front of St. Joseph's shrine on the right as you face the altar), it was remodeled and enlarged between 1845 and 1851 by J. N. B. de Pouilly. It is of Spanish design, with a tower at each end and a higher central tower, and its construction is of brick covered with stucco to protect the mortar from dampness. Inside, look for the six stained-glass windows depicting the life of St. Louis (French King Louis IX), the cathedral's patron saint. There's also a spectacular painting on the wall above and behind the main altar, showing St. Louis proclaiming the Seventh Crusade from the steps of Notre Dame.

HISTORIC BUILDINGS

✪ Old Absinthe House
240 Bourbon St. ☎ **504/523-3181.** Free admission. Daily 10am–2am.

Two blocks from Canal Street, the Old Absinthe House was built in 1806 by two Spaniards and is still owned by their descendants (although they live in Spain and have nothing to do with running the place). The drink for which it was named is outlawed in this country now, but with a little imagination you can sip a modern-day libation and visualize Andrew Jackson and the Lafitte brothers plotting the desperate defense of New Orleans in 1815. It's the custom here to put your calling card on the wall, and the hundreds and hundreds of browning cards form a covering not unlike tattered wallpapers. It was a speakeasy during Prohibition, and when federal officers closed it in 1924, the interior was mysteriously stripped of its antique fixtures, including the long marble-topped bar and the old water dripper (used to drip water into absinthe), all of which just as mysteriously reappeared down the street at a corner establishment called, oddly enough, the Old Absinthe House Bar (400 Bourbon). It, too, follows the calling-card custom. If you can't keep all that straight, just remember that if you're in an Old Absinthe House that doesn't have entertainment, you're in the original *house*—if you see that grand brass water dripper on a marble-topped bar, you're in the new home of the original bar and fixtures.

Beauregard-Keyes House

1113 Chartres St. ☎ **504/523-7257.** Admission $4 adults, $3 seniors and students, $1.50 children 12 and under. Mon–Sat 10am–3pm. Tours are offered on the hour.

This "raised cottage," with its Doric columns and handsome twin staircases, was built in 1826 as a residence by a wealthy New Orleans auctioneer, Joseph Le Carpentier. La Carpentier was grandfather to world-famous chess champion Paul Morphy, who was born to his daughter in 1837. Confederate Gen. P. G. T. Beauregard lived in the house with several members of his family for 18 months between 1865 and 1867. From 1944 until 1970 it was the residence of Frances Parkinson Keyes, who wrote many novels about this region. One of them, *Madame Castel's Lodger,* is directly concerned with the general's stay in the house. *Dinner at Antoine's,* perhaps her most famous novel, also was written here. Mrs. Keyes left the house to a foundation, and the house, rear buildings, and garden are now open to the public. The gift shop has a wide selection of Frances Parkinson Keyes's novels.

Cabildo

701 Chartres St. ☎ **504/568-6968.** Admission $4 adults, $3 students and seniors, children 12 and under free. Tues–Sun 9am–5pm.

On Jackson Square, the Cabildo is the site of the signing of the Louisiana Purchase Transfer. Reopened in 1994 following an extensive restoration in the wake of a fire, the National Historic Landmark now houses a comprehensive new exhibit that traces Louisiana's past from exploration through the Civil War and Reconstruction from a multicultural perspective.

Gallier House Museum

1132 Royal St. ☎ **504/523-6722.** Admission $4 adults, $3 seniors and students, $2.25 children 5–11, children under 5 free. Mon–Sat 10am–4:30pm, Sun noon–4:30pm. Last tour begins at 4pm.

The Gallier House Museum was built by James Gallier Jr. as his residence in 1857. The carefully restored town house contains an early working bathroom, a passive ventilation system, and furnishings of the period. The adjoining building houses historical exhibits, as well as films on decorative plaster work, ornamental ironwork, wood-graining, and marbling. There is also a gift shop, a cafe, and plenty of free parking at the museum. Special seasonal programs are available.

Old Ursuline Convent

1114 Chartres St. ☎ **504/529-3040.** Admission $4 adults, $2 students and seniors, children under 8 free. Tours Tues–Fri 10 and 11am and 1, 2, and 3pm; Sat–Sun 11:15am, 1, and 2pm.

Across from the Beauregard-Keyes House is the Archbishop Antoine Blanc Memorial, which includes the Old Ursuline Convent. The Sisters of Ursula were for years the only teachers and nurses in New Orleans—they established the first schools for Catholic girls, for African Americans, and for Native Americans, and they set up the first orphanage in Louisiana. The nuns moved out of the convent in 1824 (they're in an uptown location these days), and in 1831, the state legislature met here. It now houses Catholic archives dating from 1718. Especially noteworthy is the fact that this is the oldest building of record not only in New Orleans but also in the entire Mississippi Valley, and it is the only surviving building from the French colonial effort in what is now the United States. Included in the complex is the beautiful restored old Chapel of the Archbishops, erected in 1845, and still used as a house of worship.

The Old U.S. Mint

400 Esplanade Ave. ☎ **504/568-6968.** Admission $4 adults, $3 seniors and students, children under 12 free. Tues–Sun 9am–5pm.

The Old U.S. Mint houses exhibits on New Orleans jazz and on the city's Carnival celebrations. These displays contain a comprehensive collection of pictures, musical instruments, and other artifacts connected with jazz greats—Louis Armstrong's first trumpet is here. Across the hall there's a stunning array of Carnival mementos, from ornate Mardi Gras costumes to a street scene complete with maskers and a parade float. Entrances to the Mint are on both Esplanade Avenue and Barracks Street.

Pontalba Apartments

In the 1850 House, 523 St. Ann St. ☎ **504/568-6968.** Admission $4 adults, $3 seniors and students, children 12 and under free. Tues–Sun 10am–5pm.

These historic apartments are located in the Lower Pontalba Buildings, in a restored house of the period. They're authentically furnished from parlor to kitchen to servants' quarters.

Presbytère

751 Chartres St. ☎ **504/568-6968.** Admission $4 adults, $3 seniors and students, children 12 and under free. Tues–Sun 9am–5pm.

Located on Jackson Square, the Presbytère was planned as housing for the clergy but was never used for that purpose. It exhibits the paintings of Louisianan artists as well as displays on local history and culture.

Spring Fiesta Historic House

826 St. Ann St. ☎ **504/945-0322** (use ☎ 581-1367 on Fri.) $4 donation requested. By appointment only.

This historic mid–19th-century town house is owned by the New Orleans Spring Fiesta Association. It is furnished with lovely antiques of the Victorian era and many outstanding objets d'art from New Orleans's golden age of the 1800s. It's a lovely peek backward in time.

MUSEUMS

In addition to the museums listed here, you might be interested in visiting the Germaine Wells Mardi Gras Museum, located at 813 Bienville St. (on the second floor of Antoine's Restaurant), where you'll find a private collection of Mardi Gras costumes and ball gowns dating from around 1910 to 1960. Admission is free, and the museum is open during restaurant hours. The House of Broel in the Garden District (see Chapter 9, "Walking Tour 2," Stop 1) also displays a few Mardi Gras costumes, as does the Old U.S. Mint (see "Historic Buildings" above), which also houses a collection of jazz memorabilia.

✪ Historic New Orleans Collection—Museum/Research Center

533 Royal St. ☎ **504/523-4662.** Free admission. Tours $2, given Tues–Sat at 10 and 11am and 2 and 3pm. Wheelchair accommodation is available. Tues–Sat 10am–4:45pm. Closed major holidays and Mardi Gras.

The Historic New Orleans Collection is located within a complex of historic French Quarter buildings. The oldest, constructed in the late 18th century, is one of the few structures to escape the disastrous fire of 1794. Today, the collection serves the public as a museum and research center for state and local history with history-related gifts in the shop. The Williams Gallery, free to the public, presents changing exhibitions that focus on Louisiana's history and culture. Guided tours are available of both the founders' residence, one of the "hidden" houses of the Vieux Carré, and the Louisiana History Galleries. The History Gallery Tour is a must for all visitors who would like to learn more about Louisiana's colorful and exciting past.

Musée Conti Wax Museum

917 Conti St. ☎ **504/525-2605.** Admission $5.75 adults, $5.25 seniors over 62, $3.50 children 4–17, children under 4 are free. Daily 10am–5pm. Closed Christmas and Mardi Gras Day.

This museum offers New Orleans history depicted by life-size wax figures with authentic costumes and settings of Louisiana legends (Andrew Jackson, Jean Lafitte, Huey Long, Louis Armstrong, and Pete Fountain), plus an added "Haunted Dungeon" illustrating well-known horror tales. You'll also be able to see fabulous Mardi Gras Indian costumes.

✪ New Orleans Historic Voodoo Museum

724 Dumaine St. ☎ **504/522-5223.** Admission $5 adults, $4 students and seniors. French Quarter tour $18 per person, cemetery tour $10 per person. Daily 10am–dusk.

If tales of Marie Laveau have captured your imagination, you'll definitely want to stop by the Voodoo Museum, in the heart of the Vieux Carré. The dark, musty interior seems exactly the right setting for artifacts of the occult from all over the globe and a fitting place in which to learn more of that curious mixture of African and Catholic religions and rituals brought to New Orleans in the late 1700s by former Santo Domingan slaves.

There's a guided voodoo walking tour of the French Quarter that leaves the museum at 1pm daily and visits Congo Square (now Beauregard Square) and a pharmacy displaying voodoo potions. There is another tour that leaves at 1:30pm and takes you on a visit to Marie Laveau's reputed grave. The museum can arrange psychic readings and visits to voodoo rituals if you want to delve deeper into this subject, which has bedeviled New Orleans for centuries.

New Orleans Pharmacy Museum

514 Chartres St. ☎ **504/565-8027.** Admission $2 adults, $1 seniors and students, children under 12 are admitted free. Tues–Sun 10am–5pm.

Founded in 1950, the New Orleans Pharmacy Museum is an interesting stop on a tour of the French Quarter. In 1823, the first licensed pharmacist in the United States, Louis J. Dufilho, Jr., opened an apothecary shop here at 514 Chartres St. The Creole-style town house doubled as his home, and in the interior courtyard he cultivated the herbs he would need for fabricating his medicines. Inside the museum you'll find old apothecary bottles, pill tile, and suppository molds as well as the old glass cosmetics counter (pharmacists of the 1800s also manufactured make-up and perfumes). There's even an 1855 black and rose Italian marble soda fountain.

PARKS

Washington Artillery Park

Between Jackson Square and the Mississippi River. ☎ **504/529-5284.** Free admission. Dawn to dusk.

Just past Jackson Brewery, pretty riverside Washington Artillery Park, with its splashing fountains, has always been a "promenade" for New Orleanians, and now the elevated area has been renamed the Moon Walk (for Mayor "Moon" Landrieu).

There are attractive plantings and benches from which to view the city's main industry—its busy port (second only to Amsterdam for tonnage handled each year). To your right you will see the Greater New Orleans Bridge and the World Trade Center of New Orleans (formerly the International Trade Mart) skyscraper, as well as the Toulouse Street wharf, departure point for excursion steamboats.

Woldenberg River Park

Along the Mississippi River in the French Quarter. ☎ **504/861-2537.** Free admission. Dawn to dusk.

Some 13 acres of the riverfront, from Canal Street to St. Peter Street, have been converted into the Woldenberg River Park. This oasis of greenery in the heart of the city is centered by a large lawn, with a brick promenade leading to the Mississippi and more than 600 trees—oaks, magnolias, willows, and crape myrtles—and 1,400 shrubs to beautify this tranquil spot. The park is now the setting for the Aquarium of the Americas (see above).

2 Outside the French Quarter

UPTOWN & THE GARDEN DISTRICT

Outside the borders of the French Quarter lies "American" New Orleans. It came into being because of Creole snobbery. You see, those semiaristocratic French Quarter natives had no use for the crass Americans who came flooding into the city after the 1803 Louisiana Purchase, so they presented a united and closed front to keep "their" New Orleans exclusive. Not to be outdone, the newcomers simply bought up land in what had been the old Gravier plantation upriver from Canal Street and set about building their New Orleans. Exhibiting the celebrated Yankee flair for enterprise, they very soon dominated the business scene, centered on Canal Street itself, and constructed mansions different from the traditional Quarter residences but surrounded by beautiful gardens. In 1833, what we now know as the Garden District was incorporated as Lafayette City, and—thanks in large part to the New Orleans–Carrollton Railroad, which covered the route of today's St. Charles Avenue trolley—the Americans kept right on expanding until they reached the tiny resort town of Carrollton. It wasn't until 1852 that the various sections came together officially to become a united New Orleans.

To become better acquainted with another of the city's main areas of interest, turn to Chapter 9 and take one of the walking tours of the Garden District or follow the streetcar tour.

✪ Superdome

1500 block of Poydras St. ☎ **504/587-3810** for tour information. Hourly guided tours run daily 10am–4pm (except during events). Admission $6 adults, $5 seniors, $4 children ages 5–10; free for children under 5.

As tall as a 27-story building, with a seating capacity of 76,000, the windowless structure has a computerized climate-control system that uses more than 9,000 *tons* of equipment. It is one of the largest buildings in the world in diameter (680 feet), and its grounds cover some 13 acres. Inside, no posts obstruct the view for spectator sports such as football, baseball, and basketball, and movable partitions and seats give it the flexibility to form the best configuration for almost any event. Most people think of the Superdome as a sports center only, but this big flying saucer of a building plays host to conventions, trade shows, and large theatrical and musical productions as well. Entertainment and instant replays are provided via two Diamond Vision screens.

Bayou St. John & Lake Pontchartrain

Bayou St. John is one of the most important reasons New Orleans is where it is today. When Jean-Baptiste Le Moyne, Sieur de Bienville, was commissioned to establish a settlement that would protect the mouth of the Mississippi River for the French Crown against British expansion, he recognized the strategic importance of the "back-door" access to the Gulf of Mexico provided by the bayou's linkage to Lake Pontchartrain. Boats could enter the lake from the Gulf, then follow the bayou to within easy portage distance of the mouth of the Mississippi River. Area Native American tribes had used this route for years, and Bienville was quick to see its advantages.

The path from city to bayou back in those early days is today's Bayou Road, an extension of Governor Nicholls Street in the French Quarter. The modern-day Gentilly Boulevard, which crosses the bayou, was another Native American trail— it led around the lake and on to settlements in Florida after a relatively short boat trip.

As the new town grew and prospered, planters moved out along the shores of the bayou, and in the early 1800s a canal was dug to connect the waterway with the city. It reached a basin at the edge of Congo Square. The lake itself became a popular recreation area, with fine restaurants and dance halls (as well as meeting places for voodoo practitioners, who held secret ceremonies along its shores). Gradually the city reached out beyond the French Quarter and enveloped the whole area—farmlands, plantation homes, and resorts. So on your exploration of this part of New Orleans, you'll see traces of that development. The canal is gone, filled in long ago, and the bayou itself is no longer navigable (even if it were, bridges were built too low to per-mit the passage of boats of any size), but residents still prize their waterfront sites, and rowboats and sailboats make use of the bayou's surface.

The simplest way to reach the Bayou St. John from the French Quarter is to drive straight out Esplanade Avenue about 20 blocks. Just before you reach the bayou, you'll pass St. Louis Cemetery No. 3 (it's just past Leda Street), at which rest many prominent New Orleanians—among them are Thomy Lafon, the black philanthro-pist who bought the old Orleans Ballroom as an orphanage for African-American children and thus put an end to its infamous "quadroon balls," and Father Adrien Rouquette, who lived and worked among the Choctaw. Just past the cemetery, Esplanade reaches Moss Street, and a left turn will put you on that street, which runs along the banks of Bayou St. John.

Drive along Wisner Boulevard, along the bank of Bayou St. John, and you'll pass some of New Orleans's grandest modern homes, which provide a sharp contrast to those over on Moss Street. Stay on Wisner to Robert E. Lee Boulevard, turn right, and drive to Elysian Fields Avenue, then turn left. That's Louisiana State University's New Orleans campus on your left (its main campus is in Baton Rouge).

Turn left onto the broad concrete highway that is Lakeshore Drive. It runs for $5^1/2$ miles along the lake, and in summer the parkway alongside its seawall is usually swarming with swimmers and picnickers. On the other side are more luxurious, ultramodern residences.

Lake Pontchartrain itself is some 40 miles long and 25 miles wide. Native Americans once lived along its shores on both sides, and it was a major waterway long before white people were seen in this hemisphere. You can drive across it over the Greater New Orleans Causeway, the $23^3/4$-mile-long bridge, the longest in the world.

When you cross the mouth of the Bayou St. John, you'll be where the old Span-ish Fort was built in 1770. Its remains are now nestled amidst elegant modern homes. In the early 1800s there was a lighthouse here, and in the 1820s a railroad brought

New Orleanians out to a hotel, a casino, a bandstand, bathing houses, and restaurants that made this a popular resort area.

Look for the Mardi Gras fountain on your left. Bronze plaques around its base are inscribed with the names of Mardi Gras krewes, and if you time your lake visit to coincide with sundown, you'll see the fountain beautifully lit in Mardi Gras colors of purple (for justice), green (for faith), and gold (for power).

Down at the end of Lakeshore Drive, when you come to the old white coast guard lighthouse, you'll know you've reached West End. This is an interesting little park that's home for several yacht clubs, a marina, and restaurants, many of which have been here for years and look just like lakeside restaurants should (not too fancy—more interested in the view out over the water and good eating than in "decorator-style" interiors). This old fishing community has, over the years, become the main pleasure-boating center of New Orleans, and the Southern Yacht Club here was established in 1840, making it the second oldest in the country. After the railroad began bringing pleasure-seekers here from the city in the 1870s, showboats and floating circuses would often pull up and dock for waterside performances. West End is an excellent place to stop for a bite to eat, if indeed it isn't your destination when you set out for the lakeside with a fresh seafood dinner in mind.

To reach Buckstown, which lines the bank of a narrow canal behind the restaurants on the western side of West End park, turn to the left on Lakeshore Drive at the coast guard station, then turn right on Lake Avenue (it's the first street you come to). Buckstown is another small fishing community that still retains its old-time atmosphere. There are also many good seafood restaurants here.

CEMETERIES

In the beginning, burials were made along the banks of the Mississippi, but when the little settlement of New Orleans began to grow, more cemetery space was a necessity. However, there was a big problem: The soggy ground was so damp that graves would fill with water even before the coffins could be lowered. To solve that problem aboveground tombs were constructed. The coffin would be put in place on the ground, walls of brick would be built around it, and then the walls would be plastered and whitewashed. The entrances to the tombs were closed by marble tablets, and many were enclosed with iron fences. Some were even finished off with rounded roofs or topped with eaves—like tiny, windowless houses. It is easy to see why the cemeteries came to be called "Cities of the Dead" because they are arranged along narrow paths, many of which have "street" names. These miniature cities even have their "skyscrapers," since upper floors would be added as members of the same family passed away and were entombed right on top of the existing vault. Along the outer walls of the cemeteries, you'll see rows of wall vaults, or "ovens," which hold the remains of the city's poor. Incidentally, you may be perplexed by the long list of names for just one tomb—that's because, to economize on space, New Orleanians use the same tomb over and over, simply moving the old remains to a lower level after two years have passed and interring a fresh body in the vacated space.

St. Louis Cemetery No. 1, in the 400 block of Basin Street, was the first, established in the 1740s; you may be familiar with it through the film *Easy Rider*. Marie

Laveau I spends eternity here—followers mark her grave located just a few steps from the Basin Street entrance with red crosses. **St. Louis Cemetery No. 2** is a few blocks away down from Conti Street on Claiborne Avenue (from Iberville to St. Louis streets). If you see one of the unmarked "ovens" with red crosses on its concrete slab, that's the place where Marie Laveau II, daughter of the original voodoo queen, may be resting from her voodoo activities (though almost all other Protestant and Catholic cemeteries in town also claim to house her remains). It seems that no matter how many times the slab is painted over, the faithful keep coming back to mark it and ask Marie's favors. **Lafayette No. 1 Cemetery** is in the Garden District bounded by Washington, Prytania, and Coliseum streets. Perhaps the most beautiful of all is **Metairie Cemetery,** at the intersection of Pontchartrain Boulevard and Metairie Road—and it wouldn't be here at all except for one New Orleanian's pique at being denied admission to the exclusive Metairie Jockey Club at the racetrack that once operated on these grounds. He was an American who, to strike back at those uppity Creoles who wouldn't let him in, bought up the land, turned it into a burial ground, and swore that from then on only the dead would gain admittance.

Before leaving this subject, I must add one word of warning. Because a lot of crime has been associated with the cemeteries, particularly St. Louis Cemeteries No. 1 and No. 2, it is best not to walk in them alone. Join one of the walking tours listed under "Organized Tours," later in this chapter, if you're interested in viewing the tombs up close.

CHURCHES

Sometimes people don't realize that St. Louis Cathedral (see "The French Quarter," above) isn't the only church in New Orleans. Below, you'll find a few others that you might want to stop in and have a look at.

St. Alphonsus Church
2029 Constance St. ☎ **504/522-6748.**

The Irish built St. Alphonsus Church in 1855, and the gallery and columns may vaguely remind you of the St. Louis Cathedral in the French Quarter. A beloved Redemptorist priest, Fr. Francis Xavier Seeles, is buried in the church. He is credited with the working of many miracles; if you visit the church, you're likely to see letters of petition on his tomb.

St. Patrick's Church
724 Camp St. ☎ **504/525-4413.**

St. Patrick's was founded in a tiny wooden building to serve Irish Catholics in the parish. The present building, begun in 1838, was constructed around the old one, which was then dismantled inside the new building. The distinguished architect James Gallier Sr. designed much of the interior, including the altar. It opened in 1840, proudly proclaimed as the "American" Catholics' answer to the St. Louis Cathedral in the French Quarter (where, according to the Americans, God spoke only in French).

Church of St. John the Baptist
1139 Dryades St. ☎ **504/525-1726.**

Because you wouldn't be human if you didn't wonder about that gilded dome so prominent against the skyline (especially as you drive on the elevated expressway), I'm including the Church of St. John the Baptist. It was built by the Irish in 1871, and its most noteworthy features (besides the exceptional brickwork of the exterior) are the beautiful stained-glass windows crafted by artists in Munich, and the Stations of the Cross and sacristy murals that were painted during and after World War II by Belgian artist Dom Gregory Dewit.

Our Lady of Guadalupe International Shrine of St. Jude
411 N. Rampart St. ☎ **504/525-1551.**

Located on the corner of Rampart and Conti streets, this building was put up in 1826 as a chapel convenient to the St. Louis Cemetery No. 1—funeral services were held here rather than in the St. Louis Cathedral so as not to spread disease within the confines of the Quarter, and it became known as the "Burial Chapel." In the intervening years it has been renovated, and it now houses an International Shrine of St. Jude (the saint of impossible causes, he is often thanked publicly for favors in the "Personals" column of the *Times-Picayune*). Another saint is honored here by a statue next to the main altar. His name is St. Expedite, a name that legend says was given to the statue when it arrived at the church in a packing crate with no identification but stamped "Expedite."

HISTORIC BUILDINGS

Pitot House
1440 Moss St. ☎ **504/482-0312.** Admission $3 adults, $2 seniors, $1 children under 12. Wed–Sat 10am–3pm.

The Pitot House is a typical West Indies–style plantation home, restored and furnished with Louisianan and American antiques dating from the early 1800s. Dating from 1799, it originally stood where the nearby modern Catholic school is now. In 1810 it became the home of James Pitot, the first mayor of incorporated New Orleans, and it is now known by his name. It has wide galleries on the sides and large columns supporting the second floor.

Jackson Barracks
6400 St. Claude Ave. ☎ **504/271-6262,** ext. 242, or 504/278-6242. Free admission. Mon–Fri 7:30am–3:30pm.

On an extension of Rampart Street downriver from the French Quarter is this series of fine old brick buildings with white columns. They were built in 1834–35 for troops who were stationed at the river forts. Some say Andrew Jackson, who never

---

❓ Did You Know?

- The St. Charles streetcar line is the oldest working streetcar in the world—more than 150 years old.
- Tom Dempsey of the New Orleans Saints kicked the longest field goal—a 63-yarder—in the history of the NFL.
- New Orleans was handed over to Spain by Louis XV of France in 1762 as card game winnings.
- The French Market is the oldest city market in the United States.
- People in New Orleans are "buried" above ground in tombs, rather than underground, because proper graves cannot be dug into the swampy terrain.
- Every Monday most people in New Orleans eat red beans and rice for dinner.
- If it weren't for levees and canals surrounding the city, New Orleans would be completely under water.

Margaret in Marble

At the corner of Camp and Prytania streets, you'll see a statue of one Irish immigrant, Margaret Haughery, who toiled in a bakery and dairy and devoted every spare minute to the care of orphans. When she died, she left all her hard-won earnings to charity. The Carrara marble statue, whose inscription is simply "Margaret," was unveiled in 1884; it was one of the first statues dedicated to a woman anywhere in the country. Appropriately there's a day nursery that dates from 1850 on the edge of the small park that holds Margaret's monument.

---

quite trusted New Orleans Creoles, planned the barracks to be as secure against attack from the city as from outside forces. The barracks now serve as headquarters for the Louisiana National Guard, and there's a marvelous military museum in the old powder magazine, which has an extensive collection of military items that span the American wars. It's best to call before you go to confirm that the barracks and museum are open. The museum recently underwent an expansion, and the complex now consists of the original powder magazine and a new annex that holds exhibits from World War II to Operation Desert Storm.

MUSEUMS & GALLERIES

Confederate Museum
929 Camp St. ☎ **504/523-4522.** Admission $4 adults, $2 children under 12. Mon–Sat 10am–4pm.

Located not far from the French Quarter, the Confederate Museum was established in 1899, close enough to the end of the Civil War for many donations to be in better condition than is sometimes true of museum items. There are battle flags, weapons, personal effects of Confederate President Jefferson Davis (including his evening clothes), part of Robert E. Lee's silver camp service, and many portraits of Confederate military and civilian personalities. A series of detailed pictures traces Louisiana's history from secession through Reconstruction.

✪ Contemporary Arts Center
900 Camp St. ☎ **504/523-1216.** Admission $3 general, $2 students and seniors, free to members. Admission is free to all on Thurs. Performance prices range from $3–$15. Mon–Sat 10am–5pm, Sun 11am–5pm.

Located outside the French Quarter, in what used to be the warehouse district and is now the Arts District, the Contemporary Arts Center exhibits the artwork of regional, national, and international artists. The CAC also presents theater, performance art, dance, and music concerts. Exhibitions change every six to eight weeks, and performances are weekly.

✪ New Orleans Museum of Art
Lelong Ave. ☎ **504/488-2631.** Admission $6 adults, $3 seniors and children, free to all on Thurs. Tues–Sun 10am–5pm.

Located in City Park, this museum is in a neoclassical building housing pre-Columbian, Renaissance, and contemporary art exhibited to show the history of art development. The columned main building is a beauty inside and out. Its first-floor Delgado Great Hall leads to a branched staircase at the back that rises to a mezzanine overlooking the hall. Notice, too, the bronze statue of Hercules as an archer just outside the entrance. The original building, about 80 years old, has been expanded by the addition of three wings, and the art inside does justice to its housing. There's a lovely portrait of Estelle Musson, a relative of the French impressionist painter Edgar Degas, who painted this likeness on one of his visits to the city. The 22 sections of the Kress Renaissance collection, pre-Columbian art, and bronzes by Rodin mix well with 20th-century art. NOMA recently underwent a $23 million expansion project that created more gallery space for portions of the museum's collection (both western and nonwestern art from the pre-Christian era to the present) that had previously been relegated to storage. In addition, there is now an entire floor devoted to nonwestern and ethnographic art, including Asian, African, pre-Columbian, Oceanic, and Native American art.

MUSEUMS IN ALGIERS & KENNER

✪ Blaine Kern's Mardi Gras World

223 Newton St., Algiers Point. ☎ **504/361-7821.** Admission $5.50 adults, $4.50 seniors, $3.25 children. Daily 9:30am–4:30pm. Closed on Mardi Gras, Easter Sunday, Thanksgiving, and Christmas.

When I was a kid, Mardi Gras floats fascinated me. I marveled at their elaborate detail and I wondered who could possibly create such incredible works of art. Well, now I know, and you will too if you make the trip to Blaine Kern's Mardi Gras World where you can see floats being made year-round. Take one of the tours and you'll get to see sculptors at work, first making small "sketches" of the figures and then finally creating and painting the enormous sculptures that adorn Mardi Gras floats each year. A film about Mardi Gras is presented, and you can even dress up in a Mardi Gras costume or have your picture taken with one of the colossal float figures.

To get to Blaine Kern's Mardi Gras World, take the Canal Street Ferry, which is free, across the river. The ride takes about 10 minutes. Look for the free shuttle that will take you from the dock to Mardi Gras World. The last ferry returns at around 11:15pm. Check the schedule before you set out, however.

RIVERTOWN

Best known because it's where the airport is, Kenner also has a few interesting attractions for those of you who want to check out the surrounding suburbs. The series of buildings known as Rivertown are located right on the Mississippi River, and they house several small museums of interest. The **Louisiana Toy Train Museum** at 519 Williams Blvd. (☎ 504/468-7223) is a great place to take the kids. Here you'll find six operational layouts of toy trains as well as interesting photographs, slide shows, and a toy carousel. The kids will also enjoy the planetarium and observatory at the **Freeport McMoRan Daily Living Science Center,** 409 Williams Blvd. (☎ 504/582-4000). Shows are offered at 2pm on Tuesday through Friday, and there are three shows daily on Saturday and Sunday. The observatory is open Thursday, Friday, and Saturday night from 7:30 to 10:30pm for viewing the night sky. In addition, there are many educational hands-on activities that focus on the environment and human health. If you didn't get your aquarium fix in downtown New Orleans, head into the **Louisiana Wildlife and Fisheries Museum,** 303 Williams Blvd. (☎ 504/468-7232), where you'll find hundreds of different types of animals as well as an aquarium. Also at the Louisiana Wildlife and Fisheries Museum is Cannes Brulee, where interpreters dressed in period attire (ca. 1750–1850) demonstrate their cultural heritage through folk traditions, rituals, domestic and occupational crafts, and foodways. There is yet another Mardi Gras Museum here as well. It's the **Mardi Gras Museum of Jefferson Parish,** 407 Williams Blvd. (☎ 504/468-7258), and if you didn't get a chance to take part in this year's Mardi Gras celebration, you can do so here. Catch a throw and sample some of that famous king cake. Children will love

Children's Castle, 503 Williams Blvd. (☎ **504/468-7229**) where they can see puppet shows, mimes, magic, and take part in storytelling on Saturday afternoons. Finally, if you're a football fan, or more precisely, a Saints fan, **Rivertown's Saints Hall of Fame Museum,** 409 Williams Blvd. (☎ **505/468-6617**) is the place to go. The museum exhibits all sorts of Saints memorabilia and video clips are shown.

All of the museums at Rivertown are within walking distance of each other and are open Tuesday through Saturday from 9am to 5pm and Sunday from 1 to 5pm (the football museum is closed on Sundays during football season). Admission to each of the museums is $3 for adults and $2 for seniors and children 12 and under. If you plan on visiting all the museums located here, the multimuseum ticket will save you a few bucks. It's $10 for adults and $5 for seniors and children 12 and under.

A PANORAMA

World Trade Center of New Orleans

2 Canal St. ☎ **504/581-4888.** Admission $2 adults, $1 children 6–12, children under 6 free. Daily 9am–5pm.

Down at the river, the World Trade Center of New Orleans is the center of the city's maritime industry as well as the home of most international consulates. On the 31st floor there's an observation deck that looks out onto the city and a harbor scene that might include naval vessels (from submarines to aircraft carriers), cruise ships (those that simply ply excursions in local waters and those that leave for faraway ports), and freighters flying flags from around the world. For a stunning ride up, use the outside elevator. The observation deck, called Viewpoint, is open every day except Christmas, Mardi Gras, and Thanksgiving. This is truly an incomparable view. There are high-power telescopes to zoom in on your favorite site for only 25¢. For more relaxed viewing, go on up to the 33rd-floor revolving cocktail lounge (see Chapter 11).

PARKS & GARDENS

✪ Audubon Park

6500 Magazine St. ☎ **504/861-2538.** Free admission. Daily 6am–10pm.

Across the street from both Loyola and Tulane, Audubon Park sprawls over 340 acres, reaching from St. Charles Avenue all the way to the Mississippi River. This tract of land once belonged to Jean-Baptiste Le Moyne, the founder of New Orleans, and later was part of the Etienne de Bore plantation, where sugar was granulated for the first time in 1794. The city purchased it in 1871; a golf course now lies on the section where the World's Industrial and Cotton Centennial Exposition was held in 1884–85. In spite of having what was then the largest building in the world (33 acres under one roof) as its main exhibition hall, the exposition was such a financial disaster that everything except the Horticultural Hall had to be sold off. (The Horticultural Hall fell victim to a hurricane a little later.) After that, serious work was begun to make this into a park. Although John James Audubon, our country's best-known ornithologist, lived only briefly in New Orleans (in a cottage on Dauphine Street in the French Quarter—his studio was located on Barracks Street), the city has honored his contributions in the naming of both Audubon Park and Audubon Zoo.

The huge trees with black bark you see here are live oaks, and some go back to the days when this was a plantation. They're evergreens and shed only once a year, in early spring. Their spreading limbs turn walkways into covered alleys, and there are winding lagoons, fountains, and statuary, as well as a very nice zoo (see later in this section). Scattered about are gazebos, shelters, and playground areas—and that funny-looking mound over near the river, actually in the zoo, is called "Monkey Hill," constructed so that the children of this flatland city could see what a hill looked like. The pavilion on the riverbank is one of the most pleasant places from which to view the Mississippi.

As far as I'm concerned, the trees and wandering paths and general atmosphere of peace and quiet are quite enough for any park, but if you're looking for recreation facilities, you'll find those here, too. There's an 18-hole golf course in the front half, picnic facilities, tennis courts, a 1.8-mile jogging track, 18 exercise stations, and horseback riding. The Audubon Zoo is toward the back of the park.

When you reach the end of St. Charles Avenue (where the streetcar turns onto Carrollton Avenue), the green hill over by the river is the levee—if the water happens to be high enough, you'll see the tops of ships as they pass by.

Note: In spite of the fact that the park is open until 10pm, it is not advisable to be there after it gets dark.

✪ City Park

1 Dreyfous Ave. ☎ **504/483-9358.** Free admission. Daily 6am–7pm.

Right at the entrance is a statue of Gen. P. G. T. Beauregard, whose order to fire on Fort Sumter opened the Civil War and whom New Orleanians fondly call the "Great Creole." The park was once part of the Louis Allard plantation, and the huge old oaks looked down on a favorite pastime in New Orleans during the 1700s: dueling.

The extensive, beautifully landscaped grounds hold a botanical gardens and conservatory, four golf courses, picnic areas, a restaurant, lagoons for boating and fishing, tennis courts, horses for hire for the lovely trails, a bandstand, two miniature trains, and Children's Storyland, an amusement area with a carousel ride for children (see "Especially for Kids" in this chapter for more details). You'll also find the New Orleans Museum of Art on Lelong Avenue in City Park in a building that is itself a work of art (see "Museums and Galleries" earlier in this chapter for more details).

City Park's Dueling Oaks

To the proud Creoles, nothing, not even death, was to be feared so much as the loss of honor. When a dispute ended with a heated "under the oaks at sunrise," it was often in City Park, under what came to be called the Dueling Oaks, that the rendezvous was kept. The practice persisted into the early 1800s (there were, in fact, 10 duels fought on just one Sunday morning in 1837), but duels changed very much in character after Americans arrived on the scene. Creoles observed a very formal and strict dueling etiquette, using the meetings to demonstrate their expertise with rapiers, broadswords, or pistols (fists were never used among gentlemen), and only seldom was either party actually killed. With the Americans, however, came a whole new concept—duels became a fight to the death, with such "rude" weapons as rifles, shotguns, clubs, and even axes. Dueling died out after the Civil War; it had always been forbidden by both church and law (strictures heretofore completely ignored by the proud participants), and after the war there was a stricter enforcement of the laws. One of the mighty oaks became known during the bleak Reconstruction era as the "Suicide Oak" because of its popularity as the setting for that action. Another, McDonogh Oak, is believed to be more than 600 years old, and has a 142-foot branch spread.

Chalmette National Historical Park

8608 West St. Bernard Hwy. ☎ **504/589-4430.** Free admission. Daily 8:30am–5pm.

To reach the park, continue on St. Claude Avenue until it becomes St. Bernard Highway. The park will be on your right. On these grounds the bloody Battle of New Orleans was waged on January 14, 1815. Ironically, the battle should never have been fought at all, since the War of 1812 had by then been concluded by a treaty signed two weeks before in Ghent, Belgium. The treaty was not, however, in effect, and word had simply never reached Congress, the commander of the British forces, or Andrew Jackson, who stood with American forces to defend New Orleans and the mouth of the Mississippi River. The battle did, however, succeed in bringing New Orleanians together more than they had ever been and in making Andrew Jackson a hero forever in this city.

You can visit the battleground and see markers that will let you follow the course of the battle in detail. In the Beauregard plantation house on the grounds, you will find interesting exhibits, and the Visitor Center presents a film and other exhibits on the battle. There also is a National Cemetery here, which was established in 1864; it holds only two American veterans of the Battle of New Orleans, but some 14,000 Union soldiers who fell in the Civil War are buried here. For a really terrific view of the Mississippi River, climb the levee in back of the Beauregard House.

Joe Brown Memorial Park (& the Louisiana Nature Center)

Nature Center Dr., New Orleans East. ☎ **504/244-4663** or 504/246-5672. Admission $4 adults, $3 seniors, $2 children. Tues–Fri 9am–5pm, Sat 10am–5pm, Sun noon–5pm.

Part of the Audubon Institute, Joe Brown Park is an 86-acre tract of Louisiana forest where guided walks are given daily (except Monday). Weekdays a nature film is shown, and weekends offer additional activities as well (canoeing, bird-watching, arts and crafts workshops, and others). Three miles of trails are available for public use. There is a wheelchair-accessible raised wooden walkway for shorter walks. The Louisiana Nature Center offers changing exhibits and hands-on activities. There is a planetarium with shows on Saturday and Sunday, and on Friday and Saturday nights there are laser rock shows. Call 504/246-STAR for the current planetarium schedule. To get there, take I-10 to Exit 244; pass the Plaza Shopping Center and make a left onto Nature Center Drive.

Longue Vue House & Gardens

7 Bamboo Rd. ☎ **504/488-5488.** Admission $7 adults, $6 seniors, $3 children and students. Mon–Sat 10am–4:30pm, Sun 1–5pm. Closed New Year's Day, Mardi Gras, July 4, Labor Day, Thanksgiving, and Christmas Day.

Just off of Metairie Road, you'll find the lovely, eight-acre Longue Vue Estate, one of the most beautiful garden settings in this area. The mansion is built in the classical tradition. As with the great country houses of England, it was designed to foster a close rapport between indoors and outdoors, with vistas of formal terraces and pastoral woods. Some parts of the enchanting gardens were inspired by those of the Sultans' summerhouse, Generalife, in Granada, Spain; besides the colorful flowering plants, there are formal boxwood parterres, fountains, and a colonnaded loggia. Highlights are the Canal Garden; Walled Garden; Wild Garden (which features native iris); and Spanish Court (with pebbled walkways, fountains, and changing horticultural displays). Longue Vue House and Gardens is listed on the National Register of Historic Places and is accredited by the American Association of Museums.

A DAY AT THE ZOO

✪ Audubon Zoo

6500 Magazine St. ☎ **504/861-5101.** Admission $8 adults, $4 seniors 65 and older and children 2–12. Admission to the Butterflies in Flight exhibit is $2 additional. Daily 9:30am–5:30pm (the zoo remains open until 6pm on Sat and Sun in the summer). The last ticket is sold 1 hour before closing. Closed holidays.

The Audubon Zoo is one of the top five zoos in the country. Here, in a setting of subtropical plantings, waterfalls, and lagoons, some 1,800 animals (including rare and endangered species) live in natural habitats. Don't plan to spend less than two or three hours—more if you have time to spare—in this delightful oasis of animal culture. The new Butterflies in Flight exhibit is a glorious butterfly garden replete with lush, colorful vegetation. It houses more than 1,000 butterflies as well as a pupae hatchery. A terrific way to visit is to arrive on the sternwheeler *John James Audubon* (see "Organized Tours" later in this chapter) and depart via the St. Charles streetcar, which is reached by way of a lovely stroll through Audubon Park or on a complimentary shuttle bus. During your visit to the zoo look for the bronze statue of John James Audubon. It's in a grove of trees, and the naturalist is shown with a notebook and pencil in hand.

3 Especially for Kids

New Orleans is a great place for kids; there's so much for a child to learn in a city so filled with history. Below I've listed some places I think your kids might enjoy (chances are that you will, too). In addition to the attractions listed below, **Accents on Arrangements,** 938 Lafayette St., no. 410 (☎ **504/524-1227**), also offers tours specially designed to meet the needs and interests of children.

All kids love the French Market because it's small and there's so much to look at. Take them on a horse-and-buggy ride around the Vieux Carré: You'll all learn about the fascinating and amusing history of the city. The Riverfront streetcar and a ferry ride on the Mississippi River are fun—you can get kids to imagine that they're playing a part in the lives of Huck Finn and Tom Sawyer. Finish it off with a visit to Aquarium of the Americas (see "The French Quarter" earlier in this chapter).

Some children might like a visit to a museum or two, and I'd suggest the Confederate Museum, the New Orleans Historic Voodoo Museum, or the Musée Conti Wax Museum—all with complete listings earlier in this chapter.

If you're in the Central Business District for the day, take them over to the Superdome and go on one of the tours that are offered daily (see "Organized Tours" later in this chapter for details); they'll love seeing where some of their heroes play ball, and they'll be in absolute awe of the enormity of the building.

If they're getting restless being inside so much and the weather is nice, take them to one of the parks listed above and have a picnic lunch.

Below I've listed a couple of things that are absolutely child oriented and are worth a visit.

✪ Louisiana Children's Museum

420 Julia St. ☎ **504/523-1357.** Admission $5. Tues–Sat 9:30am–5pm, Sun noon–5pm. Mon June–Aug, 9:30am–5pm.

People of all ages will delight in exploring more than 45,000 square feet of dynamic "hands-on" exhibits—it's not your ordinary playhouse! Visitors might play with and meet new friends in the toddler area, explore the powers of math and physics through the 45 exhibits in "The Lab"; or take in a performance in science, drama, dance, art, or puppetry in the Times-Picayune Theatre.

Children's Storyland

In City Park. ☎ **504/483-9381.** Admission $1.50 children and adults, children under 2 free. Wed–Fri 10am–12:30pm, Sat–Sun 10am–4:30pm, except Jan and Feb when it's only open on Sat and Sun.

This is an enchanted playground where youngsters can slide down Jack and Jill's hill, climb Little Miss Muffet's spiderweb, or have an imaginary sword fight on Captain Hook's pirate ship. Larger than life fairy-tale figures such as Puss-n-Boots, Rapunzel, and Jack (of Beanstalk fame) will delight young children. It's right across from the tennis courts on Victory Avenue.

4 Organized Tours

As I've said earlier in this book, the very best way to see the French Quarter is on foot. But once you leave the confines of the French Quarter, sightseeing tours can save a lot of time, to say nothing of wear and tear on the nerves, especially if you're the one behind the wheel. Buses will pick you up at your hotel and deliver you back there, and guides can be depended on for complete, accurate information (as well as occasional entertainment through amusing anecdotes and legends about the city). Another marvelous way to view the city is from the riverboats that cruise the harbor and a little stretch of the Mississippi River. Docks are at the foot of Toulouse and Canal streets, and there's ample parking for the car while you sit back and relax on the water. Reservations are required for all these tours, and I would remind you once more that the prices quoted here are those in effect at press time and are subject to change.

For tours of the plantation houses outside New Orleans, see Chapter 12.

Aside from the walking tours given in Chapter 9, there's an excellent walking tour offered by the nonprofit volunteer group **Friends of the Cabildo** (☎ 504/523-3939). This tour furnishes guides for a two-hour, on-foot exploration that will provide a good overview of the area. Leaving from in front of the Museum Store, 523 St. Ann St., your guide will "show and tell" you about most of the Quarter's historic buildings' exteriors and the interiors of selected Louisiana State Museum buildings. You're asked to pay a donation of $10 per adult, $5 for seniors over 65 and children from 13 to 20 (those 12 and under are free). Tours leave Tuesday through Sunday at 10am and 1:30pm and Monday at 1:30pm, except holidays. No reservations are necessary—just show up, donations in hand. Tickets may be purchased in advance.

Tours by Isabelle, P.O. Box 740972, New Orleans, LA 70174 (☎ 504/391-3544), conducts small groups on a three-hour city tour in a comfortable, air-conditioned minibus. The tour covers the French Quarter, the cemeteries, Bayou St. John, City Park and the Lakefront, the universities, St. Charles Avenue, the Garden District, and the Superdome. The fare is $30, and departure times are 9am and 1:30pm. You should call as far in advance as possible to book. For $35 you can join her afternoon Combo Tour, which adds Longue Vue Gardens to all of the above.

Stop by the ✪ **Jean Lafitte National Park and Preserve's Folklife and Visitor Center** at 419 Decatur St. (☎ 504/589-2636) for details of the excellent free walking tours on a variety of topics conducted by National Park Service rangers. The History of New Orleans tour covers about a mile in the French Quarter and brings to life New Orleans's history and the ethnic roots of the city's unique cultural mix. No reservations are required for this tour or the Tour du Jour (also in the Quarter),

Swamp Tours

In addition to the tour providers listed below, Jean Lafitte and Gray Line both offer a swamp tour (see "Organized Tours"). On all of the following tours you're likely to see alligators, bald eagles, waterfowl, egrets, owls, herons, osprey, feral hogs, otter, beaver, frogs, turtles, minks, raccoons, black bear, deer, and nutria.

Half Pint's Swamp Adventures, McGee's, 1337 Henderson Levee Rd., Breaux Bridge, LA 70517 (☎318/228-2384), offers private guided tours of the "beauty, serenity, and exotic wildlife" of the Atchafalaya Basin, the nation's largest swamp. Appearing to be more folk hero than man, Half Pint's tours come highly recommended.

Lil' Cajun Swamp Tours, Rt. 1, Box 397-A, Hwy. 301, Crown Point, LA 70072 (☎ 504/689-3213 or 800/725-3213), offers a good tour of Lafitte's bayous. Captain Cyrus Blanchard, "a Cajun French-speaking gentleman," knows the bayous like the back of his hand—mostly because it's where he lives. The tour lasts two hours and will run you about $16 for adults, $14 for seniors, and $12 for children if you drive yourself to the boat launch. If you need transportation it will cost you $30 for adults, $15 for children ages 6 to 12. (Note that the boat used on the Lil' Cajun Swamp Tours is much larger than the boat used on many of the other tours— it seats up to 67 people.)

Honey Island Swamp Tours, 106 Holly Ridge Dr., Slidell, LA 70461 (☎ 504/ 641-1769 or 504/242-5877), will take you by boat into the interior of Honey Island Swamp's "most beautiful and pristine areas" to view wildlife with native, professional, naturalist guides. Tours are approximately two hours long. Prices are $20 for adults, $10 for children under 12. Hotel pick-ups in New Orleans are available for a fee, or you can drive to the launch site yourself.

Gator Swamp Tours, P.O. Box 2082, Slidell, LA 70459 (☎ 504/484-6100 or 800/875-4287), claims to offer the "longest and most personal swamp tour in the New Orleans area." Gator Swamp Tours takes visitors on a ride through Honey Island Swamp, beyond the bounds of the average swamp tour, into "the wilderness." Prices are $20 for adults, $10 for children under 12. Gator Swamp Tours now also offers a short nature walk in addition to boat tours. Like the other tour groups, Gator Swamp Tours offers hotel pick-ups for a fee.

which is a "ranger's choice" that varies from day to day. You must book, however, for the Faubourg Promenade Tour which takes you for a walk in the Garden District. This tour is popular, so book a couple of days ahead.

○ **Magic Walking Tours** (☎ 504/593-9693) at 1015 Iberville St. offers several guided walking tours daily. You might take a tour of St. Louis Cemetery No. 1, the French Quarter, or the Garden District. Or, if you're feeling a little more adventurous, try the Voodoo Tour or the Haunted House, Vampire, and Ghost-Hunt Walking Tour. The tour guides are excellent—not only do they enjoy their jobs, but they are extremely well educated about the city. Reservations are not necessary, but you should call ahead for tour schedules. Meeting places vary according to the tour you choose. Tours cost between $9 and $13 for adults and all children tour free.

Hidden Treasures Tours, 1915 Chestnut St. (☎ 504/529-4507), offers guided tours of the Garden District and the Lower Garden District. You'll get to take a tour of one of the cemeteries, view monuments, and enjoy fine examples of southern architecture. Tours cost $12 per person, and advance reservations are required. Hidden Treasures specializes in women's history tours, which include monuments to women and the homes of women authors.

"Roots" of New Orleans, A Heritage City Tour, 1750 St. Charles Ave., no. 202 (☎ **504/522-7414** or 800/229-1872), offers two black heritage tours daily from Thursday through Saturday. (At press time there were plans to offer the tours six days a week, so call ahead to see if the schedule has changed.) Experienced tour guides take visitors to some of Marie Laveau's favorite haunts, through the French Quarter, to the cemeteries, to the very roots of New Orleans jazz, and more. Rates are $27 for adults and $23 for children.

Gray Line, 2 Canal St., Suite 1300 (☎ **504/587-0861** or 800/535-7786), has tours of the entire city, including the French Quarter, in comfortable motor coaches. But take my word for it: The Quarter will demand a more in-depth examination than a view from a bus window. Take one of these excellent (and very informative) tours only after you've explored the Quarter in detail or as a prelude to doing so.

Gray Line's trolley tour begins in the French Quarter with an informative narration on historic buildings as well as the Creole cottages and elegant mansions along the way. You'll also go to City Park and then on to Longue Vue House and Gardens. The cost is $15 for a one-day pass and $25 for a two-day pass (cost includes unlimited boarding and departing privileges).

Gray Line also offers a tour that includes a two-hour cruise on the steamboat *Natchez.* You'll have lunch on board (cost not included in the tour price) as you take in the sights and sounds of the world's second busiest port. They also make complimentary pick-ups at various hotels throughout the city. Additionally, you can arrange to go on the River Road Plantation Tour, which departs daily at 9am or the Oak Alley Tour which leaves at 1pm daily. The plantation tours operate on a different schedule during December and January, so call for details.

Gray Line has also added walking tours to its offerings, including one of the Garden District and one of the French Quarter. Call for times and departure points.

BOAT TOURS

The steamboat *Natchez,* 1340 World Trade Center of New Orleans (☎ **504/586-8777** or 800/233-BOAT), a marvelous three-deck sternwheeler docked at the wharf behind the Jackson Brewery, offers two two-hour daytime cruises daily. The narration is by professional guides, and there are cocktail bars, an optional Creole buffet, and a gift shop aboard. The fares are $14.75 for adults ($18.75 in the evening not including dinner) and $7.25 for children ($10.75 in the evening not including dinner). Those under three ride free. Call for sailing schedule. Also, there is a jazz dinner cruise every evening. The buffet is optional. Call for schedules and prices.

The sternwheeler *John James Audubon,* 1300 World Trade Center of New Orleans (☎ **504/586-8777** or 800/233-BOAT), offers a real departure in the cruise world: the exciting Aquarium-Zoo Cruise. Passengers travel the Mississippi by sternwheeler, tour the busy port, and dock to visit both the Audubon Zoo and the Aquarium of the Americas. There are four trips daily. Tours depart from the Riverwalk in front of the Aquarium at 10am, noon, 2pm, and 4pm. Return trips from the zoo are scheduled at 11am, 1pm, 3pm, and 5pm. Tickets for one-way or return trips can be purchased with or without aquarium and zoo admission. There is a combination ticket available that will save you several dollars. Call for prices, exact sailing schedule, and to make reservations.

The paddle-wheeler *Creole Queen,* 27 Poydras St. Wharf (☎ **504/524-0814** or 800/445-4109), departs from the Poydras Street Wharf adjacent to Riverwalk at

10:30am and 2pm for three-hour narrated excursions to the port and to the historic site of the Battle of New Orleans. There is also a 7pm jazz dinner cruise. The ship has a covered promenade deck, and its inner lounges are air-conditioned and heated. Buffet and cocktail services are available on all cruises. The fares are $14 for the daytime cruises and $39 for the nighttime jazz cruise (children $7 daytime, $18 night-time; children under three are free). Call to confirm sailing schedules and current fares.

CARRIAGE TOURS

If you have even one romantic bone in your body, you'll find it hard to resist the authentic old horse-drawn (most are actually mule drawn, but who cares) carriages that pick up passengers at Jackson Square. Each horse is decked out with ribbons, flowers, or even a hat, and each driver is apparently in fierce competition with all other drivers to win a "most unique city story" award. No matter which one you choose, you'll get a knowledgeable, nonstop monologue on historic buildings, fasci-nating events of the past, and a legend or two during the $2^1/4$-mile drive through the French Quarter. They're at the Decatur Street end of Jackson Square from 9am to midnight in good weather; the charge is $8 per adult and $5 for children under 12.

Note: The carriage ride described here is *not* the one that will take you on your own private tour. Private horse-carriage tours offered by **Good Old Days Buggies** (☎ **504/523-0804**), which include hotel or restaurant pick-up, will cost you signifi-cantly more.

ANTIQUING TOURS

Antiquing in New Orleans can be a completely overwhelming experience, especially if you've never been to the city before. There are so many shops in the French Quar-ter and on Magazine Street that it's almost impossible to find what you're looking for without a little help. That's why Macon Riddle founded **Let's Go Antiquing!**, 1412 Fourth St. (☎ **504/899-3027**), in the mid-1980s. She'll organize and custom-ize antique shopping tours to fit your needs. Hotel pick-up is standard on her tours, and if you're interested, she'll even make your lunch reservations for you. If you find something and you want it shipped home, she'll even take care of that. There's no doubt in my mind, Macon Riddle is the best in the business.

5 Outdoor Activities

Even in a major city like New Orleans there are plenty of outdoor activities available to the sports enthusiast and the health conscious. New Orleans has several parks and gardens for hiking, biking, and even horseback riding. The list below will help you find what you're looking for.

BIKING

Since it's sometimes difficult to park in and around the French Quarter, biking is a good way to get from place to place without the added burden of having to worry about where you're going to park when you get there. You might also find it enjoy-able to ride through the Garden District (for safety reasons, keep to the main streets and if possible, ride with someone else). I've enjoyed riding along the levee in the Carrollton section of the city. If you're just interested in a quiet, leisurely ride, City Park and Audubon Park are both lovely places to take your bicycle.

Bicycles can be rented at **Olympic Bike Rentals,** 1506 Prytania St. (☎ **504/523-1314**). They will deliver 18- and 21-speed mountain bikes to your hotel and provide safety equipment, children's seats, and water bottles, as well as routed maps. If you've got children in tow, they have bikes for kids too. And, like some car rental companies, they'll provide roadside assistance in the event of a breakdown. Rentals are also available through **Bicycle Michael's** at 622 Frenchmen St. (☎ **504/ 945-9505**). They charge by the hour or by the day depending on your preference.

Safety is always a concern when biking in a city, but in New Orleans you shouldn't only be concerned about speeding cars. Potholes in some sections of the city are large enough to swallow a bicyclist whole, particularly along Magazine Street between the French Quarter and the Garden District.

BOATING

Well, you probably won't be taking a raft out on the Mississippi, but you can rent pedal boats and canoes by the half hour or by the hour for use on the lagoons in City Park. Pedal boats rent for $8 an hour or $6 per half hour. Canoes are $6 an hour, and a $5 (refundable) deposit is required on each boat. Call **City Park's** boating and fishing department (☎ 504/482-4888) for rental hours and to confirm prices.

If you're a little more adventurous, you might consider taking a canoe tour. **Bayou Barn "Cajun Canoeing and Dancing"** (☎ 504/689-2663) offers guided and self-guided tours as well as moonlight tours throughout Jean Lafitte National Historical Park.

The smooth waters of Lake Pontchartrain make it a favorite spot for city sailors. You can rent boats from **Murray Yacht Sales/Boat Rentals,** 402 S. Roadway Dr. (☎ 504/283-2507). If you're an experienced sailor but need some help getting started, Murray Yacht Sales will give you a quick refresher course; there are also courses available for beginners. Sailing courses are available from March to November.

FISHING

Fishing is quite popular in the New Orleans area. Appropriate temporary licenses must be obtained by nonresidents from the **Louisiana Department of Wildlife and Fisheries,** which maintains an office at 400 Chartres St. in the French Quarter (☎ 504/568-5636), open weekdays only. Separate licenses must be purchased for saltwater fishing and freshwater fishing. Additionally, you may have to get another license altogether if you intend to do shrimping and crabbing. Crawfishing does not require licensing.

As with many of the other outdoor activities listed here, City Park is a good place to start. There you can fish (with a permit obtained from the park's boating and fishing department; call **504/482-4888**) for bass and catfish year-round. Costs for fishing in City Park are $2 for a park permit, good for the day, and $6.50 for a temporary state fishing license. Both can be purchased in the park. Fishing in the park is from the shore, not from boats, and gear rental is available.

You can also fish the Mississippi River. A good spot is up in the Carrollton area near the levee, where you can just drop your line. In addition, there are several tour operators who will take you deep-sea or bayou and swamp fishing. Unless you have your own equipment and are an experienced boater, these charters are the best way to go. **Captain Nick's Fishing Charters** (☎ 504/361-3004 or 800/375-FISH) operates fishing charters daily all year-round. All equipment is provided, and Captain Nick's will pick you up at your hotel. The tours are personalized, with no more than five people per boat. **Cajun Fishing Adventures,** 163 Asphodel Dr., Luling, LA 70070 (☎ 504/837-8245 or 800/989-4843), organizes charters in 18- and 20-foot bass boats. Both inland saltwater and freshwater fishing are available. If a little history and folklore would make your fishing trip more complete, you should call **Ripp's Inland Charters,** Box 231, Barataria, LA 70036 (☎ **504/689-2665**). Ripp Blank, a native resident of Lafitte, organizes all-day fishing trips through the area's swamps and bayous. Speckled trout and redfish are the most commonly caught. All gear is provided.

FITNESS CENTERS

Many of the hotels in New Orleans have fitness centers, but if your hotel doesn't have one, you can work out at the **New Orleans Athletic Club,** 222 N. Rampart St. (☎ **504/525-2375**). In addition to a selection of exercise equipment (free weights, Nautilus, a variety of cardiovascular machines), the club offers aerobics classes, racquetball courts, jogging tracks (both indoor and outdoor), and a lap pool. There is also a steam room and sauna. Additionally, the **New Orleans Hilton** (☎ **504/584-3880**) will allow the general public to use its health club (jogging track; pool; racquetball, tennis, and squash courts; and fitness equipment) for a fee.

GOLF

Whether you bring your clubs or rent them in New Orleans, you'll be able to get in a good round of golf at several public courses around the city. **City Park** (which features one of the top 100 golf shops in the country) has four 18-hole courses. Rentals are available, as are private lessons. There is also a 100-tee lighted driving range. For information call **504/483-9396. Audubon Park** (☎ **504/865-8260**) also has a public course. **Bayou Oaks Golf Courses,** 1040 Filmore Dr. (☎ **504/483-9396**), has four 18-hole courses as well as a 100-tee lighted driving range. If you feel like making a trip to the West Bank, **Joe Bartholomew Golf Course,** 6514 Congress Dr. (☎**504/288-0928**), is a good choice. The **Bayou Barriere Golf Club,** 7427 Highway 23, Belle Chase, LA 70037 (☎ **504/394-0662** or 504/394-9500), is considered to be the best public golf course in the area. The 27-hole championship course isa challenge to any player, and clubs are available for rental. The **Bluffs at Thompson Creek,** La. Hwy. 965 at Freeland Rd, 6 miles east of U.S. 61 (☎ **504/634-3410**), is two hours from the city, but it offers a great course designed by Arnold Palmer. You must reserve tee times well in advance by calling the pro shop at 504/634-5551.

HIKING

Several trails are maintained by the Louisiana Nature and Science Center in Joe Brown Park (see above). Additionally, **Jean Lafitte National Historical Park and Preserve,** Barataria Unit, 7400 La. Hwy. 45 in Marrero (☎ **504/589-2330**), has some lovely trails (maintained by the National Park Service) that wind through the Louisiana wetlands. You'll get to see some beautiful water lily–dotted bayous and moss-draped cypress trees, as well as palmettos and oaks. Park rangers conduct guided tours that take visitors to some interesting historical and archaeological sites. To get there, take the Crescent City Connection bridge to the West Bank.

HORSEBACK RIDING

Cascade Stables in Audubon Park, 6500 Magazine St. (☎ **504/891-2246**), rents horses for riding in the park by the hour. You can also ride with an experienced guide.

IN-LINE SKATING

Rent skates, safety gear, and take lessons at **Park Skate,** 6108 Magazine St. (☎ **504/891-7055**). After you're fully outfitted, head to City Park.

JOGGING

There are many places to jog in New Orleans. The first one that comes to mind is Woldenberg Park at the outer edge of the French Quarter. Of course, a quiet run along the levee in the Carrollton area (uptown) is also pleasant. Additionally, City Park and Audubon Park also have excellently maintained trails. Remember, however, that New Orleans has its share of crime, so always exercise good judgment: It's best to jog with a partner, and only during daylight hours.

TENNIS

Audubon Park Tennis Center in Audubon Park (☎ **504/895-1042**) has 10 well-maintained courts; enter on Magazine Street. **City Park Tennis Center** (Wisner Tennis Courts in City Park; ☎ **504/483-9383**) has 39 lighted courts. There is a small court fee, and private lessons are available. If you'd rather play indoors, which is preferable in the summer especially, there are eight indoor (as well as three outdoor) courts on top of the Hilton's garage. There is a court fee, and if you don't have a game partner, the Hilton will match you up with someone. Views of the river are excellent. Inquire at the **New Orleans Hilton** (☎ **504/587-7242**).

6 Spectator Sports

Some people think Mardi Gras is New Orleans's spectator sport. Football, basketball, and baseball fans know otherwise. For years a visit to New Orleans for sports fans has been less than satisfying, but all of that is about to change. The Louisiana State Legislature approved $215 million for sports development in 1993. Out of that, a training facility for the New Orleans Saints, as well as a stadium for its minor league baseball team, have already been built. The Superdome is currently undergoing a $20.5 million renovation, and plans have been laid to build a new sports arena behind the Superdome (to host professional hockey events, boxing, and pro and collegiate basketball games).

BASEBALL

New Orleans doesn't have a major league team, but it does have the **New Orleans Zephyrs** (☎ **504/282-6777**), the AAA-class farm team of the Milwaukee Brewers. They play from April to September in their new $20 million, 15,000-seat stadium located in East Jefferson. The four-year-old team spent its first two years playing at the University of New Orleans's Privateer Park.

FOOTBALL

New Orleans's NFL team, the **Saints,** plays in the Superdome every year from August to December. Tickets for games are fairly easy to come by, but I'd recommend calling TicketMaster at **504/522-5555** (or 504/733-0255 for information) well before you plan to arrive in New Orleans to find out what availability is.

Every year, two college football teams participate in the **Sugar Bowl,** which is played in the Superdome. Last-minute tickets are virtually impossible to get, but if you make plans far enough in advance, you shouldn't have a problem. Odd-numbered years, Tulane University and Louisiana State University duke it out on the field in the Superdome, and on Saturdays during football season, Tulane University plays its home games on the field in the Dome. Just call, or stop by, the Superdome and ask for schedules and prices (☎ **504/587-3810**).

Note: New Orleans is hosting Super Bowl XXXI in 1997. If you want to get your name in for the Super Bowl ticket lottery, send a certified letter to the National

·Football League, c/o Super Bowl Tickets, 410 Park Ave., New York, NY 10022, and say your prayers.

HORSE RACING

If horse racing is your thing, head to the **Fairgrounds,** 1751 Gentilly Blvd. (☎ **504/ 944-5515**). Races take place there at one of the oldest thoroughbred racing tracks in the country. Races are run from Thanksgiving to the middle of April. Fire destroyed the permanent buildings (clubhouse and grandstand among others) a few years back, and rebuilding is expected to take a year or so more to complete. The races continue, even in the absence of these facilities.

9

City Strolls

New Orleans really lends itself to walking, and it's absolutely the best way to get to see and do as much as you can during a short period of time. If you try these walking tours, you're sure to leave New Orleans feeling like you know something about the city and its layout.

WALKING TOUR 1
The French Quarter

Start: The intersection of Royal and Bienville streets.
Finish: Jackson Square.
Time: Allow approximately 1½ hours, not including time spent in shops or historic homes.
Best Times: Any day of the week after 10am because the French Quarter takes a little while to awaken in the mornings.
Worst Times: The only bad time to do this walk is at night, because some attractions won't be open and you won't be able to get a good look at the architecture.

Taking a stroll through the French Quarter is an absolute must during any visit to New Orleans—this is the most colorful part of what is arguably the most interesting city in the United States. This tour will take you along a number of the streets, to old buildings and other landmarks, and will give you a taste of the mixture of history and legend that is so much a part of the French Quarter's fame.

From your starting point at the corner of Royal and Bienville streets, head into the Quarter to:

1. **339 Royal St.,** the old Bank of the United States, which was built in 1800—notice its fine hand-forged ironwork.

   On the right-hand corner of Royal and Conti streets you'll see:

2. **The Bank of Louisiana,** 334 Royal St. The old bank was erected in 1826 by Philip Hamblet, Tobias Bickle, and Benjamin Fox. Since the bank's liquidation in 1867, the building has suffered a number of fires (in 1840, 1861, and 1931) and has served the community as the Louisiana State Capitol, an auction exchange, a criminal court and then a juvenile court, and a social hall for the American Legion. At the present time it houses the police station for the Vieux Carré.

The French Quarter

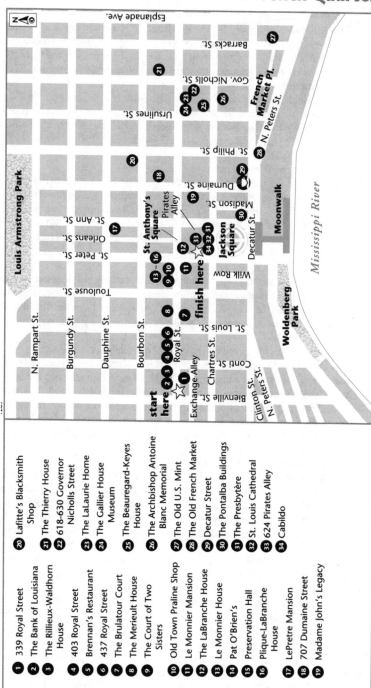

- **1** 339 Royal Street
- **2** The Bank of Louisiana
- **3** The Rillieux-Waldhorn House
- **4** 403 Royal Street
- **5** Brennan's Restaurant
- **6** 437 Royal Street
- **7** The Brulatour Court
- **8** The Merieult House
- **9** The Court of Two Sisters
- **10** Old Town Praline Shop
- **11** Le Monnier Mansion
- **12** The LaBranche House
- **13** Le Monnier House
- **14** Pat O'Brien's
- **15** Preservation Hall
- **16** Plique-LaBranche House
- **17** LePretre Mansion
- **18** 707 Dumaine Street
- **19** Madame John's Legacy
- **20** Lafitte's Blacksmith Shop
- **21** The Thierry House
- **22** 618-630 Governor Nicholls Street
- **23** The LaLaurie Home
- **24** The Gallier House Museum
- **25** The Beauregard-Keyes House
- **26** The Archbishop Antoine Blanc Memorial
- **27** The Old U.S. Mint
- **28** The Old French Market
- **29** Decatur Street
- **30** The Pontalba Buildings
- **31** The Presbytère
- **32** St. Louis Cathedral
- **33** 624 Pirates Alley
- **34** Cabildo

151

Stay on Royal Street and you'll come to:

3. **The Rillieux-Waldhorn House,** 343 Royal St. Now the home of Waldhorn Antiques (est. 1881), it was built between 1795 and 1800 for Vincent Rillieux, the great-grandfather of the French Impressionist artist Edgar Degas. Note the wrought-iron balconies—they are a lovely example of Spanish colonial workmanship.

Cross Conti Street and head onto the next block of Royal Street and you'll see:

4. **403 Royal St.** Designed by Benjamin H. Latrobe, one of the architects of the Capitol in Washington, this structure opened in 1821 as home of the Louisiana State Bank. The bank was chartered in 1818 with a capital of $2 million. In 1870 it became State National Bank.

Just ahead you'll see the famous:

5. **Brennan's Restaurant,** 417 Royal St. Brennan's has been housed in this building, also built by Vincent Rillieux, since 1955 (see Chapter 7 for full listing). This was one of many buildings erected after the fire of 1794 destroyed more than 200 of the original architectural beauties along this street. From 1805 to 1841 it was home to the Banque de la Louisiane. Later, it was also home to chess champion Paul Morphy.

Next, take a look at:

6. **437 Royal St.** Masonic lodge meetings were held regularly in a drugstore here back in the early 1800s. But something more important to American culture also happened here, when the druggist Antoine A. Peyehard served after-meeting drinks to lodge members in small egg cups, whose French name (*coquetier*) was Americanized to "cocktail."

Cross St. Louis Street and on the right, about midblock, you'll see:

7. **The Brulatour Court,** at 520 Royal St. It is a splendid home built in 1896 for wine merchant François Seignouret. WSDU-TV now maintains offices here, but you're welcome to walk into the courtyard, one of the few four-walled courtyards in the French Quarter. Notice the elaborate, fan-shaped ironwork on the right end of the third-floor balcony. Incidentally, the wine merchant is virtually revered today for the fine furniture he produced (with a graceful "S" worked into the ornamentation of every piece).

On the other side of the street is:

8. **The Merieult House,** at 533 Royal St. Built in 1792, this was the only building in the area left standing after the fire of 1794. The first owner's wife very nearly became the mistress of a French castle when Napoleon offered one in exchange for her hair, which was flaming red—he wanted it for a wig to present to a Turkish sultan. This dignified and beautiful New Orleans residence must have been quite enough for Madame Merieult, however, for she flatly refused the emperor. Nowadays this is home to the Historic New Orleans Collection—Museum/Research Center (see Chapter 8 for tour times and information).

If you continue along Royal Street across Toulouse Street, you will soon come to one of the best-known landmarks in the Quarter:

9. **The Court of Two Sisters,** 613 Royal St. It was built in 1832 for a local bank president on the site of the 18th-century home of an earlier French governor. The two sisters were Emma and Bertha Camors (whose father owned the building), and from 1886 to 1906 they ran a curio store here. When you spot the:

10. **Old Town Praline Shop,** at 627 Royal St., walk through the shop entrance to the back of the store to see another of New Orleans's beautiful courtyards. This 1777 building is where Adelina Patti, the opera singer, came for a visit and stayed to become something of a local heroine in 1860. Only 17 at the time, Adelina saved

the local opera company from financial ruin when she stepped in as a last-minute replacement for an ailing lead soprano in *Lucia de Lammermoor*. She was a tremendous hit, and the season was an assured success.

On the right side at the corner of Royal and St. Peter streets (before crossing St. Peter) is:

11. Le Monnier Mansion, at 640 Royal St., which once towered above every other French Quarter building as the city's first "skyscraper," all of three stories high when it was built in 1811. A fourth story was added in 1876. At this same intersection, also on the right, but on the other side of St. Peter is:

12. The LaBranche House (now the home of the Royal Café), 700 Royal St., probably the most photographed building in the Quarter—and no wonder. Take a look at the lacy iron grillwork, with its delicate oak leaf and acorn design, that fairly drips from all three floors. Actually, there are 11 LaBranche buildings, three-story brick row houses built between 1835 and 1840 by wealthy sugar planter Jean Baptiste LaBranche. Eight face St. Peter Street, one faces Royal, and two face Pirates Alley; it was only when wrought-iron balconies came into vogue about 1850 that they were added to the St. Peter and Royal Street facades. If you plan to preserve them on film, the best vantage point is diagonally across Royal Street so that both street exposures will show in your picture.

After getting a good look at the LaBranche House, go left down St. Peter Street to:

13. Le Monnier House at No. 714. Built in 1829 by a prominent physician who carried this name, it was the home for several years during the 1860s of Antoine Alciatoire, who ran a boarding house here. His cooking became so popular with locals that he later gave up catering to open the famous Antoine's restaurant, which is run, even today, by his descendants.

A few doors down is:

14. Pat O'Brien's, 718 St. Peter St., the famous New Orleans nightspot (see Chapter 11). The building was known as the Maison de Flechier when it was built in 1790 for a wealthy planter. Later Louis Tabary put on popular plays here, and it is said that the first grand opera in America was performed within its walls. Sightseeing in New Orleans just wouldn't be complete without a look at the gorgeous courtyard, even if you don't want to indulge in a hurricane or two.

15. Preservation Hall, at 726 St. Peter St. Scores of people come to hear some of the best jazz in the country after 8pm, but a daytime stop will give you a glimpse through the big, ornate iron gate of a lush tropical courtyard in back.

Continue walking to the:

16. Plique-LaBranche House at No. 730. This house, which was built in 1825 and sold to Giraud M. Plique, was bought by Jean Baptiste LaBranche in 1829. Originally, it was the site of New Orleans's first theater, the St. Peter Street Theatre, which burned down in the fire of 1816.

Turn right off of St. Peter Street to begin your walk up Dauphine (pronounced *DAW-feen*) Street. The first stop is:

17. LePretre Mansion, 716 Dauphine St. No one has ever reported the presence of ghosts in this house, but they may well be there. As in the LaLaurie house over on Royal Street, the walls here could tell a tale of horror. Back in 1792 there arrived in New Orleans a Turk, the brother of a sultan. That he was enormously wealthy was immediately apparent, and his entourage included many servants, as well as a "family" of five beautiful young girls. They all landed in the Crescent City in the *Youseff Bey*, a Turkish freighter that evidently had been hired for their exclusive passage. Rumors quickly spread that this Turk's riches, as well as the girls, were actually the stolen property of the sultan. The Turk rented the LePretre house for the summer when its owner left to spend the season on his downriver plantation, and the palatial home very quickly became the scene of lavish entertainments with guest lists that included the cream of society. On one fateful night, however, shrieks were heard by neighbors, followed by complete silence the next morning, with no signs of activity. Eventually neighbors entered the house and found the summer tenant's body lying in a pool of blood surrounded by the bodies of the five young beauties. There was no sign of his servants. To this day no one knows if they were responsible for the murders. In 1968 this tale of terror was the Mardi Gras theme of the Krewe of Niobe.

Continue along Dauphine, crossing Orleans and St. Ann streets. Go right at the corner of Dauphine and Dumaine streets and you'll find an interesting little cottage at:

18. **707 Dumaine St**. Focus your attention on this building's roof. After the 1794 fire, all houses in the French Quarter were required by law to have flat tile roofs, and although most have since covered them with conventional roofs, this one is still in compliance with that long-ago ruling.

Down the street is a house known as:

19. **Madame John's Legacy,** 632 Dumaine St. There are those who say this is the oldest building on the Mississippi River. Others dispute that claim, saying that only a few parts of the original building survived the 1788 fire and were used in its reconstruction. In any case, the house was erected in 1726, just eight years after the founding of New Orleans, and the reconstruction follows the original design meticulously. Its first owner was a ship captain who died in the 1729 Natchez Massacre; upon his death the house passed to the captain of a smuggling ship. It has had no fewer than 21 owners since. The present structure is a fine example of a French "raised cottage." The above-ground basement is built of brick-between-posts construction (that simply means that bricks were used only to fill in a wooden frame because locally made bricks were too soft to be the primary building material), covered with boards laid horizontally. The hipped, dormered roof extends out over the veranda. Its name, incidentally, comes from a fictional quadroon who was bequeathed the house in "Tite Poulette," a Creole short story written by George Cable. Now a part of the Louisiana State Museum complex, it is open to the public on a regular basis.

Go left at the corner of Dumaine and Chartres streets and follow Chartres to the next corner; make a left onto St. Philip Street and walk until you get to the corner of St. Philip and Bourbon streets.

Opposite, you will see:

20. **Lafitte's Blacksmith Shop,** at No. 941. For many years now, it has been a bar (for the full story, see Chapter 11), but the legend is that Jean Lafitte and his pirates posed as blacksmiths here while using it as headquarters for selling goods they'd plundered on the high seas. It has survived (thanks to the loving care of its owners in recent years) in its original condition, and you can still see the brick-between-posts construction. Step inside and the dusky interior will kindle your imagination—it's a tribute to its modern-day owners that they haven't let the age of chrome and plastic come anywhere near this old place.

Go right on Bourbon Street and make a right turn onto Governor Nicholls Street. You will then see:

21. **The Thierry House,** 721 Governor Nicholls St., which was built in 1814 and started an architectural trend that spread throughout the entire state. Designed by architect Benjamin Henry Latrobe when he was just 19 years old, the house is in the Greek Revival style and features a classic portico.

On the next block of this street is:

22. 618–630 Governor Nicholls St. Henry Clay's brother, John, built a house for his wife here in 1828, and in 1871 this two-story building was added at the rear of its garden. It was in this later building that Frances Xavier Cabrini (later sainted by the Catholic Church) conducted a school.

Backtrack to the corner of Royal and Governor Nicholls streets. Take a left onto Royal and look for:

23. The LaLaurie Home, at 1140 Royal St. You may want to be sure you walk by this house in broad daylight—after dark you might be disturbed by ghostly moans or the savage hissing of a whip; you might even catch a glimpse of a small African American child walking on the balcony. This is the Quarter's haunted house. Its story is a New Orleans tale of horror: It seems the very beautiful and socially prominent Delphine LaLaurie lived here and entertained lavishly, until one night in 1834 when a fire broke out and neighbors crashed through a locked door to find seven starving slaves chained in painful positions, unable to move. Presented with undeniable evidence of Delphine's torture of her slaves, the rescuers began to doubt the validity of her stories of past slaves "committing suicide." When the next day's newspapers suggested that the dazzling hostess might have set the fire herself, a mob assembled outside the house. Madame LaLaurie and her family escaped their neighbors' wrath; however, they still fled the city. Several years later she died in Europe and her body was returned to New Orleans—and even then she had to be buried in secrecy.

A few doors down is:

24. The Gallier House Museum, at 1132 Royal St. This was built by James Gallier Jr. as his residence in 1857 (see Chapter 8 for more details).

At the corner of Royal and Ursulines streets, take a left and continue down to Chartres until you get to:

25. The Beauregard-Keyes House, 1113 Chartres St. Notice its Doric columns and handsome twin staircases. This "raised cottage," was built as a residence in 1826 by Joseph Le Carpentier, though it has several other claims to fame (see Chapter 8 for the details).

Across the street is:

26. The Archbishop Antoine Blanc Memorial, 1114 Chartres St., which includes the Old Ursuline Convent and the Archepiscopal Residence and was completed in 1752 (see Chapter 8 for more information).

Continue walking along Chartres Street until you get to Esplanade (pronounced *es-pla-NADE*) Avenue. Esplanade served as the parade ground for troops quartered on Barracks Street. It is a lovely, wide avenue lined by some of the grandest town houses built in the late 1800s. (If you're interested in viewing some of the aforementioned town houses, "Walking Tour 4," below, concentrates on the architecture of the Esplanade Ridge.) The entire 400 block of Esplanade is occupied by:

27. The Old U.S. Mint. This was once the site of Fort St. Charles, one of the forts built to protect New Orleans in 1792. (Its troops also used Esplanade as a parade ground.) It was here that Andrew Jackson reviewed the assortment of "troops" (comprised of pirates, volunteers, and a nucleus of trained soldiers) he would lead in the Battle of New Orleans (more information on this museum can be found in Chapter 8).

Follow Esplanade and turn right at the corner of North Peters Street. Follow North Peters until it intersects with Decatur Street—at this point you will have reached the back end of:

28. **The Old French Market.** This European-style market has been here for well over 150 years, and today it has a farmer's market, innumerable shops, restaurants, coffee stands, and some nonpareil people-watching. Take your time and shop; you'll probably find some souvenirs.

Across from the Old French Market is:

29. **Decatur Street.** A large section of this street—from Jackson Square all the way over to Esplanade—was not too long ago a seedy, run-down area of wild bars and cheap rooming houses. No more. An exciting renaissance resulted in all sorts of interesting shops and old-time eateries, such as Tujague's (823 Decatur). Decatur Street is far from "finished," but it's already drawing a local clientele with a slightly bohemian flavor; as more casual/smart bars open and nightlife assumes a relaxed respectability, it will no doubt attract even larger crowds. At any rate, as you walk toward St. Ann Street, follow Decatur Street and allow some time to stroll and browse. And as you pass 923 and 919 Decatur St., let your imagination conjure up the Café de Refugies and Hôtel de la Marine that were here in the 1700s and early 1800s—gathering places for pirates, smugglers, and European refugees (some of them outlaws), it was a far cry from today's scene.

☕ **TAKE A BREAK**   If you're walking in the area of 923 Decatur around lunchtime, pop into the **Central Grocery** and pick up a muffaletta sandwich. You can get them at many restaurants and delis around the city, but the ones at Central are far and away the best. There are little tables at which to eat inside Central Grocery, or you can take your food and sit outside. If you had something else in mind, there are actually a number of restaurants along this stretch that can ease any number of gastronomic cravings.

Decatur Street will take you to Jackson Square. Turn right onto St. Ann Street; those twin, four-story, red-brick buildings here as well as on the St. Peter Street side of the square are:

30. **The Pontalba Buildings,** with some of the most beautiful cast-iron balcony railings in the Quarter. Their history reflects the determination of a plucky New Orleans woman to compete with those upstart American "uptowners" and keep business concerns in the Quarter by providing elite-address shops and living quarters on the square. Indeed, these are said to be the first apartment buildings in the country—they were designed by Baroness Micaela Almonester Pontalba (she was the daughter of the Don Almonester responsible for rebuilding the St. Louis Cathedral; see Chapter 8). They were begun in 1849 and built under her direct supervision; you can see her mark today in the entwined initials "a p" in the lovely ironwork. The row houses on St. Ann Street, now owned by the State of Louisiana, were completed in 1851.

At the corner of St. Ann and Chartres streets, turn left and continue around Jackson Square; you will see:

31. **The Presbytère,** at 751 Chartres St., originally designed to be the rectory of the cathedral. The baroness's father financed the building's beginnings, but he died in 1798, leaving only the first floor done. In 1813, the building was completed. It was never used as the rectory, but instead it was first rented and sold to the city in 1853 only to be used as a courthouse.

Cast Iron Art: New Orleans's Ironwork

The use of cast iron as an architectural embellishment was introduced to this country in the early 19th century by the Spanish. Wrought iron had to be worked by hand, and it was significantly less durable and fire resistant than cast iron, which could be poured into molds and fashioned into almost any shape imaginable.

This new method of shaping iron made it easy for blacksmiths to achieve the intricate designs seen around the Garden District and French Quarter today. Molds at that time were hand carved from wood, so homeowners could quite easily request a custom design for use on their galleries or fences. If you examine some of the ironwork carefully you'll see a large variety of patterns and decorative motifs—everything from family crests to fruits and vegetables (like the Cornstalk Fence at the Cornstalk Hotel in the French Quarter). Everyone who was building a home in or around New Orleans in the 1800s wanted some sort of cast-iron decoration for their house, and during that time ships often carried up to 500 tons of pig iron to the city in one day!

Next you'll come to:

32. **The St. Louis Cathedral.** The building standing here today is the third erected on this spot. The first was destroyed by a hurricane in 1722, the second by fire in 1788. Rebuilt in 1794, and remodeled and enlarged between 1845 and 1851, it is of Spanish design. (See Chapter 8 for more information.) On the other side of the cathedral you'll come to Pirates Alley. Go right down Pirates Alley to:

33. **624 Pirates Alley, Faulkner House Books.** In 1925 the literary great William Faulkner lived here and worked on his first novel, *Soldiers' Pay.* While here he contributed to the *Times-Picayune* and to a literary magazine, the *Double Dealer.* Currently the home of Faulkner House Books, this is a great stop for Faulkner lovers and collectors of great literature. (See Chapter 10 for more information.)

   If you continue this way along Pirates Alley, you'll reach Royal Street. Turn left and at the corner of Royal and St. Peter streets, turn left again and follow St. Peter back to Chartres. On the right side of the cathedral (as you face the Mississippi River), also facing Jackson Square, is the:

34. **Cabildo,** on the corner of Chartres and St. Peter streets. It has been, in turn, a French police station and guardhouse, the statehouse of the Spanish governing body (the "Very Illustrious Cabildo"), New Orleans's City Hall, and the Louisiana State Supreme Court. Since 1911 it has been the permanent home of the Louisiana State Museum.

   One further note: If you think those old Civil War cannons out front look pitifully small and ineffective by modern standards, you might like to know that in 1921, in a near-deadly prank, one was loaded with powder, an iron ball was rammed down its muzzle, and it was fired in the dead of night. That missile traveled from the Cabildo's portico across the wide expanse of the Mississippi and some six blocks inland before landing in a house in Algiers, narrowly missing its occupants.

   ☕ **WINDING DOWN**   You've finished! Now, go back across Decatur Street to **Café du Monde**—you shouldn't miss a stop here for the beignets and coffee; no trip to New Orleans is complete without them. If you've still got a little bit of energy left after you've indulged yourself, take a walk over to the river and relax on a bench for a while.

WALKING TOUR 2
The Garden District

Start: Jackson and St. Charles avenues.
Finish: First and Prytania streets.
Time: 45 minutes to 1½ hours, depending on your pace.
Best Times: Anytime during the day.
Worst Times: After dark, when the area is not as safe as it could be.

Behind the grand exteriors of the mansions along St. Charles Avenue and its side streets are such ornate fixtures as mahogany banisters, mantels of rosewood or Italian marble, winding staircases, crystal chandeliers, and priceless antiques. The large colonnaded and balconied homes of the Garden District—many with lavish formal gardens—are well worth a look.

To reach the Garden District, catch the St. Charles streetcar at Canal and Carondelet streets and get off at Jackson Avenue. From the corner of Jackson and St. Charles, walk up St. Charles to:

1. **2220 St. Charles Ave.**, the House of Broel. Today it's a bridal shop, but this stately home dates from 1850. Inside you can view a gasolier that is original to the house (it has since been converted to electric) and you'll be able to see an enormous mirror that was bought for the home after it was purchased by the Liberty Shop in 1920. The owner of the House of Broel also has a private collection of art from around the world. The admission fee for the tour is $5 (it's a short tour), and the house is open Monday through Saturday from 10am to 4pm.

After exiting the House of Broel (if you decided to take the tour), follow St. Charles Avenue to First Street, and make a left. As you walk along First Street you'll cross Prytania and Coliseum streets (notice the exceptional wrought iron on 1315 First Street), as well as Chestnut Street before you get to:

2. **1239 First St.** Can you believe that this house was built for only $13,000? Of course, that was in 1857. The architect was James Calrow; the original owner was Albert Hamilton Brevard. The interior woodwork is especially notable. The hexagonal wing (housing the library and a bedroom) off to one side was an afterthought, added in 1869 by the Clapp family, the second owners of the home. Mrs. Clapp resided here for more than 65 years. Notice the beautiful ironwork embellished with a rose pattern.

On the other side of the street is:

3. **1236 First St.** This Greek Revival house was constructed in 1847 by John Gayle for his bride, and it's thought to be one of the oldest homes in the Garden District. Note the beautiful double galleries, fluted Corinthian columns, and detailed ironwork. Its interior features elaborate plaster ceiling medallions, black marble mantelpieces, bronze and crystal chandeliers, and wide pine floors.

On the next block across Camp, at the right-hand corner of Camp and First streets, look for:

4. **1134 First St.** Dating from 1850, this home was also one of the first built in the area, which would explain its seeming lack of decorative architectural features—it wasn't until later that competition to build the biggest and most ornate home began among neighbors here. This building is also noted as the place where

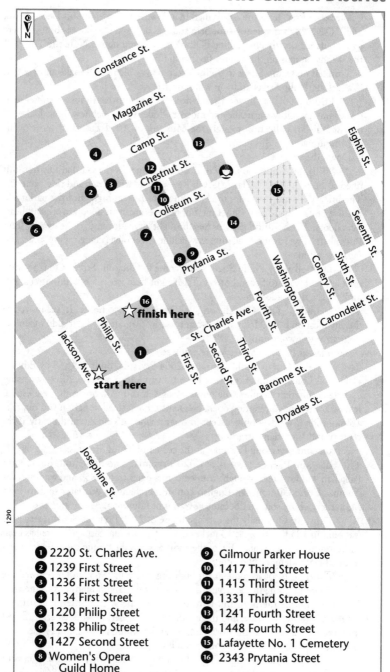

1. 2220 St. Charles Ave.
2. 1239 First Street
3. 1236 First Street
4. 1134 First Street
5. 1220 Philip Street
6. 1238 Philip Street
7. 1427 Second Street
8. Women's Opera Guild Home
9. Gilmour Parker House
10. 1417 Third Street
11. 1415 Third Street
12. 1331 Third Street
13. 1241 Fourth Street
14. 1448 Fourth Street
15. Lafayette No. 1 Cemetery
16. 2343 Prytania Street

Confederate Pres. Jefferson Davis died in a downstairs bedroom on December 6, 1889. Davis was a frequent visitor here and it is believed that he was brought here by ambulance shortly after falling ill at his Mississippi home. Note the Tower of the Winds capitals on the second-floor columns.

Turn left on Camp Street to Philip Street, onto which you'll make another left. Walk along Philip Street and you will soon see:

5. **1220 Philip St.** This all-wood residence was built in the 1850s. A subsequent owner was a wealthy sugarcane and molasses dealer whose nephew, Isaac Delgado, donated his art collection to start the Museum of Art. Isaac spent most of his growing-up years in this house.

Down the street is:

6. **1238 Philip St.** Similar to many of the other homes in the Garden District, this one was built in 1853 in classic Greek Revival style with front and side verandas. The brick walls are 18 inches thick, ceilings are 14 feet high, and the parlor is a massive 18 feet by 40 feet. Other interior features are cypress woodwork and heart pine floors. The beautiful gardens here brought citywide fame to the owner, John Rodenberg. Trees around the property include sweet olive, crape myrtle, pear, and Japanese plum.

As you stroll along Philip Street you'll come to Chestnut Street. On Chestnut, turn left and walk to Second Street. Turn right here, cross Coliseum Street, and look on the right side for:

7. **1427 Second St.** This is not the original site of this 1845 house. It was moved to the city location from Mrs. Jane Fawcett's nearby plantation, and it didn't gain the decorative ironwork until the 1930s.

Turn left at Prytania Street where you'll see:

8. **The Women's Opera Guild Home,** at 2504 Prytania. Built in 1858 by Edward Davis, this home is primarily Greek Revival in architectural style. After ownership by several different families, the home was given to the Women's Opera Guild. It now holds some interesting opera mementos. For a small donation you can take a look inside (Mondays only, except in August when it's closed) at the early 19th-century and Victorian furnishings.

As you continue along Prytania, at the corner of Third Street is:

9. **The Gilmour Parker House,** at 2520 Prytania. The light pink home with Palladian windows and wrought-iron balconies dates from 1853 and was built for Thomas Corse Gilmour, an English cotton merchant. It was later sold to John M. Parker, whose son later became governor of Louisiana. Also at this corner is:

10. **1417 Third St.** Originally the carriage house of 2520 Prytania St., this structure was built in 1853, with walls 13 inches thick. The original carriage house has been added on to over the years. One of the additions was the dining room which measures 38 feet in length. Next door is:

11. **1415 Third St.** A tobacco merchant built this house in 1865, and it featured the first indoor plumbing in the city. It is also one of the largest mansions in the area. Be sure to notice the beautiful curved double gallery. The interior features a gorgeous winding staircase, and there's an interesting carved wooden eagle, fished from the river after a violent storm, adorning the dining room chimney piece.

Cross Coliseum and on the corner you'll see:

12. **1331 Third St.** James Gallier designed this Italian villa-style home for in-laws of Edgar Degas, the French Impressionist painter, in the 1850s. In 1884 its elaborate stables out back and the cast-iron galleries were added, to make it one of the most outstanding houses in the Garden District. The teak mantelpiece in the living room is hand-carved and has a secret compartment on each side.

When you get to Camp Street, turn right to reach Fourth Street, where you turn right again. At the corner of Chestnut, on the right is:

13. 1241 Fourth St., which dates from the mid-1800s. Louis Herman, a New Orleans cotton broker, started building this house from the back. The kitchen and slave quarters went up in 1844; then when the "big house" was added up front at a later date, the two were connected.

Continue along Fourth, crossing Chestnut and Coliseum streets. If your French Quarter sightseeing included the Cornstalk Hotel on Royal Street, you'll see a twin to that fence at:

14. 1448 Fourth St. This house was built in 1859 for Col. Robert Short of Kentucky. Interestingly, Short's home was confiscated from him during the Civil War, but was returned to him when the war ended. Its double parlors measure a spacious 43 by 26 feet, and the cast-iron fence with the motif of cornstalks entwined with morning glories was cast in Philadelphia. Today it would cost more than $100 a foot to have it reproduced.

At Prytania Street, turn left. If you need a breather, go into The Rink Shopping Mall on the other side of Prytania. There are a few benches, a great bookstore, and a place to get light refreshments. Turn left again onto Washington Avenue and soon, on your right, you'll see:

15. Lafayette No. 1 Cemetery. With its aboveground tombs, it is reminiscent of Père Lachaise Cemetery in Paris. This particular cemetery was laid out in 1833. The tombs, with their spectacular architectural details, almost resemble some of the homes here in the Garden District. The wide aisles between the tombs were designed to accommodate large funeral processions. In just under 20 years from the time the cemetery was laid out, yellow fever victims had it almost completely filled. Many tombs here hold the remains of entire families, and some even hold members of various societies, organizations, or clubs. The tomb for the Jefferson Fire Company No. 22 is a good example of this. Only the very wealthy could afford tombs of cast iron or marble, so most of the tombs here were built of brick and plaster and then whitewashed. On All Saints Day city residents clean up the cemeteries and decorate family tombs with flowers. The little wooden mortuary first served as a Catholic church at another location—it dates from 1844 (see Chapter 8 for more information). *Note:* For safety reasons I would advise that you stay outside the cemetery; see suggestions for guided tours listed in Chapter 8 for a safe way to visit the city's cemeteries.

☕ **TAKE A BREAK** At the corner of Washington Avenue and Coliseum Street, you'll find **Commander's Palace,** which was built as a restaurant in 1880 by Emile Commander and has from the start been a favorite with New Orleanians (see Chapter 7 for a full discussion). You could stop here for lunch, but proper dress and reservations are required.

When you're finished at Commander's Palace, head back to Prytania and go right. Follow Prytania to:

16. 2343 Prytania (now the Louise S. McGehee School for girls). Wealthy sugar planter Bradish Johnson built this elegant town house, and it cost him $100,000 even back in 1872. This Free-Renaissance–style home was probably designed by Paris-trained architect James Freret. Before a deadly hurricane in 1815, the magnolias out front were said to be the largest in the country. Oddly enough, the inside of the house has never seen a birth, a death, or a marriage. The Louise S. McGehee School acquired the building in 1929.

Keep walking and when you get to Josephine Street, turn left to reach St. Charles Avenue and the streetcar; or, if your feet aren't hurting too much, pick up where you left off on the next walking tour, which is a tour of the Lower Garden District. It will also take you back to St. Charles Avenue and to the streetcar.

WALKING TOUR 3
The Lower Garden District

Start: First and Prytania streets.
Finish: St. Charles Avenue and Melpomene.
Time: 1¹/₂ hours.
Best Times: Anytime during the day.
Worst Times: After dark, when the area is not as safe as it could be.

The Lower Garden District is a particularly interesting area because of its wonderful collection of 19th-century Greek Revival architecture. Unfortunately, the neighborhood has become run down and some of the most incredible beauties have been demolished. Still, I hope that with this walk you'll get a good feel for what the Lower Garden District used to be like. Try to imagine the gardens, which no longer exist, as you walk. *Note:* Because the Lower Garden District has seen better days, you should be alert to any and all activity around you. Remember, you're in a major city and you must keep your physical safety in mind as you explore.

To reach the starting point, take the St. Charles streetcar all the way to First Street. When you leave the streetcar, walk one block on First Street to your left (if you're facing the direction in which the streetcar was running when it dropped you off) to Prytania Street and your first stop will be at:

1. **2343 Prytania St.,** (now the Louise McGehee School). Originally built as a private home in 1872, it was made an all-girl school in 1929. (See the last entry of the walking tour of the Garden District for more details.)

Continue along Prytania Street to:

2. **2221 Prytania,** which is a beautiful residence. In particular, note the Corinthian columns.

Continue on Prytania, crossing Jackson. If you stop at:

3. **2127 Prytania,** you'll get to see a typical Greek Revival raised villa. There are some remarkable features on this house, most notably the cast-iron fence and gallery, as well as the carved lintel. This house also has wonderful Corinthian columns.

On the corner of Josephine and Prytania you'll see:

4. **The Gospel Temple Church** (now the Fellowship Missionary Baptist Church), at 2101 Prytania St. It was built in 1901, originally as a Presbyterian church, and is a lovely stone church—perhaps Renaissance Revival would best describe this heavy but beautiful piece of architecture.

Continue walking on Prytania Street. Look for a three-story masonry building at:

5. **1823 Prytania St.** Now a home for the elderly, this building was once known as St. Anna's Asylum, a home for "destitute" women and their children. The asylum cared not about religious preference but about the women and their children—and apparently it advertised itself as such. It was officially recognized by the state as an organization in 1853 and was built on land donated by William Newton Mercer. Note the Doric portico raised on scored piers, as well as the cupola on the roof.

The Lower Garden District

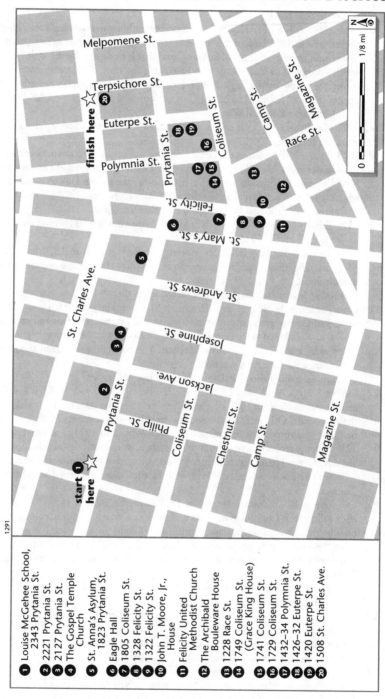

1. Louise McGehee School, 2343 Prytania St.
2. 2221 Prytania St.
3. 2127 Prytania St.
4. The Gospel Temple Church
5. St. Anna's Asylum, 1823 Prytania St.
6. Eagle Hall
7. 1805 Coliseum St.
8. 1328 Felicity St.
9. 1322 Felicity St.
10. John T. Moore, Jr., House
11. Felicity United Methodist Church
12. The Archibald Bouleware House
13. 1228 Race St.
14. 1749 Coliseum St. (Grace King House)
15. 1741 Coliseum St.
16. 1729 Coliseum St.
17. 1432–34 Polymnia St.
18. 1426–32 Euterpe St.
19. 1420 Euterpe St.
20. 1508 St. Charles Ave.

On the next block is:

6. **Eagle Hall**, at 1780 Prytania St., a commercial building that was built for Philip Meyer, who in 1851 bought the triangular site created by the intersecting streets. It was built to be a commercial building, and that is evidenced by the wide facia, which was meant to hold a large sign advertising the store. The structure was occupied for a time by the Eagle Hall, a civic organization. Lafayette Volkstheater opened here in August 1862, and German political meetings were held here during and after the Civil War.

Turn right when you get to Felicity Street. At the corner of Felicity and Coliseum, on the right, is:

7. **1805 Coliseum St.** Built in the mid-1850s, this classic raised villa with Greek and Italianate features was built for Edward Nave, a native Virginian and a prominent New Orleans commission merchant. If you can, take a close look at the doors, which hold the type of etched glass that came into vogue after 1870.

Continue on Felicity. On the right is an Italianate villa at:

8. **1328 Felicity St.** It was built in 1869 for John Augustus Braffer and was restored between 1977 and 1979. A few doors down is:

9. **1322 Felicity St.** This Italianate masonry house was built in 1870 for John McGinty. The unique cast-iron gallery and Corinthian columns are extraordinary in their detail.

Another Victorian Italianate house on the left is the:

10. **John T. Moore, Jr., House**, at 1309 Felicity St. Erected in 1880, it is a great study for the admirer of architecture. It has a wonderful overhanging roof and what is known as a scalloped verge board. The iron cresting on top is particularly interesting to look at because it forms a belvedere. You could probably stand and look at this house for hours and not notice every detail.

Continue along Felicity and you can't help but notice the:

11. **Felicity United Methodist Church**, at 1226 Felicity, a late Gothic Revival–style church that was built in 1888 after an earlier church on the same site burned down the year before. Originally there stood two steeples atop the towers on the present building—unfortunately, a hurricane blew them down in 1915. The building at 1217 Felicity, across the street from the church, is worth noticing—I think its triangular shape is interesting, although it is not recognized as a historical landmark.

When you reach the corner of Felicity and Camp, take a left onto Camp Street. The next stop is:

12. **The Archibald Bouleware House**, at 1531 Camp St. Built in 1854, it's a two-story gallery with Corinthian columns on both levels, which is quite uncommon—usually, these houses might have Corinthian columns on one level, but not the other. Another interesting feature of this house is the arched iron trellis out front—it is one of a very few surviving examples of this once-common decorative piece for the garden.

As you continue down Camp Street, you'll run into Race Street—take a left at the corner. Look for the three-story house at:

13. **1228 Race St.**, dating from 1867. Because the gallery on the second floor is wooden, you would assume that it is much older than it is. It is actually the replacement for the original simple cast-iron balcony and was built there after 1900.

Follow Race Street to Coliseum Street. Go right to:

14. **1749 Coliseum St.** This was the house of Grace King, noted Louisiana historian, fiction writer, scholar, and essayist. King, born in New Orleans in 1852, is noted for having written *Memories of a Southern Woman of Letters* (1932). The fluted columns out front often welcomed such friends as Mark Twain and Sherwood

Anderson. King never married, and she lived in this house for many years with her two sisters. For about 30 years the house was a meeting place for the artists and writers who lived in New Orleans at the time. Nearby is:

15. **1741 Coliseum St.**, known as the Hugh-Wilson House. This building was originally owned by a commission merchant. Note the front gallery with Ionic columns above and Doric columns on the ground floor.

On the corner of Polymnia, notice the house at:

16. **1729 Coliseum St.** This particular house was originally built in the 1830s and stood at 904 Orange St. In 1981 it was moved to its present location and was restored. It is one of very few restored homes in the area.

In 1858 the house was purchased by Henry Hope Stanley, born in Britain, who came here to begin a career as a cotton merchant. At some point, he met and took into his home a Welsh cabin boy who had jumped ship. Stanley and his wife decided to make the boy a part of their family and named him Henry Morton Stanley. When the Civil War began young Henry left New Orleans and became a member of the Confederate Army. After having been a prisoner of war he was released and then found himself in New York, where he became a journalist. His newspaper sent him to Africa, at which point he searched for and found Dr. David Livingston—it was he who asked, "Dr. Livingston, I presume?" He eventually earned a knighthood for his other African adventures.

After taking a left from Coliseum onto Polymnia, look for a Greek Revival house at:

17. **1432–34 Polymnia St.** (between Coliseum and Prytania streets). Notice the full-length pillars that support the gallery. This house is a good example of what the whole neighborhood looked like before the implementation of cast iron became so widespread after 1850. Before the use of cast iron, wood cisterns, gazebos, picket fences, and galleries gave the neighborhood a feeling entirely different from that of the later Garden District, when homes began to drip with cast-iron balconies, fences, and the like. Be sure to look at the unique side carriage entrance to 1434.

At the corner of Polymnia and Prytania streets, take a right and walk down to Euterpe. Go right again. As you walk along Euterpe Street, have a look at the Greek Revival row houses at:

18. **1426–32 Euterpe St.** They are a good example of the row houses typical of the Lower Garden District. Also note the "shotgun" double houses at 1423–25 and 1427–29 Euterpe. An architectural style much used in New Orleans, the "shotgun house" is so named because the rooms fall one directly behind the other. A bullet fired through the front door could go right out the back, passing through every room in the house without hitting a wall.

As you walk along, look at the house that occupies the site of:

19. **1420 Euterpe St.** (on the right between Coliseum and Prytania streets). This house dates from the early 1850s and was the residence of John Thornhill, a prominent commission merchant and cotton factor.

When you get to Coliseum Street, go left. Follow Coliseum to Terpsichore. Turn left on Terpsichore and follow it across Prytania to St. Charles Avenue. Turn right at the corner of St. Charles Avenue and at:

20. **1508 St. Charles Ave.**, you'll see what once was probably a stunning three-story Victorian. Note the dormer and semioctagonal bay. It has some great detail work. This particular house was built in the late 1800s or early 1900s and it is currently home to a doll museum.

Here you can wait for the streetcar—there's a stop right across St. Charles from the doll museum.

WALKING TOUR 4
Esplanade Ridge

Start: 2023 Esplanade Ave., in front of Mechling's Guest House.
Finish: City Park.
Time: Allow approximately 1½ hours, not including museum, cemetery, and shopping stops.
Best Times: Monday through Saturday early or late morning.
Worst Times: Sunday when attractions are closed. Also, don't walk in this area after dark—be sure to start the walk early enough.

A stroll down Esplanade Avenue to City Park offers a look at a sampling of New Orleans architecture in an area that is not often explored. Many of the proud homes on Esplanade no longer house just one family, but have become boarding houses, apartments, and restaurants. Recent improvements to the Esplanade area indicate that it is experiencing a much-needed revitalization. I've been told that restorations to this area are ongoing, and it will indeed be a great pleasure to residents and visitors alike if Esplanade Avenue is returned to its former glory.

From the French Quarter, stroll up Esplanade Avenue to your first stop:

1. **2023 Esplanade Ave.** Once a plantation home, this building is now under the ownership of Kelly and Taina Mechling (pronounced *MEK-ling*). Kelly and Taina are in the process of renovating the home, which they are running as a guest house (see Chapter 6 for a full listing). Down the street a bit is the:

2. **Widow Castanedo's House,** at 2033–35 Esplanade Ave. Widow Castanedo lived in this home, on land purchased by her grandfather, Juan Rodriguez, in the 1780s, until her death in 1861. She is famous for having battled the city against the extension of the Esplanade. (It is believed that her house was moved to its present location when the Esplanade was finally extended.)

   The house has a late Italianate appearance, similar to the Mechling residence, and is split down the middle and inhabited today by two sisters. This splitting of a house was very common at one time, and a pair of siblings often lived one on each side.

   Continue along and at the corner of Miro and Esplanade is:

3. **2139 Esplanade Ave.** This building is a great example of typical "Esplanade Ridge Style." The home was built for William Chambers, most likely a short time after the Civil War. Note the Ionic columns on the upper level. On the opposite side of the same corner is:

4. **2176 Esplanade Ave.,** a simple, classic-style town house. It was the second Bayou Road home built by Hubert Gerard, the man who built the Mechling Guest House at 2023.

   Veer left at the fork at Miro Road to stay on Esplanade and look for the statue of the:

5. **"Goddess of History—Genius of Peace,"** which is on the triangular piece of land at the crossover of Bayou Road, Esplanade Avenue, and Miro Street. In 1886 the piece of land was given to the city by Charles Gayarre, and George H. Dunbar donated the original statue to be placed there. Purchased from the Audubon Park Cotton Centennial Commission, the statue was destroyed in 1938, and the present one is a replacement.

   No one knows why, but only half of the house at:

6. **2306 Esplanade Ave.** has survived. At present, the house is most notably known as the Musson-Degas House because the home was originally purchased by

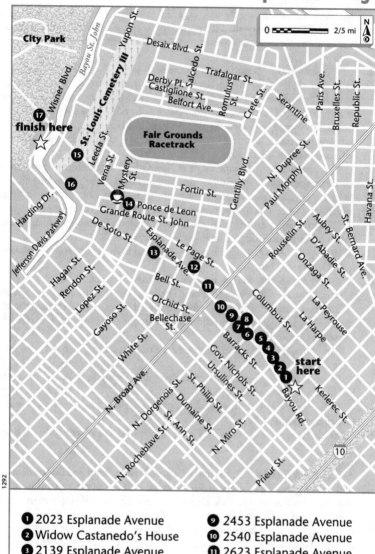

City Park

Fair Grounds Racetrack

finish here

start here

1 2023 Esplanade Avenue
2 Widow Castanedo's House
3 2139 Esplanade Avenue
4 2176 Esplanade Avenue
5 "Goddess of History–
Genius of Peace"
6 2306 Esplanade Avenue
7 2326 Esplanade Avenue
8 2337 Esplanade Avenue

9 2453 Esplanade Avenue
10 2540 Esplanade Avenue
11 2623 Esplanade Avenue
12 2809 Esplanade Avenue
13 2936 Esplanade Avenue
14 3330 Esplanade Avenue
15 St. Louis Cemetery No. 3
16 Pitot House
17 City Park

the uncle of Edgar and René Degas. Edgar Degas, French impressionist painter, is said to have painted the portrait of René's wife, Estelle Musson (which is now in the New Orleans Museum of Art), during the time he spent living at 2306.

Next door to the Musson-Degas House is:

7. 2326 Esplanade Ave., the home of a well-known local artist. You'll know the house by the collection of small metal houses, cinder-block sculptures, and a beautiful metal-crafted marlin on the front porch. The house, known as the Reuther House, was owned by Joseph Reuther, a baker, in 1913.

In passing, take a look at 2325, 2329, and 2331—all are interesting examples of Creole cottages. Nearby is:

8. 2337 Esplanade Ave., showing a style of New Orleans architecture that was dominant during the late 19th century—the shotgun house. Take a close look at:

9. 2453 Esplanade Ave. Although this house at the corner of Dorquenois Street (which used to be one of a pair until the other house was demolished) has been changed extensively architecturally, it's one of the few remaining mansard-roofed homes on Esplanade Ridge. The lovely home at:

10. 2540 Esplanade Ave. was built in the 1850s and is an example of simple classic style. On the next block is:

11. 2623 Esplanade Ave., a classical revival Victorian that was built in 1896 by Louis A. Jung. Note the Corinthian columns. The Jungs donated the triangular piece of land at the crossover of Esplanade Avenue, Broad Street, and Crete Street to the city on the condition that it would remain a public piece of land. It is officially known as DeSoto Park.

Continuing along in a lakeside direction along Esplanade, take notice of these three houses:

12. 2809 Esplanade Ave., one of the more decorative Victorian Queen Anne center-hall houses on Esplanade Ridge.

13. 2936 Esplanade Ave., a little less than a block away and a nice example of what's known as a Gothic villa.

14. 3330 Esplanade Ave., built in the Creole cottage style and a lovely galleried, frame home.

☕ **TAKE A BREAK**   At the intersection of Mystery Street and Esplanade you'll find a little grouping of shops and restaurants. If you're in the area at lunchtime you might want to stop at **Café Degas** for a leisurely meal. If you're more health conscious and don't mind eating outside, I'd highly recommend **Wholefoods**—stop in and get a quick sandwich or salad. If you're not ready for lunch, stop in at **Brew Time,** which is located behind Café Degas, for a cup of coffee and some pastry.

When you're done exploring and have gathered enough energy, continue walking along Esplanade. In a few minutes you'll see the:

15. St. Louis Cemetery No. 3 on your right. If you've been putting off going into the cemeteries because of the crime associated with them, this is one you can explore in relative safety. You can pick up brochures in the office there.

After you've spent some time in the cemetery, head back out to Esplanade and continue walking toward City Park. When you get to the bridge, you can go left, following the signs, to see:

16. Pitot House, which is open for public viewing (see Chapter 8 for a description), or you can continue walking straight into:

17. City Park, where you can explore the amphitheater, museum, and gardens (see Chapter 8 for more details).

A STREETCAR TOUR

Start: St. Charles Avenue and Canal Street.
Finish: Audubon Park.
Time: 45 minutes, not including time spent wandering at any of the stops or eating.
Best Times: Around 11am, since this will allow for a leisurely morning and afternoon spent wandering and exploring, enabling you to return back to the Central Business District or the Vieux Carré in time to get dressed for dinner.
Worst Times: Morning and evening rush hours, when the cars are packed.

One of the best ways to see the most historic and architecturally interesting neighborhoods of New Orleans is to ride the famous streetcar that runs along St. Charles Avenue. It will take you through the Garden District, past the universities and Audubon Park to Riverbend and Carrollton.

On the corner of Canal and St. Charles, while you wait for the streetcar, have a look at:

1. The Crescent Billiard Hall, 115 St. Charles Ave. It was built in 1826, and in 1865 the whole thing was remodeled, turning the inside into an enormous billiard hall. The Pickwick Club, founded in 1857 (incidentally, the members of the Pickwick Club had a hand in founding the Krewe of Comus in the same year), took over the building in 1950.

Once on the streetcar, notice:

2. Kolb's Restaurant, at 121–123, 125–127 St. Charles. The building at 125–127 St. Charles was originally a museum (ca. 1844); however, it closed shortly after opening. Kolb's Restaurant (presently housed in both buildings—121–123 was built in 1853) began as a saloon and has been in operation since 1898. The cast-iron balconies of this German restaurant are typical of those found in New Orleans in the 19th century.

From your perch in the car take note of:

3. Lafayette Square, located on your left between stops 3 and 4 and next door to the Federal Court of Appeals. Bounded by Camp Street, North Street, South Street, and St. Charles Avenue, it is the oldest public square in New Orleans. Oddly enough, there is no monument to Lafayette in the park. Across from Lafayette Square is:

4. Gallier Hall, 545 St. Charles Ave. Also between stops 3 and 4, but on the right side, the impressive Greek Revival building was the inspiration of James Gallier Sr. Erected between 1845 and 1853, it served as City Hall for just over a century. After the completion of the building's basement the city ran out of money to fund the project so construction was delayed. A roof was placed over the finished basement and the police department occupied it until money was raised for its completion. Afterward, it took two years to finish, and on May 10, 1853, it was dedicated. The building measures 90 feet in width, 215 feet in depth, and stands three stories high. It is constructed of Tuckahoe marble and features two impressive rows of fluted Ionic columns. Several important figures in Louisiana history are entombed in Gallier Hall, including Jefferson Davis and General Beauregard.

Soon after Gallier Hall (between stops 6 and 7), the streetcar will go screeching around:

5. **Lee Circle,** at St. Charles and Howard avenues. If you look out the window to the left, you will be able to see the statue of Robert E. Lee atop an impressive pedestal and column—take note that he's facing *north* (that's so his back will never be to his enemies). It was officially raised and dedicated in 1884. Also between stops 6 and 7, you'll notice on your right side:

6. **The K&B Plaza,** at St. Charles Avenue and Lee Circle. Look for the collection of sculpture outside the K&B headquarters building. There is an equally magnificent collection inside the lobby, which is open to the public from 9am to 5pm during the week. If you're an art lover, this is one place you should hop off the streetcar and have a look. Inside you will find works by many noted sculptors, including Henry Moore. Some say that it is one of the finest collections in the country.

From here on, it's fun to watch the homes that line the avenue as they change from Greek Revival to Victorian to early 1900s. The Garden District begins at Jackson Avenue, and you may want to get off the trolley to explore it fully. Even while riding by, however, you'll see many lovely homes in their garden settings, beginning with:

7. **2265 St. Charles Ave.,** on your right. The famed James Gallier Jr. was one of the architects of this house, built in 1856; the wide wing was added later.

8. **2336 St. Charles Ave.** is on your left. When this cottage was built in the 1840s, the avenue was a dirt road known as Nyades, nothing like the broad street you see today.

9. **The Christ Church Cathedral,** 2919 St. Charles Ave., on your right is one of the oldest Protestant churches in the Mississippi Valley. This is the fourth building on the site, and it suffered the loss of a steeple in a 1915 hurricane.

10. **2926 St. Charles Ave.** is on your left. This house was built in 1882, with a gallery for every room and an early air-conditioning system—a 12-inch space between inner and outer walls. Don't be confused by the number 710 above the front door—it's left over from an outdated numbering system.

On your right between stops 21 and 22, you'll see:

11. **The Columns,** at 3811 St. Charles; this is the spot where *Pretty Baby* was filmed (accommodations are offered here; see Chapter 6). You'll know it by the enormous columns and the sprawling front porch.

Soon afterward, you'll look out the right side of the streetcar and wonder what that huge brick building with the cupola is; it's the:

12. **Sacred Heart Academy,** 4521 St. Charles, between stops 24 and 25. This is a prestigious all-girl Catholic school that was built in 1899.

For a look at one of the oldest buildings on St. Charles, look out on the right between stops 27 and 28 and you'll see the:

13. **Orleans Club,** at 5005 St. Charles. It is a private social and cultural women's club, but it was built in 1868 by a Colonel Lewis as a wedding gift for his daughter. It is sometimes used for debut teas and wedding receptions.

The interesting neo-Italianate mansion on your left at:

14. **5120 St. Charles Ave.** was built in 1907 by the owners of one of the largest department stores in New Orleans. It changed hands a number of times (one owner was the silent-screen star Marguerite Clark) before it was finally donated to the New Orleans Public Library. If you'd like to get a good look at the inside, get off at stop 27 or 28 and poke around inside the library—it's worth it just to see the painted ceiling and the paneling.

A Streetcar Tour

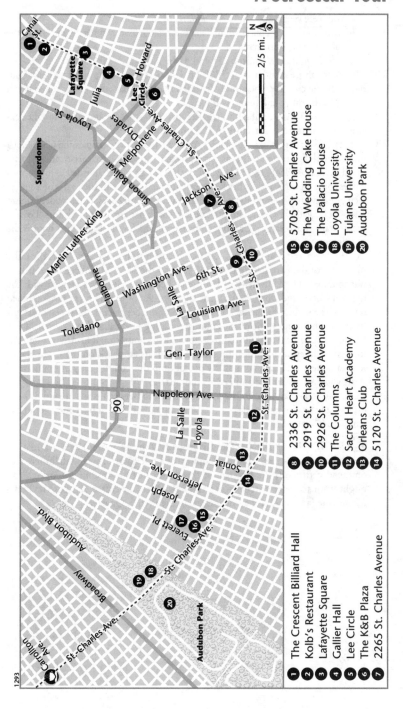

1. The Crescent Billiard Hall
2. Kolb's Restaurant
3. Lafayette Square
4. Gallier Hall
5. Lee Circle
6. The K&B Plaza
7. 2265 St. Charles Avenue
8. 2336 St. Charles Avenue
9. 2919 St. Charles Avenue
10. 2926 St. Charles Avenue
11. The Columns
12. Sacred Heart Academy
13. Orleans Club
14. 5120 St. Charles Avenue
15. 5705 St. Charles Avenue
16. The Wedding Cake House
17. The Palacio House
18. Loyola University
19. Tulane University
20. Audubon Park

If you were swept away by *Gone with the Wind,* stop at:

15. 5705 St. Charles. A replication of Tara is located between stops 30 and 31 on the right side. It was constructed in 1941.

On your right between stops 31 and 32 is:

16. The Wedding Cake House, 5809 St. Charles, one of the most talked about houses in the city. It's a beautiful Victorian mansion that you couldn't miss if you tried. Nearby on your left you will see:

17. The Palacio House, at 5824 St. Charles, between stops 31 and 32. It is a nice example of Italianate architecture. A few stops down is:

18. Loyola University, 6363 St. Charles Ave. The university occupies the 6000 block of St. Charles Avenue on the site of a preparatory school, Loyola Academy, that stood there from 1904 to 1911, when the university was established. The campus covers some 14 acres and its brick-front main buildings form three sides of a square facing the avenue. Behind these buildings the modern Dana Center student union is a popular gathering spot, and its cafe and snack bar are open to visitors. Loyola, incidentally, is the largest Catholic university in the South. Right next door is the prestigious:

19. Tulane University, at 6823 St. Charles, between stops 36 and 37. It is the older university of the two, dating from 1834, when the Medical College of Louisiana was founded. The University of Louisiana, begun in 1847, was merged with the medical school, and when Paul Tulane left a bequest of $1 million to the combined schools, the name was changed in gratitude to the benefactor. That generous gift financed what is now one of the country's leading medical and law schools. (The medical school has since moved to a downtown campus on Tulane Avenue.) An interesting facet of the education offered here is its emphasis on the Code Napoleon, a rather peculiar system of law practiced in this country only in Louisiana.

As you pass by Tulane and Loyola the entrance to:

20. Audubon Park can be seen on your left (it is also between stops 36 and 37)—it extends all the way to the levee at the Mississippi. For more information about the park, see Chapter 8.

WINDING DOWN   The Riverbend (stops 43 and 44) area is a marvelous little spot for a rest, a bit of shopping, or a bite to eat. I would definitely recommend getting off the streetcar at this point, just to do some exploring. You might want to get a burger at the **Camellia Grill** or coffee and pastries at **La Madeleine** (a branch of the one located in the French Quarter).

Shopping 10

Like everything else in New Orleans, shopping is fun. I say that as a dedicated nonshopper. Still, the shops in this city are so different, so intriguing, that I'm in and out of them all along the streets. Almost anything you could want is for sale in New Orleans. And if you can't find what you're looking for, you can find someone to make it for you: The place is loaded with craftspeople and artisans who use such disparate materials as cast iron, wood, leather, fabric, brass, plastic, and precious metals.

Antique shops are really special here, many with patios and gardens that actually seem to enhance their goods. Some are located in old French Quarter homes, giving another dimension to browsing. And the emphasis that was always placed on fine home furnishings in New Orleans has left some of the loveliest antiques I've ever viewed. Many came from Europe in the early days; others were crafted right in the city by cabinetmakers, internationally known for their exquisite pieces. Antiquing has become so popular in New Orleans that there are even people who will take you on a personalized guided tour of city shops (for more information see "Organized Tours" in Chapter 8). In addition, the **Royal Street Guild** (☎ **504/949-2222**), an association of some of the city's antique dealers, has put together brochures that are available at most hotels.

Because New Orleans is an international port city, its shops are filled with a rich variety of imported items from countries around the world. Home furnishings, kitchen utensils, pottery, designer clothes, whatever else you can name—the world's best is on sale here. Art galleries, too, display the works of leading artists as well as those from the area. The creation of fine jewelry is a much-practiced art; some of the jewelry shops will seem more like art galleries.

You'll also notice an abundance of gift shops that stock postcards, sunglasses, and T-shirts of all sorts, shapes, and varieties. There are so many of these shops in certain areas of the city that it's almost becoming offensive. Bourbon Street in particular is a haven for those interested in purchasing T-shirts and tacky souvenir items.

The following list is far from complete; if you don't see a particular category that is of special interest to you, be assured that you'll more than likely find it when you arrive in New Orleans. For convenience, I'll describe first the major shopping centers, followed by shops grouped by category.

The hours for most shops are Monday through Saturday from 10am to 5pm. Many, however, are open later on Saturday night and Sunday afternoon, especially in the French Quarter, where souvenir shops are likely to remain open until 11pm every day of the week.

1 The Shopping Scene

CANAL PLACE   At the foot of Canal Street (365 Canal St.) where it reaches the Mississippi River, this stunning shopping center holds more than 50 shops, many of which are branches of some of this country's most elegant retailers. The three-tiered mall has polished marble floors, a landscaped atrium, fountains, and pools. Stores in this sophisticated setting include Brooks Brothers, Jaeger, Bally of Switzerland, Saks Fifth Avenue, and Laura Ashley. Open Monday to Wednesday and Friday to Saturday from 10am to 6pm; Thursday from 10am to 8pm; and Sunday from noon to 6pm.

THE ESPLANADE   The Esplanade, 1401 West Esplanade, houses more than 150 stores and specialty shops. Big-name stores that are represented include Macy's, Dillard's, Mervyn's, Yvonne LaFleur, and The Limited. There is also a large food court. Open Monday to Saturday from 10am to 9pm, and Sunday from noon to 6pm.

THE FRENCH MARKET   Shops within the Market begin on Decatur Street across from Jackson Square, and include candy, cookware, fashions, crafts, toys, New Orleans memorabilia, and candles. Open from 10am to 6pm (Farmer's Market Café du Monde open 24 hours).

JACKSON BREWERY   Just across from Jackson Square at 600–620 Decatur St., the old brewery building has been transformed into a joyful jumble of shops, cafes, delicatessens, restaurants, and entertainment. The 125 shops and eateries within its walls include fashions, gourmet and Cajun-Creole foodstuffs, toys, hats, crafts, pipes, posters, and souvenirs. The latest addition to this mall is a branch of the theme restaurant Planet Hollywood. Keep in mind that many shops in the Brewery close at 5:30 or 6pm, before the Brewery itself closes. Open Sunday to Thursday from 10am to 10pm, and Friday to Saturday from 10am to 9pm.

JULIA STREET   From Camp Street over toward the river on Julia Street, you'll find great contemporary art galleries lining the street. Of course, some of the works are a bit pricey, but there's a lot that's absolutely affordable if you're interested in collecting. You'll find many of them listed below.

MAGAZINE STREET   This major uptown thoroughfare runs from Canal Street to Audubon Park, with some 6 miles of more than 140 shops (some of which are listed below), some in 19th-century brick storefronts, others in quaint cottagelike buildings. Among the offerings are antiques, art galleries, boutiques, crafts, and dolls.

NEW ORLEANS CENTRE   New Orleans's newest shopping center, New Orleans Centre at 1400 Poydras features a glass atrium and includes upscale shops like Lord and Taylor and Macy's. There are three levels of specialty shops and restaurants. Open Monday to Saturday from 10am to 8pm and Sunday from noon to 6pm.

RIVERBEND   The Riverbend district is in the Carrollton area. To reach it, ride the St. Charles Avenue streetcar to stop 44, then walk down Maple Street one block to Dublin Park, the site of an old public market once lined with open stalls. Nowadays, renovated shops inhabit the old general store, a produce warehouse made of bargeboard, and the town surveyor's raised-cottage home. Among the outstanding shops are Yvonne LaFleur, whose romantic fashions have appeared on TV and movie screens; and the Cache Pot, with a concentration of unusual, high-quality gifts.

RIVERWALK   This popular shopping development at 1 Poydras St. is an exciting covered mall that runs right along the river from Poydras Street to the Convention Center. Among the 140 specialty shops at this location, you'll find Eddie Bauer, The Limited, The Sharper Image, and Banana Republic, plus several eateries and periodic free entertainment. Open Monday to Thursday from 10am to 9pm, Friday and Saturday from 10am to 10pm, and Sunday from 12:30pm to 5:30pm.

2 Shopping A to Z

ANTIQUES

Audubon Antiques
2025 Magazine St. ☎ **504/581-5704.** Mon–Sat 10am–5pm; Sun noon–5pm.

Audubon has everything from collectible curios to authentic antique treasures at reasonable prices.

✪ Aurat Antiques
3009 Magazine St. ☎ **504/897-3210** or 800/676-8640. Mon and Wed–Sat 10am–5pm.

Owners Robert and Martha Lady collect and import incredibly beautiful Indo-Portuguese and Anglo-Indian colonial furniture as well as Oriental rugs, dhurries, kilims, and other collectibles.

Boyer Antiques—Dolls & Buttons
241 and 328 Chartres St. ☎ **504/522-4513.** Daily 9:30am–5pm.

In addition to an assortment of antiques, you'll find an enchanting collection of old dolls and doll furniture.

Charbonnet & Charbonnet, Inc.
2929 Magazine St. ☎ **504/891-9948.** Mon–Sat 9am–5pm.

If country pine is what you're looking for, you'll find it at Charbonnet and Charbonnet. They have some beautiful English and Irish pieces. In addition, custom furnishings are made on-site.

French Antique Shop
225 Royal St. ☎ **504/524-9861.** Mon–Fri 9am–5pm; Sat 10am–3pm.

This shop specializes in 18th- and 19th-century French furnishings, mirrors, statues, lighting fixtures, and marble fireplace mantels. Other items include Oriental porcelains and collectibles.

Kiel's Antiques
325 Royal St. ☎ **504/522-4552.** Mon–Sat 9am–5pm.

This lovely antique shop has a fine collection of French and English antiques, as well as decorative items.

Le Wicker Gazebo
3436 Magazine St. ☎ **504/899-1355.** Daily 10am–4pm.

New and antique wicker furnishings, including miniature versions for children.

✪ Lucullus
610 Chartres St. ☎ **504/528-9620.** Mon–Sat 9am–5pm.

An unusual shop, Lucullus has a wonderful collection of culinary antiques as well as 17th-, 18th-, and 19th-century furnishings to "complement the grand pursuits of cooking, dining, and imbibing."

Magazine Arcade Antiques

3017 Magazine St. ☎ **504/895-5451.** Mon–Sat 10am–5pm.

This large and fascinating shop once housed the Garden District's classiest mercantile. Today it holds an exceptional collection of 18th- and 19th-century European, Asian, and American furnishings; music boxes; dollhouse miniatures; European and Oriental porcelain; cloisonné and lacquer; cameos; opera glasses; old medical equipment; wind-up phonographs; antique toys; and scores of other items. Try to plan plenty of time to browse through it all.

Manheim Galleries

403–409 Royal St. ☎ **504/568-1901.** Mon–Sat 9am–5pm.

At Manheim Galleries you'll find an enormous collection of Continental, English, and Oriental furnishings. There is also a collection of porcelains, jade, silver, and fine painting. Manheim Galleries is also the agent for Boehm Birds.

Miss Edna's Antiques

2029 Magazine St. ☎ **504/524-1897.** Call for hours.

Miss Edna's has a wonderful selection of furniture, specialty items, and curios.

✪ Rothschild's Antiques

241 and 321 Royal St. ☎ **504/523-5816** or 504/523-2281. Mon–Sat 9am–5pm.

Some of the most interesting things you'll find here are antique and custom-made jewelry pieces. There's also a fine selection of antique silver, marble mantels, porcelains, and English and French furnishings.

Royal Antiques

307–309 Royal St. ☎ **504/524-7033.** Mon–Sat 9:15am–5:30pm.

Royal specializes in 18th- and 19th-century French and English furnishings as well as chandeliers and brass and copper accessories. There's another location at 715 Bienville St.

Sigle's Antiques & Metalcraft

935 Royal St. ☎ **504/522-7647.** Mon–Fri 10am–4pm.

If you've fallen in love with the lacy ironwork that drips from French Quarter balconies, this is the place to pick out some pieces to take home. In addition, Sigle's has converted some of the ironwork into useful household items, such as plant holders.

Whisnant Galleries

222 Chartres St. ☎504/524-9766. Mon–Sat 9:30am–5:30pm.

The quantity and variety of merchandise in this shop is mind-boggling. You'll find all sorts of unusual and unique collectibles, including items from Morocco, Ethiopia, Russia, Greece, South America, North Africa, and the Middle East.

ART GALLERIES

In addition to those listed below, there are a great number of galleries in what used to be the warehouse district and is now a center for the arts. You can pick up a brochure called "Arts in the Warehouse District" that lists a fairly large number of galleries on Julia Street and some of the surrounding streets. Though there are many wonderful galleries on Royal Street, don't forget the old warehouse district, especially if you're interested in contemporary art.

American Indian Art

824 Chartres St. ☎ **504/586-0479.** Mon and Wed–Fri 10am–5pm; Sat 10am–6pm; and Sun noon–5pm.

If you're a collector of Native American arts and crafts, this is the place for you. American Indian Art carries a wide variety of antique and modern Native American baskets, jewelry, sculpture, beadwork (Plains and Woodlands), kachinas, pottery, and weavings. Louisiana tribes represented include Koasati and Chitimacha. The work of the Zuni, Navajo, and Hopi Indians is also shown here.

Ariodante

535 Julia St. ☎ **504/524-3233.** Mon–Sat 11am–5pm. Closed Mon during daylight saving time.

A contemporary craft gallery, Ariodante features hand-crafted furniture, glass, ceramics, jewelry, and decorative accessories by nationally acclaimed artists. Rotating shows offer a detailed look at works by various artists.

Arius Art Tiles

504 St. Peter St. ☎ **504/529-1665.** Daily 9:30am–5:30pm.

If you've been to Santa Fe you might recognize some of the art tiles that are being sold here—many of the tiles are made in Santa Fe, and Arius has a sister gallery in New Mexico. Southwest as well as Louisiana designs are available. Custom orders are taken.

Bergen Galleries

730 Royal St. ☎ **504/523-7882** or 800/621-6179. Daily 9am–9pm.

Bergen Galleries has the city's largest selection of posters and limited-edition graphics—including New Orleans works; Mardi Gras; jazz; and artists such as Erté, Icart, Nagel, Maimon, Tarkay, as well as a large collection of works by sought-after African-American artists. The service from Margarita and her staff is friendly and extremely personable.

Bryant Galleries

524 Royal St. ☎ **504/525-5584.** Sun–Wed 10am–5:30pm; Thurs–Fri 10am–8pm; Sat 10 am–10pm.

This gallery represents renowned artists Ed Dwight, Fritzner Lamour, and Leonardo Nierman. Contemporary art is what you'll find here, including jazz bronzes, glasswork, and graphics.

✪ Casey Willems Pottery

3919 Magazine St. ☎ **504/899-1174.** Mon–Sat 10am–5pm.

Watch Casey Willems create functional art pottery before your very eyes as you browse his gallery. You'll find the usual vases and teapots, but Willems has been known to create some uniquely functional items as well.

Circle Gallery

316 Royal St. ☎ **504/523-1350.** Mon–Sat 10am–6pm; Sun 11am–6pm.

This gallery features contemporary sculpture, graphics, and paintings by internationally known artists like Yaacov Agam, Victor Vasarely, Sandro Cia, Rene Gruau, Yvari, and Erte.

✪ The Davis Galleries

3964 Magazine St. ☎ **504/897-0780.** Tues–Sat 10am–5pm.

The Davis Galleries features Central and West African traditional art. Works on display might include sculpture, costuming, basketry, textiles, weapons, and jewelry.

Dixon & Dixon of Royal

237 and 318 Royal St. ☎ **504/524-0282** or 800/848-5148. Mon–Sat 9am–5:30pm; Sun 10am–5pm.

Dixon and Dixon features 18th- and 19th-century European fine art, antiques, jewelry, clocks, and Oriental rugs.

Dyansen Gallery

433 Royal St. ☎ **504/523-2902.** Mon–Thurs and Sun 10am–6pm; Fri–Sat 10am–9pm.

A branch of the Dyansen family galleries (there are others in San Francisco and New York), this gallery features graphics, sculpture, and original gouaches by Erté. Other artists represented include Richard Estes, Leroy Neiman, and Paul Wegner.

Endangered Species

619 Royal St. ☎ **504/568-9855.** Mon–Sat 10am–5pm; Sun 11am–4pm.

The owners of Endangered Species have traveled the world (35 countries) collecting art objects and artifacts. Here you'll find tribal masks, unusual jewelry, carved ivories, and hand-woven textiles.

Galerie Royale, Ltd.

312 Royal St. ☎ **504/523-1588.** Daily 10am–6pm (open at 11am on some Sundays).

If you appreciate the works of William Tolliver (whether you just want to browse or buy), you'll find his museum-quality work here, as well as some work by Chagall, Dali, and Miró.

Galerie Simonne Stern

518 Julia St. ☎ **504/529-1118.** Tues–Fri 10am–6pm.

Galerie Simonne Stern features paintings, drawings, and sculptures by contemporary artists. Recent shows included the works of Sam Gilliam, George Dunbar, Richard Johnson, James McGarrell, Lynda Benglis, Albert Paley, and Arthur Silverman.

A Gallery for Fine Photography

322 Royal St. ☎ **504/568-1313.** Daily 10am–6pm.

A Gallery for Fine Photography specializes in 19th- and 20th-century rare photographs and books, and regular exhibits include the works of Ansel Adams, Alfred Stieglitz, and Edward Curtis. Recent exhibits included Walker Evans, Berenice Abbott, Helmut Newton, O. Winston Link, and Diane Arbus.

Hanson Gallery

229 Royal St. ☎ **504/524-8211.** Mon–Sat 10am–6pm; Sun 11am–5pm.

Hanson Galleries shows paintings, sculpture, and limited-edition prints of contemporary artists such as Peter Max, Frederick Hart, Pradzynski, Anoro, Thysell, Deckbar, Zjawinska, Erickson, LeRoy Neiman, Richard MacDonald, and Behrens.

Hilderbrand Gallery

4524 Magazine St. ☎ **504/895-3312.** Daily 10am–9pm.

Hilderbrand Galleries features contemporary works of fine art in all mediums by international, national, and local artists, including the works of Ding Massimo Boccuni, Walter Rutkowski, Christian Stock, Robert Rucker, Robert Griffeth, Cort Savage, Lynda Freese, Mark Westervelt, Janet Glodner, and Karl Heinz-Strohle.

Importicos

736 Royal St. ☎ **504/523-3100.** Daily 10am–6pm.

If you're interested in hand-crafted imports from Central America and Indonesia, stop by Importicos, where you'll find a selection of hand-crafted silver jewelry, pottery, textiles, antique and museum reproduction earrings, and leather, wood, stone, and metal items. There's another store at 517 St. Louis St. (☎ 504/523-0306).

Kurt E. Schon, Ltd.

523 Royal St. ☎ **504/524-5462.** Mon–Sat 9am–5pm.

Here you'll find this country's largest inventory of 19th-century European paintings. Works include French and British Impressionist and post-Impressionist paintings as well as art from the Royal Academy and The French Salon. Only a fraction of the paintings in the gallery's inventory are housed at this location, but if you're a serious collector you can make an appointment to visit the St. Louis Street gallery.

Nahan Galleries

540 Royal St. ☎ **504/524-8696.** Mon–Sat 9:30am–6pm; Sun 11am–6pm.

Nahan specializes in works of major contemporary artists and publishes graphics for Tobiasse, Papart, Coignard, Olbinski, and others.

✪ New Orleans School of Glassworks

727 Magazine St. ☎ **504/529-7277.** Mon–Sat 11am–5pm.

This place is difficult to categorize, simply because it serves multiple purposes—allowing artists and blossoming artists in the area of glasswork to give and take classes. Accomplished glass artists and master printmakers who teach at the school are allowed to show and sell their pieces here in the gallery. Absolutely unique to the area, it is worth a visit during gallery hours. Here, within 20,000 square feet of studio space, are a 550-pound, hot molten tank of glass and a pre–Civil War press. Daily glassblowing, fusing, and slumping demonstrations are offered. Classes in glassblowing, kiln-fired glass, hand-engraved printmaking, papermaking, and bookbinding are offered.

The Rodrigue Gallery of New Orleans

721 Royal St. ☎ **504/581-4244.** Daily 10am–6pm.

If you're visiting New Orleans there's no way you'll miss Cajun artist George Rodrigue's "Blue Dog," even if you want to. Rodrigue began painting portraits of his dog (a terrier-mix that had already died) for a children's book in 1984, and he hasn't stopped since. His work is known internationally and he is represented in galleries in Munich as well as Yokohama. You will either be instantly charmed by the dog's image (as millions are) or you'll quickly grow weary of seeing its likeness all around the city.

Shadyside Pottery

3823 Magazine St. ☎ **504/897-1710.** Mon–Sat 10am–5pm.

If you want to see another master potter at work, Shadyside Pottery is an excellent place to stop. Charles Bohn, who apprenticed in Japan, can be seen at his wheel all day on weekdays and until midafternoon on Saturday. In addition to Bohn's own work, he carries a selection of Japanese kites (by Mitsuyoshi Kawamoto) as well as some glass work.

Trade Folk Art Import Export

828 Chartres St. ☎ **504/596-6827.** Daily 10am–5pm.

Taina and Kelly travel to Mexico frequently and bring back some wonderful pieces of folk art. If you know nothing about Mexican folk art, you really should stop by and look around. Trade Folk Art also features southern folk artists. They'll also give you an education if you ask.

BOOKS

For literary enthusiasts there are the **Maple Street Bookshop,** 7523 Maple St. (☎ **504/866-4916**), which has three locations including the Maple Street Children's

Book Shop next door at 7529 Maple St. (☎ 504/861-2105), and Maple Street's Old Metarie Book Shop in Old Metairie Village, 701 Metairie Rd. (☎ 504/832-8937); **De Ville Books and Prints,** 1 Shell Square (☎ 504/525-1846); and **Beaucoup Books,** 5415 Magazine St. (☎ 504/895-2663). **Little Professor Book Center of New Orleans,** 1000 S. Carrollton Ave. (☎ 504/866-7646), stocks one of the best general collections.

Beckham's Bookshop
228 Decatur St. ☎ 504/522-9875. Daily 10am–6pm.

Beckham's has two entire floors of old editions and some rare secondhand books that will tie up your whole afternoon or morning if you don't tear yourself away. The owners also operate Librairie Bookshop, 823 Chartres St., which you'll surely have found if you're a book lover. Beckham's also has thousands of classical LPs.

Bookstar
414 N. Peters St. ☎ 504/523-6411. Daily 10am–midnight.

Bookstar is a large, attractive chain bookstore in the Jackson Brewery complex. Without doubt, it stocks one of the largest selections of books and magazines in the city, and its enthusiastic and knowledgeable staff can help you find the printed word on virtually any subject you can name.

✪ Faulkner House Books
624 Pirates Alley. ☎ 504/524-2940. Daily 10am–6pm.

This is a small bookstore with a big history. It was here that southern fiction writer and Nobel Prize winner William Faulkner lived while he was writing *Soldiers' Pay.* Today the shop holds a large collection of first-edition Faulkners, including copies of *The Sound and the Fury,* as well as rare and first-edition classics by many other authors. For book lovers, this shop is a must stop on a trip to New Orleans.

George Herget Books
3109 Magazine St. ☎ 504/891-5595. Mon–Sat 10am–5:30pm.

George Herget Books is another of New Orleans's great bookstores. More than 20,000 rare and used books covering absolutely every subject imaginable are available for your browsing and collecting pleasure.

Old Children's Books
734 Royal St. ☎ 504/525-3655. Mon–Sat 10am–1pm.

Just as its name indicates, Old Children's Books carries thousands of antique and rare children's books from the 19th century through the 1970s. Ring the buzzer to gain entrance to the shop. The courtyard alone is worth the visit.

Olive Tree Book Store
927 Royal St. ☎ 504/523-8041. Daily 10am–10pm.

I love this bookstore because it is absolutely piled high, wall to wall, with books—there's hardly room to walk around. They carry old and rare books, as well as records and magazines.

CANDIES & PRALINES

Aunt Sally's Praline Shops
810 Decatur St. ☎ 504/524-5107. Daily 8am–8pm.

At Aunt Sally's, in the French Market, you can watch skilled workers perform the 150-year-old process of cooking the original Creole pecan pralines right before your eyes. You'll know they're fresh. The large store also has a broad selection of regional cookbooks, books on the history of New Orleans and its environs, Creole and Cajun foods, folk and souvenir dolls, and local memorabilia. In addition, Aunt Sally's has a collection of zydeco, Cajun, rhythm and blues, and jazz CDs and cassettes. They'll ship any of your purchases, which can considerably lighten the load going home.

Laura's Original Praline & Fudge Shoppe

115 Royal St. ☎ **504/525-3880.** Daily 9am–9pm.

Laura's is said to be New Orleans's oldest candy store, established in 1913. There are seven varieties of pralines on sale here, plus hand-dipped chocolates, rum-flavored pecans, Vieux Carré foods, and their great praline sauce.

✪ Leah's Candy Kitchen

714 St. Louis St. ☎ **504/523-5662.** Mon–Sat 10am–10pm.

While the other candy stores listed above are all good, Leah's, in my opinion, has the best pralines in the city. (You might prefer one of the others, though—I suggest you torture yourself and try them all.) Everything, from the candy fillings to the incredible chocolate-covered pecan brittle, is made from scratch.

CANDLES

Creole Carved Candles

600 Decatur St. ☎ **504/524-1055.** Daily 10am–9pm.

Looking for a Mardi Gras mask? Try Creole Carved Candles. They have a whole selection of colorful Mardi Gras mask candles, as well as a variety of scented floating candles (the magnolia ones are especially nice). All the candles here are made locally, and if you can't find what you're looking for they take special orders.

French Market Gift Shop

824 Decatur St. ☎ **504/522-6004.** Daily 9am–9pm.

Here you'll find a delightful collection of hand-crafted beeswax candles in beautiful artistic shapes and sizes. Brass candlesticks and other candle-related items, as well as a large array of gift items and collectibles, make this much more than just a candle shop.

COSTUMES & MASKS

A number of shops specialize in Mardi Gras finery. One tip to remember is that New Orleanians often sell their costumes after Ash Wednesday, and you can sometimes pick up a one-time-worn outfit at a small fraction of its cost new.

✪ Little Shop of Fantasy

523 Dumaine St. ☎ **504/529-4243.** Mon–Tues and Thurs–Sat 10am–6pm; Sun 1–6pm.

In the Little Shop of Fantasy, owners Mike Stark, Laura and Anne Guccione, and Jill Kellys host a number of local artists and more than 20 mask makers. Mike creates the feathered masks, Jill does the velvet hats and costumes, and Laura and Anne make homemade toiletries. Some of the masks and hats are just fun and fanciful, but there are some extraordinary and beautiful ones as well.

Mardi Gras Center

831 Chartres St. ☎ **504/524-4384.** Mon–Sat 10am–5pm.

Mardi Gras Center carries sizes 2 to 50 and has a wide selection of new, ready-made costumes as well as used outfits. It also carries all accessories such as beads, doubloons, wigs, masks, hats, makeup, jewelry, and Mardi Gras decorations. Mardi Gras Center is also a good place to stop for Halloween supplies.

FASHION

A legacy of New Orleans's elegant past is the locals' love of fashion; shops around the city accommodate them by providing everything from high-fashion designer clothes to the latest funky styles.

Body Hangings

835 Decatur St. ☎ **504/524-9856.** Daily 10am–6pm.

This place has a great collection of capes, scarves, and cloaks for the whole family. Joan Braun makes them in wool, cotton, corduroy, and velveteen.

Kruz

432 Barracks St. ☎ **504/524-7370.** Daily 11am–6pm.

If you've got a thing for ethnic fashion, Kruz probably has what you're looking for. In stock are clothing and accessories from around the world.

Saks Fifth Avenue

301 Canal St. (Canal Place Shopping Center). ☎ **504/524-2200.** Mon–Wed and Fri–Sat 10am–6pm; Thurs 10am–8pm; and Sun 1–6pm.

In addition to the high-quality fashion and accessories for men and women for which they are nationally known, Saks also offers a personalized shopping service, the Fifth Avenue Club.

Yvonne La Fleur—New Orleans

8131 Hampson St. ☎ **504/866-9666.** Mon–Sat 9:45am–6pm; Wed–Thurs 9:45am–8pm.

Yvonne La Fleur, a confessed incurable romantic, is the creator of original designs so beautifully feminine that they'll invite fantasies of past golden ages. Her custom millinery, silk dresses, evening gowns, lingerie, and sportswear are surprisingly afford-able, and all are enhanced by her own signature perfume. Her store is located in the Riverbend district.

FOOD

Café du Monde Coffee Shop

800 Decatur St. ☎ **504/581-2914.** Daily 24 hours.

If you want to try your hand at making those scrumptious beignets, you can buy the mix at the Café du Monde, in the French Market. To make it complete, pick up a can of their famous coffee, a special blend of coffee and chicory. The shop also has a very good mail-order service (☎ 800/772-2927 or fax 504/587-0847).

Creole Delicacies Gourmet Shop

533 St. Ann St. ☎ **504/523-6425.** Mon–Thurs 9:30am–9pm; Fri–Sat 9:30am–10pm; Sun 10am–6pm.

Cajun and Creole packaged foods and mixes are what you'll find here. Fill your shop-ping basket with everything from jambalaya and gumbo mix to rémoulade and hot sauces. Creole Delicacies is also located at Riverwalk Marketplace.

Louisiana Potpourri

Canal Place Shopping Center, 333 Canal St. No. 202. ☎ **504/524-9023.** Mon–Wed and Fri–Sat 10am–6pm; Thurs 10am–8pm; and Sun noon–6pm.

If you want to take home a potpourri of New Orleans flavors, this is a great place to begin shopping. They have everything from gumbo flavoring to Cajun hot nuts (one of my favorites). Gift baskets are available, and Louisiana Potpourri will ship things home for you.

Orleans Coffee Exchange

712 Orleans Ave. ☎ **504/522-5710.** Mon–Fri 8am–6pm; Sat 9am–6pm; Sun 10am–6pm.

Java junkies won't be able to leave New Orleans without a visit to the Orleans Coffee Exchange. The 500 varieties of coffee beans here come from all over the world. There are also more than 350 flavored coffees as well as scores of exotic teas.

GIFTS

There are literally hundreds of gift shops in New Orleans, with merchandise ranging from very expensive to very tacky. The following are the ones I found most attractive.

Angel Wings

710 St. Louis St. ☎ **504/524-6880.** Mon–Sat 10am–10pm; Sun 10am–6pm.

If you're looking for something other than the typical New Orleans tourist souvenir, you should stop by Angel Wings. They have a wonderful, large collection of jewelry, accessories, and curios.

The Black Butterfly

727 Royal St. ☎ **504/524-6464.** Mon–Sat 10:30am–6pm.

The Black Butterfly is somewhere you might stop if you're a collector of miniatures. This third-generation shop is filled with porcelain, brass, wood, and pewter figures, as well as dollhouse furniture and accessories.

Hempstead Company Store

607 Chartres St. ☎ **504/529-HEMP.** Mon–Fri 10am–6pm; Sat–Sun 10am–7pm.

I'm not sure if this qualifies as a "gift shop," but you might find something of interest to take home to a cannabis worshiper. Everything in this place is made from hemp grown in China and Hungary—even the soap (from hemp oil).

Kruz

432 Barracks St. ☎ **504/524-7370.** Daily 11am–6pm.

Kruz (mentioned above for clothing and accessories) has a collection of international pieces, including books, incense, musical recordings from various countries, as well as handbags, musical instruments, and clothing. It's a great little store that's worth a stop.

Latin's Hand

1025 N. Peters St. ☎ **504/529-5254.** Daily 9am–6pm.

All the items in this shop are made, not surprisingly, in Latin America. You'll find goods from Brazil, El Salvador, Guatemala, Bolivia, and Mexico. It's easy to get lost amidst the hammocks, clothing, and leather goods here.

HATS

In addition to the shops listed below, you can also get fun costume hats at Little Shop of Fantasy, listed above.

Meyer the Hatter

120 St. Charles Ave. ☎ **504/525-1048** or 800/882-4287. Mon–Sat 9:45am–5:45pm.

Meyer's has one of the largest selections of fine hats and caps in the South. Men will find distinguished head wear with labels such as Stetson, Dobbs, and Borsalino in this fine shop, which opened in 1894 and is now run by third-generation members of the same family.

Rine Chapeaux

Riverwalk No. 1 Poydras St. ☎ **504/523-7463.** Mon–Thurs 10am–9pm; Fri–Sat 10am–10pm; Sun 10am–7pm.

> Here you'll find more than 300 different styles of hats and caps for men and women. Women will also enjoy browsing through the sizable collection of hair accessories.

JEWELRY

✪ Bedazzle

635 St. Peter St. ☎ **504/529-3248.** Daily 10:30am–6pm.

> If you like contemporary jewelry, head for Bedazzle, where they have "jewelry as art." They've got everything you'd find in a traditional jewelry store, only it's a lot more interesting. It's worth a stop, and the staff is extremely helpful and friendly.

Joan Good

809 Royal St. ☎ **504/525-1705.** Daily 10am–6pm.

> I love Joan Good for its wonderful collection of antique jewelry. While they do have some fairly typical pieces, like their competitors on Royal Street, they also have some very unusual pieces. I saw some cameos in there that were exquisite, as well as some uniquely designed rings and lovely old hat pins.

Mignon Faget Ltd.

Canal Place, Level One. ☎ **504/524-2973.** Mon–Wed and Fri–Sat 10am–6pm; Thurs 10am–8pm; Sun noon–6pm.

> The striking originals of New Orleans's own Mignon Faget have won national fame, and a visit to her studio display room, at Level One, Canal Place, is a real treat. Handcrafted designs in gold, silver, and bronze d'oré include pendants, bracelets, rings, earrings, shirt studs, and cufflinks.

Quarter Moon

918 Royal St. ☎ **504/524-3208.** Daily 10am–6pm. May close on Tuesdays or Sundays in summer.

> Much of the jewelry in the shop is handmade by the owners, Michael and Ellis Shallbetter. The pieces are interesting and entirely unique; since they're handmade, you won't find anything like them anywhere else. Michael and Ellis have recently expanded the shop to include contemporary crafts and wearables by local artists.

Rumors, Ltd.

513 Royal St. ☎ **504/525-0292.** Daily 10am–6pm.

> Chances are, you won't miss Rumors. They've got an incredible selection of earrings—they call it "art for ears." I'm still amazed at their stock. If you're crazy about earrings, you should stop in; no doubt something will strike your fancy.

MUSIC

> In addition to **Tower Records** at 408 N. Peters (☎ **504/529-4411**), there are a few other places you should check out for music, especially if you've still got a turntable.

Beckham's Bookshop

228 Decatur St. ☎ **504/522-9875.** Daily 10am–6pm.

> It's better known for its fine collection of used books (see above), but Beckham's also has a large selection of second-hand classical music records.

Louisiana Music Factory

225 N. Peters. ☎ **504/523-1094.** Daily 10am–7pm.

This popular music store carries a large selection of regional tunes, including Cajun, zydeco, R&B, jazz, blues, and gospel. There's also a collection of books, posters, and T-shirts.

Record Ron's
1129 Decatur St. ☎ **504/561-9444.** Daily 11am–7pm.

Record Ron's has a good selection of classic rock LPs, as well as jazz, Cajun, zydeco, R&B, and blues. At Record Ron's you'll find thousands of 45s, CDs, and cassettes. There's also a large collection of T-shirts, posters, sheet music, rubber stamps, music memorabilia, and jewelry. Record Ron's Stuff, another store, is located at 239 Chartres Street (☎ 504/522-2239).

THE OCCULT

The Bottom of the Cup Tearoom
732 Royal St. ☎ **504/523-1204.** Mon–Sat 9am–9pm; Sun 11am–7pm.

At the Bottom of the Cup Tearoom, psychics and clairvoyants specialize in palm reading, crystal gazing, tea-leaf reading, and tarot. You can also get your astrological chart done. It's been open since 1929 and bills itself as the "oldest tearoom in the United States." In addition to having a psychic consultation you can also purchase books, jewelry, crystal balls, tarot cards, crystals, and healing wands here.

Marie Laveau's House of Voodoo
739 Bourbon St. ☎ **504/581-3751.** Sun–Thurs 10am–11:30pm; Fri–Sat 10am–12:30 or 1:30am.

Marie Laveau's House of Voodoo is the perfect place to stop if you're looking for some "touristy" voodoo items to take home to friends. You'll find all sorts of mojos and voodoo dolls here. In addition, there's an on-site psychic and palm reader.

PIPES & TOBACCO

Ye Olde Pipe Shoppe
306 Chartres St. ☎ **504/522-1484.** Mon–Sat 10am–5pm.

Mr. Edwin Jansen's shop won my heart in about two seconds flat (or maybe it was Mr. Jansen himself). His grandfather, August, founded this place way back in 1868 and at one time repaired Jefferson Davis's pipes. Nowadays, *my* Mr. Jansen handmakes beautiful briar pipes, repairs broken pipes, and sells pipe accessories and enough tobacco blends to keep you puffing all year long. This is a warm, comfortable stopping-off place for pipe lovers. While you're there, take a look at the marvelous collection of antique pipes put together by his father and grandfather. Over the years Mr. Jansen has developed a firm philosophy about pipes and their smokers and has written an excellent book (free for the asking) about them. If pipes are your thing, don't fail to search this place out.

PUPPETS

Pontalba Historical Puppetorium
514 St. Peter St. ☎ **504/522-0344** or 504/944-8144. Daily 9:30am–5:30pm.

There's an excellent puppet presentation of New Orleans history here in Jackson Square, but you can also purchase puppets. In fact, the puppetorium has the largest collection in the United States.

TOYS

Le Petit Soldier Shop
528 Royal St. ☎ **504/523-7741.** Mon–Sat 10am–4pm.

Local artists create the two-inch-high masterpieces in this shop. The miniatures depict soldiers from ancient Greece up to Desert Storm, and many of the miniatures actually resemble major figures in military history, like Eisenhower, Grant, Lee, Hitler, and Napoleon. There's a large collection of medals and decorations.

The Little Toy Shoppe
900 Decatur St. ☎ **504/522-6588.** Daily 9am–8pm. Closed Christmas, Mardi Gras, Thanksgiving, and Easter.

The dolls here are some of the most beautiful I've ever seen, especially the Madame Alexander and Effanbee ones, and the New Orleans–made bisque and rag dolls. In addition to "heroes" wood toys from Germany and "All God's Children" collectibles, there are cuddly stuffed animals, tea sets, toy soldiers, and miniature cars and trucks.

UMBRELLAS

The Umbrella Lady
1107 Decatur St. ☎ **504/523-7791.** Hours vary, so call ahead.

They call her "The Umbrella Lady," but her real name is Anne B. Lane. You'll find her in her upstairs studio. A Quarter fixture, she's the creator of wonderful Secondline umbrellas as well as fanciful "southern belle" parasols. Look for the umbrellas displayed on her balcony.

WOODCRAFTS

Idea Factory
838 Chartres St. ☎ **504/524-5195** or 800/524-IDEA. Mon–Sat 10am–6pm; Sun noon–5pm.

One of my favorite shops in the French Quarter, the Idea Factory features all sorts of hand-crafted wood items, including toys, kinetic sculptures, door harps, signs, boxes, and office supplies (business-card holders, in/out trays, etc.). Many of the items are made right on the premises so if you're lucky you might get to see one of the craftspeople at work. Also featured is the jewelry of Thomas Mann.

New Orleans After Dark

11

Jazz, hurricanes, Pat O'Brien's, strippers, and cross-dressers: the French Quarter, in all its glory. New Orleans earned its Bacchanalian reputation and still deserves it—it's the only city in the country where it's legal to drink alcohol in the streets. The French Quarter seems to remove inhibitions as quickly as a triple bourbon: Anything goes here, and often does until sunrise. (New Orleans has no closure laws, so some bars and clubs stay open throughout the night, particularly during Carnival.)

Jazz was born here in Storyville cathouses, and while the brothels are gone, the music still lingers. At the moment when Buddy Bolden blew the first notes of jazz from his cornet near the end of the last century, New Orleans was guaranteed its reputation as a music city. In years to come jazz greats such as Louis Armstrong, Jelly Roll Morton, and later Harry Connick, Jr. and the Marsalises were to hone their skills in French Quarter clubs. In the past several decades, however, musicians such as the Neville brothers and Dr. John have broadened the focus of the music scene beyond its original jazz roots. Today, jazz and blues share the music marquee with Cajun, zydeco, R&B, world beat, rock, and pop.

That's not to imply, though, that jazz has abandoned the place of its birth. Performers, both black and white, both newcomers and old-timers, join together to keep the traditional sound alive at all hours in the French Quarter and after dark outside the Quarter. You'll still find uninhibited dancers performing in the streets outside jazz spots (sometimes passing the hat to onlookers); jazz funerals for departed musicians (the trip to that final resting place accompanied by sorrowful dirges and "second liners" who shuffle and clap their hands to a mournful beat); the return (a joyful, swinging celebration of the deceased's "liberation"); and occasionally a street parade (even when it isn't Carnival), complete with a brass band.

The bars and clubs listed below are hot spots at the time this edition was updated; however, the notoriously fickle fortunes of the nightclub business make it your best bet to walk Bourbon Street and follow the sounds of your favorite type of music and the loudest (or quietest) crowd to a spot you might like to try. Most places open for happy hour, around noon in most cases, and stay open until the wee hours.

Note: For safety reasons, it's best to take a cab to and from any and all of the night spots outside the French Quarter.

For up-to-date information on what's happening around town when you're there, look for current editions of *Where*, *Gambit*, and *Offbeat*, all of which are free and are distributed in most hotels. You can also check out *Offbeat* magazine on the internet (http://www.nola.com). Once you get to the nola home page, go to the music and entertainment section, and you'll have no trouble finding the magazine there. Other sources include the *Times-Picayune's* daily entertainment calendar as well as Friday's *Lagniappe* section of the newspaper. Additionally, **WWOZ** (90.7 FM) broadcasts the local music schedule several times throughout the day. If you miss the broadcasts, call **504/840-4040,** WWOZ's "Tower Records's Second Line," for the same information.

1   Jazz & Blues

This being New Orleans, jazz and blues are everywhere—you just have to look a little harder than you had to in the good old days. The clubs listed below feature jazz and/ or blues on a nightly (or almost nightly) basis, but there are other places worth consideration that may only offer live music once or twice a week. **Court of Two Sisters** (see Chapter 7) has a great jazz brunch, as does **Cafe Sbisa,** 1011 Decatur St. (☎ **504/522-5565**), on Sundays. In addition, **Joe's Cozy Corner,** 1532 Ursuline's (☎ **504/561-9216**), in the Treme section of New Orleans, has live jazz on Sundays (not a great neighborhood though); and **Crescent City Brewhouse,** 527 Decatur St. (☎ **504/522-0571**), features modern jazz bands in the afternoons on Friday, Saturday, and Sunday. Many hotel lounges and bars also feature live jazz performances, so be sure to check with your concierge.

THE FRENCH QUARTER & THE FAUBOURG MARIGNY

Cosimo's Bar

1201 Burgundy St. ☎ **504/561-8110.** Cover $5–$10.

If you're just sticking to the heart of the French Quarter, you're going to miss a great place for traditional jazz jams. Cosimo's is in the Quarter, but on the outer edges, so it's still relatively safe; but if you're walking, try to go with someone and stay with the crowd if possible. Live music begins at 8pm on Wednesday, Friday, and Saturday and goes until about midnight.

Donna's

800 N. Rampart St. ☎ **504/596-6914.** Cover varies according to performer.

Located right on the edge of the French Quarter, Donna's is known for showcasing talented local brass bands. This place is definitely worth a stop for serious music lovers.

Fritzel's European Jazz Pub

733 Bourbon St. ☎ **504/561-0432.** No cover (one-drink minimum per set, per person).

You might walk right past this small establishment, but that would be a big mistake, for this 1831 building brings some of the city's best musicians to play on its tiny stage in back. In addition to the regular weekend program of late-night jazz (Friday and Saturday from 10:30pm, Sunday from 10pm), there are frequent jam sessions here in the wee hours during the week, when musicians end their stints elsewhere and gather to play "Musicians' Music." The full bar also stocks a variety of Schnapps (served ice-cold) and German beers on tap and in bottles.

French Quarter Nightlife

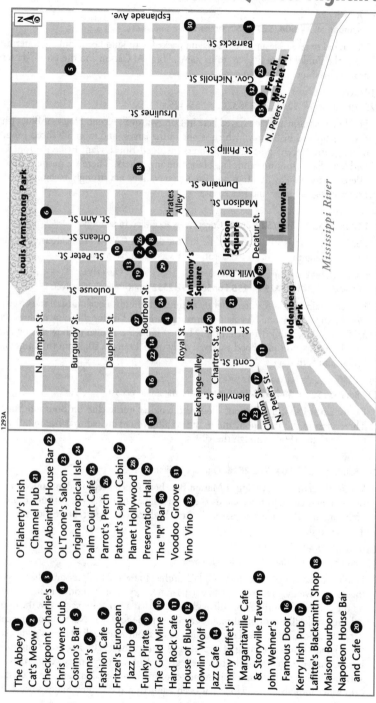

The Abbey **1**
Cat's Meow **2**
Checkpoint Charlie's **3**
Chris Owens Club **4**
Cosimo's Bar **5**
Donna's **6**
Fashion Cafe **7**
Fritzel's European Jazz Pub **8**
Funky Pirate **9**
The Gold Mine **10**
Hard Rock Cafe **11**
House of Blues **12**
Howlin' Wolf **13**
Jazz Cafe **14**
Jimmy Buffet's Margaritaville Cafe & Storyville Tavern **15**
John Wehner's Famous Door **16**
Kerry Irish Pub **17**
Lafitte's Blacksmith Shop **18**
Maison Bourbon **19**
Napoleon House Bar and Cafe **20**
O'Flaherty's Irish Channel Pub **21**
Old Absinthe House Bar **22**
OL'Toone's Saloon **23**
Original Tropical Isle **24**
Palm Court Café **25**
Parrot's Perch **26**
Patout's Cajun Cabin **27**
Planet Hollywood **28**
Preservation Hall **29**
The "R" Bar **30**
Voodoo Groove **31**
Vino Vino **32**

1293A

189

Funky Pirate

727 Bourbon St. ☎ **504/523-1960.** Cover $5 .

Decorated to resemble a pirates' den, and packed with loud beer-drinking fraternity types, the Funky Pirate lives up to its name. "Big" Al Carson and the Blues Masters provide live blues entertainment.

✪ House of Blues

225 Decatur St. ☎ **504/529-2583.** Cover $5–$25.

Live blues performances are staged here in Dan Aykroyd's second House of Blues (the first was opened in Boston), which is one of the largest and most advanced venues of its genre. Recent musical performers included Bob Dylan, Eric Clapton, Bo Diddley, Fats Domino, and Taj Mahal among others. There's a gospel brunch offered every Sunday at 11am and 2pm (reservations are strongly recommended). Friday brings $1 beers and free snacks.

Jazz Cafe

411 Bourbon St. ☎ **504/522-7623.** Cover varies according to performer.

For live jazz and R&B, the best time to visit the Jazz Cafe is in the afternoon. The sound and lighting here are excellent; there's a decent bar as well.

Jimmy Buffett's Margaritaville Cafe & Storyville Tavern

1104 Decatur St. ☎ **504/592-2565** or 504/592-2552 (concert line). No cover.

Live entertainment is featured nightly at Jimmy Buffett's. Local musical stars Marva Wright and Charmaine Neville perform regularly, and nationally known blues acts are frequently scheduled as well; Jimmy Buffett himself is known to show up and play a set from time to time. Food is served daily from 11am to 10:30pm (midnight on Friday and Saturday).

John Wehner's Famous Door

339 Bourbon St. ☎ **504/522-7626.** One-drink minimum per set.

Extant since 1934, the Famous Door is the oldest music club on Bourbon Street. There's jazz in the afternoon, and in the evening you're invited to dance to jazz and blues from the 1960s through the 1990s.

Maison Bourbon

641 Bourbon St. ☎ **504/522-8818.** One-drink minimum.

You might start your evening at Maison Bourbon, which keeps its doors open to the sidewalk and employs three bands every day to play from 2:15 or 3:15pm to midnight or 2am. Big-time jazz players include Wallace Davenport, Steve Slocum, and Tommy Yetta.

Old Absinthe House Bar

400 Bourbon St. ☎ **504/525-8108.** No cover.

Don't confuse this place with the Old Absinthe House at 240 Bourbon. That's right, they both have the same name, and what's more, they're both entitled to it. The one on the corner of Bourbon and Bienville streets (that's No. 240) can claim the original site, while all the original fixtures are now to be found at No. 400, on the corner of Bourbon and Conti. That situation came about when federal agents padlocked the original (it was operating as a speakeasy) during the 1920s, and some enterprising soul broke in, removed the bar, the register, 19th-century prints, ceiling fans, an antique French clock, and a handsome set of marble-based fountains once used to drip water into absinthe (which has been banned in the United States since 1918 because it's a narcotic). They all turned up soon afterward in the establishment on the corner a block away, and New Orleans was blessed with two "original" Old Absinthe Houses. Anyway, it's the one at 400 Bourbon where you'll find rhythm and blues and progressive jazz—and you'll only find drinks at the other. Beginning at 9pm nightly, the music is continuous, sometimes with as many as three groups alternating, until all hours. There's no legal shutdown time in New Orleans, and it isn't unusual to find things still going strong here as dawn breaks. On weekends there's also daytime music. Blues dominate on the bandstand. Drinks start at $2.

Palm Court Café
1204 Decatur St. ☎ **504/525-0200.** Cover $4 per person at tables; no cover at bar.

This is one of the most stylish jazz haunts in the Quarter. Nina and George Buck have created an oasis of civilized dining (linen on the table, lace curtains at the street windows, and international cuisine—see Chapter 7 for details) in which to present top-notch jazz groups Wednesday through Saturday. One very special feature is the collection of jazz records for sale in a back alcove, many of them real finds for the collector.

Praline Connection Gospel & Blues Hall
901 South Peters St. ☎ **504/523-3973** for reservations and information.

You can't, and shouldn't, miss the Praline Connection's colorfully painted exterior. The 9,000-square-foot Praline Connection Gospel and Blues Hall offers live entertainment on Thursday, Friday, and Saturday nights. Every Sunday brings a great gospel brunch (served buffet style). Reservations are strongly recommended.

☻ Preservation Hall
726 St. Peter St. ☎ **504/523-8939.** Cover $3.

Dear to the hearts of all jazz devotees (and I count myself among them) is Preservation Hall, where jazz is found in its purest form, uncluttered by such refinements as air-conditioning, drinks, or even (unless you arrive very early) a place to sit. The shabby old building offers only hot, foot-tapping, body-swaying music, played by a solid core of old-time greats who never left New Orleans. Nobody seems to mind the lack of those other refinements—indeed, not only is the interior always packed, but its windows are frequently lined by the faces of those who stand on the sidewalk for hours just to listen.

Admission is unbelievably low, and if you want to sit on one of the much sought-after pillows right up front or a couple of rows of benches just behind them, be sure to get there a good 45 minutes before the doors open at 8pm. Otherwise, you must stand. The music goes on until 12:30am, with long sets interrupted by 10-minute breaks. The crowd continually changes as parents take children home at bedtime (the kids *love* the hall) and sidewalk listeners move in to take vacant places. There's a good collection of jazz tapes and CDs on sale.

Snug Harbor
626 Frenchmen St. ☎ **504/949-0696.** Cover $8–$15, depending on performer.

On the fringes of the French Quarter (one block beyond Esplanade), Snug Harbor has earned top popularity from residents and visitors alike for its nightly presentation of contemporary jazz. Seating is on two levels to provide good viewing of the bandstand, and there's full dinner service featuring regional specialties as well as a light menu of sandwiches. The acts change every night. Shows are at 9 and 11pm nightly.

OUTSIDE THE FRENCH QUARTER

Bottom Line

2101 N. Claiborne Ave. ☎ **504/947-9297.** Usually $5 cover.

Bottom Line attracts a youngish (25 and up) crowd and has three huge floors offering R&B and jazz. Saturday is ladies night.

Carrollton Station

8140 Willow St. ☎ **504/865-9190.** $5–$15 cover.

This little nightclub not only has one of the best beer selections in New Orleans, but it also offers great live music Wednesdays through Sundays beginning at 10pm. Expect to hear anything and everything from acoustic blues to fusion jazz.

Lion's Den

2655 Gravier St. ☎ **504/821-3745.**

The Lion's Den fills up unbelievably fast on Friday and Saturday nights when owner Irma Thomas performs. Call ahead for hours and prices.

Pampy's

2005 N. Broad St. ☎ **504/949-7970.** Call for current cover charge.

Live jazz is offered in this tiny club Thursday through Sunday. It's a great little hole in the wall frequented mainly by locals.

Pete Fountain's

In the New Orleans Hilton, 2 Poydras St. ☎ **504/523-4374** or 504/561-0500. Cover varies; call for rates and to confirm show times.

Pete Fountain is one of those loyal native sons who has never been able to sever hometown ties. For more than 20 years he held forth in his own Bourbon Street club, but these days you'll find him here, in a re-creation of his former Quarter premises, which seats more than twice the number that could be accommodated in the old club. The plush interior—gold chairs and banquettes, red velvet bar chairs, lacy white iron-railinged gallery—sets the mood for the popular nightspot, located at the Mississippi River. Pete is featured in one show a night, Tuesday to Saturday at 10pm. You'll need reservations.

Tipitina's

501 Napoleon Ave. ☎ **504/895-8477,** concert line 504/897-3943. Cover $4–$15 depending on the performer.

Here there's jazz, rhythm and blues, and almost every other form of music. At Tip's, it all depends on the artist playing, and that covers a *lot* of territory. Past performers in this New Orleans staple have included the Neville Brothers and Bo Diddley. Back in its 1977 beginnings this was home for the revered Professor Longhair until his death in 1980—it was named after one of his songs—and you'll be greeted by a bronze bust of the beloved musician as you enter. *Note:* As this book goes to press Tip's is for sale.

Vic's Kangaroo Cafe

636 Tchoupitoulas St. ☎ **504/524-4329.**

As you might have guessed, the owner of this nightspot is a native of the land - down under. In addition to serving meals, Vic's offers excellent blues music on Thursday from 10pm to 2am and on Saturday from 11pm to 3am. Vic's also has darts and a pool table located on the back patio (also known as the "Beer Garden").

2 Cajun & Zydeco

Maple Leaf Bar

8316 Oak St. ☎ **504/866-9359.** Cover $3–$10, depending on day of week and performer.

Uptown in the Carrollton area, the Maple Leaf Bar may be the best place outside the bayous to hear Cajun music. Thursday nights and some weekends celebrate the lively music and dancing with standouts such as the Filé Cajun Band and the zydeco renditions of Dopsie and his Cajun Twisters. Other nights it might be rhythm and blues, rock and roll, or reggae. Dancing is "encouraged," so you may find yourself out on the floor two-stepping to that Cajun beat. Before the bands start at 10pm, there's a jukebox offering an eclectic mix of musical styles, from classical to jazz to ragtime to Cajun, and there's a strong tradition of good conversation ranging from literary subjects (poetry readings every Sunday afternoon feature local and visiting poets and writers) to music, sports, or almost any topic you choose.

Michaul's on St. Charles

840 St. Charles Ave. ☎ **504/522-5517.** No cover.

You'll find good Cajun music here in the Warehouse District. If your feet begin tapping to the catchy rhythms but you're uncertain of the steps, Michaul's will give you free dance lessons. The cuisine is as Cajun as the music.

Mulate's

201 Julia St. ☎ **504/522-1492.** No cover.

This Cajun restaurant, which has been popular in other parts of Louisiana, has recently opened in New Orleans. There's a huge central bar and a stage for live Cajun music performances. Cajun dancing takes place nightly.

Patout's Cajun Cabin

501 Bourbon St. ☎ **504/529-4256.** One-drink minimum.

Located right on Bourbon Street, Patout's Cajun Cabin features the music of Cajun Country as performed by The Can't Hardly Play Boys and Mudbug Deluxe. Drinks have equally odd names—try the Swamp Water. Music begins around 7pm every night.

3 Rock & the Rest of the Music Scene

IN THE FRENCH QUARTER & THE FAUBOURG MARIGNY

Cafe Brasil

2100 Chartres St. ☎ **504/947-9386.** Cover varies according to performer.

Live music ranging from rock to Latin, Caribbean, and jazz is featured here nightly. The crowd is eclectic and multicultural, and the atmosphere is friendly and welcomes all lifestyles and varieties of people. Shows begin between 10 and 10:30pm every night.

Cafe Istanbul

534 Frenchmen St. ☎ **504/944-4180.** Cover varies according to performer.

If your choices in music are varied, Cafe Istanbul (a Turkish restaurant by day) is just the place. You'll be able to hear anything from hip-hop to reggae to Latin music. Entertainment is live. Call ahead for the current schedule of events.

Cat's Meow

701 Bourbon St. ☎ **504/523-1157.** No cover.

Cat's Meow is always full, and it's no wonder—they play popular rock songs all night long. The interior is bright and colorful, and the crowd the club attracts is young and loud. Karaoke is a favorite activity here, and you can even get a video tape of your performance.

Checkpoint Charlie's
501 Esplanade Ave. ☎ **504/949-7012.** No cover.

There's live entertainment every night at Checkpoint Charlie's, and there's never a cover charge. Food and drink are plentiful, there are pool tables, and there's even a Laundromat and book exchange here. The fun never stops, whether you're doing laundry, playing video games, or kicking back at the bar, because Checkpoint Charlie is open 24 hours.

The Gold Mine
701 Dauphine St. ☎ **504/586-0745.** Cover charge varies according to performer.

Famous for its "flaming Dr. Pepper" shooters (you have to see it to believe it), The Gold Mine keeps up with current trends in popular music. There are pool tables and a dance floor.

Howlin' Wolf
828 S. Peters ☎ **504/523-2551.** Cover $4–$8 .

Every night beginning around 10pm local college students gather here to listen to progressive rock bands.

Voodoo Groove
216 Bourbon St. ☎ **504/523-2020.** Cover $5 most nights.

If you've visited New Orleans before, you'll recognize this place as the old Club Second Line. It's primarily a dance club, but if you're lucky, you might arrive on a night when they're featuring an alternative rock band. Voodoo Groove is absolutely enormous.

OUTSIDE THE FRENCH QUARTER

Abstract Bookshop & Cafe
1306 Magazine St. ☎ **504/522-2665.** Cover charge varies according to performer.

Located virtually under the highway overpass (I-10), the Abstract Bookshop and Cafe is one of the city's only genuine alternative rock/punk venues. Hours vary, so call ahead for details.

Amberjack's Down Under
7306 Lake Shore Dr. ☎ **504/282-6660.** Cover on weekends only.

On most nights Amberjack's, which is located on the Lake Pontchartrain marina, is a favorite watering hole of local boaters. However, on Friday and Saturday nights singles hang out here listening to live classic rock and oldies while sipping tropical drinks. Pizzas and sandwiches are available.

Bart's on the Lake
8000 Lake Shore Dr. ☎ **504/282-0271.** Cover on weekends only.

Offering exceptional views, pool tables, and video poker, Bart's on the Lake is a favorite of the 20- and 30-something crowd. It's located right next door to the New Canal Lighthouse, and on Friday and Saturday live entertainment is offered in the bar area, while on Sunday afternoon bands play on the dock. During the rest of the week a disc jockey keeps the place hopping.

City Lights

310 Howard Ave. ☎ **504/568-1700.** $5 cover after 9pm.

City Lights is located in the Warehouse District, and as this book goes to press it is the most popular spot in New Orleans for the well-heeled 30-something crowd. Music runs the gamut from oldies to present-day Top 40.

Mid-City Lanes Rock & Bowl

4133 S. Carrollton Ave. ☎ **504/482-3133.** Bowling: day rates $8 per hour; evening rates Sun–Thurs $8 per hour, Fri–Sat $10 per hour. Admission to dance club is usually $5.

Another popular spot for some good ol' rock and roll is Mid-City Lanes Rock and Bowl. Yes, you guessed it, it's a rock club and a bowling alley—you literally rock *and* bowl. In 1995 Mid-City Lanes Rock and Bowl was named the best dance club by New Orleans Magazine. Mid-City opens around noon and stays open until everyone gets too tired to lift the ball.

4   The Bar Scene

It's sometimes hard to distinguish the bars from the music hot spots in New Orleans, but there are quite a few places you can go to relax and have a few drinks while shooting pool or playing a good game of foosball. There are also some upscale bars suitable for a business meeting or a quiet drink before or after dinner. In addition to the places listed below, most of the hotels have their own bars and lounges that are open to the general public.

IN THE FRENCH QUARTER & THE FAUBOURG MARIGNY

Apple Barrel

609 Frenchmen St. ☎ **504/949-9399.** No cover.

If you're on your way up to Alberto's, an Italian restaurant located above the Apple Barrel (see Chapter 7 for a full listing), you might want to stop in here for a drink. Locals love this place and can often be found playing darts here.

Fashion Cafe

619 Decatur St. ☎ **504/522-3181.** No cover.

If you just can't get enough of theme restaurants and bars, you won't be disappointed to find that the Fashion Cafe has just opened in New Orleans. Fashion memorabilia decorates all surfaces here, and there are two bars featuring oh-so-creatively named drinks like "The Catwalk" or "The Cover Girl." Fashion Cafe offers a full menu.

Hard Rock Cafe

418 N. Peters St. ☎ **504/529-5617.** No cover.

Everyone knows what the Hard Rock Cafe is about by now. The focal point here is a guitar-shaped bar. A jukebox provides the music, and on Wednesdays you can get $1 longnecks.

Kerry Irish Pub

331 Decatur St. ☎ **504/527-5954.** Call for cover charge.

First and foremost this place is a traditional Irish Pub; however, you can also hear live Irish and "alternative" folk music.

Lafitte's Blacksmith Shop

941 Bourbon St. ☎ **504/523-0066.** No cover.

Lafitte's dates from 1772. Legend has it that the privateer brothers Pierre and Jean Lafitte used the smithy as a "blind" for their lucrative trade in contraband (and, some

---

Pat O'Brien's & the Mighty Hurricane

Pat O'Brien's, 718 St. Peter St. (☎ **504/525-4823**), has been famous for as long as I can remember for its gigantic, rum-based Hurricane drink, served in 29-ounce hurricane lamp–style glasses. They may have outdone themselves now, though, with the three-gallon Magnum Hurricane. It's served with a handful of straws and takes a group to finish it—all of whom must drink standing up. Watch frat boys try this and drop one by one.

Pat O's let-your-hair-down conviviality has earned it a special place among so many residents that it sometimes has a neighborhood air usually associated with much smaller places—yes, locals drink here. There are three bars: the main bar at the entrance, a patio bar, and a large lounge located just off the entrance. The lounge is the center of a Pat O'Brien's entertainment. The fun comes from several teams of pianists alternating at twin pianos and an emcee who tells jokes. The entertainers seem to know every song ever written, and when they ask a patron, "Where're you from?" quick as a wink they'll break into a number associated with the visitor's home state. Requests are quickly honored, and sing-alongs develop all night long. There's no minimum and no cover, but if you buy a drink and it comes in a *glass* you'll be paying for the glass until you turn it in at the register for a $2 refund.

---

say, slaves they'd captured on the high seas). It had pretty much deteriorated by 1944, when a honeymooning visitor fell in love with it and devoted most of the rest of his life to making it a social center for artists, writers, entertainers, and journalists. He did this all without changing one iota of the musty old interior—even today you can see the original construction and "feel" what it must have been like when it was a privateers' hangout. Unfortunately Tom Caplinger's penchant for treating good friends such as Tennessee Williams and Lucius Beebe to refreshments "on the house" was stronger than his business acumen, and he eventually lost the building. All this is history, but I think it helps explain the comfortable, neighborhood air that still pervades Lafitte's. The interior is all exposed brick, wooden tables, and an air of authenticity. It's a good drop-in spot any time of day, but I especially enjoy relaxing in the dim, candlelit bar at the end of a festive night when "Miss Lily" Hood holds forth at the piano.

Napoleon House Bar & Cafe
500 Chartres St. ☎ **504/524-9752.** No cover.

This landmark place is a favorite hangout of locals and tourists alike. Atmosphere is a big draw here. See Chapter 7 for a more complete listing.

O'Flaherty's Irish Channel Pub
514 Toulouse St. ☎ **504/529-1317** or 504/529-4570. No cover.

The haunted courtyard in this 18th-century building is a big draw, but so is the Irish atmosphere. Irish dancing is offered every Saturday night.

Ol'Toone's Saloon
233 Decatur St. ☎ **504/529-3422.** No cover.

It's not very atmospheric, but Ol'Toone's is a great place to go shoot pool and choose your tunes on the well-stocked jukebox.

Original Tropical Isle
738 Toulouse St. ☎ **504/525-1689.** No cover.

If you're looking for a good, strong drink in a "tropical" setting, stop by the Original Tropical Isle and grab a "hand grenade." Other drinks have equally creative names—the "horny gator" is also very popular. Live music is featured here frequently.

Parrot's Perch

721 Bourbon St., second floor. ☎ **504/529-4109.** No cover.

Margaritas and Corona and tequila shooters keep them coming back to Parrot's Perch every night. Sunday to Wednesday billiards are free.

Planet Hollywood

620 Decatur St. ☎ **504/522-7826.** No cover.

Yes Virginia, there is a Planet Hollywood in New Orleans (they seem to be everywhere these days). Drinks are named for film and movie characters.

The "R" Bar

1431 Royal St. ☎ **504/948-7499.** No cover.

The "R" Bar is the quintessential neighborhood bar. It attracts a varied clientele who come for the large selection of imported beers and the friendly, comfortable atmosphere.

Vino Vino

1119 Decatur St. ☎ **504/529-4553.** No cover.

As its name suggests, Vino Vino is a wine bar—a huge step above the rest of the bars listed here. It's a great place for a pre- or postdinner drink.

OUTSIDE THE FRENCH QUARTER

Audubon Tavern II

6100 Magazine St. ☎ **504/895-9702.** No cover.

The clientele at Audubon Tavern II is mainly from neighboring college campuses. Dancing is virtually a requirement if you're going to stop here for a drink.

The Boot

1039 Broadway Ave. ☎ **504/866-9008.** No cover.

Definitely a college bar (mainly due to its proximity to Tulane University), the atmosphere in The Boot is something like a frat party—Jell-O shooters being a favorite "libation." The drinks, as expected, are inexpensive, and specials are offered every day of the week.

Bruno's Bar

7601 Maple St. ☎ **504/861-7615.** No cover.

For more than 60 years Bruno's has been a gathering place for fun-loving locals of all ages. Head to Bruno's for a few games of darts and a jukebox playing music spanning the last four decades.

The Bulldog

3236 Magazine St. ☎ **504/891-1516.** No cover.

Yet another bar for the college crowd, The Bulldog has a fantastic selection of beers—currently more than 50 brews are offered. Video games and ear-splitting music make conversation difficult at best, but that's not why people hang at The Bulldog.

Hyttops Sports Bar

500 Poydras Plaza (in the Hyatt Hotel). ☎ **504/561-1234.** No cover.

Sports fans take notice: Hyttops Sports Bar has seven big-screen TVs and no fewer than 11 smaller TVs all tuned, via satellite, to sporting events around the country. This is a great place to hang out after a Saints game.

Joe's Jungle Bar
510 Gravier St. ☎ **504/524-9485.** No cover.

If you're in the Central Business District at quitting time, Joe's Jungle Bar will be jam packed with locals stopping for a drink on their way home from work. Nothing unusual here, just your regular bar drinks, a juke box, and video poker.

Madigan's
800 S. Carrollton Ave. ☎ **504/866-9455.** No cover most nights.

Located in the Uptown section of New Orleans, Madigan's is a casual watering hole that's home to blues musician John Mooney on Sundays.

Nick's
2400 Tulane Ave. ☎ **504/821-9128.** No cover.

The slogan here is "Looks like the oldest bar in town!," and it does. Behind the barroom you'll find billiards and infrequent performances by live musicians. Special drink prices are offered on weekdays.

Philips
733 Cherokee St. ☎ **504/865-1155.** No cover.

Another favorite of the local university students, Philips offers good music and a number of video poker machines.

The Polo Lounge
300 Gravier St. (in the Windsor Court Hotel) ☎ **504/523-6000.** No cover.

The Windsor Court is, without a doubt, the city's finest hostelry, and the Polo Lounge is the place to go if you're feeling particularly stylish. Sazeracs and cigars are popular here.

Saturn Bar
3067 St. Claude Ave. ☎ **504/949-7532.** No cover.

The Saturn Bar has been around for almost 40 years, but it's only recently that celebrities like John Goodman and Nicolas Cage have made it famous. These days, it's the place to be for celebrity hounds. There's a good selection of imported beers available.

Sazerac Bar
In the Fairmont Hotel, University Place. ☎ **504/529-4733. No cover.**

Located in the posh Fairmont Hotel, Sazerac Bar is a favorite with the city's young professionals. The African walnut bar and murals by Paul Ninas complete the upscale atmosphere. The Sazerac Bar was featured in the movie *The Pelican Brief.* Wines and champagnes are available by the glass, and a dessert menu is available.

Sitting Duck
5130 Freret St. ☎ **504/895-1400.** No cover.

All I can say is shots, shots, and more shots. The college crowd simply delights in the wide variety of shots offered here. The music is always very, very loud.

BREWHOUSES

These days brewhouses are popping up all over the country, and New Orleans is no exception. **Crescent City Brewhouse** (527 Decatur St., ☎ **504/522-0571**), primarily due to its central French Quarter location, is popular with tourists. The balcony, which faces Decatur Street, is always packed, and there are several original Crescent City beers on tap. A jazz combo plays here, and Happy Hour during the week brings two-for-one beer specials. There is a full menu.

Acadian Brewhouse, 201 N. Carollton Ave. (☎ 504/483-9003) is a relative new-comer to the up-and-coming midcity area. All sorts of specialty beers, from Purple Haze to Blackened Voodoo are offered.

PIANO BARS

The Bombay Club
830 Conti St. ☎ **504/522-5522** or 504/586-0972. No cover.

This posh piano bar features New Orleans jazz on Friday and Saturday evenings. Martinis at The Bombay Club are hailed as the best in town. Jeans and shorts are not acceptable attire.

Esplanade Lounge
In the Royal Orleans, 621 St. Louis St. ☎ **504/529-5333.** No cover.

For a nightcap to the strains of top-notch piano music in one of the city's loveliest settings, stop by the Esplanade.

A BAR WITH A VIEW

Top of the Mart
World Trade Center of New Orleans, 2 Canal St. ☎ **504/522-9795.**

The view is breathtaking any time of day, but especially so after dark, from the Top of the Mart, at the river. The world's largest revolving cocktail lounge located on the 33rd floor makes a complete circle about every 90 minutes. From up there you'll see the bend in the Mississippi that gives New Orleans its "Crescent City" title, and the reflected lights of ships in the harbor remind you that this is not only a fun town, but also a busy port. As you revolve, the layout of the city unfolds all the way to Lake Pontchartrain. There's no admission charge and no cover. Children aren't permitted. Top of the Mart is open daily until midnight or 1am.

5 Burlesque & Strip Clubs

As much a part of French Quarter lore as Mardi Gras and jazz are the legendary skin shows of Bourbon Street. There are a number of establishments offering this sort of entertainment in the 300 and 400 blocks of Bourbon; you'll be able to tell what you're getting into before you go in—club owners frequently open their doors to try to lure in the paying public with music and a more or less unobstructed view of the dancers inside. There is also a traditional cabaret theater in New Orleans; see below.

Chris Owens Club
735 St. Louis St., corner of Bourbon St. ☎ **504/523-6400.** Cover $11 (includes show and one cocktail; $15 on New Year's Eve). Show times are Mon–Sat at 10pm and midnight.

If you like your entertainment on the sexy side but aren't quite game for Bourbon Street's strippers, this is the place to go. The talented and very beautiful Chris Owens, backed by a great group of musicians, puts on a show of fun-filled jazz, popular, country and western, and blues while (according to one devoted fan) revealing enough of her physical endowments to make strong men bay at the moon. Between shows, there's dancing on the elevated dance floor. Audience participation is encouraged—join in the conga line, which is popular with visitors and locals alike. Trumpeteer Al Hirt now performs at the Chris Owens Club several times a week. Hirt's shows usually begin at 8pm. Call to make reservations.

6 Gay Nightlife

Below you'll find listings of New Orleans's most popular gay nightspots. For more information you can check *Ambush*, which is a great source for the gay community in New Orleans and for those visiting. Ask around at some of the locally owned gay bars and restaurants, and they'll tell you where to find the latest copy of *Ambush*.

BARS

In addition to those listed below, you might also try **Bus Stop,** 542 North Rampart St. (☎ **504/522-3372**), popular with the local African-American gay crowd; **The Golden Lantern,** 1239 Royal St. (☎ **504/529-2860**), a nice neighborhood spot where the bartender knows the clientele by name; and **Mrs. and Mr. B's on the Patio,** 515 St. Philip St. (☎ **504/586-0644**), popular with the local gay clientele for its beautiful patio (it's open 24 hours and has a happy hour from 4 to 9pm). If Levi's and leather is your scene, **The Rawhide,** 740 Burgundy St. (☎ **504/525-8106**), is your best bet; during Mardi Gras, this place hosts a great Gay Costume Contest that is not to be missed.

Bourbon Pub Parade
801 Bourbon St. ☎ **504/529-2107.**

The Bourbon Pub attracts a young male crowd, offering a video bar (with "dancing boys" on the weekend). Upstairs features a high-tech dance floor complete with lasers and smoke. Sunday nights bring a weekly T dance. It's open 24 hours and every time I've ever been in or been by, the place is packed.

Café Lafitte in Exile
901 Bourbon St. ☎ **504/522-8397.** No cover.

When Tom Caplinger lost Lafitte's Blacksmith Shop, friends say that it broke his heart. But he rallied and a little later opened a new place down the block toward Canal Street called the Café Lafitte in Exile (the exile is his own, from that beloved blacksmith shop). The new digs flourish as an elite gay bar even after his death. It is, in fact, the oldest gay bar in the country. There's a bar downstairs, and upstairs you'll find a pool table and a balcony that overlooks Bourbon Street.

Charlene's
940 Elysian Fields. ☎ **504/945-9328.** No cover.

Charlene's is known as the only lesbian bar in town. It's a little out of the way if you're staying in the Quarter, but there's dancing and live entertainment, so you might think it worth the trip. Take a cab.

Good Friends Bar & Queens Head Pub
740 Dauphine St. ☎ **504/566-7199.** No cover.

This is a good place to begin if it's your first visit to New Orleans. The local clientele is happy to offer suggestions as to where you might find the type of entertainment you're looking for. Downstairs there's a mahogany bar and a pool table. Upstairs is the quiet Queens Head Pub.

LeRoundup
819 St. Louis St. ☎ **504/561-8340.** No cover.

LeRoundup attracts the most diverse crowd around. Here you'll find transsexuals lining up at the bar with drag queens and well-groomed men in khakis and Levi's. The atmosphere is friendly and very, very open, and in spite of the fact that it's only a half a block from the Bourbon Street scene, the clientele is primarily local. The bar is open 24 hours.

The Mint
504 Esplanade Ave. ☎ **504/525-2000.** Cover charge varies according to performer.

A popular spot within the gay community in New Orleans, the Mint is always full. There's live entertainment all the time (including impersonation), so you should ask around or look in *Ambush* to find out what's happening during your visit. There's a very popular happy hour nightly from 5 to 9pm, and the club itself is open Monday through Friday from noon until the wee hours, Saturday and Sunday from 10am on.

DANCE CLUBS

Oz
800 Bourbon St. ☎ **504/593-9491.**

One of New Orleans's newest dance clubs, Oz was the place to see and be seen at press time. It was ranked as the city's number-one dance club by *Gambit* magazine, and *Details* magazine ranked it as one of the top 50 clubs in the country. The music is great, there's an incredible laser light show, and from time to time there's a dancing boys show atop the bar.

Rubyfruit Jungle
640 Frenchmen St. ☎ **504/947-4000.**

The 80-foot copper-topped bar is enough of an attraction to make this place one of the city's hottest gay and lesbian dance clubs, but what everyone really comes for is the great music and high-tech lighting and sound. Each night brings a different kind of entertainment: Some nights offer New York warehouse-style dancing, others bring country and western, and still others feature comedy and other local gay talent.

Wolfendale's
834 N. Rampart St. ☎ **504/523-7764.**

Popular with the city's gay African-American population, Wolfendale's has a lovely courtyard, a raised dance floor, and a pool table. Most don't come to lounge around in the courtyard or by the pool table. People come here to dance. Take a cab.

7 Gambling

So, you're probably wondering where you can go to gamble in New Orleans now that Harrah's highly touted casino has gone bust—before it even officially opened, I might add. Well, there's still a riverboat casino that remains in operation (see below), and if you're willing to make a short drive, you can visit the **Boomtown Belle Casino,** located on the West Bank (call **504/366-7711** for information and directions), or the **Treasure Chest Casino,** docked on Lake Pontchartrain in Kenner (call **504/443-8000** for information and directions).

Flamingo Casino New Orleans
Riverwalk Marketplace, next to the New Orleans Hilton Riverside Hotel on Poydras Street at the river. ☎ **800/587-luck** or 504/587-5777. Admission $5. Call for cruise times or to see if the boat will be remaining dockside.

The *Flamingo* is an authentic re-creation of a 19th-century riverboat casino complete with authentic period detailing. There are 75 gaming tables and 1,333 slot machines. Table games include blackjack, craps, roulette, pai gow poker, and others. The boat actually cruises the Mississippi—it's not permanently docked, though there are times that it does remain docked, and at those times you're allowed unlimited boarding. Cruises last 90 minutes and take place about every three hours, beginning at 8:45am. I would strongly advise buying your tickets in advance, especially for the evening cruises, so you won't have to wait in line (lines can be enormously long), and getting there as soon as the doors open for boarding so you can stake out your machine before the masses beat you to it. Slot machines are the most popular form of gambling on the boat, and they range from 5¢ to $100 slots. At the time of my last visit, Lucky Dogs, Mother's, and the Italian restaurant Andrea's were the three food vendors represented. Drinks are free during your cruise, and there are smoke-free gaming rooms. Live Dixieland jazz is performed from time to time as well. Children are not allowed in the gaming rooms.

8   The Performing Arts

There's more to New Orleans than its heady nightlife. Its rich French heritage, strongly spiced by the Italians who've become such a part of its life, has left a real love of classical music and opera. Theater, too, plays a part in New Orleans entertainment. Although it's a little off the regular routes for touring Broadway shows, New Orleans attracts some very good national companies, and there's surprisingly good local theater. You'll find opera, as well as concerts by top performers and symphony orchestras, ballets, and recitals by local and imported talent in one of two buildings: the New Orleans Theatre of the Performing Arts or the New Orleans Municipal Auditorium (see below).

Note: Because ticket prices vary widely according to performance, your best bet is just to call the numbers listed below before you go.

MAJOR CONCERT HALLS & AUDITORIUMS

New Orleans's **Municipal Auditorium** is located at 1201 St. Peter St. (☎ 504/565-7470 or 504/565-7490 for ticket information), just across a flowered walkway from the Theatre of Performing Arts in the Cultural Center complex in Louis Armstrong Park. It is used for just about every kind of entertainment—from the circus to touring theatrical companies to ballets and concerts. This is also where most of the marvelous, elaborate Mardi Gras balls are held.

The **Mahalia Jackson Theatre of the Performing Arts**, 801 N. Rampart St. (☎ 504/565-7470), has become the favored venue for lavish touring musical shows as well as concerts. Opera and ballet also appear here in season. General-audience shows such as circuses, prize fights, ice shows, and the popular summer pops symphony concerts are also accommodated here. The theater is a part of the 32-acre New Orleans Cultural Center complex in Louis Armstrong Park, adjacent to the French Quarter.

PERFORMING ARTS COMPANIES
OPERA

Light opera appeared in New Orleans as early as 1810, and grand opera was first sung here in 1837. Opera enjoyed its peak years during the Gay Nineties and the early part of this century and thrived until a fire destroyed the famous French Opera House in 1919. It wasn't until 1943 that the **New Orleans Opera Association** (☎ 504/529-2278) was formed to present several operas a season. Stars from New York's Metropolitan Opera Company frequently appear in leading roles, supported by talented local voices. If you're an opera buff and in town during one of the local offerings, don't pass it up—there's nothing amateurish about these productions. Occasionally, the Met's touring company will also book performances in New Orleans.

DANCE

The **New Orleans Ballet Association** (☎ 504/522-0996), which merged recently with the Cincinnati Ballet, is the city's professional ballet company. The excellent performances are held at the New Orleans Theatre of the Performing Arts. Check the newspapers for current performances.

CLASSICAL MUSIC

The **Louisiana Philharmonic Orchestra** (☎ 504/523-6530) plays a subscription series of concerts during the fall-to-spring season, and the pops concerts on June and July weekends.

THEATERS

In addition to the listings below, possibilities for theatrical performances and concerts include **True Brew** (see coffeehouses below) and the **Louisiana Superdome** (☎ 504/587-3810), which frequently hosts entertainment not even remotely connected with sports.

Contemporary Arts Center
900 Camp St. ☎ **504/523-1216.**

Located in the Warehouse District, the Contemporary Arts Center is best known for its changing exhibitions of contemporary art, but also located on the premises are two theaters where dance performances and concerts are frequently given. Also featured are experimental works by local playwrights. Call for the current schedule.

Le Petit Théatre du Vieux Carré
616 St. Peter St. ☎ **504/522-2081.**

If you hear people talking about "The Little Theater" right in the heart of the French Quarter, this is it. It's one of the oldest nonprofessional theater troupes in the country and periodically puts on plays that rival the professionals in excellence. Check when you're here to see if the footlights are up.

Saenger Theatre
143 N. Rampart St. ☎ **504/525-1052**.

The Saenger Theatre is *the* theater news in New Orleans. First opened in 1927, it was regarded as one of the finest in the world, and it has now been completely restored in all its finery. The decor is Renaissance Florence, with Greek and Roman sculpture, fine marble statues, and cut-glass chandeliers. The ceiling is alive with twinkling stars and realistic looking clouds drifting by. It's a setting the likes of which are fast disappearing from the American theater scene, and New Orleans is to be congratulated for preserving such opulence. Touring Broadway productions play here regularly.

Southern Rep Theatre
Canal Place Shopping Centre, 3rd level. ☎ **504/861-8163.**

The Southern Rep Theatre, New Orleans's newest theater, primarily presents the work of southern playwrights and actors. Located near the Canal Place movie theater, the Southern Rep is comfortable and intimate, and is easily accessible from all downtown and French Quarter hotels. During the summer new playwrights get a chance to show their stuff as part of the theater's New Playwrights series. Ample parking is available in the shopping center garage.

Theatre Marigny
616 Frenchmen St. ☎ **504/944-2653.**

This little theater is known for its presentations of avant-garde works. Both little-known and well-established playwrights are given the opportunity to present their productions here.

9 Coffeehouses with Live Entertainment

Several of the city's coffeehouses offer live entertainment at various times throughout the week. I enjoy the coffeehouses—they are nice places to relax without getting beer spilled on you by some underage college student who has had a few too many.

Kaldi's Coffee House and Museum at 941 Decatur St. (☎ **504/586-8989**) offers jazz and gospel music on the weekends. Beginning at 8pm you can listen to live jazz while sipping a cup of java and munching on pastries. Kaldi's is open Sunday through Thursday from 7am to midnight, Friday and Saturday from 7am to 2am.

In the Warehouse District the place to go is **True Brew Cafe and Theater** at 200 Julia St. (☎ **504/524-8441**), where live music and one-act plays (featuring local actors) are presented weekly to patrons enjoying coffees, teas, and pastries. The cafe is open every day from 7am until 8pm and on weekends until 1am.

Uptown at 5110 Daneel St. you'll find **Neutral Ground Coffee House.** The comfort level in this 1960s throwback cafe is high—overstuffed chairs are one of the main attractions. Open-mike night brings all sorts of musicians and performers, while at other times, more well-known musical talents are featured. Neutral Ground is open every day except Monday from 8pm until midnight or 1am.

If poetry readings are more to your liking, try **Cafe Brasil** at 2100 Chartres St. (see "Rock & the Rest of the Music Scene," above, for a complete listing).

10 An Evening Cruise

One of the loveliest evenings out in New Orleans is to be found out on the water. The *Creole Queen* (☎ **504/524-0814** or 800/445-4109) is a paddle wheeler built in the tradition of its forebears, which made its debut at the 1984 World's Fair and now offers superb Creole dinners and jazz cruises nightly. Departures are at 8pm (boarding at 7pm) from the Canal Street Wharf. The fare is $39 per person (which includes a sumptuous Creole buffet, $18 without the meal), and there's continuous bar service, as well as live jazz and dancing against a backdrop of the city's sparkling skyline. Schedules are subject to change, so call ahead to confirm days and times.

Plantation Homes & Cajun Country: Side Trips from New Orleans

12

New Orleans can serve as the hub for two interesting side trips. The first centers on the great plantation homes that line the banks of the Mississippi; the second will take you a little more than 100 miles west of New Orleans to the heart of Acadiana, where the unique culture of the Cajuns lives on. Although a day trip is enough to see some of the plantation houses that are open to the public, the other trip will probably require an overnight stop; both, though, may very likely lure you to stay for more than just one night. Should you become hooked on the romanticism of the plantations, it is quite possible to keep rambling north of the River Road to visit those in the St. Francisville area, an exploration that also calls for an overnight stay. This chapter will tell you about old homes in which you can actually spend the night if you plan ahead.

1 The Plantations Along the Great River Road

In the beginning, the planters of Louisiana were little more than rugged frontiers people. As they spread out along the Mississippi from New Orleans, they cleared swamplands with a mighty expenditure of sweat and muscle. Indigo, the area's first cash crop, had to be transported downriver to New Orleans before there was any return on all that backbreaking work. Even today, as you drive on the modern highways that course through some of the bayous, it's not hard to imagine what it must have been like for those early settlers.

In spite of all the obstacles, however, fields were cleared, swamps were drained, and crops were planted. Rough flatboats and keelboats (with crews even rougher than their vessels) were able to get the produce to market in New Orleans—sometimes. Once the boats were on the river, if they weren't capsized by rapids, snags, sandbars, and floating debris, there was the danger that their cargoes would be captured by murdering bands of river pirates. It was the crudeness of these men (and a few extraordinary women) who poled the boats to New Orleans; collected their pay for the journey; and then went on wild sprees of drinking, gambling, and brawling, that first gave the Creoles of the French Quarter their lasting impression of Americans as barbarians. And it was this impression that was later to influence the growth and development of the city.

By the 1800s Louisiana planters had introduced farming on a large scale, based primarily on their use of (and dependence on) slave labor—a fact that would ultimately bring about their downfall. With large numbers of African Americans performing the back-breaking work in the fields, more and more acres went under cultivation, and King Cotton, which proved to be the most profitable of all crops, arrived on the scene. Sugarcane, too, brought huge monetary returns, especially after Etienne de Bore discovered the secret of successful granulation. Rice became a secondary crop. Always there were natural dangers that could spell disaster for planters—a hurricane could wipe out a whole year's work, and the capricious river could, and did, make swift changes in its course, inundating entire plantations. Nevertheless the planters persevered, and for the most part they prospered.

THE RIVERBOATS

After 1812, the planters turned to the newfangled steamboat for speedier and safer transportation of their crops to the market. When the first of these (the *New Orleans*, built in Pittsburgh) chugged downriver belching sooty smoke, it was so dirty, dangerous, and potentially explosive that it was called by some a "floating volcano." Before long, however, vast improvements were made, and over a 30-year period the image of the steamboats changed to that of veritable floating pleasure palaces. Utilitarian purposes (moving goods to market and the planters and their families to town) were always primary, but the lavish staterooms and ornate "grand salons" put a whole new face on river travel and made a profound change in plantation life. A planter could now travel in comfort with his wife, children, and slaves, which induced many to spend the winters in elegant town houses in New Orleans. After months of isolation in the country, where visitors were few, the sociability of the city—with its grand balls, theatrical performances, elaborate banquets, and other entertainments—was a welcome relief. Also, it became possible to ship fine furnishings back upriver to plantation homes, and thus the planters could enjoy a more comfortable and elegant lifestyle along the banks of the river.

Those wonderful floating pleasure palaces did, alas, add another element of danger to the lives of some planters. For along with the prosperous plantation families, northern merchants, carpetbag-carrying peddlers, European visitors, and poor immigrant families who made up passenger lists, came the most colorful and dramatic passenger of all: the riverboat gambler. Plantation owners were drawn like magnets to the sharp-witted, silver-tongued professionals. Huge fortunes were won and lost on Ole Man River, and more than once when cash, luggage, and jewelry were depleted, the deed to a plantation went on the table, to be raked in by a well-dressed, cigar-smoking pro. During one famous game, which went on for three days without interruption, it was said that more than $37,000 in gold was on the table at one point.

THE PLANTATION HOUSES RISE

It was during this period of prosperity, from the 1820s until the beginning of the Civil War, that most of the impressive plantation homes were built. Each was usually intended to be the focal point of a self-sustaining community and almost always was located near the riverfront, with a wide, oak-lined avenue leading from its entrance to a wharf. On either side of the avenue would be *garçonnières* (much smaller houses, sometimes used to give adolescent sons and their friends privacy; others were guest houses for travelers who stopped for a night's lodging). Behind the main house, the kitchen was built separately because of the danger of fire, and the overseer's office was close enough for convenience. Some plantations had, behind these two structures, pigeon houses, or dovecotes—and all had the inevitable slave quarters,

Plantations Along the Great River Road

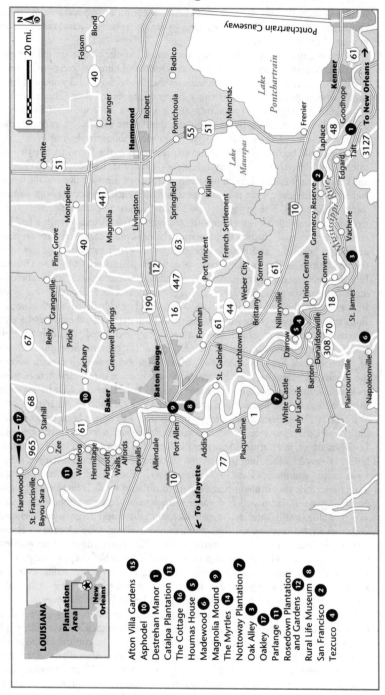

Afton Villa Gardens 15
Asphodel 10
Destrehan Manor 1
Catalpa Plantation 13
The Cottage 16
Houmas House 5
Madewood 6
Magnolia Mound 9
The Myrtles 14
Nottoway Plantation 7
Oak Alley 3
Oakley 17
Parlange 11
Rosedown Plantation and Gardens 12
Rural Life Museum 8
San Francisco 2
Tezcuco 4

usually in twin lines bordering a lane leading to cotton or sugarcane fields. When cotton gins and sugar mills came along, they were generally built across the fields, out of sight of the main house.

In the beginning, the main houses were much like the simple "raised cottage" known as Madame John's Legacy, on New Orleans's Dumaine Street—with long, sloping roofs, cement-covered brick walls on the ground floor, and wood and brick (brick between posts) used in the living quarters on the second floor. They suited the sultry Louisiana climate and swampy building sites and made use of native materials. There's a distinct West Indies architectural influence seen in houses of the colonial period, very unlike the grander styles that were to follow in the 1800s.

In the 1820s, homes were built that combined traces of the West Indian style with some Greek Revival and Georgian influences—a style that has been dubbed Louisiana Classic. Large rounded columns usually surrounded the main body of the house, wide galleries reaching from the columns to the walls encircled upper floors, and the roof was dormered. The upper and lower floors consisted of four large rooms centered by a wide hall. They were constructed with native materials, with a few imported interior details, such as fireplace mantels. Remember that there were no stone quarries in Louisiana, and if stone was used (which wasn't very often), it had to be shipped from New England and transported up the Mississippi from New Orleans. But the river flowed through banks of clay, and with so many slaves, bricks could be made right on the spot. Cypress, too, was plentiful, and such a water-loving wood was perfect for the hot, humid climate, which could quickly deteriorate less impervious woods. To protect the homemade bricks from dampness, they were plastered or cement covered, and sometimes the outer coating was tinted, although more often it was left to mellow into a soft, off-white color. The columns were almost always of plastered brick, but very occasionally of cypress wood. Even their capitals were of these materials, except for a rare instance when cast iron was used. These houses, then, took some features from European architecture and some from the West Indian styles that so well suited the location and adapted them to local building materials.

By the 1850s, planters were more prosperous, and their homes became more grandiose. The extravagance of Victorian architecture was embraced and given a unique Louisiana flavor, the features of northern Italian villas crept in, and some plantation homes followed Gothic lines (notably the fantastic San Francisco Plantation, sometimes called "steamboat Gothic"). As planters and their families traveled to Europe more frequently, they brought home ornate furnishings for their houses, which had begun to grow in size as well as elegance. European masters were imported for fine woodworking, until Louisiana artisans such as Mallard and Seignouret developed skills that rivaled or surpassed those from abroad. Ceilings were adorned by elaborate "medallions" from which glittering crystal chandeliers hung, and on wooden mantels and wainscoting the art of *faux marbre* ("false marble") began to appear. In short, plantation owners seemed determined to make their country homes every bit as elegant as their New Orleans town houses. They were developing a way of life dedicated to graciousness and hospitality unlike any other in American history.

As they grew in opulence, the plantation houses expanded in size—some had as many as 30 or 40 rooms. They were so large partly because families were quite large in those days. But even more important, any social life in the country had to come from neighbors or friends visiting for several days or weeks. After all, travel was difficult, and there just was no such thing as "popping in for a call." But there were other reasons, too, and they had to do with that well-known southern pride. Madewood, for example, on Bayou Lafourche, was built for no other reason than to outshine Woodlawn, the beautiful home of the builder's brother.

Underneath the planters' enormous wealth and power lay an economy built on the backs of slaves. It was, as world history has many times shown, an unhealthy foundation, and inevitably it crumbled with the beginning of the Civil War. Farming on a scale as large as was practiced on the plantations was impossible without that large, cheap labor base. And when plantation owners went away to war, the management of the plantations deteriorated even where slaves stayed on. During Reconstruction, lands were often confiscated and turned over intact to those unable for financial or other reasons to run the large-scale operations; many were broken up into smaller, more manageable farms. Increasing international competition began to erode the cotton and sugar markets that had built such large fortunes. And as industrialism moved south, there was no place for life as it had been lived in the golden plantation years.

It is hard to remember when you walk through the grand old homes left in the wake of the plantation era that the culture they embody began, reached a lofty pinnacle, and then died away in the span of less than 100 years.

THE PLANTATION HOUSES TODAY

Since the beginning of this century, several of these houses have been the victims of fires or floods. Some have been torn down to make way for other things, such as industrial plants. Others, too costly to be maintained in modern times, have been left to the ravages of dampness and decay. But for a few, fate has been more kind—wealthy families have bought the houses and restored them with love and affection. The encroachment of modernity has been restricted primarily to the installation of plumbing and electricity. Some are used only as private residences, but you can visit others for a small admission fee (which, in some instances, supplements the owner's own resources to keep up the old house).

PLANNING YOUR TRIP

All the plantation homes shown on the map are within easy driving distance of New Orleans. How many you take in on any one day will depend, I suspect, on your endurance behind the wheel, your walking stamina (you'll cover a lot of ground touring the houses), and how early you set out. You'll be driving through "country" Louisiana, and I might as well warn you that some of what you'll see is really quite tacky—the modern, industrial economy that prevails through most of the area just isn't pretty to look at. Also, don't expect to enjoy broad river views as you drive along the Great River Road (the name given to the roadway on *both* sides of the Mississippi); you'll have to drive up on the levee for that. You will, however, pass through little towns that date from plantation days, and in your own car you'll have the luxury of turning off to inspect interesting old churches or aboveground cemeteries that can only be glimpsed from a tour bus window.

If you should happen to be in New Orleans on Christmas Eve and drive along River Road, your way will be lit by huge bonfires on the levees—they're to light the way for the Christ Child (an old Latin custom), and residents along here spend weeks collecting wood, trash, and anything that's flammable to make the fires blaze brightly.

Because not all Louisiana plantations actually bordered the Mississippi River (many were on bayous that also provided water transportation), some of the grand old homes have survived at locations too far away from New Orleans to be visited in a single day. I'm listing those separately, with the recommendation that you try to stay overnight at one that offers guest accommodations. I'll also include accommodations in Baton Rouge and St. Francisville, either of which can serve as a convenient tour base.

ORGANIZED TOURS

For some it might be a good idea to take a plantation house bus tour from New Orleans before setting out on your own. Most of the tours visit only one or two of the houses I have described, leaving plenty for your private exploration. My experience has been that tour guides are exceptionally well informed, and the buses are an easy, comfortable way to get around in unfamiliar territory. Almost every tour company operates a River Road plantation tour.

I especially like the seven-hour River Road plantations tour offered by **Gray Line,** 2345 New Orleans World Trade Center (☎ **504/587-0861**). The two plantations visited are Nottoway and Oak Alley. All admissions are included in the $50 charge. Tours, departing at 9am on Tuesday, Thursday, and Sunday, pick you up at and deliver you to your hotel. The cost of lunch at a country restaurant, however, is not included and generally runs $8 to $10, sometimes more.

If you prefer a smaller tour group, **Tours by Isabelle,** P.O. Box 740972, New Orleans, LA 70174 (☎ **504/391-3544**), takes no more than 13 people in a comfortable minibus on an eight-hour expedition to visit Oak Alley, Madewood, and Nottoway plantations. Lunch in the elegant dining room of the Madewood Plantation mansion is included on this tour. The tour departs only when six or more people request it, so you might have to wait a day or two until they can get a large enough group together. Other tours offered by Tours by Isabelle include a 4¹/₂-hour Cajun Bayou Tour (the boat tour is 1¹/₂ hours); the five-hour Eastbank Plantation Tour (which includes a guided tours of Tezcuco Plantation with stops in front of Houmas House, Bocage, and Hermitage plantations); and the Grand Tour (a visit to Oak Alley Plantation, lunch, a Cajun Bayou Tour, and a stop in front of Destrehan plantation).

PLANTATIONS WITHIN THE NEW ORLEANS AREA

I'll start with the plantations nearest New Orleans and describe them in the order in which they appear on the map, although that is not necessarily the order in which you will view them.

A mile and a half above Destrehan, look for **Ormond** plantation house, a two-story structure with columns and gallery and a wing on each end (it's not shown on our map because it isn't open to the public). The house has in recent years been bought and beautifully restored as a private residence, but its early history is one of tragedy. Built sometime before 1790 by Pierre de Trepagnier on land granted him by the Spanish government, it witnessed the mysterious disappearance of Pierre, when he went off with a complete stranger and was never seen or heard from again; the wiping out of almost an entire family by yellow fever; and the murder of its owner during Reconstruction—his body was found riddled with bullets and hanging from a live oak tree. From all appearances the house is now seeing happier days, and its future looks bright. You can't go inside, but it is certainly worth a slowdown and long look as you pass by.

Destrehan Manor

La. 48 (P.O. Box 5), Destrehan, LA 70047. ☎ **504/764-9315.** Admission $6. Daily 9:30am–4pm.

A free person of color named Charles built this house, located 22 miles from New Orleans along the River Road, in 1787. The wings on either side were added in 1805, and between 1830 and 1840 it was renovated from French Colonial to Greek Revival. Some of the largest live oaks in the state are on the grounds. Its double galleries are surrounded by Doric columns that support the central structure's hipped roof. Inside, you can see the original woodwork and some interesting antiques. There's also a gift shop, and you can purchase light refreshments. The American Oil Company, which had bought the property, presented the house (in a state of deterioration) to the River Road Historical Society, and during its restoration some of the earliest methods of construction were uncovered. The society has left some glimpses of the construction open for visitors to see. Destrehan is the oldest plantation home remaining intact in the Lower Mississippi Valley that is open to the public. There are guided tours.

San Francisco

La. 44 (P.O. Drawer AX), Reserve, LA 70084. ☎ **504/535-2341.** Admission $7 adults, $4 children 12–17, $2.75 children 6–11, children under 6 free. Daily 10am–4pm. Closed holidays (including Mardi Gras Day).

This fantastic mansion, located 2 miles north of Reserve, was built between 1853 and 1856 by Edmond B. Marmillion. Unfortunately, Marmillion died shortly after its completion and was never able to occupy the home, which was willed to his two sons, Valsin and Charles. In 1855, while on a grand tour of Europe, Valsin met and married Louise Seybold. Valsin and Louise undertook to decorate their home in high style, and when they were finished, Valsin jokingly declared to his friends that he was "*sans fruscin*," or "without a cent" to his name. This is how the plantation home gained its first name, St. Frusquin. When the estate was sold to Achille Bougere, the name was changed to San Francisco.

Though its name has changed over the years, the legacy of Edward Marmillion is a fantasy come true, even after all these years. The Gothic three-story house has broad galleries that look for all the world like a ship's double decks, and twin stairs lead to a broad main portal much like one that leads to a steamboat's grand salon. (Novelist Frances Parkinson Keyes visited the house and used it as the setting for her novel *Steamboat Gothic*.) Inside, the owner created beauty in every room through the use of carved woodwork and paintings alive with flowers, birds, nymphs, and cherubs on walls and ceilings of cypress tongue-and-groove boards. The dazzling restoration includes English and French 18th-century furniture and paintings.

Oak Alley Plantation

3645 La. 18, Vacherie, LA 70090. ☎ **504/265-2151** or 800/44-ALLEY. Admission $7 adults, $4 students, $2 children 6–12, children 5 and under free. Mar–Oct, daily 9am–5:30pm; Nov–Feb, daily 9am–5pm. Closed Thanksgiving, Christmas, and New Year's.

On La. 18 between St. James and Vacherie, Oak Alley is 60 miles from downtown New Orleans and is probably the most famous plantation house in Louisiana. It was built in 1839 by Jacques Telesphore Roman III and named Bon Séjour—but if you'll walk out to the levee and look back at the quarter-mile avenue of 300-year-old live oaks, you'll see why steamboat passengers quickly dubbed it "Oak Alley," a name that soon replaced the original. Those trees were planted, it is thought, by an early settler; Roman was so enamored of them that he planned his house to have exactly as many columns—28 in all. The fluted Doric columns completely surround the Greek Revival house and support a broad second-story gallery. Inside, the floor plan is traditional, even to the attic, with a wide central hall flanked by two large rooms on each side. Oak Alley lay disintegrating until 1914, when Mr. and Mrs. Jefferson Hardin, of New Orleans, bought it and moved in. Then, in 1925, it passed to a Mr. and Mrs. Andrew Stewart, whose loving restoration is responsible for its National Historic Landmark designation. Both the Stewarts have passed on now, and before her death Mrs. Stewart established a private, nonprofit foundation that would, upon her death, assume the role of owner/operator of the historic mansion and the 25 acres surrounding it. Today, authentically costumed guides lead visitors on tours of the home, which is furnished just as it was during the Stewarts' lifetime, with a comfortably elegant mix of antiques and more modern pieces.

Overnight accommodations are available in several cottages at rates of $85 to $115. Also, there's a restaurant open for breakfast and lunch daily from 9am to 3pm.

Tezcuco

3138 La. 44, Darrow, LA 70725. ☎ **504/562-3929.** Admission $6 adults, $5.50 children 13–17 and seniors, $3.25 children 4–12, children 4 and under free. Guided tours daily 9am–5pm.

Just upriver from the Sunshine Bridge (55 miles from New Orleans), Tezcuco ("Resting Place") was one of the last plantation houses built before the Civil War. Although small, the raised cottage was some five years in the building, using slave labor, wood from surrounding swamps, and bricks from kilns on the plantation. Although the house follows the traditional floor plan of a central hall flanked by two rooms on either side, an unusual feature is the staircase leading to the gallery at each end, as well as the expected central stair. Outbuildings include gazebos, the Civil War Museum, shops, a commissary, a chapel, and a life-size dollhouse.

If you plan on staying overnight, accommodations here run between $60 and $160 per night. You'll be able to choose among small cottages and rooms in the main house.

Houmas House Plantation & Gardens

40136 La. 942 Burnside, Darrow, LA 70725. ☎ **505/473-7841.** Admission (including guided tour) $7 adults, $5 children 13–17, $3.50 children 6–12, children under 6 free. Feb–Oct, daily 10am–5pm; Nov–Jan, daily 10am–4pm. Closed holidays.

Fifty-eight miles from New Orleans, this lovely old house had very humble beginnings in a four-room cabin built in the 1700s on land originally owned by members of the Houmas tribe. When the massive Greek Revival main house was built out front, the original house was retained and survives today. The impressive main house is two and a half stories tall, with 14 columns on three sides supporting the wide gallery. At either side are hexagonal *garçonnières,* and a carriageway is formed where the original house is connected to the main house. The late Dr. George Crozat, of New Orleans, purchased the house some years ago and went about restoring it as a comfortable home for himself and his mother, bringing in authentic furnishings of the period in which it was built.

Magnificent live oaks, magnolias, and formal gardens frame Houmas House in a way that is precisely what comes to mind when most of us think "plantation house." It so closely fits that image that its exterior was used in the film *Hush, Hush, Sweet Charlotte.* There's an interesting gift shop out back. To get to Houmas House, take I-10 from New Orleans or Baton Rouge. Exit on La. 44 to Burnside, turn right on La. 942.

Madewood

4250 La. 308, Napoleonville, LA 70390. ☎ **504/369-7151** or 800/375-7151. Admission $6 adults, $4 children and students. Daily 10am–5pm. Closed holidays.

This magnificent house on Bayou Lafourche, just below Napoleonville, is one of the best preserved of the plantation mansions. It was built by the son of a wealthy planter who had originally come from North Carolina in 1818. Madewood, the creation of the youngest of three brothers, was built for the sole purpose of outdoing his older brother's elegant mansion, Woodlawn. Four years were spent cutting lumber and making bricks, and another four were spent in actual construction. It was finally completed in 1848, but the owner never got to gloat over his brother—he died of yellow fever just before it was finished.

The large, two-story Greek Revival house of stucco-covered brick is set on a low terrace, and on either side connecting wings duplicate its design. Inside, the ceilings are 25 feet high; the central hallways are huge, as are the bedrooms; and there's a winding carved walnut staircase. Madewood has more than 20 rooms, including a tremendous ballroom. Outside there is a carriage house and the family cemetery. Truly, it's more than worth the drive.

The overnight accommodations offered here are really rather special. If you elect to stay in one of the main-house guest rooms, you'll have the run of the place, much more like a guest in a private home than a paying member of the public. For example, you'll be greeted with wine and cheese in the library, dine by candlelight in the dining room, and have brandy and coffee in the parlor. There's no telephone or TV in your room, only antique furnishings, wonderful old canopied beds, and coffee in bed the next morning. The rate ($175 for two including meals) covers a sumptuous multicourse dinner of regional specialties and a plantation breakfast. Choose one of the three suites in an elegant 1820s raised cottage and your rooms will be a little more informal in furnishings and more secluded. Call to reserve.

WHERE TO DINE

In Donaldsonville

Lafitte's Landing Restaurant

At the foot of Sunshine Bridge on La. 70 Access Rd. (P.O. Box 1128), Donaldsonville, LA 70346. ☎ **504/473-1232.** Reservations recommended. Main courses $16.95–$27.95. DISC, MC, V. Tues–Sat 11am–3pm and 6–10pm, Sun 11am–8pm. FRENCH/CAJUN.

This huge raised cottage, built in 1797, was said to be one of Jean Lafitte's hangouts. Today there's a good restaurant and lounge in the building, a good stopping point for lunch. You might want to try the pecan-smoked shrimp to start, and as a main course, try the trout Lafitte. The desserts change daily. Since the hours can change, you might want to call ahead to check or make reservations.

In Burnside

The Cabin

La. 44 at La. 22. ☎ **504/473-3007.** Reservations not required. All items $2.75–$14.95. AE, DISC, MC, V. Mon–Wed 8am–3pm, Thurs 8am–9pm, Fri–Sat 8am–10pm, Sun 8am–6pm. CAJUN.

The Cabin is another good eating place appropriate to a day of plantation viewing. It is a slave cabin from the Monroe plantation, built about 1830. Nowadays its walls are covered with old newspapers, and antique farming equipment hangs throughout. Seafood lunches include blackened redfish, fried catfish, fried stuffed shrimp, and fried stuffed crab. There is also a po-boy menu. Specialties include crabmeat au gratin, broiled red snapper, and crawfish étouffée. Try the buttermilk pie or the homemade bread pudding for dessert.

PLANTATIONS FARTHER AFIELD

Most of the plantations described below are clustered in the area around St. Francisville, north of Baton Rouge. An overnight stay is a virtual necessity if you want to see any number of these houses, and you'll really get into the spirit of things if you plan your overnight at any of the accommodations offered by the plantations described below. You may, however, wish to stay in St. Francisville itself or even in Baton Rouge. At the end of this section, I'll tell you about accommodations in both places. If you plan to make Baton Rouge your base, the St. Francisville tour will cover approximately 100 miles, and you will want to set aside at least one full day, probably two. In Baton Rouge itself, there is one plantation home, and about 30 miles northwest there is another, both of which you may want to include in your sightseeing.

The first thing you should do is contact the **Baton Rouge Convention and Visitors Bureau,** 730 North Blvd. (P.O. Box 4149, Baton Rouge, LA 70821), Baton Rouge, LA 70802 (☎ **504/383-1825**), to ask for their useful "Baton Rouge Visitors Guide," which contains maps of attractions in the city and surrounding area.

Magnolia Mound

2161 Nicholson Dr., Baton Rouge, LA 70802. ☎ **504/343-4955.** Admission $3.50 adults, $2.50 seniors, $1.50 students, 75¢ children. Tues, Thurs, Sat 10am–4pm, Sun 1–4pm. Last tour begins at 3:15pm.

This home was built in the late 1700s as a small settler's house. As prosperity came to the lower Mississippi Valley, the house was enlarged and renovated, eventually becoming the center of a 900-acre plantation. Its single story is nearly five feet off the ground and has a front porch 80 feet across. The hand-carved woodwork and the ceiling in the parlor are authentically restored. Magnolia Mound takes its name from its setting within a grove of trees on a bluff overlooking the Mississippi. One of the oldest wooden structures in the state, it is typical French Creole in architecture and furnished in Louisiana and early Federal style. Costumed guides take you through.

Rural Life Museum

4560 Essen Lane, Baton Rouge, LA 70808. ☎ **504/765-2437.** Admission $5 adults, $4 seniors, $3 children under 12. Daily 8:30am–5pm.

Louisiana State University's Rural Life Museum is a marvelous open-air museum on Burden Research Plantation at Essen and I-10. Authentically restored buildings include an overseer's house, slave cabins, a one-room school, a country church, and a barn that holds artifacts dealing with rural life from the 18th century to the early 20th century.

Nottoway Plantation

Mississippi River Road (P.O. Box 160), White Castle, LA 70788. ☎ **504/545-2730.** Admission $8 adults, $3 children 12 and under. Daily 9am–5pm. Last tour begins at 4:30pm. Closed Christmas.

This magnificent house—located 69 miles from New Orleans and about 25 miles from Baton Rouge—has been likened to a castle, and you're likely to agree when you see its 22 enormous columns supporting the original slate roof. Built in 1859, this neoclassical house has 64 rooms and a total area of more than 53,000 square feet. It was saved from Civil War destruction by the kindness of a northern gunboat officer who had once been a guest here, and kindness still blesses it, for the present owners have lovingly restored its rooms to their former glory. The white ballroom, with its hand-carved cypress Corinthian columns, archways, delicate plaster frieze work, and original crystal chandeliers, is especially lovely.

Randolph Hall restaurant serves lunch from 11am to 3pm and dinner from 6 to 9pm; you may stay overnight in one of the restored bedrooms with private bath for $125 to $250 double occupancy, which includes a wake-up tray of hot sweet potato muffins, juice, and coffee, a full plantation breakfast served in the breakfast room, and a tour of the house.

To get here from Baton Rouge, take I-10 west to the Plaquemine exit, then La. 1 south for 18 miles. (From New Orleans, follow I-10 west to the La. 22 exit, then turn left on La. 70 across the Sunshine Bridge; exit onto La. 1 and drive 14 miles north through Donaldsonville.)

Parlange Plantation

8211 False River Rd., New Roads, LA 70760. ☎ **504/638-8410.** Admission $8 adults, $4 children 6–12. Call ahead for an appointment.

Located 29 miles northwest of Baton Rouge on Louisiana Highway 1, this plantation is one of the few that still functions as a working farm. Built in 1750 by Marquis Vincent de Ternant, the house is one of the oldest in the state, and its two stories rise above a raised brick basement. Galleries encircle the house, which is flanked by two brick *pigeonniers*. Indigo was planted here at first; then in the 1800s sugarcane became the plantation's main crop. Today, sugarcane, corn, and soybeans are grown, and the plantation also supports its own cattle. During the Civil War this house was host to generals from both sides (Gen. Nathaniel Banks of the Union and Gen. Dick Taylor of the Confederacy)—not, of course, at the same time. Parlange is designated a National Historic Landmark and is today owned by relatives of the original builders. To get to Parlange, drive 19 miles west on U.S. 190, then 10 miles north on La. 1.

Asphodel

La. 68 (mailing address: 4626 Hwy. 68), Jackson, LA 70748. ☎ **504/654-6868.** Admission $5. Mon and Fri by appointment only.

Located on La. 68 north of Baton Rouge and east of St. Francisville, Asphodel is a charming example of the Greek Revival style popular in the 1800s. Built about 1833, it consists of a raised central section with two identical wings of brick covered with a smooth plaster made with sand from a nearby creek. Doric columns line the gallery of the central section and support its gabled roof. Each wing has its own small porch. Asphodel has been seen in films such as *The Long Hot Summer*. The old Levy house (built in the 1840s) was moved to the grounds here in recent years and is now operated by Dianne and Jerry Smith as an inn and a very fine restaurant. There are leafy forest trails open to visitors.

Oakley Plantation

La. 965 (P.O. Box 546), St. Francisville, LA 70775. ☎ **504/635-3739.** Admission $2; those under 12 or over 61 free. Daily 9am–5pm. Closed Thanksgiving, Christmas Day, and New Year's Day.

Oakley Plantation, 3 miles east of U.S. 61, features the lovely old house where John James Audubon came to study and paint the wildlife of this part of Louisiana. Built in 1799, it is a three-story frame house with the raised basement so typical of that era. The two galleries are joined by a curved stairway, and the whole house has a simplicity that bespeaks its age. When Audubon was here, he tutored a daughter of the family and painted some 32 of his *Birds of America* series. When you visit the house today, you will see some original prints from Audubon's *Elephant Folio* and many fine antiques. A walk through the gardens and nature trails will explain why this location had such appeal for Audubon. Oakley is, as a matter of fact, now a part of the 100-acre Audubon State Commemorative Area, a wildlife sanctuary that would have gladdened the naturalist's heart. In the kitchen building there is now a gift shop, but you can still see the huge old kitchen fireplace where the family's meals were once cooked.

Rosedown Plantation & Gardens

I-10 and U.S. 61 (12501 Hwy. 10), St. Francisville, LA 70775-1816. ☎ **504/635-3332.** Admission $10 (house and gardens) adults, $4 children under 12. Mar–Oct, daily 9am–5pm; Oct–Mar, daily 10am–4pm. Closed Dec 24–25.

Just east of St. Francisville on I-10 and U.S. 61, you'll find Rosedown. This truly magnificent home was built in 1835 by Daniel Turnbull (whose son, William, had the distinction of having married Caroline Sanwich Butler, granddaughter of Martha Washington) on land granted by the Spanish in 1789 to a founder of the Port of Bayou Sara on the Mississippi River. The two-story house, flanked by one-story wings, combines classic and indigenous Louisiana styles. There are the typical columns and wide galleries across the front; the house is made of cement-covered brick. A wide avenue of ancient oaks, their branches meeting overhead, leads up to the house, and the formal gardens are as impressive as the house itself. The gardens at Rosedown were begun in 1835 and came to be one of the great horticultural collections of the 19th century as well as one of the nation's most significant historical gardens in the 20th century. As is fitting in such a garden, marble statues of gods and goddesses dot the winding pathways. Inside, the house still holds the massive furniture of its original owner, as well as a winding stairway and many beautiful murals and paintings. Rosedown is one of the most beautiful examples of antebellum plantation homes, and whether you're a lover of architecture, antiques, or horticulture— or simply of beauty—you'll find this an interesting stop. Overnight accommodations are available.

Catalpa Plantation

Off U.S. 61 (P.O. Box 131), St. Francisville, LA 70775. ☎ **504/635-3372.** Admission $5 adults, $2 children 6–12, children under 6 free. Daily 10am–4pm by appointment only.

This lovely old plantation is 5 miles north of St. Francisville off U.S. 61. The great oaks that line the unusual elliptical drive leading up to the house were planted from acorns by Mamie Thompson's great-great-grandfather. This charming woman, Catalpa's present owner, leads guests through her home, regaling them with stories about the many family heirlooms and priceless antiques within its walls (the slightly dented silver tea service, for example, lay buried in a pond during the Civil War, and the lovely hand-painted china was done by none other than John James Audubon). Mrs. Thompson often greets guests with sherry and homemade cheese biscuits, then invites them to linger on the front porch for coffee at the tour's end.

The Myrtles

U.S. 61 (P.O. Box 1100), St. Francisville, LA 70775. ☎ **504/635-6277.** Admission $6 adults, $3 children. Daily 9am–5pm. Closed Christmas.

A little over one mile north of the intersection with Louisiana Highway 10 along U.S. Highway 61 is this beautiful house, built in 1795. Its gallery measures 110 feet in length, and the elaborate iron grillwork is reminiscent of French Quarter houses in New Orleans. The Myrtles is in an astonishingly good state of preservation, especially inside, where the intricate plaster moldings are still intact in each room. The 1¹/₂-story house is set in a grove of great old live oaks, as is only fitting for a place that is locally believed to have at least one ghost. When this old home was restored in recent years, much attention was given to filling it with furnishings authentic to the period in which it was built. Overnight accommodations are available, with private or shared baths, at rates of $82.50 to $143 double, which includes plantation breakfast and tour. There are also "Mysteries" on Friday and Saturday evenings that are great fun; call for details and prices.

The Cottage

10528 Cottage Lane, at U.S. 61, St. Francisville, LA 70775. ☎ **504/635-3674.** Admission $5 per person. Daily 9am–5pm.

This rambling country home 5 miles north of St. Francisville is really a series of buildings constructed between 1795 and 1859. For my money, this is *the* place to make your Great River Road sightseeing headquarters (see "Where to Stay," below). The low, two-story house has a long gallery out front, a perfect place to sit and relax for an evening. The first house was built entirely of virgin cypress taken from the grounds. Many of the outbuildings date from 1811, when Judge Thomas Butler (of "the Fighting Butlers," prominent in American history) acquired the property. The judge carried on the family tradition of involvement in national affairs, as did his children. In fact, after his victory at the Battle of New Orleans, Gen. Andrew Jackson, along with a troop of officers (including no fewer than *eight* Butlers), stopped off here for a three-week stay on his way from New Orleans to Natchez.

There are several outbuildings still intact, one of them a miniature cottage that was Judge Butler's office until his death, after which it became the plantation schoolhouse. Only two of the original 25 slave cabins remain. The interior of The Cottage looks very much as it did when the Butlers lived here, with hand-screened wallpaper, a 19th-century love seat (with space for a chaperone), and needlepoint fire screens made by the ladies of the Butler family. This is a working plantation of some 360 acres. Even if you don't stay as a guest, do visit.

WHERE TO STAY

In addition to the establishments listed below, you might consider the accommodations at Madewood, Nottoway Plantation, Rosedown Plantation, and The Myrtles, all described earlier in this chapter. All should be booked well in advance.

In St. Francisville

Barrow House Inn

9779 Royal St. (P.O. Box 1461), St. Francisville, LA 70775. ☎ **504/635-4791.** 5 rms, 3 suites. A/C TV. $95 double, $115–$135 suite. Extra person $15. MC, V.

The Barrow House Inn is two guest houses, the Barrow House and the Printer's House. Both are listed on the National Register of Historic Places and located in the heart of St. Francisville's charming historic district. The Printer's House, dating from the 1780s, is the oldest in town and was built by the monks for whom St. Francisville is named. Just across the street is the New England saltbox style Barrow House (ca. 1809). Owned and operated by Shirley Dittloff and her son Christopher, the houses have been lovingly restored and furnished in 1840s to 1880s antiques. The Dittloff's offer a choice of continental or full breakfast, and their highly acclaimed gourmet dinner (guests only) is by candlelight in the historic dining room. Guests also have access to an original-edition Audubon collection and a small space museum dedicated to Shirley's father, one of the pioneers in America's space exploration.

The Cottage

10528 Cottage Lane, at U.S. 61, St. Francisville, LA 70775. ☎ **504/635-3674.** 5 rms. A/C TV. $95–$99 double. Rates include breakfast and tour of house and grounds. MC, V. Parking available.

To really get into the spirit of a plantation homes tour, you can't do better than to stay at The Cottage. A full description of the house has already been given above, but I probably should add that the owners have, rather whimsically, planted a few rows of cotton between the camellias and azaleas in the garden, so if you've never seen King Cotton in its native habitat, this is your chance. On steamy hot days you can cool off in the swimming pool. There are two rooms in the main house and three in the wing added in 1850, all furnished with lovely antiques (even some canopied four-poster beds). A highlight of any stay here is the early morning (8am) serving of steaming chicory coffee, with fresh cream and sugar, on a silver tray with bone china cups—and it comes, in old plantation style, right to your bedroom door. Half an hour later you sit down to a full plantation breakfast in the formal dining room: a splendid repast of hickory-smoked bacon, eggs, grits (naturally), coffee, and homemade biscuits—an absolutely perfect way to begin the day. There's also Mattie's House Restaurant on the grounds for dinner. This place is popular with weekenders from New Orleans and other neighboring towns, as well as with tourists, which makes it essential to book as far ahead as you possibly can.

St. Francis Hotel on the Lake

P.O. Box 440, St. Francisville, LA 70775. ☎ **504/635-3821,** 800/826-9931 in LA, or 800/523-6118 in all other states. Fax 504/635-4749. 101 rms. A/C TV TEL. $77 double. AE, DC, DISC, MC, V. Free parking.

In St. Francisville, this is your best bet. It's on the Highway 61 Bypass, with attractive guest rooms (some have TVs and facilities for the disabled), a restaurant, a coffee shop, a lounge, an outdoor pool, and dog kennels.

In Baton Rouge

Hilton Baton Rouge

5500 Hilton Ave., Baton Rouge, LA 70808. ☎ **504/924-5000.** Fax 504/925-1330. 297 rms. A/C TV TEL. $86–$95 double. Discounted family rates available. AE, DC, DISC, MC, V. Free parking.

All rooms here are Hilton quality. There is an indoor pool, a health spa, a lounge, and a dining room.

Radisson Hotel & Conference Center

4728 Constitution Ave., Baton Rouge, LA 70808. ☎ **504/925-2244.** Fax 504/930-0140. 300 rms. A/C TV TEL. $73–$103 double. Extra person $10. AE, CB, DC, DISC, MC, V. Free parking. From New Orleans, take I-10 to the College Drive exit.

This hotel is a good stop after you've spent the day driving from plantation to plantation on the way to Lafayette because it offers all the conveniences you would expect at a Radisson. Each of the rooms has cable TV, voice mail systems, a coffeemaker, an ironing board, two double beds (or one king), and a desk. There is a restaurant and a bar on premises, as well as an outdoor pool. Room service is available 24 hours a day, and there is a gift shop.

WHERE TO DINE IN BATON ROUGE

Mike Anderson's Seafood

1031 W. Lee Dr. ☎ **505/766-7823.** Reservations not accepted. Main courses $10.95–$24.95. AE, DC, DISC, MC, V. Mon–Thurs 11am–2pm and 5–9:30pm, Fri–Sat 11am–10:30pm, Sun 11am–9pm. SEAFOOD.

Mike Anderson's is one of Baton Rouge's better seafood eateries, yet it's surprisingly inexpensive. The menu features fish and shellfish of all kinds, prepared in every manner you can imagine. Freshness is everything here; the portions are quite large, and the prices are low.

Mulate's Cajun Restaurant

8322 Bluebonnet. ☎ **504/767-4794.** Reservations not required. Main courses $5.95–$16.95. AE, MC, V. Daily 7am–10:30pm. CAJUN.

If you haven't yet gotten to the Mulate's in New Orleans, there's also a branch of the famous Mulate's Cajun Restaurant (from Breaux Bridge) near I-10, with the same Cajun friendliness, great food, and live Cajun music every night of the week.

Ruth's Chris Steak House

4836 Constitution. ☎ **504/925-0163.** Reservations not required. Main courses $8.95–$23.50. AE, MC, V. Daily 11:30am–11:30pm. STEAK.

Steak lovers who became addicted to Ruth's Chris Steak House in New Orleans will be happy to know there's a branch here, with the same high-quality meats and the same moderate price range (see Chapter 7 for a full listing for this restaurant chain).

2 Cajun Country

Just what *is* Cajun Country? Its official name is Acadiana, and it consists of a rough triangle of Louisiana made up of 22 parishes (counties), from St. Landry Parish at the top of the triangle to the Gulf of Mexico at its base. Lafayette is its "capital," and it's dotted with towns such as St. Martinville and New Iberia and Abbeville and Jeanerette. You won't find its boundaries marked on any map with the name "Acadiana" stamped across it. But within those 22 parishes, there lives a people whose history and culture and way of life are so distinctive that crossing into this area is akin to stepping through the portals of another country. Even their language differs from any other in the world.

MEET THE CAJUNS

And just *who* are these Acadians, or "Cajuns"? If you've gone through the standard American schooling, you probably already know something about them. Think of Henry Wadsworth Longfellow's epic poem *Evangeline*—the story of two lovers who spent their lives wandering the face of this land searching for each other after being wrenched from their homeland. Evangeline and her Gabriel were Acadians, part of a tragic band of French Canadians who became the forefathers of today's Cajuns.

Their story began in the early 1600s, when colonists from France began settling the southeastern coast of Canada. There, in a region they named Acadia, they developed a peaceful agricultural culture based on the simple values of a strong Catholic faith, a deep love of family, and an abiding respect for their relatively small land holdings. Isolated from the mainstream of European culture for nearly 150 years, their lives were filled with hard work lightened by pleasant gatherings of families and friends—and marked by their unwavering devotion to their church. This satisfying pastoral existence was maintained until 1713, when Acadia became the property of the British under the Treaty of Utrecht. Even then, the Acadians were determined to keep to their peaceful existence under the new rulers, but that became impossible. For more than 40 years they were continually harassed by representatives of the British king who tried to force them to pledge allegiance to that monarch and to renounce Catholicism and embrace the king's Protestant religion. That course was so abhorrent to Acadians and they were so steadfast in their refusals that in 1755, the British governor of the region sent troops to seize their farms and ships to deport them. Villages were burned, husbands and wives and children were separated as ships were loaded, and a 10-year odyssey began for these sturdy, gentle people.

Some were returned to France, some went to England, many were put ashore in the English colonies along America's east coast, and some wound up in the West Indies. The deportation voyages, made on poorly equipped, overcrowded ships—none had enough food, clothing, or other provisions for their large human cargoes—took a huge toll, and hundreds of lives were lost in the process. As for the survivors, their Acadian culture was so strongly ingrained that many who were sent to France and England returned to America as much as 20 years later. Those who went ashore in Massachusetts, Connecticut, New York, and Pennsylvania went varied ways—some went into indentured service for a few years to labor-hungry colonial merchants and farmers, some immediately took to the long overland walk back to Canadian territory, but all dreamed of being reunited with the families from whom they'd been so rudely torn. Those taken to Maryland were met with a somewhat warmer welcome by colonists there and were given greater latitude in work and living quarters until they, too, could take up the search for loved ones.

Louisiana, with its strong French background, was a natural destination for Acadians hoping to reestablish a permanent home, and those who were transported to the West Indies were probably the first who headed there. By 1763 there was a fairly large contingent in the New Orleans area. The territory was under Spanish domination at the time, but the shared Catholic religion and the industriousness of the newcomers made them welcome, and many Acadians were given land grants in outlying areas. In 1765, a man named Bernard Andry brought a band of 231 men, women, and children to the region now known as Acadiana. Joseph Broussard, one of the Acadian leaders, was instrumental in making an agreement with one of the largest landowners to give each immigrant family the use of one bull and five cows with calves for six consecutive years. The Acadians agreed, at the end of that time, to return the same amount of livestock, plus one-half the increase or the money realized from the sale of one-half the increase.

The land on which they settled differed greatly from that which they had left in Nova Scotia. The swampy land was low-lying and boggy, interlaced with bayous and lakes. No one has ever come up with an exact description of the bayous (called "bayuk" by the Choctaw). Longfellow's poem comes close when he describes what the Acadians found when they arrived:

> Soon they were lost in a maze of sluggish and devious waters,
> Which, like a network of steel, extended in every direction.
> Over their heads, the towering and tenebrous boughs of the cypress.
> Met in a dusky arch, and trailing mosses in mid-air,
> Waved like banners that hang on the walls of ancient cathedrals.

Suffice it to say that a bayou is something less than a river but more than a creek; it is sluggish, with little or no current. But the swamps were forested with live oak, willow, ash, and gum, and they teemed with wildlife. Given land that mostly bounded the bayous, the Acadians went to work with a will, building small levees, or dikes, along the banks, draining fields for small farms and pastures, and taking to the swamps to hunt and trap the plentiful game for food and furs. The isolation of their new home did not bother them a bit—it was perhaps the only thing this location had in common with the land they had left.

Always attuned to family closeness, children would build homes close to parents, and thus small settlements developed. The homes they constructed were marvelously adapted to the locale. From the swamps they took cypress for their houses. To provide insulation between inner and outer walls, they again turned to natural materials, filling spaces with a mixture of mud and Spanish moss (*bousillage*). They pitched roofs high so that frequent rains would drain off, and they used the attic space thus created as sleeping quarters for the family's young men (this was called a *garçonnière*). And in order to get maximum use from every inch of interior space on the ground floor, stairways up to the garçonnières were placed outside on the front porch. The stairs did double duty as seating space when families gathered at one house (for that matter, so did the porch itself, which was many times used for extra sleeping space).

Incidentally, as far as Longfellow's poem goes, two things remain to be straightened out: The real Evangeline was Emmeline Labiche, and her sweetheart was Louis Pierre Arceneaux. And their story has a different ending from the one the poet assigned to his two lovers. Emmeline found her Louis Pierre, after many years of searching, right in Cajun Country in the town of St. Martinville. The real-life

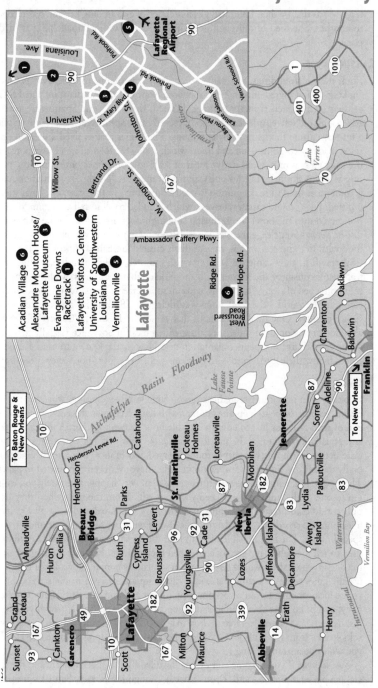

Lafayette

1. Evangeline Downs Racetrack
2. Lafayette Visitors Center
3. Alexandre Mouton House / Lafayette Museum
4. University of Southwestern Louisiana
5. Vermilionville
6. Acadian Village

tragedy was that by then Louis had given up hope of ever finding her and was pledged to another. She died of a broken heart in Louisiana, *not* in Philadelphia as in the poem.

CUISINE

From their surroundings, too, came much of what has come to be known as Cajun cooking. Using ingredients that could be locally grown, the Acadians prepared foods as their own French culinary heritage dictated, threw in some Spanish treatment, added a bit of Native American methods, picked up African secrets, and came up with a unique cuisine that is now justly famous. The dishes that evolved are based on a roux, made by combining oil and flour, which is slowly browned in a heavy pot. Into the roux go seasonings and native meat or seafood (sometimes both), and the mixture is left to simmer until (as one Cajun told me) it is "good." As a variation, okra is sometimes used to make gumbo instead of the roux. In that case, one final step is omitted: Filé (ground sassafras leaves), which is added to all roux-based gumbo when it is served into the bowl (*never* during cooking), does not appear in the okra-based dishes. Served over rice, either version is delicious. Combining various meats and seafood with rice and seasonings, the Acadians created jambalaya. And from the plentiful crawfish, they came up with crawfish étouffée, a rich blending of the small freshwater cousin of the lobster with those delectable seasonings, again serving the result on a bed of rice. What all this adds up to is some of the best, and most unique, eating in the world—the food alone is sufficient justification for an expedition into Cajun country. One final word about this wonderful feast: The Cajuns will invariably doctor any or all of these specialties with a dash of hot sauce (usually that produced on the large hot-pepper plantation near New Iberia, known to us as Tabasco). If you follow their lead, do so with caution—when they say "hot," they mean *hot!*

MUSIC

Cooking is an important ingredient of any large family gathering, whatever the occasion, whether it be to help one another with harvests or slaughtering, celebrate the end of such tasks, or just to enjoy a sociable hour or two together. Another ingredient, equally important, is the music, which any Cajun will tell you makes the food taste better. With roots probably found in medieval France, it is almost wholly an orally transmitted art form (few Cajun melodies have ever been committed to paper). The simple lyrics and strains are either very sad or very happy, and I defy you to listen to one of the numbers and keep your feet still. From the time when they used only a fiddle and triangle, Cajun musicians have expanded and now play guitars, harmonicas, accordions, and drums, but always with the distinctive sound of their special music. The best possible place to hear the music is at a *fais-dodo* (a term once used to tell the babies to "go to sleep" when they were stashed in a room apart from the one in which there would be dancing in someone's home). Nowadays a fais-dodo usually takes place in a dance hall, in a village square, or even in the streets, and if you're lucky enough to run across one, stop the car and join in—the Cajuns *love* company, and in no time at all you'll be dancing with the best of them. And if you don't just happen on a dance, feel free to drop in at any dance hall you pass, no matter what it looks like from the outside. (If you can hear live music, don't hesitate to go in, for you won't be a stranger long.)

Special note: If you become completely beguiled by this special music and the special people who play it—and if you're hardy enough for an early Saturday morning drive—there's a unique happening you won't want to miss in the little town of Mamou, some 53 miles northwest of Lafayette. (To get there, take I-10 west to the

Crowley/Eunice exit, and turn right on La. 13; Mamou is about 32 miles north of Crowley, 11 miles north of Eunice.) Every Saturday at about 8am, Cajuns from miles around congregate in **Fred's Lounge,** 420 6th St. (☎ **318/468-5411**), for a live broadcast of music, local news, and commercials, the likes of which you won't hear anywhere else. Broadcast times are 9:15 to 11am (on station KVPI, 1050 AM on the dial), but the music swings right on to 1pm. In spite of the early hour, the ambience is that of a nighttime get-together, with conviviality running high and the bar doing a brisk business. This is no slick broadcast—the "studio" is a roped-off section of the dance floor, the men behind the mikes and instruments are rugged Cajuns who work hard outdoors all week, and the audience crowds the floor dancing with friends and neighbors. It's a memorable experience! *Note:* Fred's Lounge is *only* open on Saturday. Another great place to go is **Slim Y-Ki-Ki** (☎ **504/942-9980**), located on Highway 81 in Opelousas.

PLANNING YOUR TRIP

A circular drive will allow you to take in one or two of the plantation homes en route to Baton Rouge (if you take River Road instead of I-10) before turning west on I-10 to reach Lafayette. The Interstate highway runs along the edge of Acadiana, but the little town of Breaux Bridge, just off it on La. 31, is real Cajun Country, and, of course, Lafayette is its heart. A return to New Orleans via U.S. 90 will take you right through the history, legend, and romance of this region. It's too long a drive for one day, so you'll want to book accommodations in Lafayette for at least a one-night stay. If you take I-10, the distance from New Orleans to Lafayette is 134 miles; from Lafayette to New Orleans via U.S. 90 is 167 miles. You should know in advance, however, that this is true "wandering country," which explains why I wouldn't dare set out by a step-by-step itinerary. I'll list some of the things to be sure not to miss, confident that you will find scores of other Cajun Country attractions on your own. Along the way I'll mention some of the outstanding Cajun restaurants (but rest assured, it's almost impossible to get bad food out here) and tell you about places to stay overnight.

The best tip I can give you, however, is that you write or call ahead to the **Lafayette Parish Convention and Visitors Commission Center,** P.O. Box 52066, Lafayette, LA 70505 (☎ **318/232-3808** or 800/346-1958 in the U.S., 800/543-5340 in Canada)—it'll send you tons of detailed information to make your trip even more fun. The center is open Monday to Friday from 8:30am to 5pm, and Saturday and Sunday from 9am to 5pm, if you want to stop in while you're there (the driving directions are in the section on Lafayette, below).

If there is just no way you can find time to get out to Cajun Country for an extended visit, I suggest that you take one of the excellent day tours listed below. It's a good introduction to the area, and maybe on your next New Orleans visit you'll be able to drive out for an in-depth exploration of this fascinating region.

If, on the other hand, you can get here during festival time (see Chapter 2), you'll have a terrific time, right along with native Cajuns, who enjoy their festivals with real gusto.

TOURS

And what if you simply cannot spare the time to wander around Cajun Country? If you can set aside a day for activities outside of New Orleans, a guided tour will give you a glimpse of how and where the Cajuns live. **Tours by Isabelle,** P.O. Box 740972, New Orleans, LA 70174 (☎ **504/391-3544**), specializes in small-group tours via a comfortable, air-conditioned minivan. You are driven across the Mississippi to visit Cajun Country and then provided with a 1¹/₂-hour narrated swamp tour. The Cajun Bayou Tour fare is $45 and leaves New Orleans at 1pm, returning around 6pm. Isabelle also offers a longer tour, dubbed "The Grand Tour," that includes the Cajun Bayou Tour, a guided tour of Oak Alley Plantation, lunch, and a stop in front of Destrehan Plantation.

For other Cajun Country tours, see "Organized Tours," in Chapter 8.

BREAUX BRIDGE

Just off I-10 on La. 31, this little town, founded in 1859, prides itself on being the "Crawfish Capital of the World." Its famous Crawfish Festival and Fair has drawn as many as 100,000 to the town of 4,500 permanent residents, and it's the most Cajun affair you can imagine, with music, a unique "bayou" parade, crawfish races, crawfish-eating contests, and lots more. It's such a splendiferous party, in fact, that it takes a full year to recover. It's always held the first week in May, so you're in luck if that's when you plan to come. Otherwise, you'll have to be content with stopping by for some of the best Cajun eating to be found.

WHERE TO DINE

Crawfish Town U.S.A.

2815 Grand Point Hwy., Breaux Bridge. ☎ **318/667-6148.** Reservations recommended. Main courses $7.95–$18.95. AE, DC, MC, V. Daily 11am–11pm. From Lafayette, take I-10 to Henderson (exit 115). Follow the signs, you can't miss it. SEAFOOD/CAJUN.

This restaurant is a must for anyone who wants to experience real Cajun cooking. The restaurant is housed in an early 1950s barn and was established in 1986 by natives Deanna and Jerry Guidry. Because it's in a barn, the dining room is large, open, airy, and informal. You could spend hours just looking at the Cajun memorabilia and Louisiana political posters on the walls. There's a TV in the back, and the ceilings are covered with baseball caps, T-shirts, and old license plates.

The food is as pleasant as the dining room, and they'll do it to your taste: mild, strong, or extra hot. They say that they serve the biggest crawfish in the world, and I don't doubt it. The steaming platters of boiled crawfish that come out of the kitchen by the hundreds look almost like small lobsters. The crawfish étouffée and the gumbo are delicious. Of course, you shouldn't miss the bread pudding here. And, if you just can't decide what you want, go for the "Seafood Festival Platter," which consists of a cup of gumbo, jambalaya, crawfish étouffée, grilled catfish, shrimp, seafood pie, frogs' legs, crawfish, and a crawfish patty—all served with grilled potatoes, vegetables, and garlic bread.

Mulate's Cajun Restaurant

325 Mills Ave., Breaux Bridge. ☎ **318/332-4648.** Reservations recommended. Main courses $5.95–$15.95. AE, MC, V. Mon–Sat 10:30am–10:30pm, Sun 11am–11pm. CAJUN.

This is a roadside cafe with cypress-board walls, where Cajun owner Goldie Comeaux takes great care to make every dish authentic to her heritage. Stuffed crab is a specialty. Seven nights a week and at noon on Saturday and Sunday there's live Cajun music. Mulate's is a good introduction to the Cajun world of friendliness, unique food, and music. The prices are quite reasonable.

LAFAYETTE

If you haven't written to it in advance, make your first stop at the office of the **Lafayette Parish Convention and Visitors Commission Center,** where the helpful staff will tell you everything you could possibly want to know about their region and send you out loaded with material to enlighten your stay. Turn off I-10 at

Exit 103A and go south for about a mile and you'll find the office in the center of the median at 1400 NW Evangeline Thruway (☎ **318/232-3808** or 800/346-1958 in the U.S., 800/543-5340 in Canada); it's open Monday to Friday 8:30am to 5pm, and from 9am to 5pm on Saturday and Sunday. Located near the intersection of Willow Street and the Thruway, the attractive offices are housed in Cajun-style homes set in landscaped grounds that include a pond and benches. It is a restful spot to sit and plan your Cajun Country excursion.

SEEING THE SIGHTS

Once you've met the engaging Cajuns who live in this region, you really shouldn't leave without exploring the bayous and swamps that have helped shape their hardy character. Gliding through misty bayous dotted with gnarled cypress trees dripping Spanish moss, seeing native water creatures and birds in their natural habitat, and learning just how Cajuns harvest their beloved crawfish—it's an experience not to be missed. To arrange just such a voyage, contact Terry Angelle at **Angelle's Atchafalaya Basin Swamp Tours,** Whiskey River Landing, P.O. Box 111, Cecilla, LA 70521 (☎ **318/228-8567**). His tour gives you nearly two hours in the third-largest swamp in the United States, with Cajun guides who have spent their lives thereabouts and who travel the mysterious waterways as easily as you and I walk city streets. There's a glass-enclosed boat for large groups and a small, open boat for up to 14. The fares are $8.50 for adults, $7.50 for seniors, and $4 for those under 12. Departure times are 10am, 1, and 3pm (there is also a tour at 5pm during daylight saving time). For other swamp tours, see "Organized Tours," in Chapter 8.

To reach Whiskey River Landing from I-10, take Exit 115 to Henderson, go through Henderson to the levee, and turn right. The landing is the fourth exit on the left.

If you're in Cajun Country between the first week in April and Labor Day and happen to be a devotee of the "sport of kings," you can enjoy an evening of horse racing at **Evangeline Downs,** 3 miles north of town on U.S. 167. Post time and racing days change periodically, so be sure to check. Don't bring the kids, though—no minors are allowed. For current schedules and clubhouse reservations, call **318/896-RACE.**

In the very heart of Lafayette, on the grounds of the University of Southwestern Louisiana, there's a lovely natural swamp environment. Although small, it gives the effect of being in the wild, and during warm months you'll actually see alligators. Water birds of several varieties, as well as turtles, are almost always on hand, and during April the swamp is abloom with Louisiana irises. If you want to know more about the lake and how it is used as a teaching tool, contact the **University News Service,** University of Southwestern Louisiana, Lafayette, LA 70504 (☎ **318/482-6475**). If you just want to get closer to the sort of swampland seen most often from highways, you'll like Cypress Lake next to the Student Union on the USL campus, between St. Mary Boulevard and University Avenue, Hebrard Boulevard and McKinley Street.

Acadian Village

200 Greenleaf Dr., Lafayette. ☎ **318/981-2364** or 800/962-9133. Admission $5.50 adults, $4.50 seniors, $2.50 children 6–14, under 6 free. Daily 10am–5pm. Closed holidays.

Just south of La. 342, you'll find a reconstructed (actually, reassembled) Cajun bayou community at Acadian Village. Houses have been moved from original locations to this site beside a sleepy bayou, and a footpath on its banks takes you past these historic structures. The buildings hold a representative collection of Cajun furnishings. There's a gift shop, too, where you can buy Cajun handicrafts and an interesting selection of books on this unique culture. To get here, take I-10 to Exit 97. Go south on La. 93 to Ridge Road, then take a right, followed by a left on W. Broussard.

Vermilionville

1600 Surrey St., Lafayette. ☎ **318/233-4077** or 800/99-BAYOU. Admission $8 adults, $6.50 seniors, $5 students, children under 6 free. Daily 10am–5pm. Closed New Year's Day and Christmas Day.

A recent addition to the Lafayette scene is this marvelous reconstruction of a Cajun/Creole settlement from the 1765–1890 era. Vermilionville sits on the banks of the brooding Bayou Vermilion, directly adjacent to the airport on U.S. 90. Hundreds of skilled artisans labored to restore original Cajun homes and to reconstruct others that were typical of such a village but unavailable. Homes of every level in society are represented, from the most humble to one of a well-to-do farmer. The costumed staff in each gives a vivid demonstration of daily life back then; craftspeople ply their crafts in traditional ways; and, in the performance center, authentic music, plays, dancing, and storytelling hold sway. There is a restaurant serving Cajun/Creole cuisine and a gift shop. It's a great introduction to the Cajun way of life and a pleasant way to spend an afternoon. To reach Vermilionville, take I-10 to Exit 103A. Get on the Evangeline Thruway going south and keep going until you get to Surrey Street, then follow the signs.

Alexandre Mouton House/Lafayette Museum

1122 Lafayette St., Lafayette. ☎ **318/234-2208.** Admission $3 adults, $2 seniors, $1 students of all ages. Tues–Sat 9am–5pm, Sun 3–5pm. Closed holidays.

Louisiana's first Democratic governor, Alexandre Mouton, once lived in this antebellum town house with square columns and two galleries. Today it houses the Lafayette Museum. While the main house was built in the early 1800s, its cupola, attic, and second floor were added in 1849. Inside, in addition to the antiques, paintings, and historic documents you might expect to find, there's a colorful collection of Mardi Gras costumes that were worn by Lafayette's krewe kings and queens.

Chretien Point Plantation

Chretien Point Rd., Sunset. ☎ **318/233-7050** or 318/662-5876. Admission $5.50 adults, $2.75 children 4–12, under 4 free. Daily 10am–5pm. Last tour 4pm. Closed holidays.

One of Cajun Country's most intriguing plantation mansions is only a short drive (about 15 miles) north of Lafayette. Allow yourself at least an hour to explore this columned home, built in 1831 on a 1776 Spanish land grant. The house itself is fascinating, but even more so are the tales of past owners. Its history includes links to privateer Jean Lafitte, a flamboyant gambler, his equally flamboyant widow, a ghost or two, a buried treasure (never recovered), and a Civil War battle fought right out front. And if you remember the scene in *Gone With the Wind* in which Scarlett O'Hara shoots a marauding Union soldier on the staircase at Tara, the staircase here was the one that was copied for the movie. To get here, take I-10 west to Exit 97, then go north about 8 miles through Ossun, Vatican, and Cankton. A little over 2 miles north of Cankton, turn left onto Parish Road 356 (toward Bristol), then turn right on Chretien Point Road; the plantation is about a mile farther on your left.

WHERE TO STAY

Bois des Chenes Inn

338 N. Sterling, Lafayette, LA 70501. ☎ **318/233-7816.** 5 suites. A/C TV. $75–$115 double. Extra person $20–$30. Rates include breakfast. AE, MC, V. Free parking.

In Lafayette, three suites at the Bois des Chenes Inn are in the carriage house, and two suites, one with an open fireplace, are in the 1820s Acadian-style plantation home known as the Charles Mouton House. Now listed on the National Register of Historical Houses, Bois des Chenes was once the center of a 3,000-acre cattle-and-sugar plantation. Its restoration has been a labor of love that is reflected in the careful selection of antique furnishings, most of Louisiana French design. All guest accommodations are tastefully furnished with antiques of different periods, and each has a small refrigerator and down pillows. The rates include a Louisiana-style breakfast, a bottle of wine, and a tour of the house. The owner, a retired geologist, conducts nature and birding trips into the Atchafalaya Swamp as well as guided fishing and hunting trips. Smoking is not permitted indoors. Booking as far in advance as possible is recommended.

Holiday Inn Central—Holidome

2032 NE Evangeline Thruway, Lafayette, LA 70509. ☎ **318/233-6815** or 800/942-4868. 250 rms. A/C TV TEL. $69 double. AE, CB, DC, DISC, JCB, MC, V. Free parking.

The Holiday Inn has superior guest rooms, some of which are equipped for the disabled. There is a lounge, a coffee shop, a good restaurant, an indoor pool, a whirlpool, a sauna, a game room, lighted tennis courts, a jogging track, a playground, a picnic area, and a gift shop.

ⓢ Hotel Acadiana

1801 W. Pinhook Rd., Lafayette, LA 70508. ☎ **318/233-8120** or 800/874-4664 in LA; 800/ 826-8386 in the rest of the U.S. 290 rms, 6 suites. A/C TV TEL. $70–$155 single or double. AE, DC, DISC, MC, V. Free parking. From New Orleans take I-10 west to Exit 103A. Follow the Evangeline Thruway to Pinhook Road. Go right onto Pinhook, follow Pinhook across the bridge, and you'll see the hotel on your left.

Hotel Acadiana is a great value. The rates are low, but you have all the modern conveniences you'd expect to find in a large chain hotel: two double beds or a king in each room, a minirefrigerator, cable TV, and a warm, friendly staff. You'll also be in a location central to any sightseeing you might want to do. If you really want to be in the lap of luxury, ask for a room on the Executive Floor, where you'll have access to a private lounge. The hotel's restaurant, Bayou Bistro, offers great Cajun cuisine in a New Orleans environment; Scandals is the hotel's dance club. Room service, laundry service, concierge service, and complimentary airport shuttle are provided. Facilities include an outdoor pool and a health club.

Lafayette Hilton & Towers

1521 Pinhook Rd., Lafayette, LA 70508. ☎ **318/235-6111** or 800/33-CAJUN. 327 rms. A/C TV TEL. $80–$85 single or double; $175–$250 suite. Discounted rates available on weekends and for senior citizens, students, faculty members, and military. AE, DC, MC, V. Free parking.

The centrally located Lafayette Hilton and Towers has nicely appointed guest rooms and suites. Some have private patios. There is a good restaurant overlooking the bayou; a lounge with live music and dancing Monday through Saturday; and a heated pool.

WHERE TO DINE IN & AROUND LAFAYETTE

Café Vermilionville

1304 Pinhook Rd. ☎ **318/237-0100.** Reservations recommended. Main courses $15–$24. AE, DC, DISC, MC, V. Mon–Fri 11am–10pm, Sat 5:30–10pm, Sun 11am–2pm. Closed holidays. INTERNATIONAL/CAJUN.

In a beautifully restored historic Acadian building of cypress and handmade brick that dates from 1799, Café Vermilionville seats you in a glassed-in dining room overlooking the courtyard and herb garden. The superb menu represents the best of Louisiana French and Cajun cuisines, with lots of fresh seafood, including specialties like salmon aux poivre and Louisiana crawfish madness (crawfish tails prepared in the chef's favorite ways—au gratin, étoufée, crawfish and mushroom sauté on couton, crawfish beignet, and fried).

Prejean's

3480 U.S. 167 North. ☎ **318/896-3247.** Reservations not required. Main courses $12–$21; children's menu $2–$6. AE, CB, DC, DISC, MC, V. Daily 11am–11pm. Take I-10 to Exit 103B, at which point you will get on I-49 to U.S. 167 North. Follow the signs—it's next to the Evangeline Downs Racetrack. CAJUN.

Prejean's is a place to enjoy both superb traditional and award-winning nouvelle Cajun cooking. You'll almost always find a large gathering of locals here. You can choose to be seated either in the large dining room with its stained-glass mural depicting a cypress shrimp boat on bayou waters or in the lounge with its oyster bar. The rustic setting is enhanced by an impressive collection of fish trophies from the Gulf of Mexico, waterfowl from inland, and reptiles from the swamp. In season, heaping platters of boiled crawfish come out of the kitchen in a continuous stream, along with shrimp, oysters, gumbo, alligator, steaks, and all sorts of local dishes. Every night beginning at 7pm there's live Cajun music, which transforms all those happy diners into happy party-goers at a Cajun fais-dodo.

Prudhomme's Cajun Cafe

4676 NE Evangeline Thruway, near Carencro. ☎ **318/896-7964.** Reservations not accepted. Main courses $6.95–$16.95. AE, DISC, MC, V. Tues–Sat 11am–10pm, Sun 11am–2:30pm. Take Exit 103B off I-10. Go north on I-49 to Exit 7 (three miles past racetrack). The restaurant is located on the right side of Frontage Road. CAJUN.

Set in an Acadian country home built of cypress, this restaurant is run by Enola Prudhomme, who is easily the equal of her famous brother, Paul, in the kitchen. Assisted by her son and two sons-in-law, she dishes up wonderful dishes from a menu that changes daily, according to what fresh ingredients are available at the time. Blackened tuna and eggplant pirogue (eggplant skiff filled with seafood in a luscious cream sauce) are just two of her specialties. There's ramp access for the disabled.

Randol's Seafood Restaurant Cajun Dance Hall

2320 Kaliste Saloom Rd. ☎ **318/981-7080** or 800/962-2586. Reservations recommended. Main courses $7.95–$15.95. MC, V. Mon–Fri 11am–2pm and 5:30–10pm, Sat–Sun 5:30–10:30pm. Closed holidays. Take I-10 from New Orleans to the Evangeline Thruway (Exit 103A), then follow the Thruway to Pinhook Road. Turn right onto Pinhook and follow Pinhook to Kaliste Saloom Road (right). Randol's will be on your right. CAJUN.

Randol's is a happy combination of good Cajun food and Cajun music that is sure to have you up two-stepping on the dance floor between courses. Your fellow dancers are likely to be locals enjoying their own fais-dodo at this popular place. In fact, so imbued are they with the lively Cajun spirit that they eagerly volunteer when owner Frank Randol is in need of dancers for his traveling Cajun food and dance show, which has been booked as far north as New England. Back home, seafood is the star of the menu, all of it fresh from bayou or Gulf waters, and Randol's will serve it fried, steamed, blackened, or grilled. One of the house specialties is the seafood platter, which includes a cup of seafood gumbo, fried shrimp, fried oysters, fried catfish, stuffed crab, crawfish étouffée, warm French bread, and coleslaw.

ST. MARTINVILLE

This historic old town dates all the way from 1765, when it was a military station known as the **Poste des Attakapas.** It is also the last home of Emmeline Labiche, Longfellow's Evangeline. There was a time, too, when it was known as "la Petite Paris"—many French aristocrats fled their homeland during the French Revolution and settled here, bringing with them such traditions as fancy balls, lavish banquets, and other forms of high living.

SEEING THE SIGHTS

St. Martin de Tours Church

Main St., St. Martinville. ☎ **318/394-6021** or 318/394-7334.

This is the Mother Church of the Acadians, and the building you see was constructed in 1836, on the site of the original. It is also the fourth-oldest Roman Catholic church in Louisiana. Father George Murphy, an Irish priest, was the first to associate it with its patron saint, St. Martin, back in the 1790s, and there's a noteworthy portrait of the saint behind the main altar. You'll also see the original box pews, a replica of the grotto of Lourdes, an ornate baptismal font (which some say was a gift from King Louis XVI of France), and the lovely old altar itself. Guided tours of the church, antebellum rectory, and museum are available. Contact the Petit Paris Museum at 318/394-7334 for details.

Evangeline Monument

Main St., St. Martinville.

Longfellow's heroine is commemorated by a statue to the side and slightly to the rear of St. Martin's Church. It was donated to the town in 1929 by a movie company that came here to film the epic. The star of that movie, Delores del Rio, is supposed to have posed for the statue. Legend says that the real-life Evangeline, Emmeline Labiche, lies buried here.

Evangeline Oak

Port St. and Bayou Teche, St. Martinville.

This ancient old oak is where her descendants say Emmeline's boat landed at the end of her long travels from Nova Scotia. Legend has it that it was here, too, that she learned of her lover's betrothal to another.

Longfellow-Evangeline Commemorative Area

La. 31, St. Martinville.

Situated on the banks of Bayou Teche, just north of town, the 157 acres that make up this park once belonged to Louis Pierre Arceneaux, Emmeline's real-life Gabriel. The **Acadian House Museum** on the grounds (☎ **318/394-4284**), dating from about 1765, is typical of the larger Acadian homes, with bricks that were handmade and baked in the sun, a cypress frame and pegs (instead of nails), and bousillage construction on the upper floor. You can also see the *cuisine* (outdoor kitchen) and *magazin* (storehouse) out back. Admission to the Acadian House Museum is $2, and it is open daily from 9:30am to 4:30pm.

WHERE TO STAY

Old Castillo Bed & Breakfast

220 Evangeline Blvd., St. Martinville, LA 70582. ☎ **318/394-4010** or 800/621-3017. 5 rms. A/C. $50–$80 single or double. Rates include breakfast. AE, MC, V. Free parking.

The Old Castillo Bed and Breakfast in St. Martinville appears on the National Register of Historic Places. Set on the banks of the Bayou Teche, virtually under the branches of the Evangeline Oak, the Greek Revival building began life in the early 1800s as a residence and inn and for many years served as a high school for girls. It blossomed into its present incarnation (in spite of the devastation caused by Hurricane Andrew several years back) under the loving direction of Peggy and Gerald Hulin.

The very spacious rooms at the inn are comfortably furnished with some antiques and four-poster beds that are either double or queen size. Daybeds can be furnished for an extra $10.

WHERE TO DINE

La Place d'Evangeline

220 Evangeline Blvd. ☎ **318/394-4010.** Reservations recommended. All items under $25. AE, MC, V. Mon–Tues 8am–5pm, Wed–Sat 8am–9pm, Sun 8am–2pm. FRENCH/CAJUN.

Located in the historic Old Castillo Bed and Breakfast (see above), La Place d'Evangeline is a warm, homey room where "friendly" certainly defines the service. All three meals are served. Breakfast features regional favorites of beignets, pain perdu, and café au lait. Seafood and steaks share the à la carte menu with soup-and-salad combinations, po-boys, and such traditional homemade desserts as peach cobbler and fudge pecan pie.

NEW IBERIA

This interesting town had its beginnings in 1779 when a group of 300 immigrants from the Spanish province of Málaga came up Bayou Teche and settled here. Incorporated in 1813, its history changed drastically after the arrival of the steamboat *Plowboy* in 1836. New Iberia became the terminal for steamboats traveling up the bayou from New Orleans, and it promptly developed the rambunctious character of a frontier town. In 1839, however, yellow fever traveled up the bayou with the steamboats and killed more than a quarter of the population—many more were saved through the heroic nursing of an African-American woman called Tante Félicité who had come here from Santo Domingo and went tirelessly from family to family carrying food and medicine. (She had had the fever many years before and was immune.) During the Civil War, New Iberia was a Confederate training center that was attacked again and again by Union troops. Confederate and Union soldiers alike plundered the land to such an extent it is said that local Acadians threatened to declare war on *both* sides if any more of their chickens, cattle, and farm produce were appropriated. The steamboats continued coming up the bayou until 1947 (I'll bet you didn't know the steamboat era lasted that long anywhere in the United States). New Iberia has continued its growth and is known as the "Queen City of the Teche."

SEEING THE SIGHTS

Take one of Annie Miller's **Swamp and Marsh Tours** for a unique, close-up look at the bayou and its wildlife. In a comfortable boat, you'll visit a rookery of nesting egrets and herons and say hello to "Smilin' Sam," the alligator who has come to look for his daily feeding from the friendly operators of this very personal and delightful cruise. Call **504/879-3934** for current schedules and rates, and to find out which location (there are several) is nearest you. *Note:* This is also worth a drive out from New Orleans. Take U.S. 90 west through Houma (about 57 miles), exit right at the tourist office on St. Charles Street, then turn left at the stoplight onto Southdown/Mandalay Road and proceed to Miller's Landing on Big Bayou Black.

Shadows-on-the-Teche Plantation

317 E. Main St., New Iberia. ☎ **318/369-6446.** Admission $5 adults, $4 seniors, $3 children 6–11, under 6 free. Daily 9am–4:30pm.

This beautifully preserved home was built in 1834 for David Weeks, a wealthy planter. It reflects the prevailing classical taste of the times, as seen in its Greek Revival facade. The two-story house is built of rose-colored brick and sits amid oak trees, camellias, and azaleas. One of the most authentically restored and furnished homes in the state, this is now the property of the National Trust for Historic Preservation. From New Orleans it is approximately a three-hour drive. Follow U.S. 90 to La. 14. Shadows-on-the-Teche is at the intersection of Routes 14 and 182.

Tabasco Sauce Factory & Jungle Gardens

Avery Island. ☎ **318/365-8173.** Free admission. Factory open Mon–Fri 9am–4pm, Sat 9am–noon; garden open daily 9am–5pm.

Avery Island, on La. 329, south of New Iberia, is underlaid by a gigantic salt dome and the oldest salt-rock mine in the western hemisphere. But it is the fiery-hot peppers that grow especially well here that have brought Avery Island its greatest claim to fame. Tabasco brand pepper sauce, so loved not only in Cajun country but also all over the world, is made by a closely knit family and equally close workers who cultivate and harvest the peppers, then nurse them through a fermentation process first developed by Edmund McIlhenny, founder of the McIlhenny Company. You can tour the Tabasco factory and visitor's center, which includes an old-fashioned Tabasco Country Store. You may want to take a driving or walking tour (for a fee) of the Jungle Gardens afterward. The gardens cover more than 200 acres, with something in bloom continuously from November through June. You'll see a Buddha from A.D. 1000 in the Chinese Garden, sunken gardens, a bird sanctuary (with egrets and herons), and tropical plants.

Live Oak Gardens

284 Rip Van Winkle Rd., New Iberia. ☎ **318/367-3485.** Admission $8 adults, $7 seniors, $4 children. Daily 9am–5pm (winter, daily 9am–4pm). Closed holidays.

Set on the shores of Lake Peigneur, Live Oak Gardens is a place of huge oak trees, some 350 years old or more, that are draped with Spanish moss. Known as Jefferson Island, this isn't a proper island at all but a piece of land held up higher than its surroundings. Actor Joseph Jefferson, who gained national fame for his portrayal of Rip Van Winkle, purchased the land in 1869 and erected an extravagant three-story home, much of which he designed himself. Although Jefferson did more than a little landscaping and gardening on the grounds, it was the Bayless family, which bought the estate in 1917, that was responsible for the colorful panorama you see today. The gardens were well developed when disaster struck in 1980—the lake disappeared after an oil company drilled into the salt mine, creating a gigantic whirlpool so powerful that it sucked in all the waters of the lake and huge portions of the gardens adjacent to it. Today all has been repaired; the gardens have been rebuilt; and you'll see only the glory of camellias, azaleas, crape myrtles, tulips, and even a Japanese garden.

Index

FROMMER'S COMPLETE TRAVEL GUIDES

(Comprehensive guides to destinations around the world, with selections in all price ranges—from deluxe to budget)

FROMMER'S FRUGAL TRAVELER'S GUIDES
*(The grown-up guides to budget travel, offering dream vacations
at down-to-earth prices)*

Australia from $45 a Day
Berlin from $50 a Day
California from $60 a Day
Caribbean from $60 a Day
Costa Rica & Belize from $35 a Day
Eastern Europe from $30 a Day
England from $50 a Day
Europe from $50 a Day
Florida from $50 a Day
Greece from $45 a Day
Hawaii from $60 a Day

India from $40 a Day
Ireland from $45 a Day
Italy from $50 a Day
Israel from $45 a Day
London from $60 a Day
Mexico from $35 a Day
New York from $70 a Day
New Zealand from $45 a Day
Paris from $65 a Day
Washington, D.C. from $50 a Day

FROMMER'S PORTABLE GUIDES
(Pocket-size guides for travelers who want everything in a nutshell)

Charleston & Savannah
Las Vegas

New Orleans
San Francisco

FROMMER'S IRREVERENT GUIDES
(Wickedly honest guides for sophisticated travelers)

Amsterdam
Chicago
London
Manhattan

Miami
New Orleans
Paris
San Francisco

Santa Fe
U.S. Virgin Islands
Walt Disney World
Washington, D.C.

FROMMER'S AMERICA ON WHEELS
*(Everything you need for a successful road trip, including full-color
road maps and ratings for every hotel)*

California & Nevada
Florida
Mid-Atlantic
Midwest & the Great Lakes
New England & New York

Northwest & Great Plains
South Central &Texas
Southeast
Southwest

FROMMER'S BY NIGHT GUIDES
(The series for those who know that life begins after dark)

Amsterdam
Chicago
Las Vegas
London

Los Angeles
Miami
New Orleans

New York
Paris
San Francisco